Unraveling Race, Politics, and Gender in Trinidad and Tobago's Economic Development

Jeetendra Khadan · Inder Jit Ruprah

Unraveling Race, Politics, and Gender in Trinidad and Tobago's Economic Development

palgrave
macmillan

Jeetendra Khadan
Washington, DC, USA

Inder Jit Ruprah
Washington, DC, USA

ISBN 978-3-031-54655-6 ISBN 978-3-031-54656-3 (eBook)
https://doi.org/10.1007/978-3-031-54656-3

This Palgrave Macmillan imprint is published by the registered company Springer Nature Switzerland AG
The registered company address is: Gewerbestrasse 11, 6330 Cham, Switzerland

Paper in this product is recyclable.

Acknowledgements

The authors are grateful to Amrita Deonarine, Marla Dukharan, and Gerard Johnson for their careful review of an earlier version of this book. They also thank the Inter-American Development Bank for granting access to Trinidad and Tobago's household and firm-level datasets during their tenure at the institution.

Contents

List of Figures

List of Tables

CHAPTER 1

Introduction: Is Trinidad and Tobago Unique?

1.1 Introduction

Most of us consciously or not think of our country as unique. Trinbagonians, at least, may be right. In evaluating the development of a country, analysis typically uses the evolution of performance over time in the country and compares it with other, similar countries. However, there is a problem determining a set of comparator countries for Trinidad and Tobago, TT. The problem stems from the fact that an understanding of the historic and future development of TT needs to consider the ramifications of five critical structural aspects of the country: the small size, high oil and gas dependency, an ex-British colony that was based on an extractive-plantation economic system, high ethnic polarisation, and a democratic political system. The simultaneous existence of these five features makes TT unique. It only shares the first four features with Bahrain (see Fig. 1.1). However, by adding the democracy filter, the country becomes unique as Bahrain is a constitutional monarchy where

J. Khadan and I. Jit Ruprah, *Unraveling Race, Politics, and Gender in Trinidad and Tobago's Economic Development*,
https://doi.org/10.1007/978-3-031-54656-3_1

the King of Bahrain appoints the government. So, similar countries that share these five characteristics are an empty set.[1]

However, TT is neither the smallest, the most energy-dependent, the only ex-British colony, the most ethnically diverse, nor the most democratic. Nonetheless, it is the only country with all five characteristics. The essential point is not that they make the country unique but that these

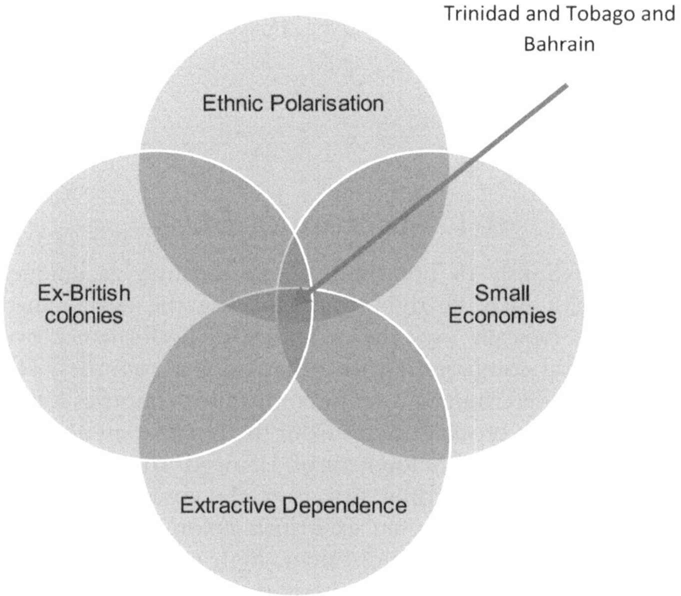

Fig. 1.1 Is TT unique? (*Note* The following filters were used in our database: Extractive dependence if the index value of Montalvo & Reynal-Querol [2005] is above the median; ex-British colony if yes; small if the country has a population of less than 3 million; and ethnic polarisation if the index value of Hailu & Kipgen [2017] is above the median. *Source* Authors' derivations based on data from Hailu & Kipgen [2017]; Montalvo & Reynal-Querol [2005]; World Development Indicators)

[1] However, in 2020 Guyana became an oil exporter, hence joining TT in having these five characteristics but did not do so for most of the period studied. Nonetheless the two countries did share one key characteristic: an ethnically polarised society, see Bissessar and La Guerre (2013).

five features, individually and together, sometimes reinforce each other or act as countervailing forces that underlie much of the country's political, economic, and social dynamics. In addition, the uniqueness makes international comparisons, a means of judging the gravity of the challenges and relative performance, problematic.[2] Uniqueness suggests that the country would take its own development course. Nonetheless, we compare TT's ranking with countries satisfying each characteristic separately to judge TT's development.

The objective of this chapter is to set the stage for the subsequent chapters of the book. We do so by focusing on three strands. First, numerically define these five features, i.e., quantify the dimensions of size, oil and gas dependency, colonial plantation economy, ethnic diversity, and democracy from an international perspective. Second, review what the existing literature expects regarding development challenges given these features. Third, briefly compare TT's relative development performance using a limited set of indicators: real economic growth, corruption, life expectancy, and a global social development index. However, the development encompasses much more than measured by these three variables; hence, it is explored in more depth and width in subsequent chapters that focus on the country's economic, political, and social development.

Specifically, we delimit the potential answers to the questions: Does the size, oil dependency, ex-British plantation colony, ethnic diversity, and democratic political system, individually and together, matter for socioeconomic success, and if so, why and through which channels? We first review these features separately. Their interactions are empirically fleshed out in more detail in the subsequent chapters.

1.2 Size

TT is a small country. The definition of the size of a country invokes cutoffs by population, GDP, and landmass or as an index using a combination of the three measures. TT has a population of 1.4 million and is the 65th largest between Estonia and Bahrain. It comprises two islands (Trinidad and Tobago) with a total landmass of 5128 sq. km (90% being Trinidad),

[2] For alternative criteria for selecting comparators see Nielson (2011) who compares the approaches taken by United Nations Development Programme, World Bank, and the International Monetary Fund (IMF). He finds these are all deficient and proposes a data-driven approach.

the 180th largest globally, between Brunei and French Polynesia. It had a Gross Domestic Product of US$21,599 million in 2019, the 115th largest in the world. Following Ruprah et al. (2014), this book defines small economies as countries with less than 3 million persons. Currently, 83 countries fit this classification of a small country. Much ado has been made about the disadvantages of being a small country.

So, does size matter for a nation's socioeconomic success, and if so, why, and through which channels?

Yes, because there are economic disadvantages of small size. Small economies have standard intrinsic features that hinder their development that larger economies do not have. Three features are often mentioned: diseconomies of scale, indivisible fixed costs, and often being in "isolated neighbourhoods". For example, Alesina (2003) and IMF (2013) list several disadvantages. Small economies' governments cost more but provide inadequate services regarding the public sector. The per capita costs of many public goods are higher in smaller countries, where fewer taxpayers can pay for them. Alesina and Wacziarg (1998) find that the share of government spending over GDP decreases with GDP; smaller countries have larger governments and more open economies.

Smaller countries cannot provide "insurance" to their sub-regions. Interregional transfers that operate through several fiscal channels and spending programmes can be sizable in large economies. The benefits of this insurance are evident in the case of natural disasters. Large countries can build redistributive schemes from more affluent to poorer regions, therefore achieving redistributions of after-tax income, which would be less available in small economies. However, the limits on insurance and redistributive functions are mitigated in TT, given rents accruing to the public sector from oil and gas. The business sector is also at a disadvantage. The size of the country affects the size of its domestic markets; smaller domestic markets often imply elevated concentration and inferior market competition. Higher fixed costs mean cost disadvantages. Foreign trade does not necessarily overcome these problems because higher fixed costs suggest higher international trade costs exacerbated by low global connectivity, particularly for a small island economy such as TT.

Nonetheless, there are possible advantages to small size. Typically, smaller countries have more homogenous preferences. As nations become larger, the heterogeneity of preferences increases, i.e., their population's diversity of preferences, culture, language, and identity. As heterogeneity increases, more individuals or regions (if differentiated by racial composition) will be less satisfied by central government policies. Different racial groups may not necessarily have other preferences over policies but may not like interactions with members of another group because of racial prejudice. However, the homogeneity of preferences is not an advantage of TT's small-population size, given its ethnic diversity.

There are political problems in small-sized countries. There is the problem of misallocation of resources due to stable rent-seeking groups. By increasing their slice of the pie (gross domestic product), these interest groups reduce the enlargement of the pie (economic growth). This misallocation of resources is achieved through influencing policy. Smaller states may be more prone to state capture.[3] These rent-seeking groups are relatively more stable in small than in large economies, as they can avoid free riders eroding their power. This power partially derives from the small absolute size of the elite, who have often studied together at school and university and hence have personal bonds that prevent others from entering their network.[4] Thus, kinships and family ties can be more prominent in small economies' politics than in larger states. "Closely knit" and "highly personalised" relationships characterise these countries' bureaucracies and business elites, further promoting rent-seeking and clientelism.

Corruption is also expected to be higher in small compared to large economies. Additionally, some sectors are more prone to corruption than others. As is the case for TT, governments that rely heavily on mining or oil-based extraction are more exposed to domestic and international bribery through public procurement, under-invoicing, and fraudulent financial practices.

Countries can overcome the negative consequences of smallness. However, in TT's case, the problems posed by smallness are accentuated by the potential resource curse of the country's oil and gas dependency (see Chapter 6 for further discussion on the resource curse).

[3] State capture refers to the attempts by powerful groups to influence state laws, policies, and regulations for their benefit by offering illicit gains to public officials.

[4] Elites refer to a small group of powerful individuals with significant wealth, privilege, political influence, or expertise, and exercises that power over the rest of the society (Mariotti, 2022).

1.3 Oil and Gas

TT is an oil and gas-dependent country.[5] Typically, economic analysts list three ways a country's dependence on the resource sector manifests itself: energy's contribution to export revenues, fiscal revenues, and value-added in GDP. These variables reveal the transmission mechanisms by which energy dependency operates and reflects the specialised production structure resulting from such dependence. We use Hailu and Kipgen's (2017) dependency index for international comparison and found that TT is the 43rd most natural resource-dependent country between Papua New Guinea and Myanmar. It consists of export revenue from oil, gas, and minerals exports as a share of total export revenue; the revenue generated by the extractive industry as a share of total fiscal revenue; total tax; and extractives industries' value-added as a share of GDP. The index also has three additional variables to capture the specialised production structure of an energy-dependent economy. It includes per capita manufacturing value-added used as a proxy for domestic industrial capability. Plus, it contains export revenues as a share of global high-skill and technology-intensive manufactured exports. It also includes revenue from non-resource income, profits, and capital gains as a share of GDP. Using the Hailu and Kipgen (2017) resource dependency index, TT is the 43rd most mining-dependent country between Papua New Guinea and Myanmar. If we take a more popular measure of energy exports as a proportion of the total exports, TT becomes the 35th most extractive-dependent country, between Colombia and Chile.

So, does energy dependency matter for the socioeconomic success of a country, and if so, through which channels? From an economic perspective, resource-based oil and gas economies are plagued by market failures, leading to a slower growth rate. Developing countries with wealth from natural resources have failed to grow faster than those without (Frankel, 2010). These failures imply that the economy and the public sector's purse are subject to the vagaries of the international price of oil and gas; hence, it must confront export revenue volatility and a market-based overvaluation of the real exchange rate. The dependence on hydrocarbons is associated with the effect of the resource curse, specifically with the Dutch disease.

[5] For a comprehensive analysis of the oil and gas sector and its effects on Trinidad and Tobago see Hosein (2021).

Dutch disease refers to the negative consequences of natural resource booms that promote deindustrialisation. The Dutch disease hypothesis postulates that a boom in the natural resource sector causes sectoral economic shifts that can harm the country's long-term sustainable growth due to an overvalued real exchange rate.

In addition, the hydrocarbon sector is often an enclave. Because oil and gas are extracted and not produced, the industry has few forward and backward linkages with the rest of the economy. The oil and gas sector is highly capital-intensive, limiting its contribution to the domestic economy. For example, in TT, the hydrocarbon sector accounts for about 4% of employment but contributes 45% of GDP. This feature has often led energy-producing countries to pursue diversification away from energy dependency.

On the political side, the importance of institutions in explaining the resource curse is another aspect of the literature that has recently gained considerable traction. Natural resources can affect the quality of institutions primarily through government or public policy, affecting economic growth (Atkinson & Hamilton, 2003; Auty, 2001; Ross, 2001). Mineral abundance penalises growth indirectly through the quality of institutions (Isham et al., 2005; Sala-i-Martin & Subramanian, 2003). The indirect effect occurs through the adverse impact of natural resources on corruption, negatively affecting economic performance (Sala-i-Martin & Subramanian, 2003). Studies have shown that resource abundance fosters corruption, undermines institutions' quality, and reduces investment in education, and research and development.

Rent-seeking behaviour creates a bias towards unproductive activities. Public policies and institutions can become binding constraints to economic growth in mineral-rich economies. The perverse incentive to use rents for short-term gain rather than investing them for long-term sustainable development projects is at the root of this challenge. This type of behaviour lowers productivity levels and slows economic growth. One of the main effects of rent-seeking is that it reduces the relative value of directly productive activities and diverts entrepreneurship towards unproductive activities (Acemoglu & Verdier, 1998).

The hostile forces of smallness compounded by oil and gas dependency may be mitigated by TT being an ex-British colony.

1.4 A British Colony

TT is an ex-British colony that was based on an extractive-plantation system. TT changed many colonial hands, including Spanish, British, French, Dutch, and Courlanders, but ended up under British control in 1814. In 1889, the consolidation of the two islands resulted in the establishment of a singular British crown colony. TT can be classified as an extractive colony by invoking Acemoglu et al. (2001) distinction between settler vs. extractive colony.[6] A plantation economy was based initially on enslaved people (from Africa) and later on indentured workers (from India).[7]

Why does it matter? There are at least four reasons one should consider the TT colonisation experience when discussing its development, particularly its institutions. The first is that the British colonised TT. Second, TT was an extractive type of colony. Third, TT is a relatively young independent country, so the lingering effects of the colonial "rules of the game" can still be significant. Fourth, the labour inputs in TT were derived through slavery and indentureship which later shaped the political system, often through ethnic rivalry.

One strand of the literature argues that British colonisation led to better outcomes than colonisation by other colonial powers.[8] The explanation that supports this view focuses on the attributes of the British legal system, which is more favourable for economic growth. There are three mechanisms through which the British legal system impacted the development of their colonies. First, the common law system provides investors and property owners greater rights. Second, British culture creates a strong commitment to enforcing those rules. Third, an independent judiciary and emphasis on the separation of powers in common law systems provide more checks on political expropriation.[9]

[6] See Acemoglu et al. (2001) who argue that Europeans implemented varying colonisation strategies across colonies, resulting in distinct institutions. These enduring institutions had significant impacts on income per capita.

[7] For the Trinidad and Tobago experience see Ryan (1972).

[8] See Lee and Schultz (2011) for a study on Cameroon which has within its borders both French and British colonised areas. They find the British areas are better off.

[9] Treisman (2000) finds that common law countries have lower levels of corruption, and he also finds some evidence that this effect is due to the cultural and enforcement-enhancing effects of British culture rather than legal tradition (since common law and British colonisation do not overlap perfectly). Hall and Jones (1999) find that output per

A typology of colonisation identifies colonies of exploitation, settlement, and conquest, creating different institutions. On one extreme was the extractive model. The primary purpose was to transfer resources from the colony to the coloniser. The institutions did not introduce much protection for private property or provide checks and balances against government expropriation. On the other extreme was the settler's model. Many Europeans migrated and settled in a few colonies, creating what historian Alfred Crosby (2004) calls "Neo-Europes".[10] The settlers tried to replicate European institutions, emphasising private property and checks against government power. Examples include Australia, New Zealand, Canada, and the United States. The feasibility of settlements influenced the colonisation strategy. In places where the disease environment was not favourable to European settlement, the cards were stacked against the creation of "Neo-Europes", and the formation of an extractive state was more likely the TT case.

The economic system was based on slavery and, later on, indentureship. Slavery was announced to be abolished in 1833, and enslaved people were freed by 1840. In the meantime, enslaved people on plantations were expected to work as "apprentices" for the next six years. Only in 1838 was the "apprenticeship" system abolished. On being freed, many ex-slaves migrated to urban areas. Workers were imported between the 1830s and 1917 to solve the ensuing labour shortage problem. Initially, Chinese, free West Africans, and Portuguese from the island of Madeira were imported. In 1839, the British government began recruiting Indian labourers, mainly Hindus and Muslims, and sending them to TT and Guyana (Look, 1993). There were two central features of the system: immigrants were contracted for long periods with a single employer, and there were penal sanctions for breaches of the contract. From 1854 until 1917, the system remained relatively consistent. A significant change for TT was granting Crown land in lieu of the free return passage between 1869 and 1880. In 1844, the period of indenture was

worker is correlated with language, with English having a particularly strong positive effect, which they see as being primarily caused by the positive economic effect of European settlement. For a review of the literature see Dippel and Khadan (2018).

[10] He explained why European colonialists were successful in establishing settler societies in temperate regions. He argued that this was due mainly to the "portmanteau biota"—disease microbes, weeds, domesticated plants, and animals—that accompanied Europeans. These devasted local populations and remade local landscapes.

extended to five years with a guarantee that, if they wished, they would get free passage home at the end of their service. In 1853, the law was again amended to allow the indentured labourers to re-indenture themselves for a second five-year term or, if they wished, to commute any portion of their contract by repayment of a proportionate part of their indenture fee. TT Indians (ITTs) began moving off the estates to become independent farmers, settling on, and cultivating lands granted to them through the land commutation scheme or purchased from the state. By 1902, more than half of the sugar cane in Trinidad was being produced by independent cane farmers, most of which were ITTs. A significant number of ITTs also went into cocoa and wet rice cultivation.

After 165 years as a colony, TT gained independence in August 1962. At that time, the country's situation was marked by the following: The British promoted and exploited a conflictive relationship between TT Africans (ATTs) and TT Indians (ITTs). ATTs and ITTs were united in the nationalist labour movements in the 1930s. However, politics became an ethnically contested terrain. In the election in 1946, the first under universal adult suffrage, less than half of the registered voters cast ballots. The trade unions did not consolidate into a cohesive political entity. The labour vote fragmented as ATTs and ITTs were divided. Subsequently, political parties and candidates appealed to ethnicity. Dr. Eric Williams (1911–1981) started the People's National Movement (PNM) in 1955 with other middle-class ATTs. Williams maintained that the PNM was a multi-ethnic party, but its interests were soon identified with ATTs. The PNM led the country to independence in 1962 and remained in power until the general elections in 1986, i.e., governed for the first 24 years as an independent country. Heading the government continuously for a quarter of a century during the country's formative years implies that Williams and the PNM are primarily responsible for much of the characteristics of TT.

The ATTs were mainly urban, and ITTs were primarily rural. Asset ownership differed between the ethnic groups as the country gained independence: ITTs had land, ATTs had education, and whites had financial resources (partly due to cash compensation for the loss of enslaved people).[11] Thus, the social-political hierarchy consisted of whites as the

[11] See Benistant (2022) who estimated the number of slaves and compensation that led to a concentration of wealth among white slave owners. The top 10% slave owners owned about 60–80% of slaves (and received around 60–80% of total compensation), and

plantation owners gradually transformed—thanks to the British compensating enslavers for the loss of their slaves—into businessmen-bankers; the Chinese, Syrians/Lebanese, and Portuguese in trading occupations; ATTs were skilled (including in civil service) professions and manual occupations comprising the majority of the urban middle class; and ITTs were mainly in agriculture concentrated in the central and south rural parts of the island of Trinidad. Ethnic diversity pertains to the discussion on Trinidad, as the population in Tobago is almost 100% ATTs.

Thus, being an ex-British colony may have given TT advantages over countries colonised by other imperial powers without undervaluing the terrible deprivations of colonisation. However, it left an ethnically diverse country.

1.5 Ethnically Diverse

Trinidadians, but not Tobagonians, often refer to citizens of the Republic of Trinidad and Tobago as "Trinidadians" or "Trinis", or occasionally, to be inclusive, as "Trinbagonians". We will use the latter term.

TT is an ethnically diverse country. Diversity stems from its colonial past, as discussed previously. Of course, there are many definitions of ethnicity. The most invoked description in socio-political discourse in TT is race-based.[12] The latter is a misnomer; we are using the category ITT as people of Indian origin, the category ATT as people of African ancestry, and MTT as mixed race.[13]

Further, the rich data in TT with race markers are a fixed choice rather than open-field identification.[14] The latter severely restricts the fluidity of

that the top 1% slave owners owned about 20–30% of slaves (and received 20–30% of compensation). The concentration was compounded by the fact that small slave holders were the most indebted, such that a significant share of compensation securities were handed over from indebted owners to their creditors.

[12] Most of the discussions in the country remain at the anecdotal level. This is surprising as both surveys and administrative data have ethnic markers. This administrative data and rich survey have been largely underused. An exception is the book by Premdas (2007).

[13] A special category is the Dougla, i.e., mixed ITT and ATT. For an ethnographic study see Barratt and Ranjitsingh (2021).

[14] For example, the LAPOP survey asks do you consider yourself: (1) White, (2) Mixed, (3) Indigenous, (4) Black, (5) Indian, (6) Others, Indian, (7) Chinese, (8) and Syrian/Lebanese. The small number of observations other than for Black (ATT), Indian (ITT), and Mixed (MTT) preclude their analysis.

ethnic identifiers, which sometimes are multiple, depending upon space and time. Thus, we are constrained by conventional categories used in TT.[15] The same goes for gender. The literature on diversity also uses language, religion, colour, and culture, which we also use.[16]

There are also different means of summarising the diversity of a country into a single figure for international comparisons. The two most common are ethnic fractionalisation[17] and polarisation (for example, Montalvo & Reynal-Querol, 2005). The fractionalisation index assumes that with more ethnic groups, there is a higher probability of ethnic conflict. Horowitz (2001) argues that the relationship between ethnic diversity and conflict is not monotonic, but less conflict exists in highly homogeneous and heterogeneous societies. Thus, in communities where a significant ethnic minority faces an ethnic majority, i.e., the minority is not divided into many different groups but is also substantial; in the case of TT, the probability of conflict will be higher. A polarisation index better captures the TT case. To these summary measures, we must add ethnic segregation—the clustering of ethnic groups across regions within a country; as we saw previously, ATTs were mainly urban and ITTs primarily rural at independence.

For an international comparison of ethnic factionalism, we use Fearon's (2003) diversity index and Montalvo and Reynal-Querol's (2005) polarisation index. A comparison between the two measurements shows that while factionalism places TT as the 140th most diverse country, the polarisation index ranks TT at the opposite side of the spectrum as the tenth most polarised country (lying between Guinea and Ecuador).

Does ethnic diversity matter for economic success, and if so, why and through which channels? The literature on the effects of ethnic diversity mainly identifies adverse effects on governance and economic development. The Human Development Index (HDI) supports the argument that diversity has its costs.[18] Of the bottom 35 countries ranked as having

[15] Croll and Gertis (2017) discusses the problems associated with fixed choice identification.

[16] See Appendix 1.1 for a list of the major databases used in the book.

[17] The indices are computed as one minus the Herfindahl index of group shares. It includes language, ethnicity, and religion.

[18] The human development index combines information on life expectancy at birth, years of schooling, expected years of schooling, and gross national income into a single measure for a single country. See United Nations (2020).

"low human development", all three are in Africa, where colonialists draw borders without regard for tribal, linguistic, or religious identities. In contrast, single-ethnicity states (30 countries do not have a religious or ethnic minority of more than 10% of the population) are strongly represented at the top of the HDI, which includes Norway, Sweden, the Netherlands, Japan, and Ireland.

Studies generally document a negative relationship between ethnic fractionalisation and measures of well-being, such as cross-country growth rates (Easterly & Levine, 1997), income per capita, public goods provision, and institutional quality. Regarding geographical and ethnic segregation within a country, Alesina and Zhuravskaya (2011) show that ethnic segregation—the clustering of ethnic groups across regions within a country—is detrimental to long-run institutional development and reduces trust among ethnic groups. Alesina, Easterly, and Matuszeski (2011) and Michalopoulos and Papaioannou (2011) show that ethnic partitioning is associated with a lower level of development.

Ethnic diversity is associated with lower social cohesion. The literature explains the cross-sectional association between diversity and cohesion by suggesting that living at higher levels of ethnic diversity causes lower cohesion among residents, and secondly, this results from processes of threat and anomie.

In TT, three ethnic groups numerically dominate in terms of the share of the population: African TTs (ATTs) and Indian TTs (ITTs), followed by Mixed TTs (MTTs). The latter is an interesting feature of TT, where there is a growing percentage of marriages between ATTs and ITTs. It is not so in other countries with a sizable Indian community, such as Fiji, Guyana, and Suriname.[19] Most of our empirical analysis will focus on these three groups. However, this is an oversimplification. Although small in population share, see Fig. 1.2, other groups may have a pivotal role.

An example is the Syrian and Lebanese communities (Barclay, 2002). This group represents only 0.08% of the population but is often associated with the moniker "from humble peddlers to captains of industry". In Antony Bourdain's Parts Unknown episode on TT, in speaking about

[19] Countries with East Indian communities representing more than 20% of the population are Mauritius (68%), TT (40%), Guyana (43%), Fiji (38%), Suriname (24%), Bahrain (24%), United Arab Emirates (21%), and Qatar (21%).

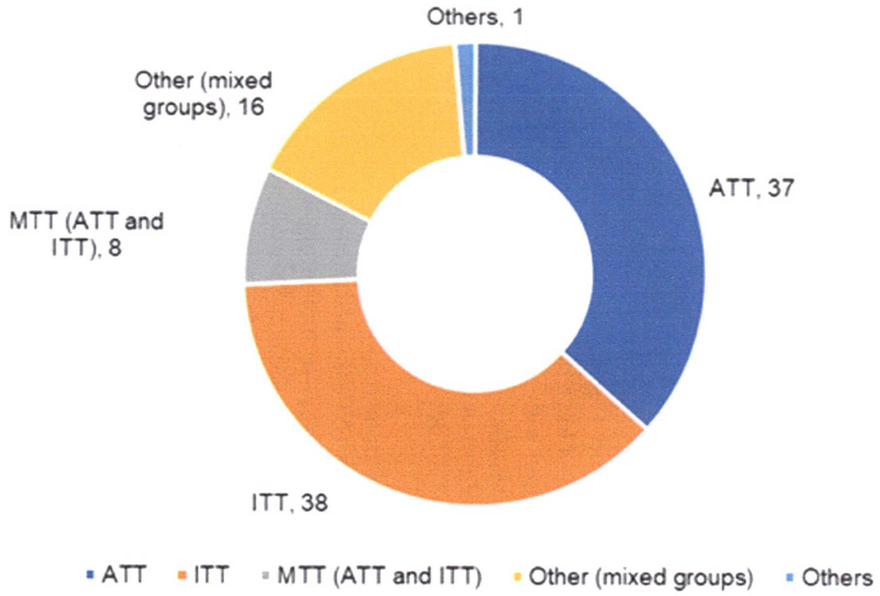

Fig. 1.2 Percentage Distribution of the Population by Ethnic Group (*Note* ATT = African Trinidad and Tobago; ITT = Indian Trinidad and Tobago; MTT = Mixed Trinidad and Tobago; Others = Caucasian, Chinese, Indigenous, Portuguese, Syrian/Lebanese, and other ethnic groups. *Source* Central Statistical Office, Trinidad and Tobago. Census 2010)

the Syrian–Lebanese history in TT, Bourdain notes that the community is likely the smallest ethnic group in the country. Sabga-Aboud, the chairman of Global Brands Group of Companies, interjected, saying, "But the most powerful, well almost the most powerful". The ensuing fallout led to him retracting the comment (Boodram, 2017). In her doctoral thesis, based on empirical analysis, Letchie (2013) argued that TT is dominated by a small and interconnected group of individuals: the elites. The network created by this group has meant that the comparatively small Chinese, White, and Syrian–Lebanese ethnic groups and a few ATTs and ITTs families have maintained a strong presence in the political and economic arena. She uses the phrase "parasitic Oligarchy" to describe that elite, a phrase used by Basdeo Panday (the first ITT prime minister) in his electoral campaign.[20]

Ethnic clustering within a country accentuates the adverse effects of ethnic diversity through spatial inequality. Spatial inequality is vital because regional income disparities can lead to voter reaction against the established system and internal disputes about the distribution of resources, undermining social and political stability (Kanbur & Venables, 2005). Fractionalisation indices do not capture the extent to which members of each group are spatially clustered, i.e., they ignore the degree of segregation within countries. Nevertheless, ethnic segregation is a relevant aspect of regional diversity, and it may affect spatial inequality, as ethnic groups often differ in economic terms (Alesina et al., 2016). In a 2007 paper entitled "E Pluribus Unum: Diversity and Community in the Twenty-first Century", Robert Putnam had a central hypothesis that ethnic diversity at the neighbourhood level leads to people "hunkering down", or being less social, trusting, and altruistic (Putman, 2007).

Ethnic groups in TT are highly concentrated in defined geographic areas. Initially, the ITTs dominated the rural areas and ATTs the urban areas. Historical events, slavery and indentureship, largely explain this

[20] The term was used by Basdeo Panday in 1994, leading up to the 1995 general election, Panday continued his parasitic oligarchy campaign, saying that they continued to control the financial institutions and to hold political sway over the government. He said the oligarchy was not necessarily French Creoles, but Africans and East Indians who held economic power. "Sometimes, they think they are white, and because of that they hold sway in the country". Indeed, the black managerial class only had office, but the parasitic oligarchy had the power, he claimed. "What I am trying to say is that every five years the black masses win the elections, but the oligarchy wins the government". See: Shaliza Hassanali The 'oligarchy' wins his heart - Trinidad Guardian; see also Parris (1985).

pattern of settlement. After slavery ended, the ATTs moved out of the sugar plantations and settled in urban areas while the ITTs replaced the ATTs on the sugar estates. Ethnic concentration in today's Trinidad still largely follows a similar pattern. Table 1.1 shows the ethnic composition by geography (electoral districts). All areas dominated by ATTs and ITTs, in 1992, remained dominated by those groups, except Arima and San Fernando. There is an increase in MTTs in almost all electoral districts (except for Changuanas and Port of Spain). The three districts reporting the largest increase from 1992 to 2013 are Sangre Grande (169%), Point Fortin (105%) and Tunapuna/Piarco (67%).

Although our discussion of ethnic groups mirrors the discourse in TT, other ethnic categories are sometimes invoked in the country: skin colour and religion. Figure 1.3 shows the distribution of skin colour by race. It is often asserted in TT that light-skinned black or brown people are still the preferred population in contemporary Trinidadian society (Bernard, 2015). They are more likely to attain high-status jobs and be perceived as attractive (Bernard, 2015). The seeds of the colour complex were planted during slavery when light-skinned enslaved captives were preferred as domestics. The unequal treatment of enslaved people fostered a light-skinned upper class and a dark-skinned lower class.[21] For ITTs, colour has been associated with the caste system perpetuated by arranged marriage encapsulated within endogamy. Hence, lightness of skin may be a factor over and above race. When searching for the term "skin lightening" in Google, Trinidad and Tobago comes at the top of the search number rankings of countries.[22] They are not necessarily acting irrationally; Fig. 1.4 shows how income falls the darker the person.

ITTs are mainly non-Christian eastern religions (Hindu and Muslim), and ATTs are mainly Christians and other faiths (see Fig. 1.5). The operative word is "mainly". Where data is not available by race, we use religion as a proxy, as some research has done, which may introduce noise in our analysis.

[21] See Doubeni (2017) for a study the negative effects of colourism on black women. She concludes that entrenched in skin tone hierarchies, the post-slavery countries of the United States and Trinidad are exemplars of how the social constructs of a racial caste system perpetuate themselves in Black communities. See also McCree (2014) who concludes the persistence of pigmentocracy among ATTs and ITTs.

[22] See http://www.buykojicacidsoap.com/how-to-get-lighter-skin/.

Table 1.1 Ethnic composition of electoral districts

	ATT		*ITT*		*MTTs*	
	1992	*2013*	*1992*	*2013*	*1992*	*2013*
Arima	46	34.9	17	15.2	36	49.3
Chaguanas	27	28.1	60	62	13	9.6
Couva-Tabaquite-Talparo	22	24.3	67	63.1	11	12.6
Diego Martin	55	46.9	10	10.5	30	36
Mayaro/Rio Claro	35	29.6	52	57.8	12	12.4
Penal-Debe	23	13.2	66	75.2	10	11.2
Point Fortin	75	77.9	18	9.8	6	12.3
Port of Spain	55	57.3	10	16.6	34	22.5
Princes Town	21	22.7	67	59.3	12	17.8
San Fernando	47	46.1	36	34.3	15	18.7
San Juan-Laventille	63	56.6	18	21.7	18	20.8
Sangre Grande	46	28.3	38	28.3	16	43
Siparia	32	26.8	55	56.9	13	16.1
Tunapna/Piarco	44	39.2	34	25.4	21	35
	Others		*Dominant ethnic group*		*Percent change (from 1992 to 2013)*	
	1992	*2013*	*1992*	*2013*	*ATT*	*ITT*
Arima	0.5	1.0	ATT	MTT	−24.1	−10.6
Chaguanas	0.2	1.0	ITT	ITT	4.1	3.3
Couva-Tabaquite-Talparo	0.0	0.0	ITT	ITT	10.5	−5.8
Diego Martin	6.5	5.0	ATT	ATT	−14.7	5.0
Mayaro/Rio Claro	0.1	0.0	ITT	ITT	−15.4	11.2
Penal-Debe	0.4	1.0	ITT	ITT	−42.6	13.9
Point Fortin	0.0	0.0	ATT	ATT	3.9	−45.6
Port of Spain	3.7	1.0	ATT	ATT	4.2	66.0
Princes Town	0.2	0.0	ITT	ITT	8.1	−11.5
San Fernando	0.9	3.0	ITT	ATT	−1.9	−4.7
San Juan-Laventille	0.8	1.0	ATT	ATT	−10.2	20.6
Sangre Grande	0.4	1.0	ATT	ATT	−38.5	−25.5
Siparia	0.2	0.0	ITT	ITT	−16.3	3.5
Tunapna/Piarco	0.5	1.0	ATT	ATT	−10.9	−25.3

Note ATT = African Trinidad and Tobago; ITT = Indian Trinidad and Tobago; MTT = Mixed Trinidad and Tobago; Others = Caucasian, Chinese, Indigenous, Portuguese, Syrian/Lebanese, and other ethnic groups

Source Central Statistical Office, Trinidad and Tobago. Continuous Sample Survey of Population (various years)

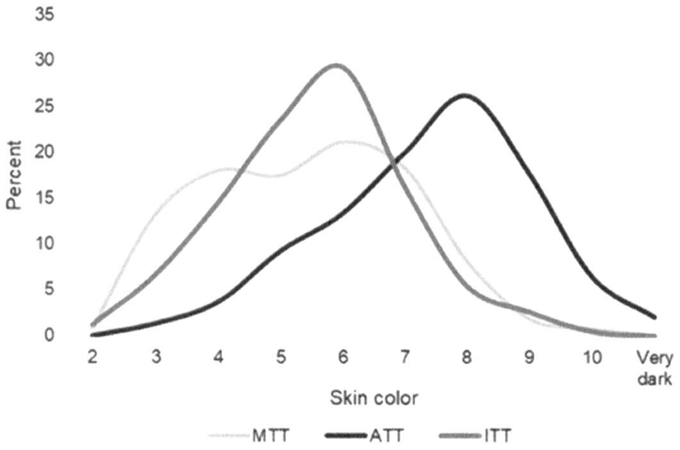

Fig. 1.3 Diversity measured by skin colour (*Note* ATT = African Trinidad and Tobago; ITT = Indian Trinidad and Tobago; MTT = Mixed Trinidad and Tobago. *Source* Latin American Public Opinion Project [LAPOP, 2012])

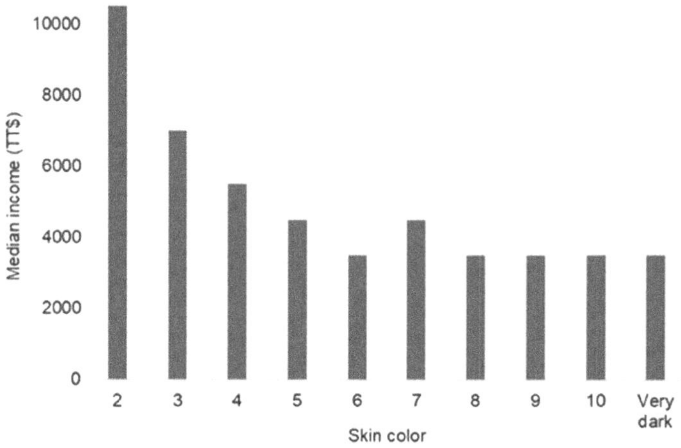

Fig. 1.4 The relationship between income and skin colour (*Note* ATT = African Trinidad and Tobago; ITT = Indian Trinidad and Tobago; MTT = Mixed Trinidad and Tobago. *Source* Latin American Public Opinion Project [LAPOP, 2012])

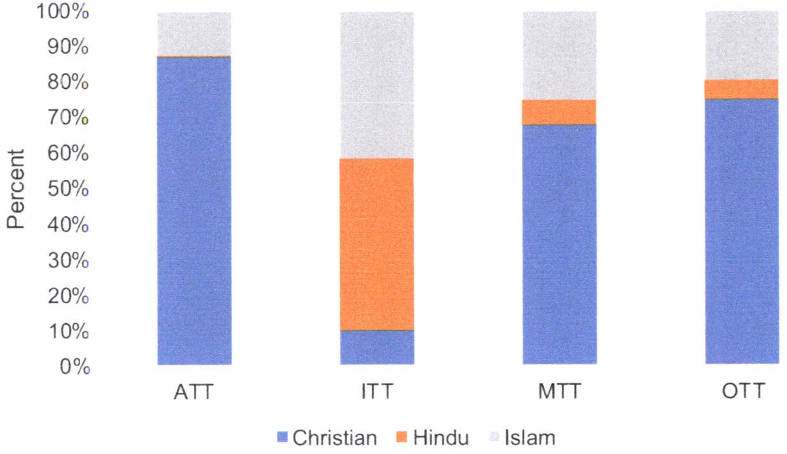

Fig. 1.5 Race and religion (*Note* ATT = African Trinidad and Tobago; ITT = Indian Trinidad and Tobago; MTT = Mixed Trinidad and Tobago; OTT = Caucasian, Chinese, Indigenous, Portuguese, Syrian–Lebanese, and other ethnic groups. *Source* Central Statistical Office, Trinidad and Tobago. Census 2010)

A vital extension of the literature on ethnic diversity is the relationship between ethnic and cultural factionalism (Desmet et al., 2017; Fearon, 2003). Ethnic diversity matters because ethnic differences make it harder for people to cooperate and coordinate. Hence, the cultural distance between ethnic groups matters. Fearon (2003) provides a measure of cultural distance between groups. He ranks TT seventh among Latin America and Caribbean countries. Desmet et al. (2017) find that ethnic identity predicts cultural values. However, the within-group variation in culture trumps between-group variation. Thus, ethnic and cultural diversity are unrelated. Nonetheless, the provision of public goods worsens when there is a significant overlap between ethnicity and culture.

In the subsequent chapters, we ask about the extent to which cultural values are shared between the ethnic groups, whether horizontal trust is a problem, whether they differ in vertical trust, and whether ethnic diversity results in civic disengagement. Is there a negative association between community ethnic diversity and indicators of social cohesion (especially attitudes towards neighbours, the community, and the country)?

Ethnic polarisation suggests opposing forces against development, which may be mitigated by democracy.

1.6 A Democracy

The political system in TT is free and democratic, based on the UK's Westminster model. How does its system compare to other countries? We use the Economist Intelligence Unit's definition of democracy (Kekic, 2007) to answer this question. Instead of a binary classification of democratic vs. non-democratic, it is a continuous index, i.e., countries have degrees of democracy. Nonetheless, the index classifies countries into four categories: full democracy, flawed democracy, hybrid regimes, and authoritarian regimes. The data for 2016 describes the state of democracy worldwide for 165 independent states and two territories. The information covers almost the entire population of the world and most of the world's 192 independent states. The democracy index is based on five categories: electoral process and pluralism, civil liberties, the functioning of government, political participation, and political culture.

TT is classified as a flawed democracy (along with 53 other countries, including the USA) and lies between Mauritius and Slovakia, according to the Economist Intelligence Unit. Bahrain (plus 54 different countries), which shares all key characteristics other than democracy with TT, is classified as an authoritarian regime.

Does the political regime matter for development, and if it does, is democracy good or bad for development? Inadequate or irrelevant is argued by some. Gerring et al. (2012) conclude that "*the net effect of democracy on growth performance cross-nationally over the last five decades is negative or null*". On the opposite side, "*The evidence suggests that democracy does cause growth and that its effect is significant and sizable*", Acemoglu et al. (2019). Thus, the empirical literature gives no consensus on the answer.

Smallness, oil and gas dependency, and ethnic polarisation suggest the country is more prone to corruption. Empirical research on the effects of bribery shows a negative relationship between crime and economic growth. A high level of corruption lowers the ratio of total and private investment to GDP and, consequently, lowers economic growth (Mauro, 1995). However, a simple electoral democracy—as in TT—does not necessarily reduce a country's level of corruption. It requires effectively operating institutions, mainly the judiciary, police force, press, and active political participation.

In TT, ethnic polarisation combined with democracy has led to ethnic-based political parties. In other words, political parties have been distinguished primarily based on who they represent rather than what they represent. When major parties are distinguished from each other primarily based on the ethnic groups they represent, the quality of democracy could be lower than where major parties are determined based on different identities (for example, class, education, and ideology). The existence of ethnic-based parties raises the question of how they reward their supporters.

1.7 Performance

So, how well does TT perform compared with other countries?[23] The answer to this question is detailed in subsequent chapters of this book. Here, as a first cut in answering the question, we consider three performance indicators: for economic development, we use real GDP growth;

[23] See Appendix 1.2 for the list of countries within each country group.

Table 1.2 TT's relative economic performance

	Life expectancy	*Corruption*	*Economic growth*
Ethnic polarisation	−37	−48	−28
Small Economies	−31	−69	−33
Ex-British colony	−30	−55	−32
Extractive dependence	−20	−18	−21

Source Authors' estimations following Borensztein (2014)

for political development, we use the level of corruption; for social development, we use the level of life expectancy. Table 1.2 shows a simple gap analysis of the three performance indicators (economic growth, life expectancy, and corruption) and the critical structural features.[24] A positive figure holds when TT performs better than expected, given its GDP per capita, and a negative figure implies a worse performance. TT performs worse for all three performance indicators for each of the five structural characteristics.

However, using a comprehensive dataset of the social progress index gives a very different picture (Harmacek et al., 2022). TT does better than all the comparator country groups (Fig. 1.6). This index measures a society's ability to meet basic human needs, establish the means that allow citizens to enhance the quality of their lives, and facilitate the conditions for all individuals to reach their full potential. The index is based on 53 individual indicators and covers 169 countries. The 53 social and environmental indicators give everyday people a clearer picture of life. The index doesn't measure traditional indicators like income or life satisfaction but focuses on actual life outcomes in areas from shelter and nutrition to rights and education.

[24] Each indicator is first standardised (regressed on per capita GDP). The gap is estimated as the difference between the predicted value (based on regressions) minus the actual value. For more detail of the methodology see Borensztein et al. (2014). Note in our case the countries for ethnic diversity and energy dependence were limited to those above the median value. For democracy, we only used countries classified as having full and flawed democracies.

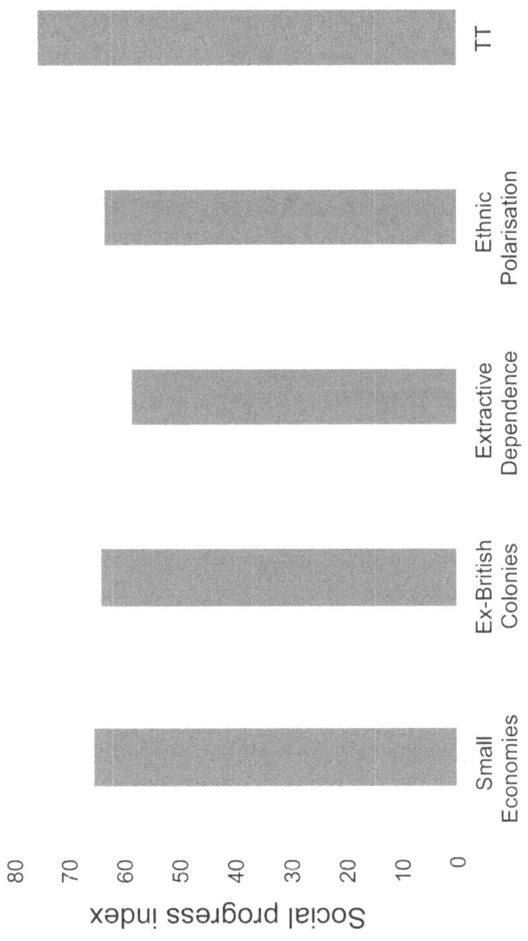

Fig. 1.6 Social Progress Index (2021) (*Source* www.socialprogress.org)

1.8 Conclusions

TT is unique because it is the only country that meets five criteria: small country, oil and energy-dependent, ethnically diverse, an ex-British colony, and a democracy. According to the literature, each feature implies adverse structural forces on diverse aspects of the country's development performance. Structural characteristics suggest forces are stacked up against success. Uniqueness also creates problems in selecting comparator countries. The previous brief literature review of the forces derived from the country's vital structural features reveals there is not necessarily an unambiguous linear, unidirectional effect on development. Often, even the sign of the impact on development is unclear. Nonetheless, in general, the forces derived from the structural features create additional problems for development compared to their absence. The general thrust of our literature review emphasised the adverse effects of TT's structural characteristics, suggesting that TT would underperform in economic, political, and social development.

The data bear out these predictions. For each characteristic, small country, oil and energy-dependent, ethnically diverse, an ex-British colony, and a democracy, TT underperforms concerning life expectancy, corruption, and economic growth concerning the relevant comparator countries; however, if we use the comprehensive social progress index, TT does better than all the comparator country groups.

In the rest of the book, we delve into more detailed potential answers to why and what to do about it? Where possible, i.e., data permitting and where relevant, we differentiate by gender and race. We first consider the country's political development. In Chapter 2, we analyse the parliamentary system and evaluate race-based politics. In Chapter 3, we discuss the size and quality of the public sector. In the following chapter, we discuss the payoffs by the political parties to their constituents through policies and the public purse, where we focus on rent-seeking and corruption. Second, we evaluate the country's economic development. Chapter 5 outlines the stages of the economic system, from agriculture to oil to gas. The following chapter discusses the country's macroeconomic performance regarding policies and outcomes, emphasising periods of economic booms and busts. In Chapter 7, we evaluate the outcomes in the labour market, including poverty and income inequality. In Chapter 8, we assess the role played by the non-energy private sector. Third, we discuss the country's social development. In Chapter 9, we focus on education. The following two Chapters discuss crime and health, respectively. In the penultimate chapter, Chapter 12, we explore the roles of culture and happiness. We end with Chapter 13, which contains the conclusions.

Appendix 1.1: Major Databases Used

Names	*Sources*	*Years*
Population census	Central Statistics Office, Trinidad and Tobago, and Tobago and Inter-American Development Bank Central Statistical Office (cso.gov.tt)	2011
Central Bank Independence and transparency index	Garriga, A. C. (2016). Central Bank Independence in the World: A New Data Set. *International Interactions, 42*(5), 849–868. http://www.tandfonline.com/doi/abs/10.1080/03050629.2016.1188813 Dincer, N., & Eichengreen, B. (2014). Central Bank Transparency and Independence: Updates and New Measures. *International Journal of Central Banking, 10*(1), 189–253. https://www.ijcb.org/journal/ijcb14q1a6.htm Dincer N., Eichengreen, B., & Geraats, P. (2022). Central Bank Transparency Data for 1998–2019. New Updated Indices Based on Revised Methodology. https://eml.berkeley.edu/~eichengr/data.shtml	2014, 2016, 2022
Continuous Sample Survey of Population (CSSP)	Central Statistics Office, Trinidad and Tobago, and Tobago and Inter-American Development Bank Central Statistical Office (cso.gov.tt)	1991–2015
Database of Political Institutions	Inter-American Development Bank IDB|Database of Political Institutions (iadb.org)	2020
Doing Business surveys	World Bank https://archive.doingbusiness.org/en/doingbusiness	2004 to 2020
Educational Outcomes	Ministry of Education, Trinidad and Tobago https://www.moe.gov.tt/	2000–2015
Global Democracy Index	Economist Intelligence Unit Democracy Index 2022|Economist Intelligence Unit (eiu.com)	2022
Health data	World Health Organization, http://apps.who.int/nha/database/DataExplorerRegime.aspx	Various years
Innovation, Firm Performance, & Gender (IFPG)	Compete Caribbean PROTEqIN & IFPG DATASETS—Compete Caribbean Partnership Facility	2020
Judicial Independence and Effectiveness	World Justice Project https://worldjusticeproject.org/our-work/wjp	2016
Latin American Public Opinion Project (LAPOP)	Vanderbilt University, AmericasBarometer, Survey Data|LAPOP|Vanderbilt University	2010, 2012, 2014

(continued)

(continued)

Names	*Sources*	*Years*
Productivity, Technology, Innovation in the Caribbean (PROTEqIN)	Compete Caribbean PROTEqIN & IFPG DATASETS—Compete Caribbean Partnership Facility	2014
The Survey of Living Conditions (SLC)	Central Statistics Office, Trinidad and Tobago, and Inter-American Development Bank Central Statistical Office (cso.gov.tt)	2005 and 2014
World Development Indicators	World Bank World Development Indicators|DataBank (worldbank.org)	Latest year available
World Economic Forum (WEF)	Global Competitiveness Report https://www3.weforum.org/docs/gcr/2015-2016/Global_Competitiveness_Report_2015-2016.pdf	2006–2015
World Economic Outlook	International Monetary Fund World Economic Outlook Databases (imf.org)	Latest year available
World Governance Indicators	World Bank www.govindicators.org	2017
World Values Survey (wave 5)	Inglehart et al. (Eds.). (2014). World Values Survey: Round Six—Country-Pooled Datafile Version: https://www.worldvaluessurvey.org/WVSDocumentationWV6.jsp	2005–2009

Appendix 1.2: Countries in Comparator Groups

Country name	*Small economies*	*Ethnic polarisation*	*Extractive dependence*	*Ex-British colonies*
Afghanistan		Yes		Yes
Albania	Yes			
Algeria			Yes	
American Samoa	Yes			
Andorra	Yes			
Angola		Yes	Yes	
Antigua and Barbuda	Yes			Yes
Argentina		Yes		
Aruba	Yes			
Australia				Yes
Azerbaijan			Yes	

(continued)

(continued)

Country name	*Small economies*	*Ethnic polarisation*	*Extractive dependence*	*Ex-British colonies*
Bahamas, The	Yes	Yes		Yes
Bahrain	Yes		Yes	Yes
Bangladesh				Yes
Barbados	Yes			Yes
Belgium		Yes		
Belize	Yes			Yes
Bermuda	Yes			
Bhutan	Yes			Yes
Bolivia		Yes	Yes	
Brazil		Yes		
British Virgin Islands	Yes			
Brunei Darussalam	Yes		Yes	Yes
Cabo Verde	Yes	Yes		
Cameroon		Yes		
Canada		Yes		Yes
Cayman Islands	Yes			
Central African Republic		Yes		
Chad		Yes	Yes	
Chile		Yes		
China		Yes		
Colombia		Yes		
Comoros	Yes			
Congo		Yes	Yes	
Curacao	Yes			
Cyprus	Yes	Yes		Yes
Czech Republic				
Democratic Republic Congo		Yes		
Djibouti	Yes			
Dominica	Yes			Yes
Dominican Republic		Yes		
Ecuador		Yes	Yes	
Equatorial Guinea	Yes		Yes	
Estonia	Yes			
Ethiopia		Yes		
Faroe Islands	Yes			
Fiji	Yes	Yes		Yes
French Polynesia	Yes			
Gabon	Yes		Yes	
Gambia	Yes	Yes		Yes

(continued)

(continued)

Country name	*Small economies*	*Ethnic polarisation*	*Extractive dependence*	*Ex-British colonies*
Ghana		Yes		Yes
Gibraltar	Yes			
Greenland	Yes			
Grenada	Yes	Yes		Yes
Guam	Yes			
Guatemala		Yes		
Guinea		Yes	Yes	
Guinea Bissau	Yes			
Guyana	Yes	Yes		
Iceland	Yes			
India				Yes
Iran		Yes	Yes	
Iraq		Yes	Yes	
Ireland				Yes
Jamaica	Yes	Yes		Yes
Jordan		Yes		
Kazakhstan			Yes	
Kenya				Yes
Kiribati	Yes			Yes
Kuwait		Yes	Yes	Yes
Latvia	Yes			
Lesotho	Yes			Yes
Libya			Yes	
Liechtenstein	Yes			
Lithuania	Yes			
Luxembourg	Yes	Yes		
Macao SAR, China	Yes			
Malawi		Yes		Yes
Malaysia		Yes		Yes
Maldives	Yes			Yes
Malta	Yes			Yes
Marshall Islands	Yes			
Mauritania			Yes	
Mauritius	Yes	Yes		
Mexico		Yes		
Micronesia, Fed. Sts	Yes			
Monaco	Yes			
Mongolia	Yes		Yes	
Montenegro	Yes			
Morocco		Yes		
Mozambique				

(continued)

(continued)

Country name	*Small economies*	*Ethnic polarisation*	*Extractive dependence*	*Ex-British colonies*
Myanmar		Yes	Yes	Yes
Namibia	Yes			Yes
Nauru	Yes			
Nepal		Yes		
New Caledonia	Yes			
New Zealand				Yes
Nicaragua		Yes		
Niger		Yes		
Nigeria			Yes	Yes
Oman			Yes	
Pakistan		Yes		Yes
Palau	Yes			
Panama		Yes		
Papua New Guinea		Yes	Yes	Yes
Peru		Yes		
Qatar	Yes		Yes	Yes
Russia			Yes	
Samoa	Yes			
San Marino	Yes			
Sao Tome and Principe	Yes			
Saudi Arabia			Yes	
Seychelles	Yes			Yes
Sierra Leone		Yes		Yes
Singapore		Yes		Yes
Sint Maarten (Dutch part)	Yes			
Slovenia	Yes			
Solomon Islands	Yes			Yes
Somalia		Yes		
South Africa		Yes		Yes
Spain		Yes		
Sri Lanka		Yes		Yes
St. Kitts and Nevis	Yes			Yes
St. Lucia	Yes	Yes		Yes
St. Vincent and the Grenadines	Yes	Yes		Yes
Sudan		Yes	Yes	Yes
Suriname	Yes	Yes	Yes	
Swaziland	Yes			Yes
Switzerland		Yes		

(continued)

(continued)

Country name	*Small economies*	*Ethnic polarisation*	*Extractive dependence*	*Ex-British colonies*
Tanzania				Yes
Thailand		Yes		
Timor-Leste	Yes		Yes	
Togo		Yes		
Tonga	Yes			Yes
Trinidad and Tobago	Yes	Yes	Yes	Yes
Turks and Caicos Islands	Yes			
Tuvalu	Yes			
UAE		Yes	Yes	Yes
Uganda				Yes
UK		Yes		
USA		Yes		Yes
Vanuatu	Yes			Yes
Venezuela		Yes	Yes	
Virgin Islands (U.S.)	Yes			
Yemen			Yes	Yes
Yugoslav		Yes		
Zambia		Yes	Yes	Yes
Zimbabwe		Yes		Yes

Note The following filters were used in our database: Extractive dependence if the index value of Montalvo and Reynal-Querol (2005) is above the median; ex-British colony if yes; small if the country has a population less than 3 million; and ethnic polarisation if the index value of Hailu and Kipgen (2017) is above the median
Source Authors' derivations based on data from Hailu and Kipgen (2017); Montalvo and Reynal-Querol (2005); World Development Indicators

References

Acemoglu, D., Johnson, S., & Robinson, J. (2001). The Colonial Origins of Comparative Development. *American Economic Review, 91*, 1369–1401.

Acemoglu D., Naidu, S., Restrepo, P., & Robinson, J. (2019). Democracy Does Cause Growth. *Journal of Political Economy, 127*(1).

Acemoglu, D., & Verdier, T. (1998). Property Rights, Corruption and the Allocation of Talent: A General Equilibrium Approach. *The Economic Journal, 108*(450), 1381–1403.

Alesina, A., & E. Zhuravskaya. (2011). Segregation and the Quality of Government in a Cross Section of Countries. *The American Economic Review, 101*(5), 1872–1911. http://www.jstor.org/stable/23045625

Alesina, A., Easterly, W., & Matuszeski, J. (2011). Artifical States. *Journal of the European Economic Association, 9*(2), 246–277. Oxford University Press. http://www.jstor.org/stable/25836066.

Alesina, A. (2003). The Size of Countries: Does it Matter? *Journal of the European Economic Association, 1*(2–3), 301–316.

Alesina, A., & Wacziarg, R. (1998). Openness, Country Size and Government. *Journal of Public Economics, 69*(3), 305–321.

Alesina, A., Harnoss, J., & Rapoport, H. (2016). Birthplace Diversity and Economic Prosperity. *Journal of Economic Growth, 21*, 101–138. https://doi.org/10.1007/s10887-016-9127-6

Atkinson, G., & Hamilton, K. (2003). Savings, Growth and the Resource Curse Hypothesis. *World Development, 31*(11), 1793–1807.

Auty, R. (2001). *Resource Abundance and Economic Development*. Oxford University Press.

Barclay L. (2002). The Syrian Lebanese Community in Trinidad & Tobago: A Preliminary Study of a Commercial Ethnic Minority. *Entrepreneurship in the Caribbean: Culture, Structure, Conjecture* (pp. 203, 212, 216–217). UWI UP.

Barratt, S., & Ranjitsing, A. (2021). *Dougla in the Twenty-First Century*. University Press of Mississippi.

Benistant, L. (2022). The Compensation of Slave Owners After the Abolition of Slavery in the French and British Colonies: a Comparative and Quantitative Perspective. APE Master Thesis, Paris School of Economics.

Bernard, A. L. S. (2015). *Happiest People Alive: An Analysis of Class and Gender in the Trinidad Carnival*. The University of Western Ontario (Canada).

Bissessar A. M., & La Guerre, J. (2013). *Trinidad and Tobago and Guyana. Race and Politics in Two Plural Societies*. Lexington Books.

Boodram, K. (2017, June 26). *Most Powerful: Saga-Aboud Apologies*. Trinidad Express.

Borensztein, E., Miller, S., Sánchez, G., & Valenzuela, P. (2014). Development Diagnostics for the Southern Cone, IDB Working Paper Series No. IDB-WP-516.

Croll, P., & Gertis, J. (2017). Race as an Open Field: Exploring Identity Beyond Fixed Choices. *Sociology of Race and Ethnicity, 5*(1).

Crosby, A. (2004). *Ecological Imperialism: The Biological Expansion of Europe, 900–1900*. Cambridge University Press.

Desmet, K., Ortuæo-Ortn, I., & Wacziarg, R. (2017). Culture, Ethnicity and Diversity. *American Economic Review, 107*(8), 2479–2513.

Dippel C., & Khadan, J. (2018). Colonisation and Institutions in the Caribbean. In D. Beuermann & M. Schwartz (Eds.), *Nurturing Institutions For a Resilient Caribbean*. IDB.

Doubeni, E. (2017). Understanding Colorism Through the Perceptions and Social Interactions of African Diasporic Women. Undergraduate Honors Thesis. Paper 1087.

Easterly, W., & Levine, R. (1997). Africa's Growth Tragedy: Policies and Ethnic Divisions. *The Quarterly Journal of Economics, 112*(4), 1203–1250. http://www.jstor.org/stable/2951270

Fearon, J. (2003). Ethnic and Cultural Diversity by Country. *Journal of Economic Growth, 8*(2), 195–222. Springer. http://www.jstor.org/stable/40215943

Frankel, J. (2010). The Natural Resource Curse: A Survey. HKS Working Paper No. RWP10-005.

Gerring, J. C., Thacker, C., & Alfaro, R. (2012). Democracy and Human Development. *Journal of Politics, 74*(1), 1–17.

Hailu D., & Kipgen, C. (2017). The Extractives Dependence Index (EDI). The Extractives Dependence Index (EDI) | Extractive Industries Transparency Initiative (eiti.org).

Hall R., & Jones, C. (1999). Why do Some Countries Produce So Much More Output Per Worker than Others? *The Quarterly Journal of Economics, 114*(1), 83–116. Oxford University Press.

Harmacek, J., Krylova, P., & Htitich, M. (2022). Social Progress Index Data. Social Progress Imperative. www.socialprogress.org

Horowitz, D. (2001). *Ethnic Groups in Conflict*. University of California Press.

Hosein R. (2021). *Oil and Gas in Trinidad and Tobago: Managing the Resource Curse in a Small Petroleum Exporting Economy*. Palgrave.

IMF. (2013). Macroeconomic Issues in Small States and Implications for Fund Engagement. The paper had two supplements: Asia and Pacific Small States—Raising Potential Growth and Enhancing Resilience to Shocks and Caribbean Small States—Challenges of High Debt and Low Growth.

Isham, J., Woolcock, M., Pritchett, L., & Busby, G. (2005). (2005) The Varieties of Resource Experience: Natural Resource Export Structures and the Political Economy of Economic Growth. *The World Bank Economic Review, 19*(2), 141–174.

Kanbur, R., & Venables, A. (2005). Rising Spatial Disparities and Development. UNU-Wider Working Papers.

Kekic, L. (2007). The Economist Intelligence Unit's Index of Democracy.

Lee, A., & Schultz, K. (2011). Comparing British and French Colonial Legacies: A Discontinuity Analysis of Cameroon. APSA 2011 Annual Meeting Paper.

Letchie, A. (2013). The Parasitic Oligarchy? The Elites in Trinidad and Tobago. Theses, University of South Carolina.

Look, L. (1993). *Indentured Labor, Caribbean Sugar: Chinese and Indian Migrants to the British West Indies, 1938–1918*. The Johns Hopkins University Press.

Mariotti, C. (2022). Elite theory. *The Palgrave Encyclopedia of Interest Groups, Lobbying and Public Affairs* (pp. 427–432). Springer International Publishing.

Mauro, P. (1995, August). Corruption and Growth. *The Quarterly Journal of Economics, 110*(3), 681–712.

McCree, R. (2014). *Race, Colour, and Class in the Caribbean Society*. Routledge International Handbook.

Michalopoulos, S., & Papaioannou, E. (2011). Divide and Rule or the Rule of the Divided? Evidence from Africa. NBER Working Paper Series 17184.

Montalvo, J., & Reynal-Querol, M. (2005). Ethnic Diversity and Economic Development. *Journal of Development Economics, 76*(2), 293–323.

Nielson, L. (2011). Classifications of Countries Based on the Level of their Development: How it is Done and How it Could by Done. WP11/31 IMF.

Parris, C. (1985). Power and Privilege in Trinidad and Tobago. *Social and Economic Studies, 34*(2), 97–109.

Premdas, R. (2007). *Trinidad and Tobago: Ethnic Conflict*. Inequality and Public Sector Governance.

Putman, R. (2007). E.Pluribas Unum Diversity and Community in the Twenty-first Century. *Scandinavian Political Studies, 30*(2), 137–174.

Ross, M. (2001). Does Oil Hinder Democracy? *World Politics, 53*(3), 325–361.

Ryan, S. (1972). *Race and Nationalism in Trinidad and Tobago*. University of Toronto Press.

Ruprah, I., Melgarejo, K., & Sierra, R. (2014). Is There a Caribbean Sclerosis. IDB.

Sala-i-Martin, X., & Subramanian, A. (2003). Addressing the Natural Resource Curse: An Illustration from Nigeria. Working Paper No. 9804, National Bureau of Economic Research.

Treisman, D. (2000). The Causes of Corruption: A Cross-National Study. *Journal of Public Economics, 76*(3), 399–457.

UN. (2020). Human Development Report. UNDP.

CHAPTER 2

Political Development: Parliament and Political Parties

This chapter first discusses the basics of TT's Westminster type of electoral system. The following section contains a discussion of race-based political parties. In the third section, we review the electoral results, including the gender composition of the Parliament. The fourth section discusses proposed reforms. We end the chapter by discussing why the country is classified as a flawed democracy.

2.1 Westminster in Trinidad and Tobago

As an ex-British colony, it is no surprise that Trinidad and Tobago, as did the other West Indian islands, opted for a bicameral parliamentary system based on the Westminster model rather than a presidential system. It could be argued that for the Caribbean leaders, there was little question that it should be otherwise. None of the early independence leaders had seriously considered an alternative to the Westminster model into whose norms they had been socialised. As illustrated by Williams' oft-cited statement, "After all, if the British Constitution is good enough for Great Britain, it should be good enough for [us]" (Williams, 1955, p. 30). Norman Girvan asserted, "[this] implanting colonial ways of thinking into native elites was one of the outstanding successes of British policy

J. Khadan and I. Jit Ruprah, *Unraveling Race, Politics, and Gender in Trinidad and Tobago's Economic Development*,
https://doi.org/10.1007/978-3-031-54656-3_2

in the Caribbean. It was key to the entrenchment of the Westminster government in the soon-to-be-independent states" (Girvan, 2011).

So, how is the political system organised? The Constitution (of 1962, modified in 1976 to introduce a president as head of state) provides for an elected president to serve as head of state and commander in chief, a bicameral legislature consisting of a Senate and a House of Representatives. The executive consists of a president and a cabinet, headed by the prime minister (with no term limits). The president is elected by the Senate and House of Representatives to serve a five-year term with no term limits. The majority party or majority coalition leader in the House of Representatives is named prime minister by the president. The prime minister chooses cabinet ministers from Parliament (Senate and House of Representatives), who the president then appoints, and he/she can change ministers and ministries at will.

Bills may be introduced in either house, apart from money bills, which must be submitted to the House of Representatives. Bills passed by the House of Representatives and the Senate and signed by the president become law. The president must call Parliament into session at least once a year and may dissolve Parliament anytime. No Parliament may sit for more than five years; in case of a vote of no confidence, Parliament must be dissolved in seven days. After dissolution, a general election to elect members to the House of Representatives must be held within three months. The prime minister can also call for a snap election within five years. There are no restrictions, as is in the UK, where most Parliament members have to vote to do so. Elections are by secret ballot, and citizens over eighteen can vote.

The Senate is an unelected body; the president appoints all thirty-one members. Sixteen senators are appointed after consultation with the prime minister, six on the advice of the opposition leader, and nine from among outstanding citizens who are at least twenty-five years old. A Senate quorum is ten, and all senators are required to leave office upon dissolution of Parliament. The House of Representatives has thirty-six members and a quorum of twelve. If the speaker is not already a house member, its number equals the number of constituencies plus the house's speaker. Two constituencies in the House of Representatives must be in Tobago. Representatives must be citizens over eighteen who have been residents of Trinidad and Tobago for at least two years. As is the case with senators, representatives must vacate their seats upon the dissolution of Parliament. Members of Parliament are protected from prosecution for "words spoken in Parliament".

2.2 Political Parties

The country has a two-party system essentially because they have formed governments. The People's National Movement, PNM, has formed governments from 1956 to 1986, 1991 to 95, 2001 to 2010 and is currently in power (since 2015). It held power for the first 25 years after independence. The other party to have formed coalition governments is the UNC. The UNC formed a government with the National Alliance for Reconstruction from 1995 to 2001 and with People's Partnership (formed by the main partners: the United National Congress, Congress of the People, the Tobago Organization of the People, and the National Joint Action Committee) from 2010 to 2015. Only one other party, the National Alliance for Reconstruction, NAR, held power from 1986 to 1991.

The significance of Dr. Eric Williams and the political party he established, the PNM, in the country's history cannot be overstated. From 1962 to 1986, politics in Trinidad and Tobago was inseparable from the story of Williams and the PNM. Even following his death in 1981, his lasting legacy played a crucial role in securing another term in office for the PNM. It would thus not be an overstatement to assert that Williams—often called the father of the nation—and the PNM, which governed for a quarter-century, established the fundamental framework that continues to shape the country today. Williams and the PNM helped create and left Trinidad and Tobago with a democratic political system, a free press, and a healthy opposition whose leaders often had been trained within PNM ranks. After independence, the opposition was splintered among different parties during the first three decades. However, a new coalition party, the National Alliance for Reconstruction (NAR), won the 1986 elections but lost to the PNM in the 1991 elections and, after that, demised.[1] UNC-led coalitions contested and won elections twice, first in 1995 and again in 2010.

It is beyond the scope of this book to give a detailed account of the formation and evolution of these and other political parties that have contested elections. An excellent, thorough blow-by-blow account is by Meighoo (2003, 2008) covering 1925 to 2001 and a more reflective account by Lieber and Ryan (1972) from 1797 to 1971, and Bissessar and La Guerre (2013), who compares TT's experience with that of Guyana. We focus instead on the question of how the political parties differ. The political party's role is to bring people together to achieve control of the government, develop policies favourable to their interests or the groups that support them, and organise and persuade voters to elect their candidates to office. Political parties could differ in their supporters' ethnic composition, ideology classified as left or right-leaning, socioeconomic class, religion, or colour.

PNM and UNC are mainly, although not exclusively, race-based political parties. Still, they differ in terms of religion and colour but do not differ significantly concerning ideology classified as left or right-leaning or by class defined by income or education. In what follows, we look at these possible explanations individually.[2]

[1] An aberration to our two-party narrative was National Alliance for Reconstruction (NAR). The party was established in 1986, aiming to be a multiracial party. The party won the 1986 elections with 66% of the national vote and winning 33 of the 36 seats. The first time the PNM had failed to win over 50% of the national votes since 1956. However, with a dramatic decline in international oil prices the government imposed fiscal austerity and neo-liberal economic policies under the auspices of an IMF Structural Adjustment Programme. The result was increased unemployment and a 10% cut in public-sector salaries. Infighting split the party and some ministers defected after a single year in power. In 1988 former ULF (United Labour Front) leader Basdeo Panday was expelled, taking with him five other former ULF members to form the ITT-dominated United National Congress. Subsequently, a further five MPs defected to become independents. In 1990, the Jamaat et al. Muslimeen attempted a coup d'état, see Abdulah (1991). NAR was defeated in the 1991 general elections, winning only two seats, both in Tobago. In the 2001 elections NAR lost its single seat. An attempt at a multiracial party had failed. After spending six years in opposition, the UNC won control of the government in 1995. The multiracial party experiment had failed and thereafter race based parties would dominate the elections.

[2] To overcome the pitfalls of individual bi-variable descriptions we estimated a multilogit regression where the effect of race (separating ATT, ITT, and OTT), was complemented by (controlled for) the individual's skin colour, religion, education, wealth, age, gender,

First, using LAPOP (2012), we consider voting and party identification by race. Figure 2.1 shows voting patterns (in the 2010 general elections) by race. ATTs voted overwhelmingly for PNM (over 70%), and ITTs did so for UNC (88%). Just over half (50.4%) of MTTs voted for PNM, with the rest casting their vote approximately evenly between UNC and others. Figure 2.2 reveals similar statistics by race and political party identification. Has race-based party identification dropped among younger voters? Fig. 2.3 shows party identification by race and age; it is U-shaped—the party identification by race peaks among the elderly and the young. Party identification by ITTs is systematically higher than for ATTs. However, ATTs are higher for the 18 to 27 age group. These figures suggest that the hypothesis of an ethnic-based political system not weakening but strengthening has empirical support. Race-based politics seems to be increasing.

Note that the political party, not necessarily the candidate's race, matters. In elections, both parties fielded candidates of both races. In constituencies where a particular race dominates, candidates are typically of the same race. Hence, PNM Parliament members are usually ATTs, and UNC Parliament members are generally ITTs, representing an electoral district dominated by their ethnic group. There are a few exceptions for both parties. For example, the UNC has traditionally fielded a few ATT candidates in ITT-dominated areas. The PNM has fielded candidates of ITT and other groups (mostly of Syrian origin) in ATT-dominated areas.

However, these figures of party affiliation by race could pick up marked differences in other characteristics that differentiate the races. It could be due to differences in ideology, socioeconomic class, colour, or religion between ethnic groups.

Therefore, we first consider differences in the supporters' ideology. Figure 2.4 shows the self-categorised ideology of the individuals surveyed (ranging from 1 a left-wing/liberal ideology to 10 a right-wing/conservative ideology). As can be seen, there do not appear to be any marked ideological differences. That would occur when there is no intersection between the curves. All individuals who voted for the PNM or

and location (urban vs. rural). What matters for political party identification are three highly correlated variables: race, religion, and colour. The other variables are statistically insignificant. See Khadan et al. (2023).

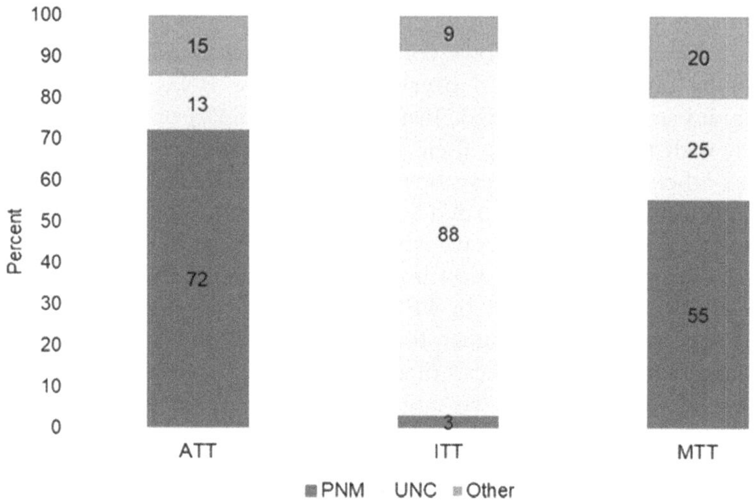

Fig. 2.1 Voting (in the 2010 election) by race (*Note* People's National Movement; UNC = United National Congress; COP = Congress of the People; Other = Congress of the People, Tobago Organisation of the People, and Movement of Social Justice; ATT = African Trinidad and Tobago; ITT = Indian Trinidad and Tobago; MTT = Mixed Trinidad and Tobago. *Source* Latin American Public Opinion Project [LAPOP, 2012])

UNC have the same distribution on the ideological scale, a normal distribution with a peak at the centre-right—however, slightly more individuals who voted for the PNM self-classify as left-leaning.

In contrast, those who voted for the UNC self-classify more as right-leaning. However, there appears to be no ideological polarisation between the two political party's bases. Therefore, it is not ideology that mainly drives the identification with political parties. Note this belies the political party's self-classification—according to their web page—where PNM classifies itself as a centre party and UNC as a centre-left party.

Party affiliation could be due to marked differences in membership of an economic class, i.e., ethnic politics are little more than class politics in disguise. Figure 2.5 shows that for those who voted for either the PNM or the UNC in the previous election, there was no skewness in their income distribution relative to the country's income distribution. Therefore, identification with political parties appears not to be economic

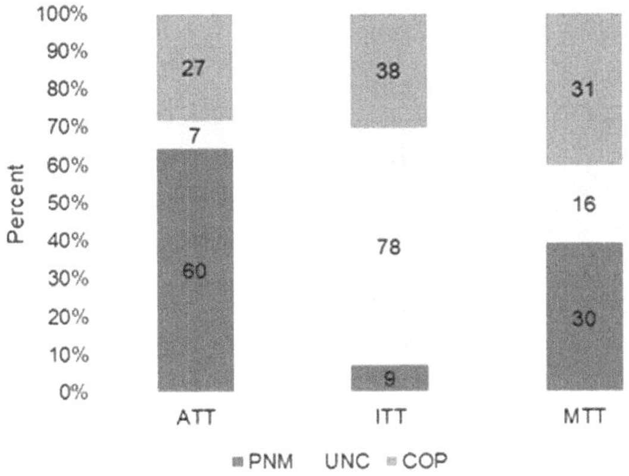

Fig. 2.2 Party identification by race (*Note* PNM = People's National Movement; UNC = United National Congress; COP = Congress of the People; ATT = African Trinidad and Tobago; ITT = Indian Trinidad and Tobago; MTT = Mixed Trinidad and Tobago. *Source* Latin American Public Opinion Project [LAPOP, 2012])

class-based. However, the latter, the Marxian-based class definition, may miss class identity. Class identity is better measured by socioeconomic status following a Weberian class definition. Figure 2.6 shows that its influence is insignificant when using education as a proxy for the Weberian class definition.

Party identification could differ by religion or by colour. Party identification by religion shows UNC supporters, Fig. 2.7, as non-Christian eastern religions (Hindu and Muslim) and PNM supporters as Christians. They also differ by skin colour (Fig. 2.8). PNM has more supporters with darker skin than UNC. Skin colour appears to matter in TT, perhaps as a hangover from slavery. However, when asked if people with dark skin colour are not good political leaders, a substantial majority of respondents disagreed, independently of the respondent being ATT, ITT, or MTT.

2.3 Electoral Results

By 2020, since independence in 1962, there have been 14 general elections. Members of Parliament (MP) for the House of Representatives are elected by a first-past-the-post system, with single-seat electoral districts

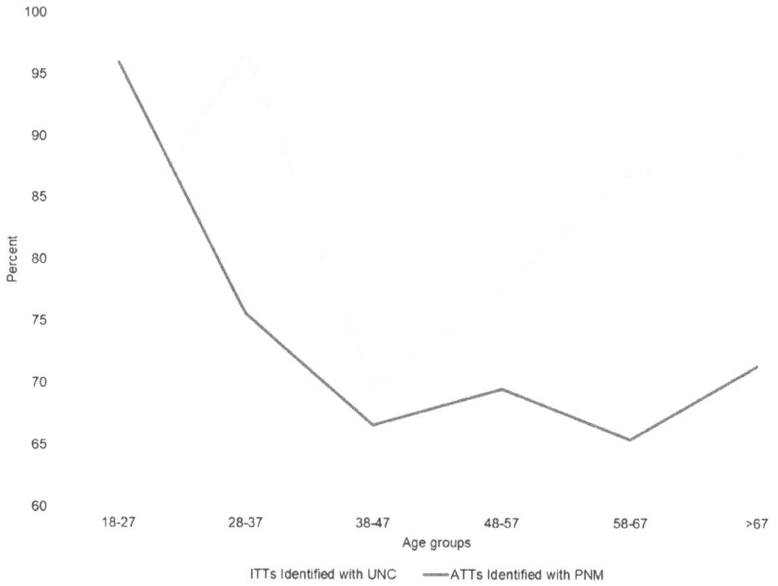

Fig. 2.3 Party identification by race and age (*Note* PNM = Peoples National Movement; UNC = United National Congress; ATT = African Trinidad and Tobago; ITT = Indian Trinidad and Tobago. *Source* Latin American Public Opinion Project [LAPOP, 2012])

as in UK General Elections with no term limits. For the House of Representatives, the election is divided into 41 (39 in Trinidad and 2 in Tobago) separate constituencies. Before 2007, there were 36 constituencies.[3] Voters are asked to choose a candidate to be the local representative in Parliament. Candidates may (or may not) be representatives of political parties. The direct result of a general election is the election of MPs

[3] The increase was recommended to the House by the Elections and Boundaries Commission (EBC), which is mandated by Section 72 of the National Constitution to review the number of boundaries of the constituencies into which the country is divided. The two Arouca seats were carved up into three constituencies, and a new seat when the eastern half of Caroni East was cut off to create La Horquetta/Talparo. Analysts suggest that the UNC will win a new seat when a slice of Chaguanas is shaved off to form the new Chaguanas East, a new seat when Oropouche is split into two seats, and a new seat when a chunk of two-thirds of Ortoire/Mayaro running along the South Coast creates the new Princes Town South/Tableland seat.

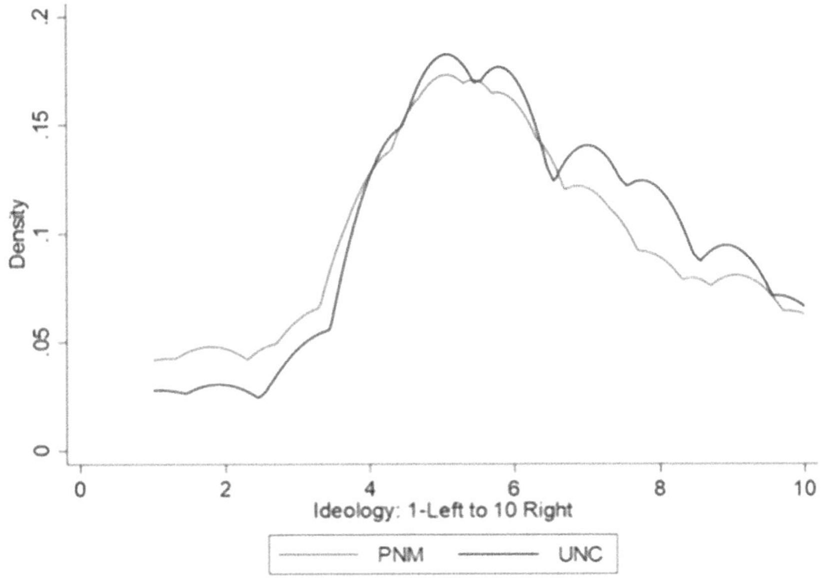

Fig. 2.4 Ideology self-classification by PNM and UNC voters (*Note* PNM = People's National Movement; UNC = United National Congress. *Source* Latin American Public Opinion Project [LAPOP, 2012])

to Parliament, the choice of a party to form the government, and the selection of a prime minister. The PNM won the first nine general elections. For eight consecutive periods, Eric Williams was the prime minister (Table 2.1).

In the case of Trinidad and Tobago, race-based political parties combined with a relatively static geographical sorting out by race into electoral districts would imply—assuming a deterministic process—that election results are preordained.[4] However, not all electoral districts are dominated in the sense of an absolute majority of a given race. Of 41

[4] Note this paragraph combines two databases: the 2011 Population Census from the Central Statistical Office of Trinidad and Tobago and the electoral results from the Election and Boundaries Commission of Trinidad and Tobago. The census does not give identifiers for parliamentary constituencies. Hence the 41 constituencies' racial profile was derived using regional corporation identifiers from the 2011 Population Census plus community addresses and the interactive electoral map of the Elections and Boundaries

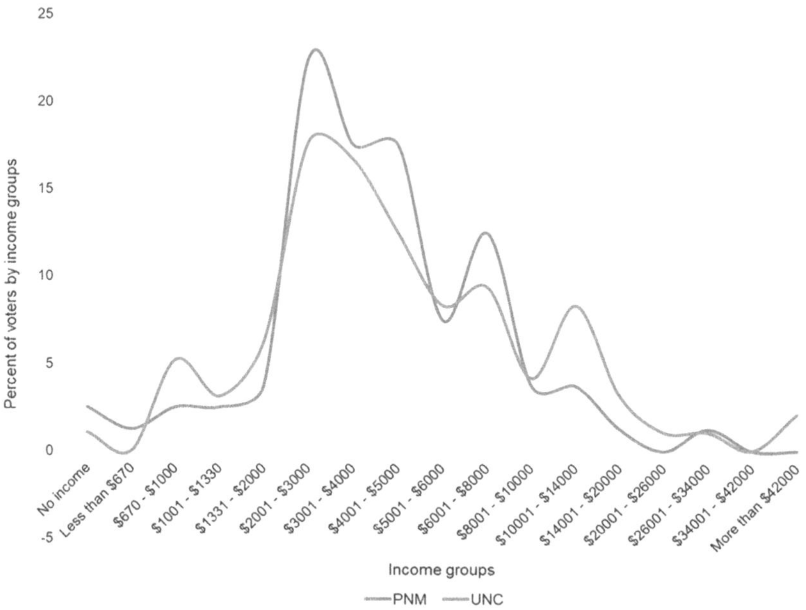

Fig. 2.5 Personal income by party voted for in the previous election (*Note* COP = Congress of the People; People's National Movement; UNC = United National Congress. *Source* Latin American Public Opinion Project [LAPOP, 2012])

constituencies (36 seats before the 2007 election), 12 have an absolute majority in ITT. These have consistently voted—in the last three elections—for UNC. Five of the rest of the constituencies have an absolute majority of ATTs. No constituency has a mixed-race absolute majority. UNC has more safe seats than PNM. However, UNC has consistently won three additional seats: St. Augustine (44.2%), Mayaro (46.4%), and Cumuto Manzanillia (45.4%)—a total of 15 safe seats for the UNC. Although the PNM only has 5 ATT majority constituencies, they won 12 safe seats in the last three elections. These are characterised by ATTs being the largest group and ITT being the smallest group, such that ATTs combined with MTTs result in an absolute majority.

Commission and Google maps. This would have introduced some degree of error in the classifications.

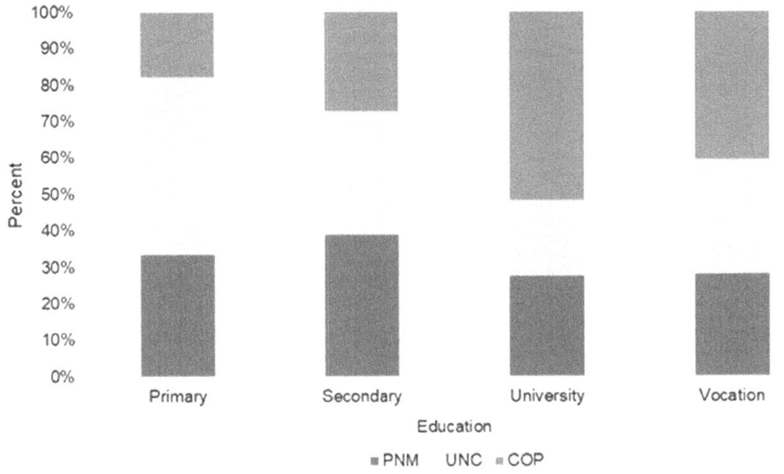

Fig. 2.6 Party affiliation by education and race (*Note* COP = Congress of the People; People's National Movement; UNC = United National Congress. *Source* Latin American Public Opinion Project [LAPOP, 2012])

These were the first elections for a House, expanded from 36 seats to 41. Previous polls were decided mainly by five marginal seats—Barataria/San Juan, Mayaro, San Fernando West, St. Joseph, and Tunapuna. The 2007 election raised the number of marginal seats to 10, with Chaguanas East, Lopinot/Bon Air West, Princes Town South/Tableland (renamed Moruga/Tableland for the 2010 election), Pointe-à-Pierre, and Tobago East ending up among the marginals.

In the last three elections, there have been over 14 seats that have switched parties.[5] In 2007, PNM won all 14, hence the general elections. In 2010, UNC won all 14 and consequently won the general elections. In 2015, PNM won 11, thus the general elections. Two types of constituencies switched from PNM to UNC and remained—3—with the UNC and those that changed back to PNM in 2015. What are the characteristics of these constituencies? Those who stayed with the UNC have the majority

[5] These are Barataria/San Juan, Chaguanas East, D'Abadie/O'Meara, Lopinot/Bon Air West, Mayaro, Moruga/Tableland, Pointe-a-Pierre, Princes Town, San Fernando West, St. Joseph, Tobago East, Tobago West, Toco/Sangre Grande, and Tunapuna.

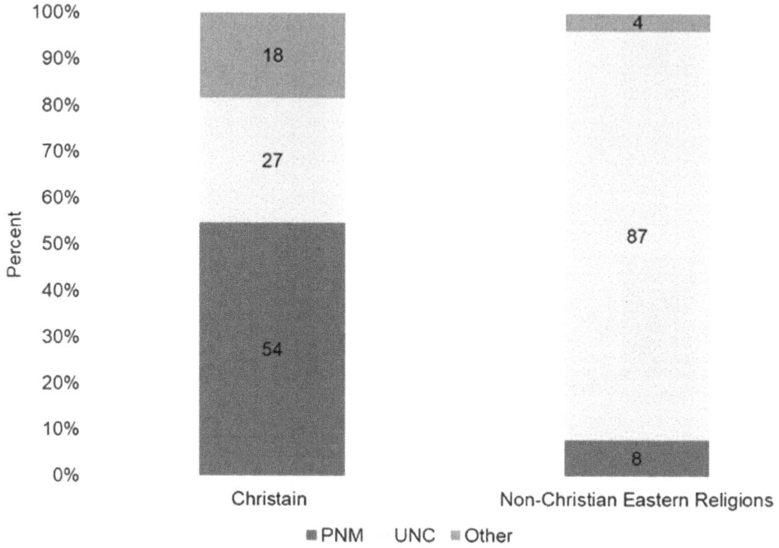

Fig. 2.7 Party identification by religion (*Note* People's National Movement; UNC = United National Congress; Other = Congress of the People; Tobago Organisation of the People; and Movement of Social Justice. The 2012 LAPOP questionnaire identifies 12 religious categories that we aggregated into three. The category not shown in the chart refers to agnostics and atheists. *Source* Latin American Public Opinion Project [LAPOP, 2012])

of ITTs (average 47.4%) with ATT (29.8%). Those that switched back to PNM had an average of ATTs at 35%, with ITTs at 26%.

A similar pattern is observed for local government elections in Trinidad. There are 14 regional corporations (Table 2.2). Six have a majority of ITTs (average 54.6%), and five have a majority of ATTs (average 47.7%).

An important aspect of electoral results is the gender of elected politicians. Gender matters for several reasons. First, it is a matter of fundamental equity and human rights, cornerstones of a democratic society. Second, the representation of women in Parliaments significantly impacts what issues are raised and how policies are shaped. Third, it creates room to reform and revise discriminatory laws against females. Today, 121 countries have some form of gender quota at the legislative level. The most common form requires a minimum number of female

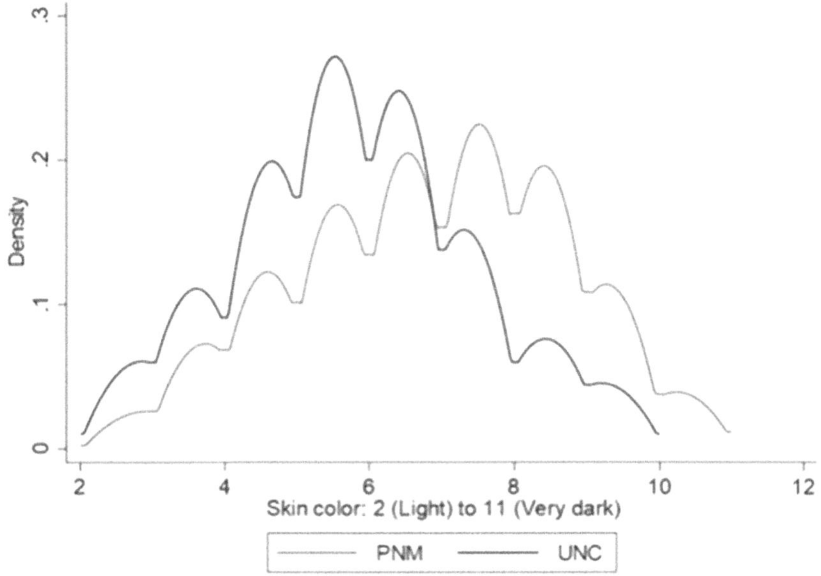

Fig. 2.8 Party identification by colour (*Note* Colour classification, as per the 2012 LAPOP questionnaire, is a scale of 1 (white) to 11 (black). *Source* Latin American Public Opinion Project [LAPOP, 2012])

candidates on party ballots, a rule that is in place in 62 countries. The most binding quota, which reserves seats for women in the national legislature, is in place in 30 countries. In TT, there are no legislated or voluntary party quotas.[6]

There is a gender gap in TT's Parliament.[7] Figure 2.9 shows female parliamentarians as a percentage of the total for TT and the median values for comparator country groups. TT has more than the median values of all comparator country groups. Yet the success benchmark should be 50% (United Nations, 1995). However, only four countries have 50% or more women in Parliament in single or lower houses: Rwanda with 61%, Cuba with 53%, Bolivia with 53%, and the United Arab Emirates

[6] See Gender Quotas Database, International IDEA.

[7] Throughout this book, where relevant and where there is data, we consider gender issues as well as ethnic ones.

Table 2.1 General election results

Year	*Prime Minister*	*Political party*	*Voter turnout*	*Votes of winning party*	*Number of seats*	*Seat margin*	*Seats gain/ Loss*
1956	Eric Williams	PNM	80.1	39.8	13	1	NR
1961	Eric Williams	PNM	88.1	57	20	5	7
1966	Eric Williams	PNM	65.8	52.4	24	6	4
1971	Eric Williams	PNM	33.2	84.1	36	18	12
1976	Eric Williams	PNM	55.8	54.2	24	6	−12
1981	Eric Williams	PNM	56.4	52.9	26	8	2
1971/ 1972	Eric Williams	PNM	33.2	84.1	36	18	12
1976	Eric Williams	PNM	55.8	54.2	24	6	−12
1981/ 1983	George Chambers	PNM	56.4	52.9	26	8	2
1986	A.N.R. Robinson	NAR	65.5	66.3	33	15	23
1991	Patrick Manning	PNM	65.5	45.1	21	3	18
1995	Basedo Panday	UNC-NAR	66.1	50.6	19	1	4
2000	Basedo Panday	UNC	63.1	51.7	19	1	2
2001/ 2004	Patrick Manning	PNM	66.1	49.9	18	0	−1
2002	Patrick Manning	PNM	69.6	50.9	20	2	2
2007	Patrick Manning	PNM	66	45.8	26	5	6
2010	Kamal Persad-Bissessar	PP	69.45	60.3	29	8	24
2015	Keith Rowely	PNM	66.8	51.7	23	2	11

Notes (1) The total number of seats was 24 in 1956, increasing to 30 from 1961 to 2002 and 36 after that, changing to 41 after 2007. (2) The PNM faced only limited opposition as the major opposition parties boycotted the election, citing the use of voting machines. (3) March 1981 Eric Williams died. Williams had maintained an iron grip over the party and forced all potential rivals out. Without a clear successor, President Ellis Clarke chose the new prime minister from among the three deputy political leaders of the party. Clarke appointed George Chambers Prime Minister. (4) Early general elections were held on 10 December 2001 after the ruling UNC lost its majority in the House of Representatives following four defections. However, the election results saw the UNC and the PNM winning 18 seats each. Although the UNC received the most votes, President A.N.R. Robinson appointed PNM leader Patrick Manning as prime minister

Source Election and Boundaries Commission of Trinidad and Tobago

Table 2.2 Local election results and ethnic composition

Ethnic composition in 2010 (%)					*Election results*		
	ATT	*ITT*	*MTT*	*OTT*	*2013*	*2016*	*2019*
Arima	31.7	15.5	7.1	45.7	PNM	PNM	PNM
Chaguanas	25.3	53.5	7.0	14.1	UNC (minority)	UNC	UNC
Couva Tabaquite Talparo	19.0	57.6	7.4	16.0	UNC	UNC	UNC
Diego Martin	43.0	9.3	8.5	39.1	PNM	PNM	PNM
Penal Debe	12.2	71.2	5.1	11.5	UNC	UNC	UNC
Point Fortin	59.5	11.6	8.9	20.0	PNM	PNM	PNM
Port of Spain	51.5	9.6	10.2	28.7	PNM	PNM	PNM
Princes Town	23.4	54.4	6.9	15.3	UNC	UNC	UNC
Rio Claro Mayaro	23.7	48.8	9.0	18.5	UNC	UNC	UNC
San Fernando	35.8	30.3	8.2	25.7	PNM	PNM	PNM
San Juan Laventille	52.6	17.7	9.3	20.4	PNM	PNM	PNM
Sangre Grande	30.1	31.0	12.9	26.0	UNC	PNM (minority)	UNC
Siparia	31.7	43.6	6.8	17.9	UNC	UNC	UNC
Tunapuna/ Piarco	32.0	27.3	6.7	34.1	PNM	PNM	PNM

Note People's National Movement; UNC = United National Congress; ATT = African Trinidad and Tobago; ITT = Indian Trinidad and Tobago; MTT = Mixed Trinidad and Tobago (ATT & ITT); OTT = Other Trinidad and Tobago

Source Census 2010, Central Statistics Office Trinidad and Tobago; Elections and Boundaries Commission of Trinidad and Tobago

with 50%. Even after 24 May 2010, when Kamla Persad-Bissessar was elected, women continued to face challenges in getting elected in TT (see Ranjitsingh, 2016).

The under-representation of women is also reflected in the appointed membership of the Senate. Figure 2.10 shows the gender composition of the 11th Parliament (2015–2020) by political party at the end of the PNM administration. Women are less than a third.

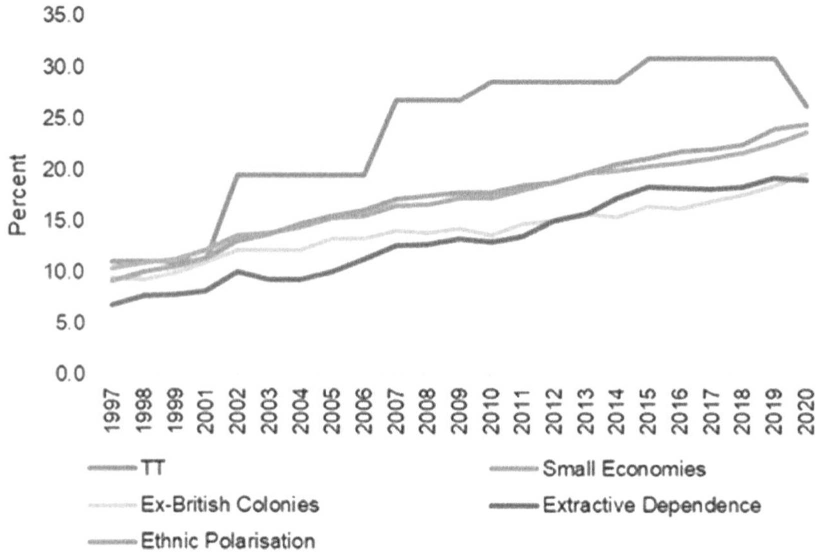

Fig. 2.9 Percentage of women in Parliaments (*Source* Authors' estimates from the Inter-Parliamentary Union)

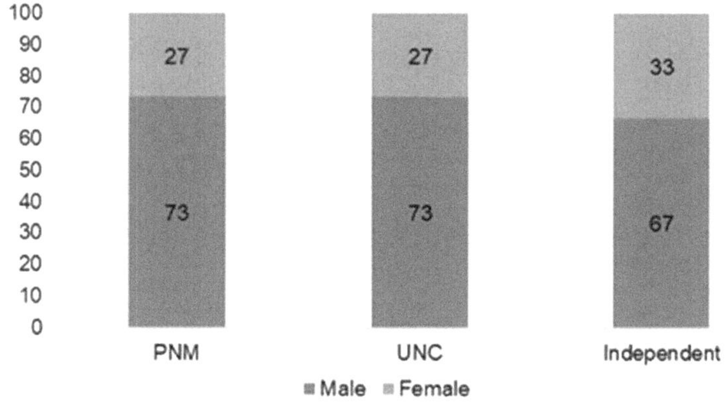

Fig. 2.10 Gender composition of the senate (2015–2020) (*Note* PNM = Peoples National Movement; UNC = United National Congress. *Source* Authors' estimates from the Parliament of Trinidad and Tobago)

2.4 Problems and Proposed Reforms: Proportional Voting and Gerrymandering

Parliamentary electoral systems differ in how they translate national votes into legislative seats. The result of an election depends on how people vote and how the ballots are counted. Majoritarian systems such as first past the post may produce an election result with a big difference between the share of the votes each party wins in the election and each party's share of votes in the Parliament.

There have been discussions of moving towards proportional representation (PR). In 1971, the government appointed a Constitution Commission headed by the then Chief Justice Sir Hugh Wooding. The Wooding Commission recognised the problem of race-based politics in the country. It recommended that Trinidad and Tobago become a Republic with a president as head of state and a prime minister as head of government. They also proposed a hybrid system of electoral representation. It also suggested that Parliament should consist of a single chamber. Half of the members will be elected from the 36 constituencies; the other half will be selected from lists by political parties contesting constituencies. However, while adopting the recommendations to abolish the monarchical system of government and establish Trinidad and Tobago as a Republic, the government rejected the Commission's recommendations for a National Assembly and proportional representation. In 1987, another Chief Justice, Sir Isaac Hyatali appointed and headed a Constitution Commission. The Commission conceded that the first-past-the-post electoral system did not always recognise the popular will and perpetrated an injustice on the electorate where the party with a minority of votes got more seats than the party with a majority of the popular votes. A solution proposed by the Hyatali Commission was to introduce a proportional representation system by distributing some of the seats in the Senate among the contesting political parties other than the party forming the government. So, both the Wooding Commission and the Hyatali Commission found that the first-past-the-post system did not inspire confidence in the electorate. The government rejected the recommendations for a partial proportional representation in the electoral system.

Such a system reduces the disparity between a party's percentage of the national vote and its share of the parliamentary ballots. Proportional representation increases minority representation, while electoral systems with single-member districts that first past the post exclude minorities from legislative representation. Lijphart (2004) argues that proportional representation is better than single-member districts and is superior to all other electoral institutions. As Lijphart explains, "The beauty of PR is that in addition to producing proportionality and minority representation, it treats all groups-ethnic, racial, religious, or even non-communal groups, in a completely equal and even-handed fashion. A simulation of "what if" the country had a strictly proportional system's electoral results is shown in addition to the actual results shown in Table 2.3. It would have only impacted the winning party in the 1991, 2007, and 2020 general elections. Instead of PNM winning, it would have been the UNC in all three cases.

In 2007, the parties contesting the election were the incumbent PNM, the official opposition UNC–Alliance (a coalition of the UNC and six smaller parties), the Congress of the People (a UNC splinter group), the Tobago United Front–Democratic Action Congress (a Tobago-based party), and the Democratic National Assembly (a new party based in Tobago). Also contesting were five independent candidates. A poll published in the Trinidad and Tobago Newsday in October 2007 showed

Table 2.3 Comparison between first-past-the-post vs. proportional system

	First-past-the-post system		*If proportional system*			
Election Year	*Winning party*	*Number of seats*	*% of votes*	*Number of seats*	*Change in seats*	*Change in winning party*
2020	PNM	22	49.1	20	−2	Yes
2015	PNM	23	52	21	−2	No
2010	UNC-PP coalition	29	60	25	−4	No
2007	PNM	26	46	19	−7	Yes
2002	PNM	20	51	18	−2	No
1995	UNC-NAR coalition	19	51	18	−1	No
1991	PNM	21	45	16	−5	Yes

Note NAR is the National Alliance for Reconstruction; PNM is the People's National Movement; and the UNC is the United National Congress

Source The authors' calculations are based on data from the Elections and Boundaries Commission of Trinidad and Tobago the Congress of the People ahead of the ruling People's National Movement by 7%. It was not to be. The PNM party, under the leadership of Patrick Manning, won 26 of the 41 seats in Parliament, receiving 45.9% of the votes. The UNC-A, under the leadership of Basdeo Panday, won the 15 remaining seats with 20.7% of the votes. The COP won no seats despite receiving 22.8% of the votes.[8] The 1991 general election result was a victory for the People's National Movement, which won 21 of the 36 seats. Voter turnout was 65.5%. In the 2020 election, the incumbent PNM, led by Prime Minister K. Rowley, won 22 of 41 seats to form a second five-year term majority government by defeating UNC's opposition leader, ex-Prime Minister K. Persad-Bissessar. PNM had led the opinion polls throughout the campaign. Voter turnout was 58%.

In 2013, Trinidad and Tobago stepped towards a proportional system for local elections the Municipal Corporations Amendment Bill that introduces proportional representation in Trinidad's local elections. Trinidad and Tobago's local government officials were previously chosen through winner-take-all rules in single-member districts. Now, under a new proportional representation system, citizens vote for political parties, with seats allocated proportionally to each party's vote share.

Trinidad's local government comprises 14 "corporations", including five municipalities, and 9 more larger regions. In these corporations, officials previously determined winners through winner-take-all methods, leading to one party often dominating with over 80% of the seats in nine out of the 14 corporations. This monopoly control is a characteristic of winner-take-all systems, where a party with the most support in a region can control its representation.

The new system, although not replacing winner-take-all elections in Trinidad and Tobago's regional corporations, will provide more opportunities for representation by having four alderpersons elected by proportional representation instead of being appointed. This change will decrease the dominant party's majority size by allowing the minority party in a district to pick up an extra position or two.

The closed-list system for the election of the alderpersons allows for each party to provide a list of candidates who will be elected if the party receives enough votes in this system. After votes are cast, the four seats in each municipality will be divided using the largest remainder

[8] The party was formed on 10 September 2006 by Winston Dookeran, after leaving the UNC.

method. Parties need to attain 20% of the votes to win a seat in Trinidad and Tobago's four-seat districts.

Another key feature of the electoral system is potential gerrymandering, i.e., setting electoral districts to establish a political advantage for a particular party by manipulating district boundaries. Partisan gerrymandering follows this logic by employing "packing and cracking", two gerrymandering tactics to force the other side to waste votes. With packing, one party's votes are concentrated into a district, resulting in wasted votes in lopsided victories. With cracking, one party's votes are split among several communities that lean safely to the other side.

The efficiency gap summarises the effect of gerrymandering by identifying all the wasted votes in victory and defeat for both parties. It then adds them up, finds the difference between the two sides, and divides that by the total number of votes in a constituency. A calculation yields a single percentage figure: the efficiency gap (Table 2.4). Note that the conversion of votes to seat symmetry isn't the same as proportionality. The efficiency asks that the parties' votes translate into seats with equal efficiency, not that their shares of votes and seats be identical as in proportionality (Stephanopoulos & McGhee, 2015).

Table 2.4 Electoral efficiency gap

Election year	*Winner*	*Efficiency gap in favour of winner (%)*
2020	PNM	4.7
2015	PNM	2.4
2010	UNC-PP	4.5
2007	PNM	17.2
2002	PNM	5.6
1995	UNC	8.5
1991	PNM	17.5

Note PNM = People's National Movement; UNC = United National Congress; UNC-PP = UNC-led Peoples Partnership. In 2007, the Congress of the People (COP) split from the UNC coalition. In the 1995 elections, UNC and PNM won 17 seats and NAR 2 seats

Source The authors' calculations are based on data from the Elections and Boundaries Commission of Trinidad and Tobago

2.5 A Flawed Democracy?

The democracy index used in the introductory chapter classifies TT as a flawed democracy. What contributes to its ranking? The index is based on five subcategories: political process and pluralism (TT is 34th out of 150 countries, lying between Panama and Brazil), government effectiveness (TT is ranked 43rd, lying between Slovakia and Siri Lanka), political participation (TT ranked 76th, laying between Slovakia and Brazil), political culture (TT ranked as 112th laying between Panama and Oman), and civil liberty (TT ranked 56th laying between Mongolia and South Africa).[9] So, the subcategories that pull down TT in the democracy index are political participation and political culture.

Figure 2.11 shows TT's overall index and subcategories of political participation and political culture and the median values for comparator country groups. TT does better than all comparator groups for overall performance, political participation, and political culture. There is only one exception: Ex-British colonies' median value of political culture is higher than TT's. However, the comparison does not help in understanding the non-stellar performance of TT.

There is another set of information by Franco and Scartascini (2014) for judging a country's political performance relative to comparator countries which helps. The *Political Institutions, State Capabilities, and Public Policy* international database produced by Franco and Scartascini (2014) provides information on key features of public policies and government capabilities that highlight the performance of countries' political system, particularly their political parties and Parliament.

The Congress Capabilities Index, which measures how much congress can effectively facilitate discussions, negotiations, and enforcement of political agreements, reveals that TT performs poorly compared to comparator countries' median values (see Figure 2.12). Congress Capabilities Index is based on answers to questions that determine legislative efficiency. These include: How effective is your national Parliament/ congress as a law-making institution? How much confidence do you have in the Parliament to determine confidence in Parliament?

The second indicator, see Figure 2.13, is the Party System Institutionalisation Index evaluates if established political parties or systems support enduring commitments and enable agreements over time within

[9] See: https://www.economist.com/media/pdf/DEMOCRACY_INDEX_2017.pdf.

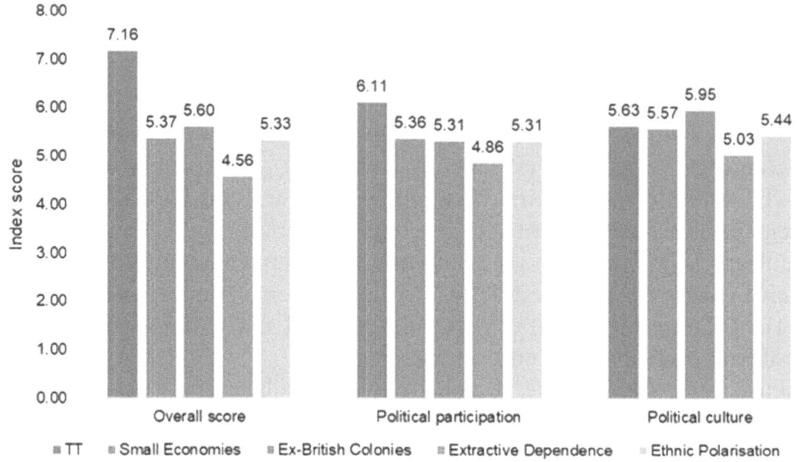

Fig. 2.11 Democracy index and political participation and culture (*Source* The authors' calculations are based on data from the Economist Intelligence Unit)

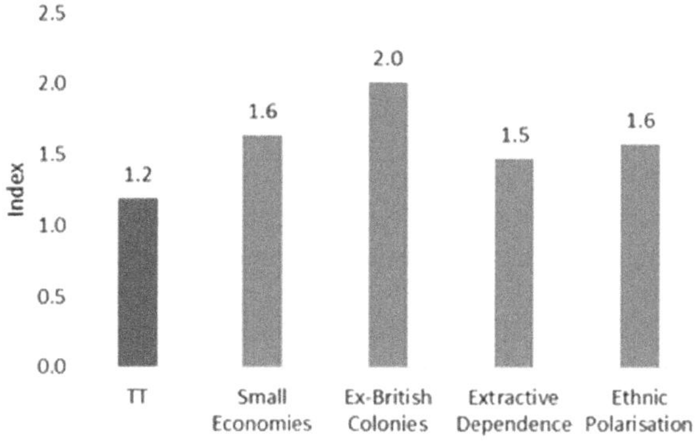

Fig. 2.12 Parliament capabilities (*Source* Authors estimates from Chuaire and Scatascini [2014])

and between parties. The index is based on the following five variables: Stable, moderate, rooted party system, confidence in political parties, vote

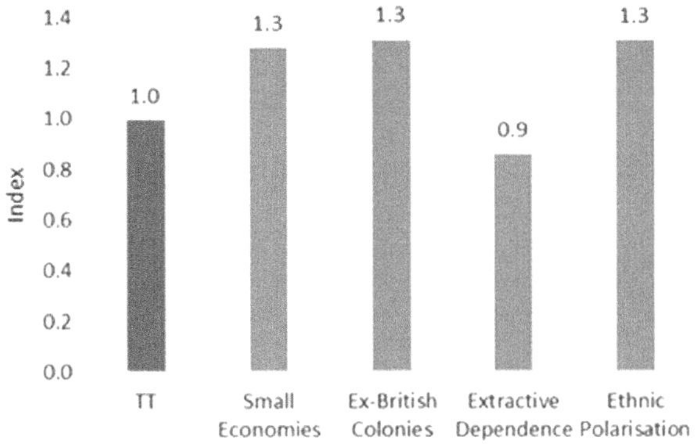

Fig. 2.13 Party system institutionalisation (*Source* Authors estimates from Chuaire and Scatascini [2014])

volatility,[10] party age, and—fairness of elections (see Franco and Scartascini, 2014 for details). Except for extractive-dependent countries, TT's index is lower than the comparator country groups median values.

The third indicator is legislative efficiency, which measures the effectiveness of law-making bodies. This index is based on the question: How effective is your national Parliament/congress as a law-making institution? TT underperforms all the comparator country groups (Figure 2.14).

Is there a significant difference in trust between the different ethnic groups? There is. ITTs are skewed towards greater trust in political parties than are ATTs and MTTs. 17% and 23% of ATTs and MTTs report zero trust in political parties (Fig. 2.15). Nonetheless, moderate and high trust percentages are 58, 85 and 59% for ATTs, ITTs, and MTTs, respectively. A similar pattern is observed for trust in Parliament. ITTs are skewed towards more trust than ATTs and MTTs (Fig. 2.16).

[10] Volatility is calculated by subtracting the percentage of the vote/seats won by every party in an election from that won in the previous election, taking the absolute value of this result, summing the results for all parties, and then dividing this total by two.

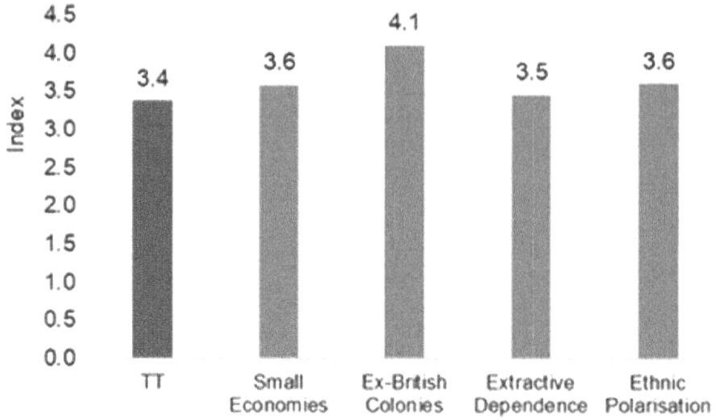

Fig. 2.14 Legislative efficiency (*Source* Authors estimates from Chuaire and Scatascini [2014])

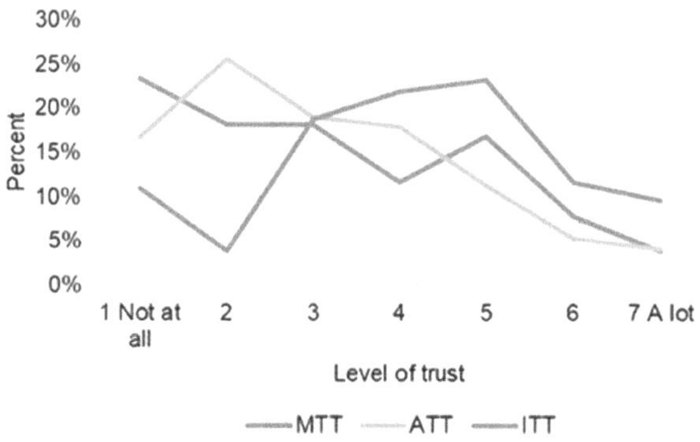

Fig. 2.15 Trust in political parties (*Note* ATT = African Trinidad and Tobago; ITT = Indian Trinidad and Tobago; MTT = Mixed Trinidad and Tobago. *Source* Latin American Public Opinion Project [LAPOP, 2012])

2.6 Conclusions

TT's political system is organised with an elected president as the head of state, a bicameral legislature consisting of a Senate and a House of Representatives, and a cabinet headed by the prime minister. The country's political system is based on a single-member constituency, with a Westminster model, using a first-past-the-post voting system and an ethnic-based political party system. Despite having free and fair elections

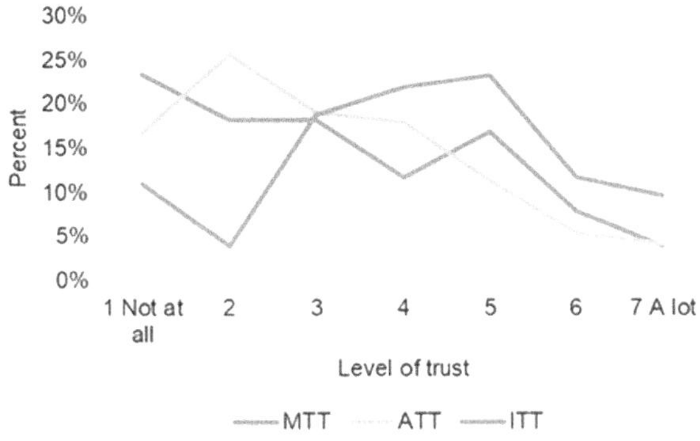

Fig. 2.16 Trust in Parliament (*Note* ATT = African Trinidad and Tobago; ITT = Indian Trinidad and Tobago; MTT = Mixed Trinidad and Tobago. *Source* Latin American Public Opinion Project [LAPOP, 2012])

and fundamental civil liberties, TT is classified as a flawed democracy due to a relatively underdeveloped political culture and limited political participation.

TT's political development has been influenced by the two political parties, the PNM, and the UNC. Both have historically dominated the political landscape, attracting support primarily based on race. The electoral results indicate predictable patterns and potential shifts, especially after the 1990s, reflecting the country's evolving political dynamics. The PNM held power for a significant portion of the country's history. Both political parties do not significantly differ regarding ideology, classified as left or right-leaning, or by class defined by income or education. Instead, the political parties are race-based, as voting patterns in general elections show a strong correlation between race and party affiliation. The pattern of race and party affiliation is high among the youth, which suggests that race-based politics is likely to persist.

The electoral results in TT since independence have seen both parties winning elections, with the PNM dominating the early years and the UNC forming governments during specific periods. The election system based on single-seat electoral districts has resulted in some seats switching between parties in different elections. The latter indicates that not all electoral districts are preordained by race-based politics. Marginal seats have played a crucial role in determining several general election outcomes.

The marginal seats have increased, indicating a more competitive electoral landscape. Switching of seats between parties has also occurred in past elections, highlighting the potential for shifts in voter preferences, especially when they are presented with a coalition among political parties.

References

Abdulah, D. (1991). Jamaat al Muslimen Insurrection in Trinidad and Tobago 1990. *Caribbean Quarterly, 37*, 814–888.

Bissessar, M., & La Guerre, J. (2013). *Trinidad and Tobago. Race and Politics in Two Plural Societies*. Lexington Books.

Chuaire, M. F., & Scatascini, C. (2014). Political Institutions, State Capabilities and Public Policy. An International Data Set. 2013 Update. IDB.

Girvan, N. (2011). Existential Threats in the Caribbean: Democratising Politics, Regionalising Governance. C.L.R. James Memorial Lecture, 12 May 2011, revised 17 May 2011.

Ruprah, K. J. I., & Godinez-Puig, L. (2023). Ethnic Cleavages and Vote Choice in Trinidad and Tobago. *Ethnopolitics, 22*(2), 222–251.

Lieber, M., & Ryan, S. (1972). *Race and Nationalism in Trinidad and Tobago: A Study of Decolonization in a Multiracial Society*. University of Toronto Press.

Lijphart, A. (2004, April). Constitutional Design for Divided Societies. *Journal of Democracy, 15*(2), 96–109.

Meighoo, K. (2008). Ethnic Mobilisation vs. Ethnic Politics: Understanding Ethnicity in Trinidad and Tobago Politics. *Commonwealth and Comparative Politics, 46*(1), 101–127.

Meighoo, K. (2003). *Politics in a Half Made Society: Trinidad and Tobago 1925–2001*. Ian Randel Publishers.

Ranjitsingh, A. (2016). Women's Political Leadership in Trinidad and Tobago: Understandings, Experiences, and Negotiations. In G. Hosein and J. Parpart (Eds.), *Negotiating Gender Policy and Politics Feminist Strategies Masculinist Relevance and Possibilities for Transformation*. Rown and Littlefield.

Franco, M., & Scartascini, C. (2014). The Politics of Policies: Revisiting the Quality of Public Policies and Government Capabilities in Latin America and the Caribbean. IDB Policy Paper, IDB.

Stephanopoulos, N. & McGhee, E. (2015). Partisan Gerrymandering and the Efficiency Gap. University of Chicago Law Review, 831 (2015), U of Chicago, Public Law Working Paper No. 493, SSRN: https://ssrn.com/abstract=2457468

Williams Eric, E. (1955). The Case for Party Politics in Trinidad and Tobago. Public Affairs Pamphlet no. 4. Port-of-Spain, Trinidad: Teachers Economic and Cultural Association, Ltd.

United Nations. (1995). Beijing Declaration and Platform for Action, Critical Area G, "Women, Power and Decision-Making".

CHAPTER 3

Political Development: The Executive's Size and Quality

The literature reviewed in the introductory chapter implies that the structural features of TT would result in a larger public sector of low quality (inefficient and ineffective). Thus, in this chapter, we first review the size of the public sector. The latter is followed by an assessment of the quality of institutions in the executive and judicial branches of the state. The third section looks at the quality of government policies in general concerning the private sector in particular. We end with the viewpoints of TT citizens on the quality of public services.

3.1 Size of the Public Sector

The structural features of TT imply the country will have a larger than usual public sector. The following ratios can measure the size of the public sector: (i) primary government expenditure to GDP, (ii) public investment to total investment, and (iii) public wage bill to GDP. Table 3.1 gives these measurements as the average values of comparator country groups relative to TT's value. Therefore, a value of more than one (1) implies TT has a larger share in that indicator relative to other comparator country groups. It also includes TT's degree of openness (exports plus

J. Khadan and I. Jit Ruprah, *Unraveling Race, Politics, and Gender in Trinidad and Tobago's Economic Development*,
https://doi.org/10.1007/978-3-031-54656-3_3

Table 3.1 Size of the public sector and openness of the economy

	General government total expenditure (% of GDP)	*Public investment (% of GDP)*	*Wage bill (% of GDP)*	*Trade (% of GDP)*
Small economies	1.1	1.1	1.2	0.8
Ex-British colonies	1.1	1.5	1.1	1.1
Extractive dependence	1.2	1.1	1.2	1.3
Ethnic polarisation	1.3	1.2	1.3	1.2

Note Data refers to the average for the period 2007–2016
Source Authors' calculations based on data from the World Development Indicators

imports to GDP) relative to comparator country groups' averages, as higher openness is associated with a larger public sector.[1]

As can be seen in Table 3.1, the predictions are borne out. Whichever measurement is used, public expenditure, investment or the wage bill, TT has a larger public sector than all the averages for comparator country groups. For example, compared to small economies, expenditure to GDP and public investment are 10% higher, and the public wage bill to GDP is 20% higher. However, it is less open; openness is only 80% of the small economies' average. Nonetheless, compared to other comparator groups, TT is more open.

The relatively larger public sector is partly due to the continued use of state enterprises and statutory bodies. The State Enterprises Sector comprises fifty-five (55) companies, of which forty-three (43) are wholly owned, eight (8) are majority owned, and four (4) in which the government has a minority shareholding.[2] These entities operate throughout the economy. They can be found in the gas and oil industry, banking and

[1] See Rodrick (1998) explains the positive correlation is due to government spending playing a risk reducing role and is strongest when the terms of trade risk are highest, as in the case of TT.

[2] For a complete list of State Enterprises in Trinidad and Tobago, see Appendix I of the State Enterprises Investment Programme 2023 report. https://www.finance.gov.tt/wp-content/uploads/2022/09/State-Enterprises-Investment-Programme-2023.pdf.

financial services, manufacturing, transport and communication, tourism, agriculture, information technology, and the provision of social services. There are approximately 32 statutory bodies. Examples include Trinidad and Tobago's Unit Trust Corporation, The Port Authority of Trinidad and Tobago, the Airports Authority of Trinidad and Tobago, and the National Carnival Commission.

But does it matter? There is evidence that governments that are too large reduce potential growth unless the functioning of government is highly effective. However, increasing the size of government, family benefits, or subsidies decreases inequality. Further, the composition of public spending matters as there is evidence that specific public spending (public investment and education) boosts potential growth while others (pensions and public subsidies) lower potential growth (Khadan, 2017a). So, comparisons of aggregate numbers as in Table 3.1 may be misleading (see Fournier & Johansson, 2016), given differences in expenditure composition.

We now turn to whether TT's public sector is effective.

3.2 Quality of Institutions and Governance

The literature finds that the quality of institutions and governance is influenced by many factors, including history (colonisation), ethnic diversity, natural resource dependence, geography, economic openness, and whether the country has democratic systems (Lehne et al., 2018).[3]

The country's structural features suggest that TT will likely perform worse on institutional quality. Table 3.2 shows TT's performance in twelve areas relative to the average values of comparator country groups. A value less than one (1) implies TT performs worse than the average of the comparator country group. This relative underperformance holds for property rights, intellectual property protection, diversion of public funds, trust in politicians, irregular payments and bribes, favouritism in decisions of government officials, the wastefulness of government spending, burden of public regulation, the efficiency of the legal framework in settling disputes, and transparency of government policymaking. TT performs

[3] See Lehne et al. (2018) who find that economic openness and commodity wealth may help non-democratic countries achieve improvements in some economic institutions. At the same time, the impact of commodity wealth on deeper economic institutions such as control of corruption remains negative.

relatively well in only one area (judicial independence). Public trust in politicians is shallow in TT, and there is a perception of favouritism in decisions made by government officials (usually perceived as favouring well-connected firms and individuals).

Furthermore, the perception of public funds diversion, along with irregular payments and bribes, is very negative. The judiciary comprises the only set of institutions that perform relatively better when compared

Table 3.2 Institution quality

	Small economies	*Ex-British colonies*	*Extractive dependence*	*Ethnic polarisa-tion*
Property rights	0.93	0.88	1.01	0.94
Intellectual property protection	0.84	0.79	0.95	0.85
Diversion of public funds	0.66	0.61	0.72	0.69
Public trust in politicians	0.59	0.54	0.57	0.62
Irregular payments and bribes	0.80	0.78	0.87	0.83
Judicial independence	1.09	0.96	1.21	1.10
Favoritism in decisions of government officials	0.60	0.57	0.63	0.63
Wastefulness of government spending	0.78	0.70	0.73	0.77
Burden of government regulation	0.98	0.90	0.99	1.00
Efficiency of legal framework in settling disputes	0.86	0.77	0.89	0.85
Efficiency of legal framework in challenging regs	0.88	0.80	0.95	0.88
Transparency of government policymaking	0.93	0.88	0.99	0.94

Note Values below one imply a lower TT score than other comparator country groups
Source Global Competitiveness Index (2015)

to the benchmark, as predicted by TT being an ex-British colony. The judiciary is widely perceived as independent from the influences of citizens, firms, and government members (Khadan & Smets, 2018).

3.2.1 *Education*[4]

The related evidence presented in Chapter 8 suggests that the quality of education matters more than quantity. Furthermore, the quality of education hinges primarily on the quality of teachers. Therefore, this section will focus not only on the ability of educational institutions to offer educational services coverage but also on the extent to which institutions ensure appropriate teacher quality in TT.

TT offers free public education from the pre-primary to the secondary level. Just over half of the 895 primary and secondary schools are managed by religious boards and funded by the government. A further 37% are owned and managed by the government, and 21% are private institutions. At the tertiary level, TT hosts two government-funded universities. The largest by enrolment, the University of the West Indies (UWI) St. Augustine Campus, offers post-graduate programmes, including PhD degrees. The Ministry of Education subsidises full tuition at the undergraduate level through the Government Assistance for Tuition Expenses (GATE) programme. This policy is reflected in the share of working-age adults (25–65 years old) with tertiary education at 67%, significantly above the levels in comparator countries: TT (67%), Small Economies (32%), Ex-British Colonies (30%), and Extractive Dependence (35%).

As mentioned above, it is the quality of education rather than the quantity that matters for development. This section documents the extent to which institutional arrangements are present in TT to ensure appropriate teacher quality.

School supervision and quality monitoring of the education system broadly fall under the Office of the Chief Education Officer within the Ministry of Education (MOE). The office comprises five units, including a unit charged with educational research and evaluation and a unit responsible for school supervision. Institutional efforts seeking to boost the quality of teaching have been undertaken in the past.

[4] See Chapter 9 for a more detailed discussion on education.

These have included delinking teachers' salaries from the general civil service, strengthening teacher training institutions, and introducing more rigorous entry requirements into the teaching profession. However, there is still ample room for improvement as no explicit and structured mechanisms to evaluate teacher effectiveness exist except for a mechanism called clinical supervision. Clinical supervision aims to help teachers improve teaching and delivery, but this is only an ad hoc tool.

Although students take several standardised examinations across primary and secondary schools, such data are not organised as individual-level longitudinal series, analysed, or used to evaluate student and teacher performance over time. In terms of measures of teacher effectiveness, if appropriately managed, the existing data of students' evaluations across time could be used to compute teacher-specific value-added measures. The latter is highly relevant, as objective evidence provided by Araujo et al. (2016) that show that value-added teacher measures based on student evaluations give better teacher effectiveness than traditional teacher assessments based on direct evaluations or observation of teachers. Implementing this type of measure, however, is usually met with resistance. Objective evidence has shown the benefits of teacher value-added evaluations in guiding policy decisions.

The recruitment of teachers for secondary schools is done through the Teaching Service Commission's Recruitment Committee. The Curriculum Division of the Ministry of Education determines an applicant's suitability for serving as a teacher in the teaching service. Candidates who have been assessed are then placed in a database according to their year of assessment. The Recruitment Committee of the Teaching Service Commission then calls candidates for interviews based on demands from the Ministry of Education in the relevant subject areas. Those candidates who are successful are placed on a priority list that is sent to the permanent secretary of the Ministry of Education. The placement of teachers in schools depends on the availability of vacancies and subject area. Teachers' career advancement is tied to academic advancement, i.e., completion of a degree programme or any other required training courses, and not to objective performance measures.

3.2.2 *Health*[5]

TT's population has access to public and private health care. Public health care is based on universal access, and citizens can access free health care services at public facilities. Health insurance is not required, and medicines are free at public health facilities. The Ministry of Health—through five regional health facilities—manages a network of nine hospitals, nine district health facilities, and 96 health centres. Basic or primary-level care is provided at health centres and district health facilities, while secondary-level care is provided at public hospitals. Primary care providers refer patients to secondary care facilities when the need arises. Tertiary care is also offered, though limited, at specific hospitals. TT also has a relatively small private health sector. About 19.5% of the population has access to private health care.[6] The private sector mainly consists of individual physicians, private pharmacies, and ten medical institutions and primarily operates on a fee-for-service basis, funded by out-of-pocket expenses or private health insurance. Private healthcare facilities are mainly located in urban areas, and there is a strong perception that private medical facilities offer better service and treatment than public facilities.

The Chemistry Food and Drug Division (CFDD) is the principal authority responsible for implementing and enforcing health regulations in TT. The CFDD is accountable for ensuring the safe quality of an equitable standard for use by food, drugs, and medical service consumers. Three different units of the CFDD carry out these responsibilities: (1) the food and drugs inspectorate, (2) the pesticides inspectorate, and (3) the laboratory service.

Besides institutional measures to maintain high-quality health services, individual-level incentives for health care providers in the public sector—e.g., performance evaluation and merit-based promotion—are lacking in TT. The lack of such arrangements may prevent medical practitioners from being incentivised to exert high effort. Introducing a retention strategy that includes continued educational opportunities and financial and non-financial incentives based on objective performance measures might thus be considered to boost quality in the health sector.

[5] See Chapter 10 for a more detailed discussion on health.

[6] Source: 2014 Trinidad and Tobago Survey of Living Conditions.

3.2.3 Central Bank Independence and Transparency

The Central Bank of Trinidad and Tobago (CBTT) is the country's monetary authority. It is managed by a Board of Directors that includes a governor, at most two deputy governors, and at least six other directors. The President of TT appoints the Board of Directors. The governor's term in office is set for five years, and deputy governors are set for a term fixed by the president. The Central Bank Act outlines a wide range of responsibilities for the central bank, including maintaining monetary and financial stability. Concerning the implementation of monetary policy, the CBTT has three primary objectives: maintaining a low and stable inflation rate, an orderly foreign exchange market, and an adequate level of foreign exchange reserves.

How central banks are governed influences these institutions' credibility and effectiveness in controlling inflation and providing a proper environment for economic growth and prosperity. The 2016–2020 strategic plan of the Central Bank of Trinidad and Tobago includes strengthening governance, transparency, and accountability as essential pillars. The bank has made noteworthy progress, especially in operational efficiency.

However, data for 2010 provided by Dincer and Eichengreen (2014) and historical data covering 1970–2012 provided by Garriga (2016) show that improvements could be made to continue to strengthen central bank independence. For instance, the Central Bank Act permits the minister of finance to issue general directives to the CBTT to give effect to government's policies. On the other hand, the Central Bank Act stipulates that the total amount of outstanding advances to the government is not to exceed 15% of annual revenue.

Objective international comparisons of central bank independence reported by Dincer and Eichengreen (2014) rank the CBTT relatively low at 77th out of 89 countries worldwide.[7] Garriga (2016) ranked the CBTT in the 106th position out of 179 countries in a study covering an

[7] This ranking is based on the Central Bank Independence Weighted Index (CBIW) for 2010 reported in Dincer and Eichengreen (2014). The CBIW is a weighted average of measures related to the following dimensions: CEO appointment (weight = 0.1), policy formulation (0.15), objectives (0.15), limitations on lending to the government (0.50), and appointment of board members (0.1). For details on the specific components of these measures, see Table 18 of Dincer and Eichengreen (2014).

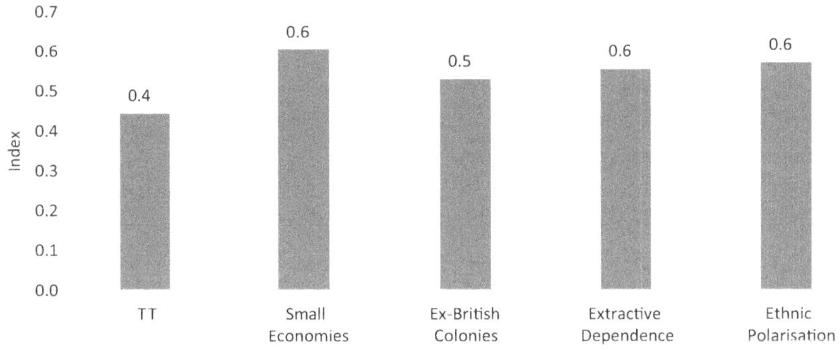

Fig. 3.1 Central Bank Independence (CBI), 2012 (*Note* The Central Bank Independence Index ranges from 0 (lowest independence) to 1 (highest independence). *Source* Garriga [2016])

extended set of countries worldwide.[8] Figure 3.1. reveals that CBTT's independence is below the averages for all comparator country groups.

Regarding legal requirements for accountability of the bank's operations, the Central Bank Act stipulates that bank accounts shall be audited annually by auditors appointed by the board and approved by the minister of finance. In addition, the minister of finance may require the auditor general to examine and report on the central bank's accounts at any time. Within three months after the financial year, the CBTT must provide the minister of finance with a report on the bank's operation for the preceding financial year and the audited financial statements certified by the auditors. The finance minister then presents the annual audited statement in Parliament and publishes it in the Gazette. The bank must also prepare and communicate its assets and liabilities weekly to the minister of finance, which must also be published in the Gazette.

[8] This ranking is for year 2012. Garriga (2016) identified four dimensions concerning the independence of central banks from political influence: who appoints the governor (weight = 0.2); whether there is direct government involvement in policy decisions (weight = 0.15); whether there are limits on the ability of the government to borrow from the central bank (weight = 0.50); and whether price stability is a core objective of monetary policy (weight = 0.15). The weighted average of these dimensions results in a central bank independence index ranging from 0 (lowest independence) to 1 (highest independence).

In terms of transparency to the public, the central bank publishes several reports with varying time frequencies. Concerning decisions about monetary policy, the CBTT has an established Monetary Policy Committee (MPC) assisted by a Monetary Policy Secretariat (MPS). The chief economist chairs the MPC, which is comprised of members from various departments of the CBTT. The MPC has the mandate to develop and implement the monetary policy framework. In addition to setting the repo rate, the MPC supervises the preparation and publication of a bi-monthly Monetary Policy Announcement and a semi-annual Monetary Policy Report. The CBTT also publishes data on macroeconomic aggregates and several other reports, such as the Annual Economic Survey, Balance of Payments Report, Business Confidence Report, Consumer Confidence Report, Economic Bulletin, Financial Stability Report, Labour Confidence Report, Statistical Digest, and Summary of Economic Indicators Bulletin. However, following Dincer and Eichengreen (2014), measures of overall transparency that include political, economic, procedural, policy, and operational transparency suggest that CBTT's transparency is lower than the averages in comparator countries other than Extractive Dependence countries (Fig. 3.2).[9]

3.2.4 *Fiscal Institutions*

TT's economy is highly dependent on the energy sector (oil, gas, and petrochemicals). For instance, during 2010–2015, the energy sector generated 40% of GDP and 50% of fiscal revenues. It is well understood that commodity-dependent countries are at a greater risk of facing significant fiscal adjustments due to price and supply shocks to the resource sector (for TT, see Khadan, 2017b).[10] As such, it is essential to establish

[9] The Central Bank Transparency Index measures compliance with 15 best practices distributed across the following areas: political transparency (practices), economic transparency (three practices), procedural transparency (three practices), policy transparency (three practices), and operational transparency (three practices). The index ranges from 0 (no compliance at all) to 15 (full compliance with the 15 best practices). For details on the specific practices and index construction, see Appendix 1 in Dincer and Eichengreen (2014).

[10] Khadan (2017a) finds asymmetrical effects of external shocks: positive energy revenue shock increases growth almost immediately; it is not sustained. A negative energy revenue shock is found to have a greater adverse effect on primary expenditure than a positive shock and this largely occurs through a reduction in capital expenditure. Transfers and

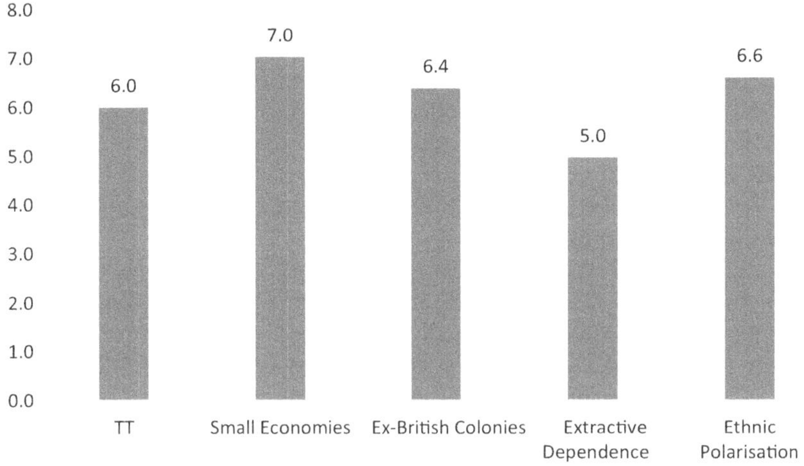

Fig. 3.2 Central Bank Transparency Index (2019) (*Note* The Central Bank Transparency Index ranges from 0 (lowest transparency) to 15 (highest transparency). *Source* Dincer et al. [2022])

strong fiscal frameworks with appropriate levels of stabilisation savings, effective spending policies, and effective use of taxation to reduce revenue volatility (IMF, 2015).[11] If properly established, objective fiscal rules, independent fiscal councils monitoring compliance with fiscal rules, and sovereign wealth funds provide a medium-term anchor that enhances the credibility of policies and supports inter-generational equity. By contrast, the lack of such institutions makes fiscal mismanagement more likely.

TT only has an explicit fiscal target for its annual budget; however, a formal publicly available multi-year rules-based fiscal framework does not exist.[12] The Ministry of Finance currently produces projections for

subsidies, and goods and services are the most sensitive components of current expenditure to positive energy shocks. With respect to the effect of expenditure on growth, transfers and subsidies significantly reduce growth in the short run, whereas other categories of expenditure are found to have a largely positive effect on growth.

[11] The latter are conclusions of IMF (International Monetary Fund, 2015) which examines the conduct of fiscal policy under the uncertainty caused by dependence on natural resource revenues.

[12] From time to time, however, the minister of finance may make broad statements on how the government would like to see the fiscal accounts develop over the medium

revenues, expenditures, and the fiscal balance for one year. The authorities make public the assumptions of commodity prices used to estimate energy revenue forecasts and the allocation of government expenditure across government ministries and by functional areas. Fiscal performance during the fiscal year is monitored and evaluated by the Ministry of Finance through the publication of a mid-year budget review debated in Parliament. While fiscal performance is publicly discussed, TT does not have an independent fiscal council.

TT can rely on a sovereign wealth fund to manage revenue volatility. TT introduced its Heritage and Stabilization Fund (HSF) in 2007, smoothing public expenditures and saving resources for future generations. It has operated chiefly as a savings fund, with US$3.5 billion—about 60% of the current stock—considered the "heritage" component, the floor below which funds cannot be accessed for stabilisation purposes. It was only in 2016 that the government of TT began to draw on the stabilisation component of the fund to finance government spending. The HSF is managed by an independent board comprised of members from the Ministry of Finance, the Central Bank, and the private sector. Operational management is delegated to the Central Bank, which publishes quarterly reports on the fund's performance.

3.2.5 *Judicial Independence and Effectiveness*[13]

The judiciary is headed by the chief justice, who is responsible for the general administration of justice. The judicial system is separated into a Supreme Court of Judicature (higher judiciary) and a Magistracy (lower judiciary). The Supreme Court of Judicature consists of the Court of Appeal and the High Court. The Magistracy comprises the Courts of Summary Criminal Jurisdiction and Petty Civil Courts. The chief magistrate is responsible for the Magistracy and reports to the chief justice. The Office of the Director of Public Prosecutions (DPP) is TT's prosecution entity.

term, although these generally lack detail on what are the key policy measures that will contribute to such an outcome. Moreover, medium-term forecasts of other macroeconomic aggregates (GDP, inflation) that are important to evaluate fiscal and macroeconomic performance are also absent from annual budget planning.

[13] See Chapter 11 for a more comprehensive discussion on crime and violence in TT.

The constitution enables the judiciary to operate independently from the executive. The president appoints the chief justice in consultation with the prime minister and leader of the opposition. The holder of the position of chief justice is also the president of the Court of Appeal, an ex-officio judge of the High Court, and chairman of the Judicial and Legal Service Commission (JLSC). The JLSC is responsible for appointing justices of appeal, High Court judges, masters of the High Court, magistrates, registrars of the Supreme Court, and the administrative secretary to the chief justice.

The Office of the DPP is established under Section 90 of the constitution and operates independently of the executive. The President of TT appoints the director of public prosecutions in consultation with the prime minister and leader of the opposition. The DPP is supported by legal staff that should number about 40 attorneys-at-law. Prosecutors are typically attorneys-at-law from the Office of the DPP. However, for criminal matters in the Magistrates Court, a police officer who has attained the rank of sergeant and above usually presents the facts of the case.

The judiciary lacks financial autonomy. Financial and administrative autonomy has been a critical concern for judicial independence in TT (Mendes, 2000). For instance, at the start of the 2014/2015 law term, the chief justice indicated that an insufficient budget allocation, low remuneration of judges, and delays in the release of funds from the central government were among the main problems facing the judiciary. Similarly, in a meeting of the Joint Select Committee of Parliament in March 2017, the director of public prosecutions lamented the lack of physical space and abysmal under-staffing that has contributed to a backlog of cases. Furthermore, the level of protection afforded to state prosecutors could be significantly improved. The concern for the safety of prosecutors became a critical issue after the assassination of a state prosecutor in 2014. Increasing the financial autonomy of the judiciary and improving the protection of state prosecutors—two areas the government is currently working on—could further enhance TT's ranking on the Judicial Independence Index (Fig. 3.3, where the value of comparator countries has been divided by the value of TT). The relative value is below comparator country groups other than marginally above the average for the Ethnic Polarisation group.

Regarding judicial effectiveness, TT does better than most comparator groups of countries other than the ex-British colonies. The situation differs between the components of civil justice, where TT performs better

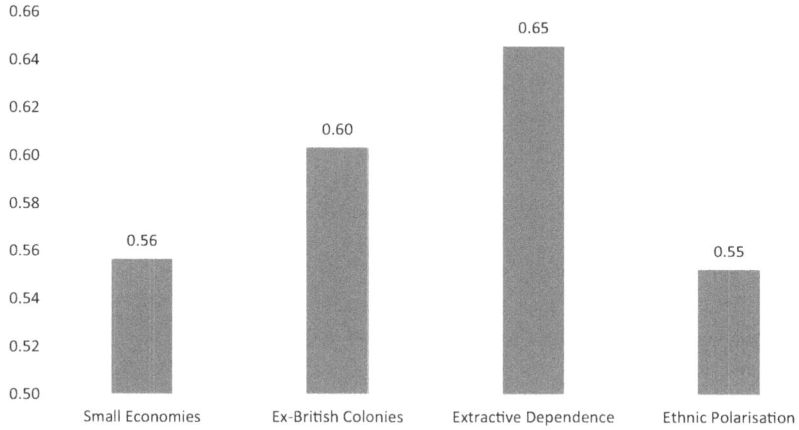

Fig. 3.3 Judicial Independence Index (*Note* Values below one imply a lower TT score than comparators. *Source* Authors' estimates from Franco & Scartascini [2014])

than all comparators, while criminal justice performs worse than the comparators (Table 3.3).

The Trinidad and Tobago Police Service (TTPS), the country's law enforcement body, falls within the ambit of the Ministry of National Security. The primary mandates of the police service are to maintain law and order, protect life and property, prevent and detect crime, and enforce all laws and regulations that fall within its remit. The TTPS comprises nine divisions and 26 branches charged with various responsibilities. There are 6500 police officers and 78 police stations in TT.

The commissioner of police is the head of the TTPS. The commissioner and deputy commissioners are appointed by the Police Service Commission (PSC) through a selection process determined by the Parliament. The PSC is an independent body established by the constitution consisting of a chairperson and four members the president appoints in consultation with the prime minister and the opposition leader. In addition, the PSC is responsible for managing the TTPS's monitoring, appointments, disciplinary, and appeals functions. The process of appointing a commissioner of police and a deputy commissioner is often described as rigorous, though convoluted and costly.

Table 3.3 Judicial effectiveness

	TT	*Small economies*	*Ex-British colonies*	*Extractive dependence*	*Ethnic polarisation*
Judicial effectiveness	46.90	46.0	50.9	37.0	44.3
Civil justice	0.58	0.55	0.56	0.49	0.52
People can access and afford civil justice	0.58	0.56	0.54	0.52	0.53
Civil justice is free of discrimination	0.63	0.56	0.55	0.50	0.53
Civil justice is free of corruption	0.72	0.56	0.62	0.47	0.54
Civil justice is free of improper government influence	0.71	0.53	0.61	0.40	0.50
Civil justice is not subject to unreasonable delay	0.34	0.46	0.44	0.46	0.42
Civil justice is effectively enforced	0.43	0.52	0.52	0.47	0.50
Alternative dispute resolution mechanisms are accessible, impartial, and effective	0.68	0.66	0.67	0.60	0.64
Criminal justice	0.32	0.47	0.50	0.39	0.44
Criminal investigation system is effective	0.21	0.42	0.45	0.34	0.39
Criminal adjudication system is timely and effective	0.22	0.48	0.49	0.42	0.44
Correctional system is effective in reducing criminal behavior	0.15	0.41	0.42	0.35	0.36
Criminal system is impartial	0.33	0.47	0.47	0.41	0.43

(continued)

Table 3.3 (continued)

	TT	*Small economies*	*Ex-British colonies*	*Extractive dependence*	*Ethnic polarisation*
Criminal system is free of corruption	0.56	0.55	0.58	0.46	0.53
Criminal system is free of improper government influence	0.44	0.48	0.56	0.32	0.46
Due process of the law and rights of the accused	0.36	0.50	0.49	0.40	0.46

Note Scores for the WJP Rule of Law Index, as well as for its component factors and sub-factors, range from 0 to 1, where scores closer to 1 indicate better performance
Source World Justice Project (WJP) (https://worldjusticeproject.org/our-work/wjp-rule-law-index/wjp-rule-law-index-2016/factors-rule-law)

Trinidad and Tobago's Police Training Academy trains recruits and conducts refresher courses for serving officers. Some courses are offered in collaboration with other agencies, such as the Ministry of Education, the Central Training Unit, and professional management consultants. The educational requirements to become a police officer require successful completion of secondary school. Applicants must also take an entrance examination and undertake several medical and physical tests. A selection panel then interviews successful applicants. Training involves an enhanced introduction programme over a 24-week cycle. Successful trainees are then transferred to a police station to begin their career as a police officer. The recruits undergo a probation period of two years, during which they are closely supervised and their performance evaluated. The opportunity to be promoted to the rank of corporal comes after three years of service. Promotion to higher levels is attained through continuous assessment.

The Crime and Problem Analysis Branch (CAPA) is the TTPS data processing unit. It analyses information from crime reports and other sources to inform the crime deterrence, disruption, and detection efforts of the Police Service. However, a diagnostic analysis by the Crime and Problem Analysis Unit found several areas for improvement: data collection, validation, and verification procedures and their application leave ample room for error (Seepersad, 2016). Victimisation surveys have not been carried out regularly in TT. In addition, complementary crime and violence data collected by other government ministries are generally not shared, published, or released, and systems to track, record, and analyse crime are lacking.

Oversight of the TTPS is performed by the Police Complaints Authority (PCA). The PCA is an independent body mandated to provide civilian oversight of law enforcement and to independently investigate complaints against police officers involved in criminal offences, police corruption, and serious police misconduct. The PCA accepts walk-in, mailed, and emailed complaints from the public. The PCA Act also allows the authority to initiate its investigations.

The number of complaints received by the PCA has increased over the past seven years. The PCA received 255 complaints in 2010 and 321 complaints in 2014. The highest number of complaints received in a single year was 491 in 2015. There are many allegations of criminal and disciplinary offences against or involving the police. From October 2014 to September 2015, the PCA received reports of 672 offences. It was estimated that 230 were allegations of criminal offences, and 442 were allegations of disciplinary offences. The breakdown of these allegations shows that 60% were related to severe police misconduct, 37% to the commission of a criminal offence by a police officer, and 3% to police corruption.

The data suggest that police effectiveness needs to be improved. Despite increasing expenditure over the years, detection rates for significant crimes remain low. TT has one of the highest homicide rates in the Americas (30.88 per 100,000 inhabitants). The number of homicides increased from 84 in 1990 to 463 in 2013. The detection rate, however, was 13% in 2013. Incidents of wounding and shootings increased from 391 to 542, while the detection rate declined from 61 to 24% from 1990 to 2013. Similar but less drastic declines in detection rates were reported for other crimes (Khadan, 2017b). The high incidence of crime and violence has been linked to drug-related activities, law enforcement limitations, lack of credibility of the police force, and a tendency to resort to violence to resolve personal grievances. Therefore, TT's Order and Security Index ranking remains low (Fig. 3.4).

In summary, this section has evidenced that several institutions related to the rule of law in TT could be improved. There is scope to enhance property protection, fundamental human rights, criminal justice, security, and order. The situation could partly erode economic agents' confidence in the rules of society, thereby hindering the ability to spur investment and

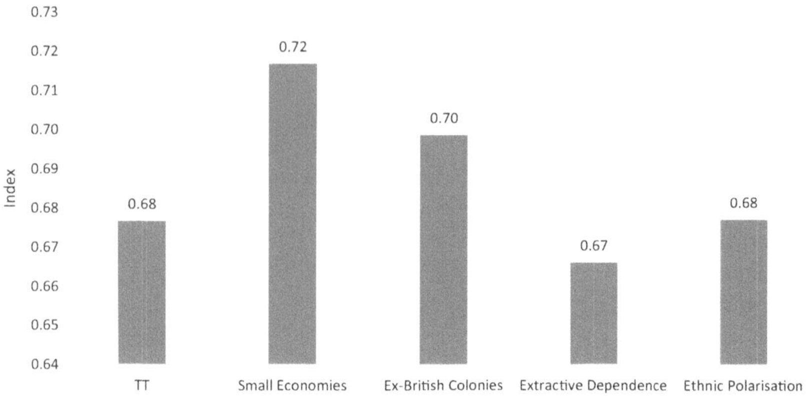

Fig. 3.4 Order and security index (*Source* Authors' calculations using the 2016 World Justice Project database)

growth. Indeed, as revealed in Fig. 3.5, the country's ranking on the 2016 Rule of Law Index ranks below the averages of Small Economies and ex-British but above the Extractive Dependence and Ethnic Dependence country groups.

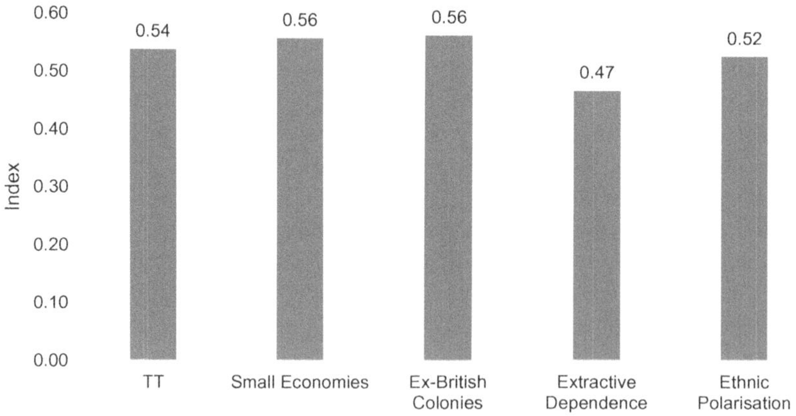

Fig. 3.5 Rule of law index (2016) (*Source* World Bank, 2017 World Governance Indicators database [www.govindicators.org])

3.3 Quality of Public Policies

We can delve more into the quality of public policies. We can contend that countries that have more capable bureaucracies, more institutionalised congresses, independent judiciaries, and institutionalised political parties tend to have policies that are more stable, adaptable, coherent, efficient, and public regarded (Scartascini et al., 2014).

According to Franco and Scartascini (2014), the quality of policies can be measured along several dimensions. These are (i) stability—the extent to which policies are stable over time; (ii) quality of implementation and enforcement—the degree to which policies are implemented and enforced correctly after approval in Parliament; (iii) efficiency—the extent to which policies reflect an allocation of scarce resources that ensures high returns; and (iv) public regardedness—the degree to which policies pursue the public interest. The four dimensions can be aggregated into one policy Index—an overall Index of Public policy quality (Franco & Scartascini, 2014).[14] Table 3.4 gives the relative values for the quality of institutions such that values below unity indicate a worse performance of TT. Generally, TT performs better for stability and efficiency but worse for implementation, public regardedness, and the overall policy index.

The features of public policies are associated with political and institutional variables such as the policymaking capabilities of the Congress,

Table 3.4 Features of public policy

	Small economies	*Ex-British colonies*	*Extractive dependence*	*Ethnic polarisation*
Stability	1.16	1.11	1.32	1.20
Efficiency	1.10	1.04	1.35	1.17
Implementation and effectiveness	0.94	0.88	1.10	1.00
Public regardedness	0.78	0.73	0.92	0.80
Policy index	1.00	0.95	1.23	1.08

Note Values below one imply a lower TT score than comparators
Source Authors' estimates from Franco and Scartascini (2014)

[14] Chuaire & Scartascini (2014) use two more indicators for the overall index but that are not available for TT.

party system institutionalisation, both of which were discussed in the previous chapter, judicial independence, and bureaucratic quality. The Congress Capabilities Index captures the degree to which Congress can serve as an appropriate arena for discussing, negotiating, and enforcing political agreements, hence facilitating the development of relatively consensual and consistent policies over time. An independent judiciary enables the inter-temporal enforcement of prior political and policy decisions according to constitutions and laws. The judiciary can improve the stability and quality of enforcement in the policymaking process. The Party Institutionalisation index captures that party systems, particularly programmatic ones, are more likely to encourage long-horizon commitments and facilitate inter-temporal bargains between parties. This index is constructed based on the following five variables: stable, moderate, and rooted party system, confidence in political parties, vote volatility, party age, and fairness of elections. High bureaucratic capabilities improve the quality of implementation of public policies as they promote fewer politics that can limit the bureaucracy's discretion and enforce long-term commitments. The Index of Government Capabilities summarises the information from the previous four indicators. Table 3.5 gives the values of TT relative to the comparator country groups, where a value below unity indicates a worse TT performance. Generally, TT performs worse than the comparators regarding the quality of public institutions, except for civil service, where it performs better than all the comparators.

Table 3.5 Quality of government institutions

	Small economies	*Ex-British colonies*	*Extractive dependence*	*Ethnic polarisation*
Congress capabilities index	0.79	0.78	1.17	0.78
Judicial independence	0.56	0.60	0.65	0.55
Party institutionalisation	0.73	0.68	0.85	0.76
Bureaucracy	1.19	1.25	1.35	1.17
Government capabilities	0.93	0.88	1.09	0.98

Note Values below one imply a lower TT score than comparators
Source Authors' estimates from Franco and Scartascini (2014)

3.4 Ease of Doing Business

Private entrepreneurship and innovation are crucial to boosting investment, growth, and development. Therefore, institutions and regulations that permit and promote private-sector development are highly relevant. As such, this section assesses the state of these issues in TT.

According to the World Bank's 2016 Doing Business Indicators, TT underperforms vis-à-vis other country groups in dimensions such as registering property, paying taxes, trading across borders, and enforcing contracts (Table 3.6). For example, the time and cost of enforcing contracts through a local first-instance court in TT are lengthy and high. On average, it takes 1340 days to enforce contracts, the 13th longest time in the world and more than twice the time in other Caribbean countries. With many procedures and elevated costs, registering property in TT is also challenging. This is reflected in the World Bank's Ease of Registering Property Index, which ranks the country 150th out of 190 countries in 2017.

According to Table 3.6, TT performs well along other dimensions, such as access to credit and protection of investors. The Companies Act of Trinidad and Tobago outlines the protection of shareholders. The act stipulates that shareholders of a company (other than an unlimited liability company) are not liable for any liability, act, or default of the company. The latter is reflected in the country's relatively good ranking in the World Bank's Ease of Doing Business Index for the protection of minority investors, at 62nd out of 190 countries.

The banking system in TT is generally well-capitalised, profitable, and highly liquid. There is a high level of penetration of banking services. Commercial bank branches per 100,000 adults are estimated at 13, compared to 15 in Latin America and the Caribbean. However, electronic and Internet banking exist at most commercial banks, facilitating greater access to citizens' banking services. These factors explain why economic agents in TT get good access to credit.

Current tax administration rules and procedures are cumbersome, as the average firm spends 210 hours and makes 39 payments annually compared to 183 hours and 24 payments annually by firms in small countries group. Sahadeo (2012) and more recent TADAT (Tax Administration Diagnostic Assessment Tool) reports note that tax administration in TT faces several challenges, including human capital constraints, lack of electronic services, and a weak revenue accounting environment, among

Table 3.6 Ease of doing business

	Small economies	*Ex-British colonies*	*Extractive dependence*	*Ethnic polarisa-tion*
Ease of doing business score	1.0	1.0	1.1	1.0
Starting a business	1.1	1.0	1.1	1.1
Dealing with construction permits	1.0	0.9	1.0	1.0
Getting electricity	1.2	1.2	1.3	1.2
Registering property	0.7	0.8	0.8	0.8
Getting credit	1.2	1.2	1.4	1.2
Protecting minority investors	1.2	1.2	1.4	1.2
Paying taxes	0.8	0.7	0.8	0.9
Trading across borders	0.9	1.0	1.2	0.9
Enforcing contracts	0.6	0.7	0.7	0.7
Resolving insolvency	1.1	1.1	1.4	1.1

Note Values below one imply a lower TT score than comparators
Source World Bank, 2016 Doing Business database

other issues (see also Muyangwa et al., 2017). TT moved from 101st to 77th on Transparency International's 2017 Corruption Perception Index regarding the latter. However, an independent and autonomous anti-corruption agency would be a further step forward and help reduce high levels of perceived corruption.

Finally, TT has produced several plans and strategies to diversify the country's exports and revenue sources. Some of the main plans in recent years include Vision 2020 and Vision 2030. These plans are generally very detailed and identify the economic challenges, provide policy recommendations, and specify the relevant authorities and agencies responsible for undertaking policy action. In addition, most strategies are derived from rigorous research and consultations with key economic stakeholders. Despite these strategies and plans, the lack of an implementation, financing strategy, and other structural features of the economy that disincentivise productive activity in the non-energy sector has contributed to slow economic diversification. As such, the quality of policies and regulations to promote private-sector development leaves room for improvement. TT is above other small economies regarding regulatory quality but still significantly below OECD levels.

3.5 Quality of Public Services by Race: What Do the Trinbagonians Say?

The LAPOP surveys allow us to measure peoples' satisfaction with government policies, specifically by race. However, one-year snapshots may pick up the "sore-loser effect". Attitudinal research on political trust and support consistently shows that electoral losers are less satisfied with how democracy works in their country than electoral winners. The same can be said of TT. To measure the "sore-loser effect", we should ideally compare at least two points in time, 2010 when PNM was in power and 2014 when UNC formed the government. If the "sore-loser effect" holds, we expect ATTs to be more satisfied when the PNM is in power and less so when the UNC is in power, and the opposite has happened for ITTs. This exercise cannot be done as questions on the level of satisfaction of neighbourhood roads, schools, and health services and the police were not asked in the 2010 survey when the PNM was in power but only in 2012 and 2014 when UNC was in power.

Instead, a proxy of the sore-loser effect can be picked up by the answers to whether the Prime Minister, Persad-Bissessar, is doing a good job in the 2014 survey. Generally, it is low. The sum of very good and good answers is only 17% but falls to a low of 9% for ATTs and 14% for MTTs but rises to 40% for ITTs. A similar pattern holds for the level of satisfaction (very satisfied plus satisfied) with neighbourhood roads, public schools, and health services. The satisfaction with roads generally is 51% but falls to 48% for ATTs and rises to 57% for ITTs. Satisfaction with public schools is high, at 57%, but slightly lower for ATTs at 55% but much higher for ITTs at 66%. Generally, it is 42% for medical services but is marginally lower for ATTs at 40% but is higher for ITTs at 47%. Satisfaction with the police stands at 61% but is lower for ATTs (54%) but higher for the ITTs (72%).

Thus, although inconclusive, public service satisfaction (roads, schools, health, and police) is generally low. Further, there appears to be a "sore-loser effect" as ATTs report lower satisfaction than ITTs with these services when UNC is in power.

3.6 Conclusions

TT's structural features imply a sizeable but low-quality public sector, i.e., inefficient and ineffective. These predictions are generally borne out. Whichever measurement is used, public expenditure, investment or the wage bill, TT has a larger public sector than all the averages for comparator country groups.

TT performs worse than the average of the comparator country group regarding public institutional quality. This relative underperformance (using perception-based measures) holds for property rights, intellectual property protection, diversion of public funds, trust in politicians, irregular payments and bribes, favouritism in decisions of government officials, the wastefulness of government spending, burden of public regulation, the efficiency of the legal framework in settling disputes, and transparency of government policymaking. TT performs relatively well in only one area (judicial independence). Public trust in politicians is shallow in TT, and there is a perception of favouritism in decisions made by government officials (usually perceived as favouring well-connected firms and individuals).

Countries with more capable bureaucracies, more institutionalised congresses, independent judiciaries, and institutionalised political parties tend to have more stable, adaptable, coherent, efficient, and public-regarded policies. Generally, TT performs worse than the comparators regarding the quality of public institutions (congress capabilities, judicial independence, and party institutionalisation), except for the civil service, where it performs better than all the comparator groups.

However, generally, it performs on par regarding the quality of policies. Policies can be viewed from different dimensions. These are stability—the extent to which policies are stable over time, in which TT does better; the quality of implementation and enforcement—the degree to which policies are implemented and enforced correctly after approval in Parliament in which TT does worse; efficiency—the extent to which policies reflect an allocation of scarce resources that ensures high returns in which TT does better; and public regardedness—the degree to which policies pursue the public interest where TT does worse.

References

Araujo, M. C., Carneiro, P., Cruz-Aguayo, Y., & Schady, N. (2016). Teacher Quality and Learning Outcomes in Kindergarten. *The Quarterly Journal of Economics, 131*(3), 1415–1453.

Franco, M., & Scartascini, C. (2014). The Politics of Policies: Revisiting the Quality of Public Policies and Government Capabilities in Latin America and the Caribbean. IDB Policy Brief, 220.

Dincer, N., Eichengreen, B., & Geraats, P. (2022). Central Bank Transparency Data for 1998–2019. New updated indices based on revised methodology.

Dincer, N., & Eichengreen, B. (2014). Central Bank Transparency and Independence: Updates and New Measures. *International Journal of Central Banking, 10*(1), 189–253.

Fournier, H., & Johansson, A. (2016). The Effect of Size and Mix of Public Spending on Growth and Inequality. ECO/WKP(2016) 68, OECD.

Garriga, A. C. (2016). Central bank independence in the world: A new data set. *International Interactions, 42*(5), 849–868.

IMF (International Monetary Fund). (2015). *The Commodities Roller Coaster: A Fiscal Framework for Uncertain Times.* International Monetary Fund, Fiscal Monitor.

Khadan, J. (2017a). An Econometric Analysis of Energy Revenue and Government Expenditure Shocks on Economic Growth in Trinidad and Tobago. *The Journal of Developing Areas, 51*(2), 183–203. https://www.jstor.org/stable/26415733

Khadan, J. (2017b). *Are Oil and Gas Smothering the Private Sector in Trinidad and Tobago?* Inter-American Development Bank.

Khadan, J., & Smets, L. (2018). Trinidad and Tobago. In D. Beuermann & M. Schwartz (Eds.), *Nurturing Institutions for a Resilient Caribbean.* Inter-American Development Bank.

Lehne, J., Mo, J., & Plekhanov, A. (2018). What Determines the Quality of Economic Institutions? Cross-Country Evidence. EBRD Working Papers No 171.

Mendes, D. (2000). Judicial Independence and the Administration of the Judiciary in Trinidad and Tobago. Caribbean Dialogue 6.

Muyangwa, M., Miller, N., Bonner, T. A., & van den Bosch, R. (2017). Trinidad and Tobago TADAT performance assessment report. International Monetary Fund, Washington, DC. https://bit.ly/2Kak3N8

Rodrick, D. (1998). Why Do More Open Economies Have Bigger Governments? *Journal of Political Economy, 106*(5), 997–1032.

Sahadeo, C. (2012). *The Case for a Revenue Authority in Trinidad and Tobago.* Unpublished.

Scartascini, C., Stein, E., & Tommasi, M. (2014). Political Institutions, Intertemporal Cooperation, and the Quality of Public Policies. *Journal of Applied Economics, 16*, 1–32.

Seepersad, R. (2016). Crime and Violence in Trinidad and Tobago. IDB Series on Crime and Violence in the Caribbean. (IDB-TN-1062). Institutions for Development and Country Department Caribbean Group.

CHAPTER 4

Political Development: Payoffs to the Voter Base and Corruption

Do the political parties play to their ethnic base, drawn from the electorate or elites? Despite many studies that have explored the historical context that shaped the country's racially based voting behaviour, none, as far as we know, have empirically examined whether and to what extent and through which channels an ethnic group benefit when "their" party controls the national purse. The latter is the question and answer we explore in this chapter.

The combination of characteristics, including rent-seeking combined with state capture, high perception of corruption, and ethnic-based political parties discussed previously, suggest that the country could be classified as an ethnic-based patronage democracy. In this system, political leaders are selected through a competitive process. The government in turn largely monopolises the provision of basic goods and services, which allows government officials discretion over how these goods and services are distributed. The public sector's role in providing goods and services in an oil economy may be more significant than in a non-oil economy.

The association between patronage democracy and ethnicity has been attributed to institutional legacies that privilege ethnic identities, a presumed cultural similarity that makes patronage transactions between co-ethnics easier than non-co-ethnics, and the functional superiority of ethnic identity networks. Patronage democracy thrives in scenarios where

J. Khadan and I. Jit Ruprah, *Unraveling Race, Politics, and Gender in Trinidad and Tobago's Economic Development*,
https://doi.org/10.1007/978-3-031-54656-3_4

many voters rely on the state for resources. Additionally, in situations where the size of ethnic groups surpasses the threshold necessary for winning or exerting leverage within the system, it becomes easier to classify groups based on their ethnicity rather than any other identity.

Voters in patronage democracies choose between parties through ethnic headcounts rather than comparing political platforms or ideologies. They expect material benefits and obtain psychic benefits (e.g., an increase in happiness and life satisfaction). In addition, ethnic parties are likely to succeed when they have competitive rules for intra-party advancement that give them a comparative advantage in representing the elites from the targeted ethnic groups.[1]

Chandra (2004, 2007, 2013) argues that the patronage ethnic-based democracy system is a self-reproducing equilibrium once established. Paraphrasing her argument, politicians bidding for the support of co-ethnic voters follow suit by sorting themselves into ethnic blocks. Therefore, there is a self-reinforcing equilibrium of ethnic favouritism in which voters mainly target co-ethnic politicians for favours, and politicians target, particularly, co-ethnic voters. Once this equilibrium is in place, there is a feedback loop with ethnic politics strengthening patronage politics. Over time, the balance would also generate additional reinforcing mechanisms that facilitate its persistence. There will be incentives for both politicians and voters to create and maintain institutions and networks to reduce co-ethnic transaction costs of communicating demands and delivering benefits.

Those benefits include both material and psychic benefits. Material benefits include public employment, public expenditure, and socioeconomic results (real wages, poverty, inequality, and unemployment). Psychic benefits include trust and life satisfaction cum happiness. Another aspect is payback to the party's elite supporters. For this, we use data on government contracts to examine political parties' preferences for certain contractors.

This chapter considers different types of payoffs to the PNM and UNC's electoral bases. First, we look at public employment. Second, we

[1] Elites refer to a small group of powerful individuals with significant wealth, privilege, political influence, or expertise within a group, and exercises that power over the rest of the society (Mariotti, 2022).

analyse public expenditure, mainly transfers to regional governments and social assistance programmes. We then discuss rent-seeking and public procurement. We end the chapter with a discussion on corruption.

4.1 Public Employment

Patronage democracy combined with ethnic-based political parties suggests that a political party winning an election delivers to its base through public employment. Do they? To answer this question, we examine changes in employment composition by race between four administrations. UNC (1995–1999) replaced PNM, which in turn replaced PNM (2000–2010), which in turn was replaced by UNC-PP (2010 to 2014).[2] We compare data from the last year of the previous administration to the end year of the administration being considered: 1994–1999, 1999–2010, and 2010–2014, thus comparing how a new government found employment by race and left it when it lost the election. The variables we look at are public employment by level of government (central government, public enterprises, and Boards). A direct way a political party can reward its base is by redirecting public jobs to its base when it gains power. The returns to patronage depend on the political party's access to resources (supply side) and voter dependence on public-sector jobs. Territorial biases can affect access to patronage if they overlap with a geographical concentration of electoral supporters of parties (Calvo & Murillo, 2004).[3] The supply side will be dependent on energy revenue. Demand will depend on whether patronage is a distributive mechanism that returns voters with different skills and labour market expectations.

The employment pattern, discussed in detail below, shows a preference by UNC for ITTs and PNMs for ATTs and, to a lesser extent, MTTs.

[2] The elections of 2001 resulted in a stalemate between PNM and UNC, each having won 18 seats. The president, Robinson, nominated PNM's Patrick Manning. He was, however, unable to build a majority and elections were held in 2002. In a highly racially tinged election, PNM won.

[3] Calvo and Murillo (2004) taking the Argentina case analyse the interaction between patronage and partisanship to explain why some incumbents are more likely to benefit from pork politics than others. They explain such differences by focusing on political parties' access to resources (supply side) and voters' dependence on fiscal largesse (demand side). They show how these differences affect the patron's choice of public-sector wages and employment.

Therefore, voting based on race is rational as it increases the probability of finding a public job when your party wins an election. This rationale is not trivial as public employment is a large part of employment, and higher wages are paid in public versus private employment.

We calculate changes between an administration's first and last years, i.e., how a government encountered public employment when it took office and left it. The data is for three periods: 1994–1999, when UNC took over from PNM; 2001–2009, when PNM took over from UNC; and 2009–2014, when UNC took over from PNM. In addition to total public employment, we analyse the level of Government (Statutory Boards, Central Government, and Public Enterprises) and low vs high-income jobs.

The degree of patronage depends upon government resources available to the party. The 1994 UNC government faced declining oil revenues. The average yearly energy revenue was 6% of GDP. The 2001 PNM government faced increasing income: energy revenue averaged 12% of GDP. The 2010 UNC government met declining energy revenue; it averaged 14.8% of GDP. Energy revenues further deteriorated during the 2015 PNM government, as energy prices collapsed; they averaged 7.2% of GDP (Fig. 4.1).

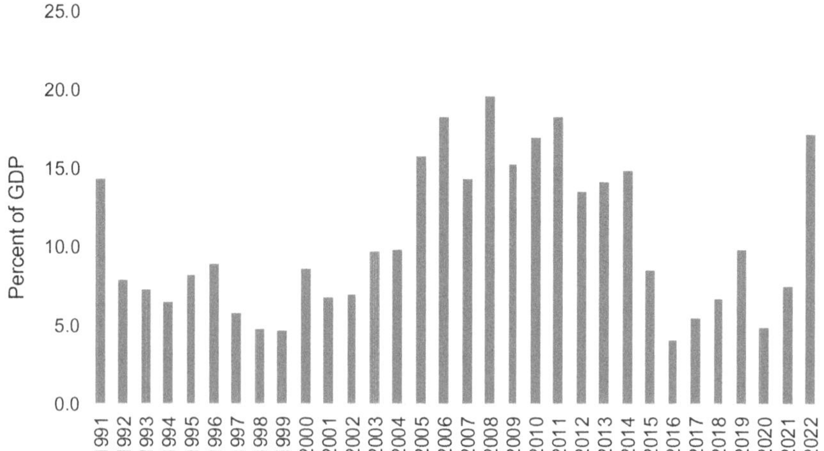

Fig. 4.1 Energy revenue by public administration (*Source* Central Bank of Trinidad and Tobago)

UNC took power in 1995 and faced declining oil revenue. By 1999, it had reduced public employment by 7.6% (Fig. 4.2), a reduction that was borne mainly by ATTs (3.7%), followed by ITTs (2.9%) and to a lesser extent by MTTs (0.9%) (Fig. 4.3). The decrease in public employment was mainly in the central government (6%; Fig. 4.4) followed by public enterprises (1%; Fig. 4.5), but employment increased in statutory boards (0.5%; Fig. 4.6).

PNM took power in 2001 and faced an uptake in oil revenue. Public employment expansion of 10% was mainly due to an increase in MTT (8.4%), followed by ATT (4.5%), while ITT was reduced (2.3%). The latter was reflected geographically in the 2.8% increase in public employment; 4% was in ATT-dominated areas, while there was a decrease in ITT-dominated areas. In the UNC period, the increase in public employment of 2.2% was more evenly distributed: 1.4% in ITT-dominated areas and 1.1% in ATT-dominated areas.

The conclusion is that it appears that political parties do redirect public employment to their base. Partisan patrons face a trade-off between hiring a large number of public employees and providing more significant

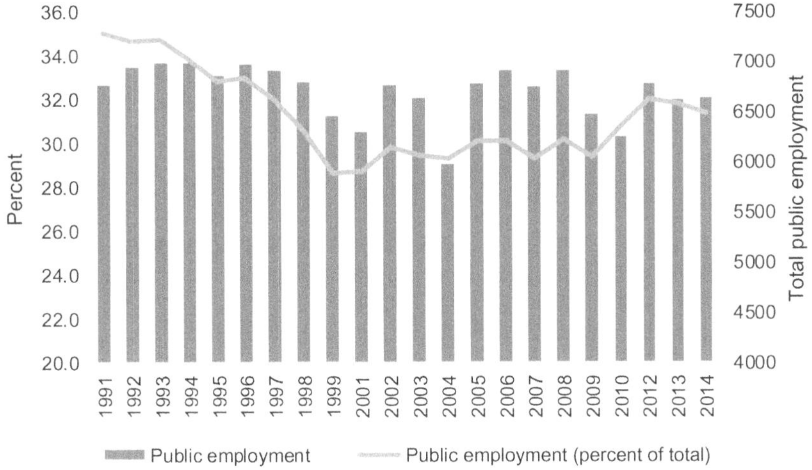

Fig. 4.2 Public employment by public administration (*Source* Continuous Sample Survey of Population [various years])

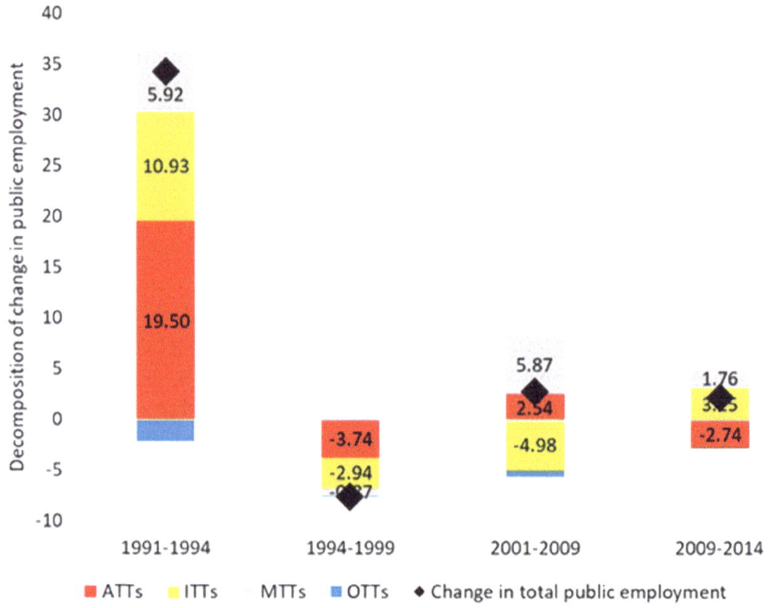

Fig. 4.3 Decomposition of Change in Public Employment by Race (*Note* ATT = African Trinidad and Tobago; ITT = Indian Trinidad and Tobago; MTT = :Mixed Trinidad and Tobago; OTT = Caucasian, Chinese, Indigenous, Portuguese, Syrian/Lebanese, and other ethnic groups. *Source* Authors' estimates from the Continuous Sample Survey of Population for Trinidad and Tobago [various years])

public-sector wages, i.e., face the trade-off of granting wage premiums to fewer high-skilled workers or a larger group of low-skilled workers (Figs. 4.7 and 4.8).

4.2 Public Expenditure

Ideally, to test the hypothesis of payoffs by redistributing public expenditure towards a particular ethnic group, we need data on public spending and beneficiaries by race or electoral district. Thus, we could determine how the government targeted its base or attempted to win votes from a different racially dominated area. Such data is not available. As a proxy,

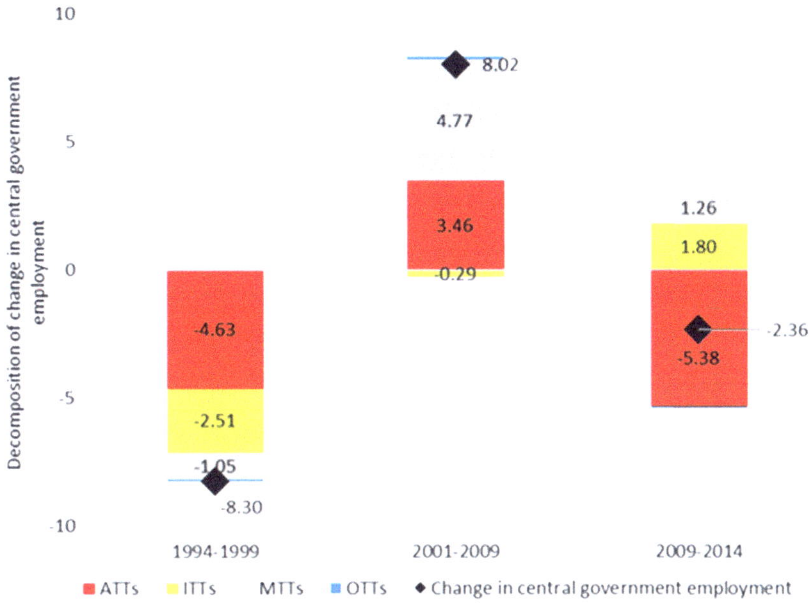

Fig. 4.4 Decomposition of change in central government employment by race (*Note* ATT = African Trinidad and Tobago; ITT = Indian Trinidad and Tobago; MTT = :Mixed Trinidad and Tobago; OTT = Caucasian, Chinese, Indigenous, Portuguese, Syrian/Lebanese, and other ethnic groups. *Source* Authors' estimates from the Continuous Sample Survey of Population for Trinidad and Tobago [various years])

we analyse the relation between the change in the budget allocated to regional corporations by the central government and the racial profile of the regional corporation (Fig. 4.9a, b). Plus, we consider the racial composition of public assistance programmes highlighted in the IDB's 2014 Survey of Living Conditions (Tables 4.1 and 4.2).[4]

Another possible mechanism of payoffs is the social safety net. Unfortunately, this is essentially a black hole, despite public expenditure on a

[4] Public assistance is a monthly subsistence grant designed to provide financial aid to adults who cannot work because of ill health. Public assistance may also be granted on behalf of needy children whose father, mother or both parents have died, incarcerated, disabled and unable to work, or have deserted the family and cannot be found.

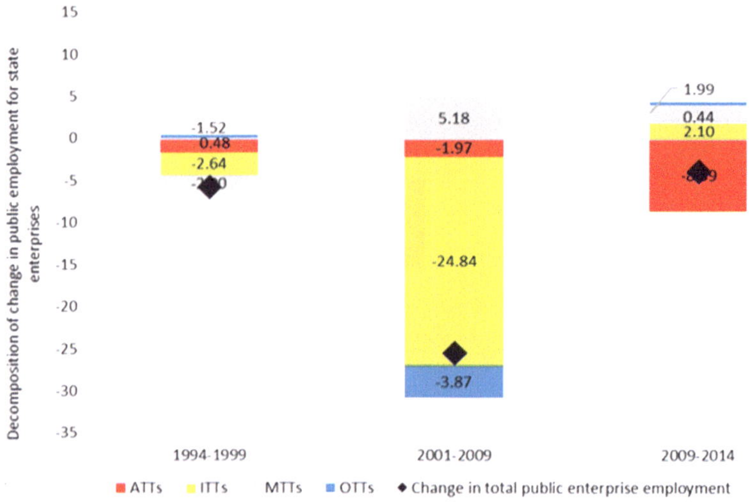

Fig. 4.5 Decomposition of change in public enterprise employment by race (*Note* ATT = African Trinidad and Tobago; ITT = Indian Trinidad and Tobago; MTT = :Mixed Trinidad and Tobago; OTT = Caucasian, Chinese, Indigenous, Portuguese, Syrian/Lebanese, and other ethnic groups. *Source* Authors' estimates from the Continuous Sample Survey of Population for Trinidad and Tobago [various years])

myriad of programmes is not trivial. Generally, little is known about these programmes, and it is often difficult to retrieve information on its impact from government administrative sources.

4.3 The Elites and Public Contracts

"Rents" are defined as rewards above that which effort and productivity would imply. Thus, rent is an unearned compensation sought through the pursuit of privilege. Although rent is personally beneficial, it means social loss because resources are used in non-productive distributive searches. When economic agents engage in rent-seeking, they distort good governance practices, engage in bribery and corruption, and transform potential entrepreneurs into rent-seekers, thus lowering productivity and constraining sustainable economic growth (Dietz et al.,

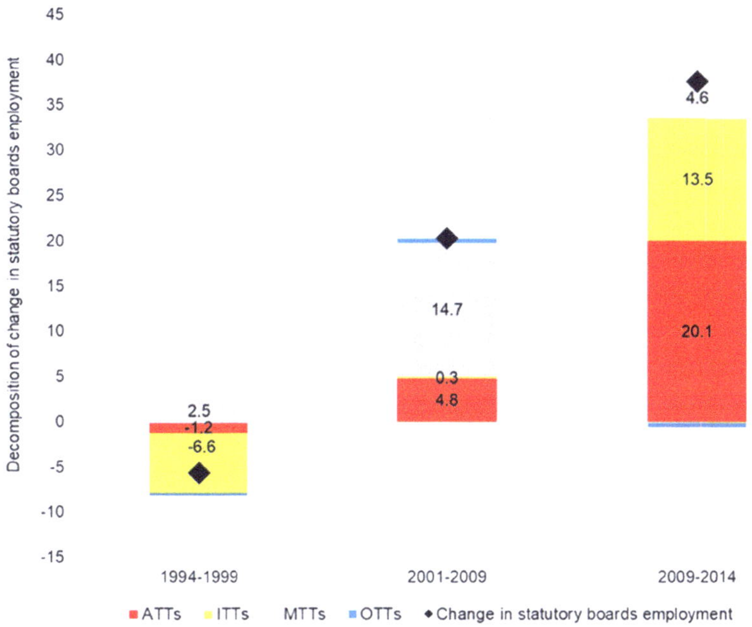

Fig. 4.6 Decomposition of change in statuary boards employment by race (*Note* ATT = African Trinidad and Tobago; ITT = Indian Trinidad and Tobago; MTT = :Mixed Trinidad and Tobago; OTT = Caucasian, Chinese, Indigenous, Portuguese, Syrian/Lebanese, and other ethnic groups. *Source* Authors' estimates from the Continuous Sample Survey of Population for Trinidad and Tobago [various years])

2007; Tullock, 1980). If the business environment is unfavourable, rent-seeking can occur if the state administers legal restraints, regulations, subsidies, taxes, tariffs, import quotas, or award contracts through public procurement. For their part, private actors are incentivised to influence the decisions of public officials in their favour, usually at the expense of others (Krueger, 1974). In societies with democratic political systems, lobbying and campaign contributions are typical methods of

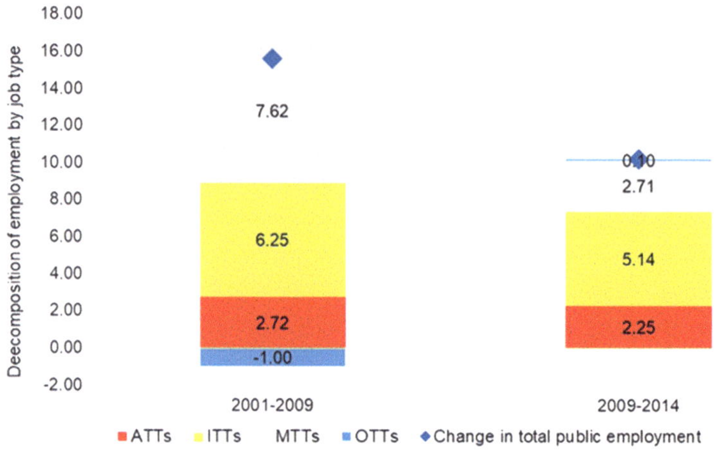

Fig. 4.7 High-income jobs (*Note* ATT = African Trinidad and Tobago; ITT = Indian Trinidad and Tobago; MTT = :Mixed Trinidad and Tobago; OTT = Caucasian, Chinese, Indigenous, Portuguese, Syrian/Lebanese, and other ethnic groups. *Source* Authors' estimates from the Continuous Sample Survey of Population for Trinidad and Tobago [various years])

influencing the government or policy outcomes.[5] Rent-seeking emphasises the efforts made by special interest groups to capture transfers created by government intervention in a private exchange.

The latter raises Olson's (1965) concept of "institutional sclerosis". It is hypothesised that special interest groups will accumulate over time in politically stable societies and eventually reduce the economic efficiency of the economy in which they operate. The latter is accentuated in a small-energy based-ethnically diverse country. Olson argued that incentives work against the formation of pro-economic growth groups. Instead, groups that advocate excludable redistribution will obtain considerable benefits for themselves while imposing costs on the broader society.

Consequently, groups encouraging redistribution are more likely to form successfully than groups advocating growth. Since it takes even

[5] In a speech in 2018, Mr. Mark Ramkerrysingh, Chairman of the Election and Boundaries Commission noted that "At present there is no real or proper regulatory system in place for accountability in the acquisition or expenditure of these (for campaign finance) financial resources".

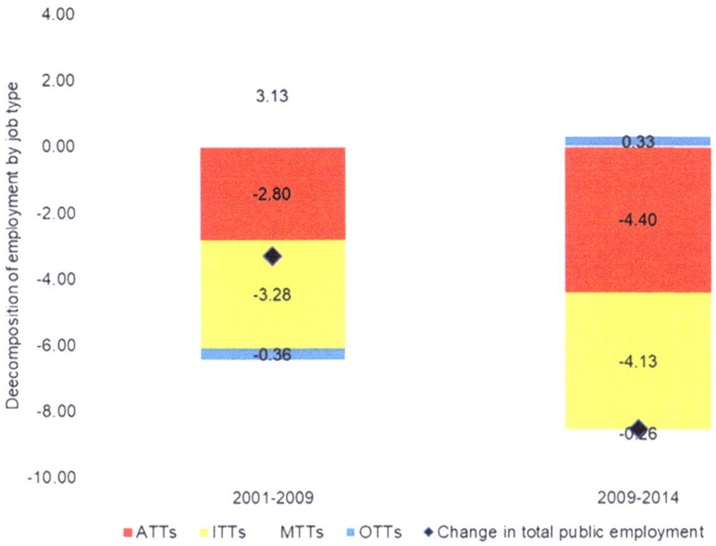

Fig. 4.8 Low-income jobs (*Note* ATT = African Trinidad and Tobago; ITT = Indian Trinidad and Tobago; MTT = :Mixed Trinidad and Tobago; OTT = Caucasian, Chinese, Indigenous, Portuguese, Syrian/Lebanese, and other ethnic groups. *Source* Authors' estimates from the Continuous Sample Survey of Population for Trinidad and Tobago [various years])

small groups to overcome their collective action problems, more special interest groups are expected to develop and engage in redistributive activities. Their impact will divert scarce economic resources away from technological advances and other growth-enhancing activities that are non-excludable towards redistributive activities. Thus, Olson predicts that economic growth will naturally decline in stable societies as groups continue to flourish through economic rents. These sclerotic effects are due to the formation of special interest organisations that overcome free-riding behaviour if they are small. Small groups would be more likely to form than large groups because free riding is more accessible to monitor in a smaller group. Hence, his arguments are more pertinent to small-population countries. Thus, the same feature that the Caribbean is proud of, namely political stability, may have created the conditions for and sustained an alliance against growth. Therefore, it is no surprise that Dookeran and Jantzen (2012) raise the problem of an "Anti-Growth

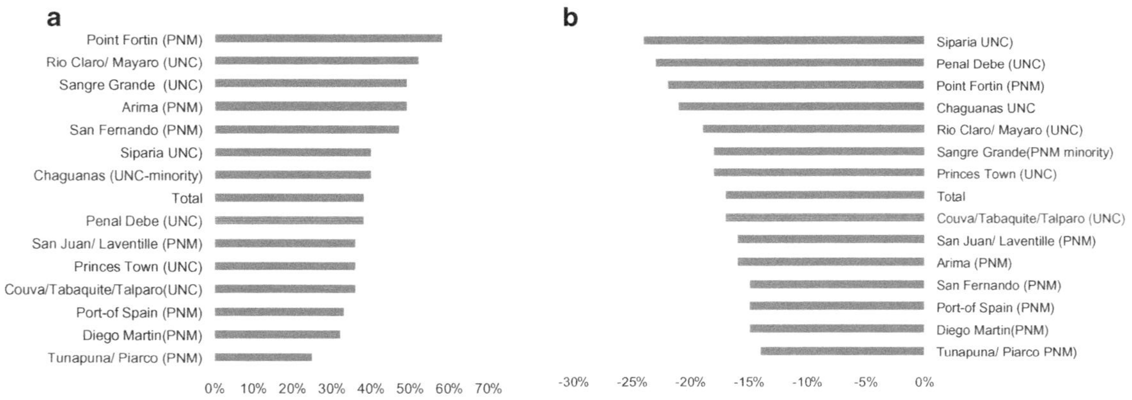

Fig. 4.9 **a** UNC Government (2011 to 2014) **b** PNM Government (2016 to 2019) (*Source* Ministry of Finance budget documents [various years])

Table 4.1 Social benefit recipients (%)

	ATT	*ITT*	*MTT*
Chronic Disease Assistance Program	29.5	51.6	18.9
Food card	47.3	36.4	16.3
Disability grant	30.4	51.8	17.8
Public assistance	31.0	49.0	20.0

(*Note* ATT = African Trinidad and Tobago; ITT = Indian Trinidad and Tobago; MTT = Mixed Trinidad and Tobago
Source IDB Survey of Living Conditions [2014])

Table 4.2 Government Work and Skills Programme (%)

	ATT	*ITT*	*MTT*
Government work programme			
URP	66.7	18.6	14.7
CEPEP	55.1	27.9	17.0
On-the-job placement	50.0	26.5	23.5
Other	51.5	33.3	15.2
None	45.8	45.8	8.3
Not stated	64.1	12.8	23.1
Skills programme attended			
YTEPP	54.0	23.9	22.1
NESC	52.6	25.3	22.1
Civilian Conservation	68.6	6.5	24.9
Servol	53.5	13.2	33.3
HYPE	59.3	11.1	29.6
YAPA	14.3	47.6	38.1
Re-afforestation	43.8	25.0	31.3
MUST	59.1	13.6	27.3
Skills retraining	55.0	21.0	24.0
Non-traditional skill	42.9	28.6	28.6
Other	61.8	20.3	17.9
Not stated	67.1	18.0	15.0

Note ATT = African Trinidad and Tobago; ITT = Indian Trinidad and Tobago; MTT: Mixed Trinidad and Tobago; URP = Unemployment Relief Programme; CEPEP = Community-based Environmental Protection and Enhancement; Programme; YTEPP = Youth Training and Employment Partnership Programme; NESC = National Energy Skills Centre; HYPE = Helping You Prepare for Employment Programme; YAPA = Youth Apprenticeship Certificate Programme in Agriculture; MUST = Multi-Sector Skills Training Programme
Source IDB Survey of Living Conditions (2014)

Alliance" as a significant factor hindering higher economic growth in the Caribbean.

One measure of the extent of rent-seeking is a state capture index. The state capture index suggests that TT is at the higher end of the spectrum. State capture is defined as the efforts of groups to shape the laws, policies, and regulations of the state to their advantage by providing illicit private gains to public officials. The state capture index ranges from zero (no capture) to unity (full capture). It is constructed by taking the average from three pillars of the World Economic Forum's Global Competitiveness Index: Pillar 1 (Institutions), Pillar 6 (Goods Market Efficiency), and Pillar 7 (Labour Market Efficiency). For each value, the minimum value (within small economies) is subtracted and then divided by the difference between the maximum and minimum values (Ruprah & Sierra, 2016). The index value for TT shows that 80% of the state is "captured" (Fig. 4.10).

Another measure of rent-seeking is public regardedness. The latter refers to the degree to which policies promote the general welfare and resemble public goods (that is, are public-regarding) or tend to channel private benefits to specific individuals or factions in the form of projects with concentrated benefits, subsidies, or tax loopholes (that is, are private-regarding). This dimension is closely tied to the fair process inequality effect, i.e., whether citizens consider that they have been fairly treated by the authorities in terms of procedures and outcomes, particularly since those favoured by private-regarding policies tend to be the elite members. The latter has the economic and political clout to skew policy decisions in their favour. Figure 4.11 shows that TT performs insufficiently on the Public-Regardedness Index, implying policies tend to favour the economic and political elites of the country. Relative to all comparator country groups.[6]

[6] The public regardedness index was created based on the following three variables: a. Government Officials' Favoritism: gcr_favorit Source: The Global Competitiveness Report-World Economic Forum; average 2001–2012 Values and Details: To what extent do government officials in your country show favoritism to well-connected firms and individuals when deciding upon policies and contracts? [1 = always show favoritism; 7 = never show favoritism] b. Government Social Transfers: govtsoc Source: The Global Competitiveness Report- World Economic Forum; 2002 Values and Details: Expert evaluation of whether government social transfers go primarily to (1 = poor people, 7 = rich people). This variable had its scale reversed to compute the index. The reverse version is govtsocr. c. Corruption Perceptions Index: cpi Source: Transparency International Corruption

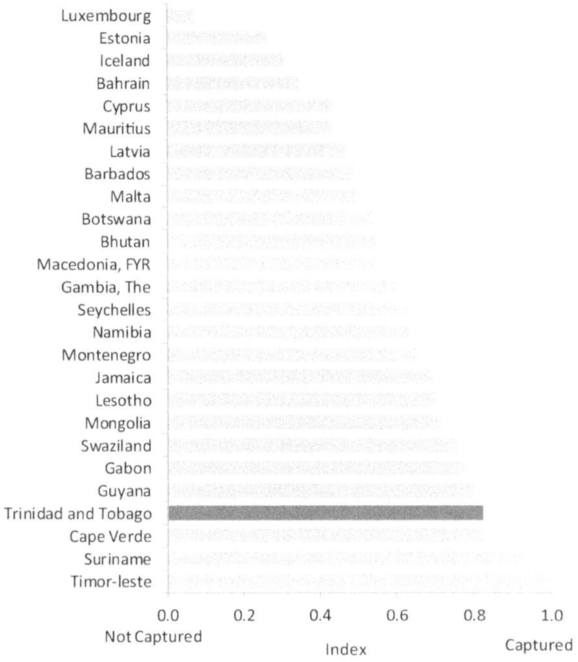

Fig. 4.10 State capture in small economies (*Source* Ruprah and Sierra [2016])

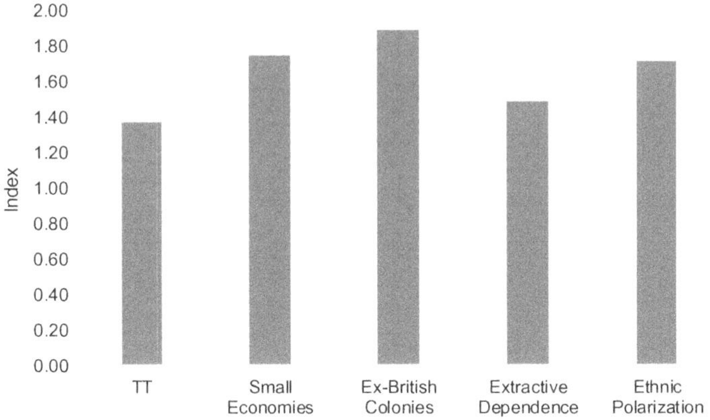

Fig. 4.11 Public regardedness (*Source* Authors' estimates from Franco and Scartascini [2014])

Another aspect is payback to the party's elite supporters. A Venn diagram, Fig. 4.12, shows the percentage of firms that received public contracts under PNM and UNC administrations exclusively and those that received contracts from both political parties. Those that received public contracts, irrespective of which party held office, was 29%, which is roughly 50% of the value of all contracts we considered from 2007–2021.

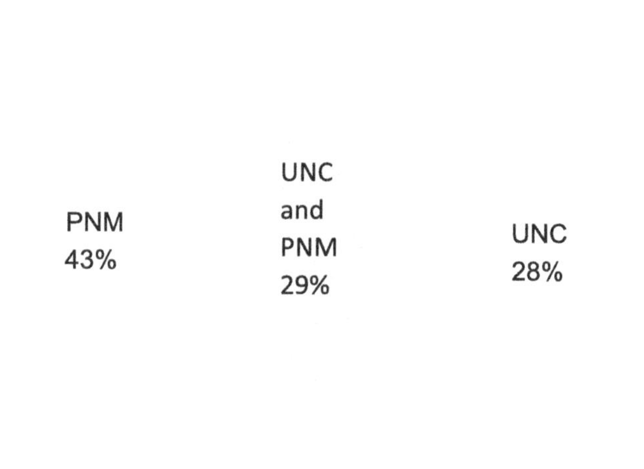

Fig. 4.12 Public contracts under different political administrations (2007–2021) (*Source* Authors' estimates using publicly available data from the Central Tenders Board of Trinidad and Tobago[7])

Perceptions Index; average 1995–2012 Values and Details: Countries are ranked based on how corrupt their public sector is perceived to be by observers from around the world and experts in the countries evaluated. This index ranges between 0 (highly corrupt) and 10 (highly clean).

[7] The number of contracts offered under different administrations could be related to many factors, including the number of years each administration held office, policy priorities, and external shocks that adversely affected government revenues.

4.4 Corruption "*Who ent tief in Trinidad? All ah we tief*"[8]

Three, namely resource dependency, ethnic polarisation, and smallness, of the five structural characteristics of TT, suggest that there will be forces towards a high level of state capture (rent-seeking), corruption, and a low level of vertical trust. Potential countervailing influences derive from the other two characteristics: an ex-British colony and a democracy. The term capture describes how public officials are dominated by and serve the interests of powerful interest groups. Corruption refers to bribery, i.e., administrative or petty corruption, or as significant embezzlement of public monies, i.e., grand corruption, including bribes paid in a public tender. Vertical trust, i.e., trust in government, is expected to be low.

The newspapers and various media outlets in TT frequently report on corruption allegations involving government officials and Parliament members, with such accusations often intensifying during election campaigns.[9] How robustly anti-corruption laws are implemented directly influences the prevalence of corruption and their overall impact. In TT, the Integrity in Public Life Act of 2000 established an Integrity Commission as an independent body that receives declarations of income assets and liabilities of government officials and provides criminal penalties for corruption by officials. None have been prosecuted successfully. Public Procurement and Disposal of Public Property Act of 2015 seeks to reform the procurement laws invoking principles of good governance, such as accountability, integrity, transparency, and value for money. It established the Office of Procurement Regulation as the governing body for public procurement and the retention and disposal of public property—the Freedom of Information Act, Chap. 22:02—gave members of the public a general right (with specified exceptions) of access to official documents of public authorities. However, despite these laws and changes in public procurement processes, continued allegations abound. The allegations are that some politicians and ministers have close relationships with gang leaders and facilitated the procurement and contracting of construction

[8] A term coined in 1986 by D. Cartey, Minister for Housing and Resettlement.

[9] For a tally of corruption accusations covering both PNM and UNC governments see D. Polo three part series in Loop PART 3: Some of the biggest, most absurd scandals to hit UNC and PNM|Loop Trinidad & Tobago (loopnews.com).

projects to companies owned and operated by criminal enterprises and, more often, relatives (US Department of State, 2020).

What are the facts? This chapter looks at the empirical evidence from three primary sources. Corruption Perception Index from Transparency International,[10] citizens' views and experience with bribery and trust are from The Latin America Public Opinion Project (LAPOP Surveys from Vanderbilt University).[11] From a businessperson's viewpoint and experience, we use The Productivity, Technology, and Innovation (PROTEqiN) Survey.[12] There is no database for the significant embezzlement of public monies.

Before discussing corruption and trust in the government, we first consider rent-seeking and the capture of the state. The capture of the state will set the stage for a fuller understanding of bribes, trust, and rent-seeking.

Rent-seeking can be, but is not necessarily, accompanied by corruption. Nonetheless, the most crucial rent-seeking behaviour is bureaucratic corruption. The latter involves the paying of bribes and the use of other forms of pressure to persuade bureaucrats to grant entrepreneurs access to economic sectors closed by government regulation, to minimise the burden of government regulation on an individual's enterprise, and to receive a public subsidy, or a transfer from the state (Mbaku, 1992).

The Corruption Perception Index measures the degree to which corruption is perceived by businesspersons and country analysts to exist among public officials and politicians. The score ranges from 100 (very clean) to 0 (highly corrupt). TT's rankings on the Corruption Perception Index, Fig. 4.13, are low and lower than the averages of comparator country groups except for extractive-dependent countries.

Citizens also see corruption as a problem. The Latin America Public Opinion Project (LAPOP 2012) Survey provides information on households' perceptions and direct experience of corruption. Specifically, this survey asks citizens if they have heard of corruption among government officials and whether they were asked to pay bribes. However, that is perceived to depend on the ethnicity of the political incumbent and the

[10] 2021 Corruptions Perceptions Index.

[11] LAPOP|Vanderbilt University.

[12] Compete Caribbean (2016).

Fig. 4.13 Corruption perception index (*Source* Authors using data from Transparency International)

citizen's race. Chang and Kerr (2009) argue that voters form their attitudes towards corruption based on their insider or outsider status. They distinguish between insiders and outsiders along with cost–benefit instrumentality and identity. The former refers to whether a voter belongs to the patronage network of the incumbent, and they posit that a patronage insider is more tolerant of corruption and perceives corruption at a higher level than patronage outsiders. Affective identity involves sharing a partisan or ethnic affiliation with the incumbent. Voters view corruption through the lens of identity, and those partisan and ethnic insiders are more likely to turn a blind eye to corruption. Finally, they argue that insiders' electoral support of the incumbent is less affected by the consequences of corruption.

The survey found that 94% of respondents in TT perceive corruption as very common (49%) or common (45%), with similar values for ATTs, ITTs and MTTs. About a quarter think giving a bribe is justified. However, when asked if they had to pay a bribe for different public services over the last twelve months, the positive answers generally were a low percentage, single digits. Responses were for government employees, military officers, workplaces, courts, health, and schools, with similar responses from different ethnic groups. The exception was at local government, where the affirmative answers were 44% (with ITTs at 64%, ATTs at 50%, and MTTs at 38%).

A firm-level analysis is based on the Productivity, Technology and Innovation (PROTEqiN) Survey that provides information on the frequency of bribe requests for eight transactions involving the government and crucial for businesses: construction permits, operating licences, import licences, water, telecommunications, electricity connections, tax inspections, and contracts. This scope of transactions allows us to determine a firm's interaction with government officials, the level of bureaucracy that firms encounter, and the extent to which public officials request bribes to speed up transactions. In TT, a high percentage of firms interact with the government, and the bureaucracy is relatively high: 77% of firms report transactions with the government. The largest share of firms (36%) report one transaction, 26% of firms say two, and 10% report three transactions. The time spent by senior management dealing with government regulations is used as a proxy for bureaucracy. Senior management in TT firms spends 10% of their time dealing with government regulations, the second-highest in the Caribbean after St. Kitts and Nevis.

Do illicit payments "grease" or "sand" the wheels in TT? To provide an answer to this question, we examine data on how long firms must wait for public services when a bribe is paid compared with when a bribe is not paid. If illicit payments grease the wheels, one expects that the waiting time of bribe payers would be significantly less than that of non-bribe payers. The average wait time for electricity is considerably higher for non-payers than for bribe-payers. Getting an electricity connection takes 35% less time with an illicit payment. For water connections, the results show that paying a bribe gets you a connection in 19 days compared with 23 days if no bribe is paid. Import licences are received in nine days when payments are made, but firms that do not pay have to wait twice as long (18 days). Telephone connections take longer when a bribe is produced, contradicting our hypothesis. Lastly, most firms (90%)

that secured or attempted to secure a government contract reported that informal payments or gifts were not requested. In instances where informal payments were requested, the cost ranged from an average of 5 to 25% of the value of the contract.

A graft index is constructed to reflect the probability that a firm will be asked for a bribe conditional on the firm undertaking one of the aforementioned transactions with the government. The index shows the proportion of instances in which firms were requested to pay bribes over the total solicitations for a public service (Ruprah & Sierra, 2016). The graft index ranks TT above the Caribbean average (23%) but below six Caribbean countries. The cost of "getting things done" is relatively lower in TT. The cost of corruption is measured by the amount that firms pay (as % of annual sales) in informal payments or gifts to public officials to "get things done." Firms in TT report that the average cost of getting things done represents 0.8% of annual sales compared to the Caribbean average of 2.6%.

4.4.1 *Vertical Trust*

Trust in authorities is typically labelled political or vertical trust. Trust in others is usually called social or horizontal trust. It is closely connected to social capital and often describes citizens' levels of horizontal trust and network activities (Prakash & Selle, 2004; Putnam, 2002).

Trust focuses on people's propensity to obey the law implemented by different authorities (e.g., the police) (e.g., Tyler & Lind, 1992). People's willingness to obey the law and trust the authorities implementing the regulations is closely related to whether they consider that the authorities have fairly treated them regarding procedures and outcomes (Tyler & Lind, 1992). This finding is called the fair process effect (Van den Bos et al., 1997). Procedural fairness concerns are closely related to trust matters. For instance, Van den Bos, Wilke, and Lind (1998) found that perceived procedural fairness is relevant for judging the outcomes received when people lack information about whether the authority can be trusted. In TT, the perception of a fair process may change by ethnic groups depending on which political party is in power. We can call this a mild form of the sore-loser effect.

Regarding vertical trust, measured by the public's trust in politicians, TT performs poorly compared to the averages of comparator country

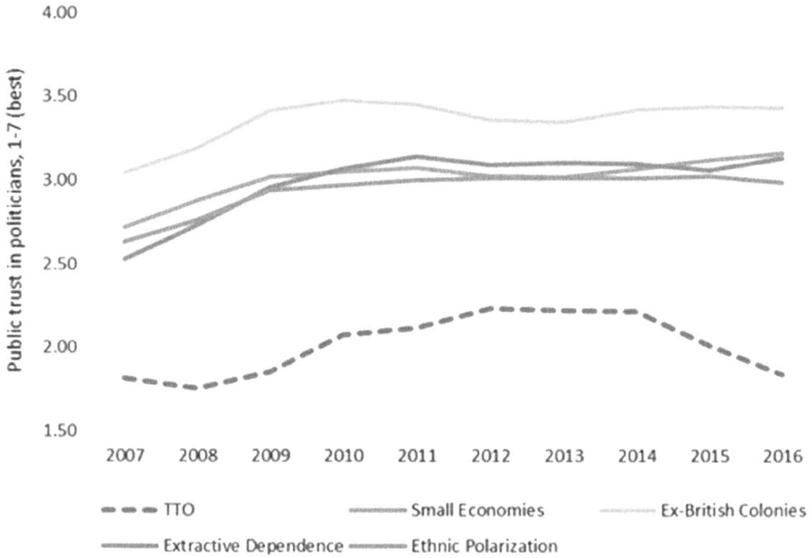

Fig. 4.14 Trust in politicians (*Source* Authors using data from the World Economic Forum)

groups (Figs. 4.14 and 4.15). Further, since 2014, the underperformance gap has started to widen. It shows higher trust during the UNC administration than when PNM was in power.

Is there a sore-loser effect? How does trust by different ethnic groups change when there is an ATT or an ITT prime minister? With an ATT prime minister (Patrick Manning) in 2010, the ITTs' low trust was 63%, and for ATTs, it was 48%. However, with an ITT prime minister (Kamala Persad-Bissessar) in 2012, low confidence fell to 9%, and high trust soared to 64%. For ATTs, the high and low trust levels remain similar between both periods (50/19 vs 49/14 per cent). If there is a sore loser effect, it is mainly held by the ITTs (Figs. 4.16 and 4.17).

4.5 Conclusions

This chapter explored the relationship between political development, voter base payoffs, and TT corruption. The findings suggest the country can be classified as an ethnic-based patronage democracy. Voters in

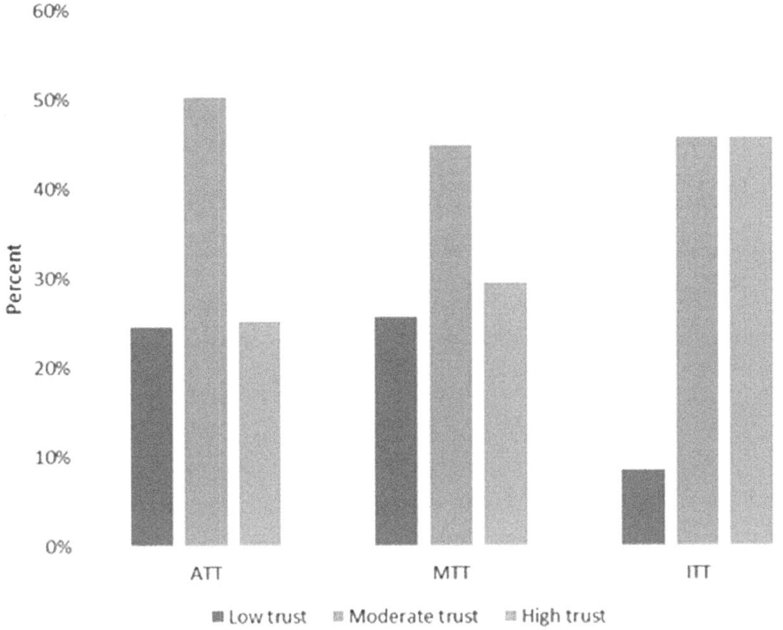

Fig. 4.15 Respect for political institutions in TT (*Source* Authors using data from LAPOP [2012])

patronage democracies primarily choose parties based on ethnic head-counts rather than political platforms or ideologies. The analysis shows that changes in employment composition by race between different administrations tend to favour the ethnicity of the voter base of that political party that holds power, and this is irrespective of political parties. This finding highlights the rationality of voting based on race, as it can increase the chances of obtaining a public job when one's party wins an election. In terms of benefits to the elites, there also appears to be a common group that benefits from the majority of public contracts, regardless of which political party holds office.

It is not surprising, therefore, to find that corruption and rent-seeking, which often involve bureaucratic corruption, are perceived to be common in TT. At the same time, TT has laws in place, such as the Integrity in Public Life Act and the Public Procurement and Disposal of Public Property Act; allegations of corruption persist, particularly during

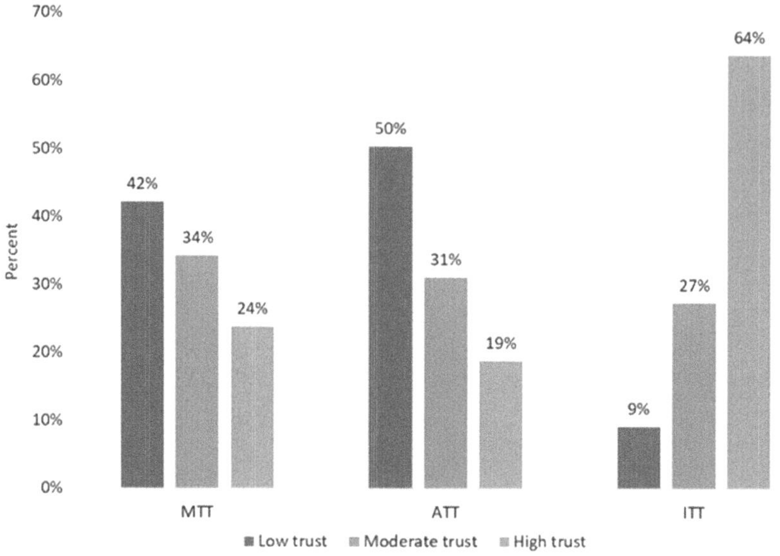

Fig. 4.16 Trust in an ATT Prime Minister (2010) (*Source* Authors using data from LAPOP [2010 and 2012]. The trusted scale ranges from one [no trust] to 7 [many trusts]. Low trust = 1 + 2; moderate trust = 3 – 5; high trust = 6 + 7)

election campaigns. We find that ethnicity and political affiliation can influence individuals' attitudes towards corruption, with insiders being more tolerant of corruption and identity playing a role in how corruption is perceived. Also, trust in the government, known as vertical trust, is low in TT compared to other comparators. However, trust levels vary depending on the ethnic background of the prime minister in power, with shifts observed between administrations. The sore-loser effect, where trust levels change based on the ruling party, appears more pronounced among ITTs.

Addressing corruption and building trust in the government are crucial for TT's development and stability. Strengthening the enforcement of existing laws, promoting transparency in public procurement processes, and fostering a culture of accountability are necessary to combat corruption. Efforts to bridge ethnic divisions and promote inclusivity can also enhance trust in the government and foster a sense of national unity. By

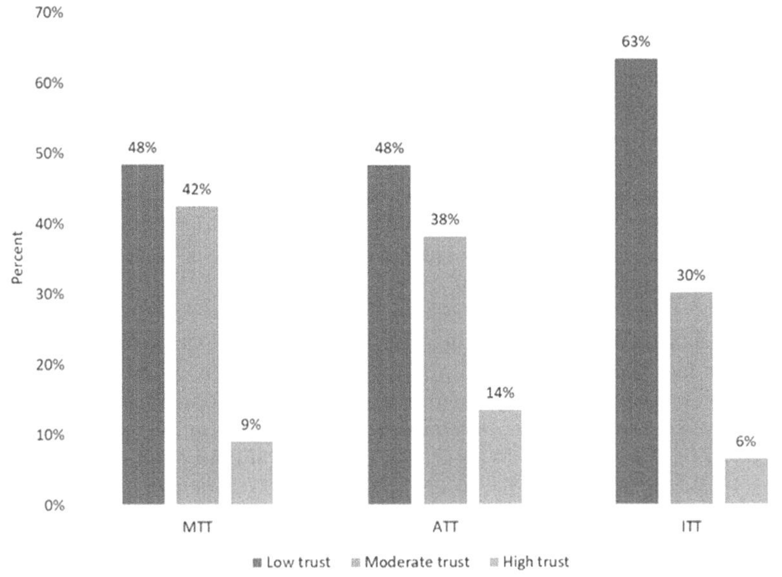

Fig. 4.17 Trust in an ITT Prime Minister (2012) (*Source* Authors using data from LAPOP [2010 and 2012]. The trusted scale ranges from one [no trust] to 7 [many trusts]. Low trust = 1 + 2; moderate trust = 3 – 5; high trust = 6 + 7)

tackling corruption and improving vertical trust, TT can work towards a more transparent and accountable governance system that serves the best interests of its citizens.

References

Calvo, E., & Murillo, M. (2004). Who Delivers? Partisan Clients in the Argentine Electoral Market. *American Journal of Political Science*, *48*(4), 742–757. https://doi.org/10.2307/1519931

Chandra, K. (2004). *Why Ethnic Parties Succeed*. Cambridge UP.

Chandra, K. (2007). Counting Heads: A Theory of Voter and Elite Behaviour in Patronage-Democracies. In Herbert Kitschelt and Steven Wilkinson (Eds.), *Patrons, Clients and Policies*. Cambridge University Press.

Chandra, K. (2013). Patronage, Democracy and Ethnic Politics in India. In D. Abente, & L. Diamond (Eds.), *Clientelism, Social Policy and the Quality of Democracy*. Johns Hopkins University Press.

Chang, E., & Kerr, N. (2009). Do Voters Have Different Attitudes Toward Corruption? The Sources and Implications of Popular Perceptions and Tolerance of Political Corruption. Afrobarometer Working Papers No 116.

Compete Caribbean. (2016). Productivity, Technology, Innovation in the Caribbean (iadb.org).

Desmond, C. (1986). Minister for Housing and Resettlement, responding to a heckler at a public meeting, quoted by Meighoo page 113.

Dietz S., Neumayer, E., & Soysa, I. (2007). Corruption, the Resource Curse and Genuine Saving. *Environment and Development Economics, 12*(1), 33–53. Cambridge University Press.

Dookeran, W., & Jantzen, M. (2012). A New Leadership Challenge. In *Power Politics and Performance: A Partnership Approach for the Development* (p. 233). Ian Rndle Publishers.

Krueger, A. O. (1974, June). The Political Economy of the Rent-Seeking Society. *American Economic Review, American Economic Association, 64*(3), 291–303.

Mariotti, C. (2022). Elite Theory. *The Palgrave Encyclopedia of Interest Groups, Lobbying and Public Affairs* (pp. 427–432). Springer International Publishing.

Mbaku, J. M. (1992). Bureaucratic Corruption as Rent-Seeking Behavior. *Konjunkturpolitik (Germany), 38*(1), 247–265.

Olson, M. (1965). *The Logic of Collective Action: Public Goods and the Theory of Groups*. Harvard University Press.

Prakash, S., & Selle, P. (Eds.). (2004). *Investigating Social Capital*. SAGE.

Putnam, R. D. (Ed.). (2002). *Democracy in Flux: Social Capital in Contemporary Societies*. Oxford University Press.

Ramkerrysingh, M. (2018). "The need for campaign finance vs society's need for transparency" speech posted on the 8th of November, Trinidad and Tobago Transparency Institute.

Ruprah, I., & Sierra, R. (2016). *An Engine of Growth? The Caribbean Private Sector Needs More than an Oil Change*. Inter-American Development Bank.

Tullock, G. (1980). Efficient rent seeking. In J. Buchanan, R. Tollison, and G. Tullock (Eds.), *Toward a Theory of the Rent-Seeking Society*. Texas A and M University Press.

Tyler, T. R., & Lind, E. A. (1992). A Relational Model of Authority in Groups. In M. Zanna (Ed.), *Advances in Experimental Social Psychology* (vol. 25, pp. 115–191). Academic Press.

US Department of State. (2020). 2020 Country Reports on Human Rights Practices: Trinidad and Tobago. Bureau Of Democracy, Human Rights, and Labor. Government Printing Office. https://www.state.gov/reports/2020-country-reports-on-human-rights-practices/trinidad-and-tobago/

van den Bos, K., Vermunt, R., & Wilke, H. A. M. (1997). Procedural and Distributive Justice: What is Fair Depends More on What Comes First Than on What Comes Next. *Journal of Personality and Social Psychology, 72*(1), 95–104.

Franco, M., & Scartascini, C. (2014). The politics of policies: Revisiting the quality of public policies and government capabilities in Latin America and the Caribbean. Policy Brief IDB-PB-220. Washington, DC, United States. Inter-American Development Bank

CHAPTER 5

Economic Development: From Sugar to Hydrocarbons and Beyond

5.1 The Beginnings of a Plantation Economy[1]

Even though Christopher Columbus encountered the islands of Trinidad and Tobago on his third voyage in 1498, it was not until 1592 that the Spanish took official possession of Trinidad and founded the then capital San José of Oruña (Saint Joseph). TT's development proceeded slowly, and the island remained largely undeveloped until the late eighteenth century when a few Spaniards and their slaves immigrated to Trinidad. The development of the sugar industry, which later became the backbone of the economy, started after the Spanish Crown proclaimed the Cedula of Population in 1783, offering land, tax incentives, and other benefits to attract settlers. After the Cedula of Population, many wealthy French planters and their slaves, including freed Africans and coloureds, immigrated to the island to establish sugar plantations. The French planters successfully expanded the island's sugar production and trade. Attracted by the success of Trinidad's plantations, the British seized the island from Spain in 1797 and continued its development as a plantation economy. Tobago's complete formation as a sugar plantation began after the island was ceded to the British in 1793—Tobago changed hands several times between the British, French, Dutch, and Courlanders before it ended

[1] For a detailed analysis of this period see Williams (2005) and Brereton (1981).

J. Khadan and I. Jit Ruprah, *Unraveling Race, Politics, and Gender in Trinidad and Tobago's Economic Development*,
https://doi.org/10.1007/978-3-031-54656-3_5

up under British control in 1814. Tobago's sugar production peaked in the 1790s. However, by 1807, sugar production began an irreversible decline, and the island's sugar industry eventually collapsed in 1889, leaving Tobago's economy in shambles. Both islands were amalgamated to form a single colony under British rule in that same year.

Nonetheless, in the early 1800s, Trinidad's economy was based on highly productive crops. Sugar production increased rapidly until a labour shortage hit the industry following the abolition of slavery in the British Empire.[2] There was competition from beet sugar produced in European countries and cheaper slave-grown sugar from other territories such as Cuba, Haiti, and Brazil. The British turned to Portuguese, Chinese, and Indian indentured workers in response. However, the Madeirans found it challenging to cope with the harsh conditions of tropical sugar plantations, and most of them turned to petty shopkeeping. At the same time, the Chinese labourers tended towards commerce rather than agriculture. After other experimental immigration schemes, the Colonial Government eventually settled on labour from the Indian subcontinent and imported East Indian workers from 1845 to 1917. The indentured Indian workers helped quadruple Trinidad's sugar production by 1895, from its 1828 level, when sugar production fell in other English-speaking islands.[3]

Although sugar was prominent, Trinidad also produced crops of cocoa, coffee, and other exports. Cocoa took over as the island's leading export crop in 1897. The rise and fall of the cocoa industry followed a path similar to that of sugar. Cocoa was first introduced to Trinidad by the Spanish in 1525. Still, only after the Spanish Cedula of Population in 1783 did its cultivation and production intensify—led by French migrants. The cocoa trade commenced in the eighteenth century. By 1830, TT was the third (after Venezuela and Ecuador) largest cocoa producer globally, accounting for 20 per cent of the world's cocoa. The cocoa industry remained buoyant and dominated the local economy from 1866 to 1920, supported by increasing world demand and attractive prices. After cocoa production peaked in 1921, the industry experienced

[2] See Wood (1968) for the period of transition from slavery to indentured workers.

[3] For an analysis of the plantation economy as applied to TT see Sudama (1979) who questions the model that was widely used to analyse the Caribbean namely the plantation economy model developed by Best (1968), which is a type of dependency analysis that focuses on the impact of imperial domination on the export-propelled economies of the Caribbean, as metropolitan interests shifted from plunder to production for trade.

a steady decline due to both external and internal factors such as the great depression of the 1920s, Witches' Broom disease in Trinidad, competition for agricultural labour from the development of the local oil industry, and a glut in the market which drove down prices. Despite efforts to rehabilitate the industry, cocoa production continued to decline steadily in the twenty-first century. The other export crops were coffee, citrus fruits, and coconuts. The expansion of coffee and citrus production coincided with the fall of cocoa in the 1930s. However, there was a drastic decline in the production of both crops during the oil boom of the 1970s. As the country entered a deep recession in the early 1980s, the output of domestic agriculture (vegetables, rice, tubers, and livestock) increased. Nevertheless, the agriculture sector continued its steady decline over the following decades, often exhibiting an inverse relationship with the oil sector's performance (Pollard, 1985).

5.2 Transition to a Hydrocarbon Economy

One of the defining moments in TT's economic history was the discovery of crude oil. The country's first oil well, and perhaps the first successful oil well ever drilled anywhere in the world, was drilled in 1857 to 280 feet by US-based Merrimac Oil Company at La Brea, Trinidad. This marked a turning point for the country's development. Crude oil, later natural gas, and petrochemicals significantly influence TT's socioeconomic development. The oil sector remained nascent until commercial production and exports of crude oil commenced in 1908 and 1909, respectively. The rapid absorption of shares of oil companies operating in TT by the London Stock Exchange and Winston Churchill's encouragement for the Royal Navy to turn to oil contributed to a significant expansion in the country's crude oil production, increasing from 37 barrels in 1908 to 7.7 million barrels by 1928. The average annual crude oil production was 1,182,536 million barrels during World War I (1913–1918), and TT had become the leading petroleum producer in the British empire by 1929. There was a significant expansion of crude oil during World War II (1939–1945) until it peaked at 230,000 barrels per day towards the end of the oil boom in 1978. Since then, crude oil production has steadily declined in the following decades, reaching 58,440 barrels per day by 2022.

In the mid-1990s, TT transitioned from an oil-based to a natural gas-based economy. This transition was supported by the establishment of one of the most extensive natural gas processing facilities in the Western Hemisphere during the mid to late 1990s (Ministry of Energy of Energy Industries).[4] Even though natural gas has been an essential part of TT's hydrocarbon resources, it remained largely undeveloped until the second half of the 1900s. In the post-World War II period, natural gas emerged as an essential low-cost fuel source to support the country's industrialisation efforts. In the 1950s, natural gas was first used as a fuel for steam generators and manufacturing cement and ammonia. The creation of the Natural Gas Company of Trinidad and Tobago in 1975 catalysed the natural gas industry's development. Natural gas production increased from 544 mmcf/d in 1993 to 4329.5 mmcf/d in 2010. The transition to natural gas was more pronounced for the economy in the 2000s as the country's second hydrocarbon boom (from 2002 to 2008) was led by increased natural gas production and prices.

5.3 The Push for Industrialisation and Nationalisation[5]

In 1950, the government introduced two significant pieces of legislation to support its industrialisation efforts: the Aid to Pioneer Industries Ordinance and the Income Tax Reform Ordinance to Benefit Industry. These measures provided a range of fiscal incentives for infant industries and marked the first time TT sought foreign capital outside Britain. By 1962, when TT became an independent nation, policymakers complemented the fiscal incentives by significantly raising tariffs to protect and encourage the growth of the nascent manufacturing sector. Similar measures were also adopted by the authorities to support the tourism sector in Tobago. These measures proved successful as more than 100 pioneer industries in bricks, beer, textiles, glass, cement, paints, and chemicals were established by the mid-1960s.

The oil boom of the 1970s enabled the government to play a larger role in the economy, including in agriculture, manufacturing, and financial sectors. The government's increased economic role was also catalysed by decades of trade unions' critique of foreign ownership and the 1970s

[4] See Ministry of Energy and Energy Industries, http://www.energy.gov.tt/historical-facts-petroleum/

[5] See Motley (2008) for a comprehensive analysis of industrial policy.

Black Power movement that challenged an economic system where skin colour dictated employment opportunities. In the 1970s, the government nationalised several foreign firms; Trinidadian citizens purchased majority shares in foreign companies, and the banking sector underwent a process of nationalisation and localisation, among others. Furthermore, between 1968 and 1974, the government intervened in the oil sector by purchasing the oil holdings of the British Petroleum Company and Shell Corporation and establishing the National Petroleum Company. One entity that symbolised the specific role of the government in the oil sector was the creation of the multibillion-dollar industrial park at Point Lisas. Although marred by cost overruns, the industrial park came onstream in the early to mid-1980s. It included a well-integrated petrochemical industry, producing steel, urea, ammonia, cement, methanol plants and an oil refinery. Beyond that, the increase in petrol revenues allowed the government to expand their role in the economy by introducing transfers and subsidies, public works programmes, expansion of state-owned enterprises, and investments in industrial projects. By the late 1970s, the state had become the largest employer in the country.

5.4 A Maturing Oil Jurisdiction with Challenges to Diversify Its Economy

After over a century in the hydrocarbon business, TT has found itself in an unenviable position of having a largely undiversified economic structure with waning hydrocarbon resources. Having transitioned from an oil-dominant to a primarily natural gas-based economy in the 2000s, TT is now a mature hydrocarbon economy whose reserves are expected to run out in the coming decade (see Boopsingh, 2014). There are clear signs that the sector has been in retreat. Perhaps one of the more telling signs is the closure of the century-old-loss-making and highly indebted petroleum refinery (Petrotrin) in 2018—TT now imports refined petroleum products it once produced. Moreover, attracting new investments for exploration is a challenge, especially given the rise of Guyana as the newest and most lucrative hydrocarbon jurisdiction in the Caribbean region. These trends will only worsen as the global energy transition accelerates in the coming years. The economy has seen the effects of these changes as energy exports fell from 60 per cent of GDP in 2011 to 30.1 per cent of GDP in 2019. The decline is not only reflective of commodity prices but also production. Crude oil production has experienced a persistent decline, dropping from its peak at a daily average of 144,000 barrels per day (bpd) in 2015 to 56,480 bpd in 2020. Natural gas production also has declined from its peak at 4,329.5 million cubic feet of gas, mmcf, per day in 2010 to 3,044 mmcf per day in 2020.

Policies to support economic diversification are usually recommended for commodity-dependent countries to help mitigate the effects of commodity price shocks and the eventual exhaustion of resources. TT has recognised the need for such policies for several decades. Economic diversification has been a key area of attention for policymakers dating back to the country's first Five Year Development Plan and subsequent ones (see Toney, 1995). While vertical diversification within the energy sector has been largely successful, horizontal diversification or diversification from the energy sector towards non-oil and gas tradable has largely failed.[6] As measured by the Herfindahl–Hirschman Index, the non-oil and non-petrochemical, tradable diversification has remained low from 1968 to 2000. But as the commodity super cycle took hold of the economy in the 2000s, the non-energy tradable sector became more concentrated in commodities and markets. The economy faces an enormous challenge to find new sources of growth in the coming decade as hydrocarbon production and proven reserves are declining or have plateaued, barring new discoveries.

5.5 Conclusions

TT's economy has transitioned from a sugar-based plantation economy in the eighteenth century to a hydrocarbon-dependent economy. The discovery of crude oil in 1857 marked a significant turning point for the country's development. The government's efforts to promote industrialisation, exemplified by establishing the Point Lisas industrial park, supported the development of upstream, midstream, and downstream energy sectors and the sector's transition from an oil-based to a natural gas-based economy in the mid-1990s. However, TT is experiencing declining energy exports and slowing sector investments as a mature hydrocarbon jurisdiction with depleting resources. These trends have highlighted the urgent need for economic diversification. In the following

[6] See Moya, Mohammed and Sookram (2010) who attempt to answer why resources are not flowing to the non-energy sector towards non-energy tradables.

chapters, we will examine the macroeconomic performance of TT over economic cycles and assess its outcomes on poverty, inequality, and the role played by the labour market and the private non-energy sector firms.

References

Brereton, B. (1981). *A History of Modern Trinidad 1783–1962*. Heineman.

Best, L. (1968). Outlines of a Model of Pure Plantation Economy. *Social and Economic Studies (University of the West Indies), 17*(3), 283–323.

Boopsingh, T., & McGuire, G. (Eds.). (2014). *From Oil to Gas*. University Press of America.

Boopsingh, T. "The Last Decade of Liquidified Gas and Its Impact" in Boopsingh, T. and G. McGuire (2014), op.cit.

Ministry of Energy and Energy Industries "Historical Facts on the Petroleum Industry of Trinidad and Tobago", Ministry of Energy and Energy Industries | Historical Facts on the Petroleum Industry of Trinidad and Tobago (https://www.energy.gov.tt/historical-facts-petroleum/).

Motley, W. (2008). Trinidad and Tobago, Industrial Policy 1950–2008. Ian Randel Publishers.

Moya, R., Mohammed, A., & Sookram, S. (2010). Productive Policies in Trinidad and Tobago: A Critical Review, IDB Working Papers WP-115.

Pollard, H. (1985). The Erosion of Agriculture in an Oil Economy: The Case of Export Crop Production in Trinidad. *World Development, 13*(7), 819–1835.

Toney, H. (1995). A Critical Review of the Manufacturing Sector in Trinidad and Tobago ECLAC, CONS/95/3.

Sudama, T. (1979). The Model of the Plantation Economy: The Case of Trinidad and Tobago, *Latin American Perspectives, 6*(1).

Williams, E. (2005). *Capitalism and Slavery*. Ian Randle Publishers.

Wood, D. (1968). *Trinidad in Transition: The Years After Slavery*. Oxford University Press.

CHAPTER 6

Economic Development: The Macroeconomic Perspective

6.1 Introduction

Two critical structural features of TT, namely resource dependency and ethnic polarisation, imply that forces are at play, leading to poor economic performance. As discussed in previous chapters, resource dependency and ethnic polarization result in a reallocation effect through the political process, and via the fiscal policy channel.[1] Regarding resource dependency, the most common economic explanation is that these economies are subject to high volatility, which reduces economic growth.

TT's story is that economic growth has been highly volatile, mainly reflecting the vagaries of international commodity prices. Several studies have found that growth volatility reduces economic growth (Ramsey & Ramsey, 1995; Philippe & Rogers, 1995). This negative relationship derives from the inverse relationship between volatility and the riskiness of investments, which leads to a decline in aggregate demand and growth. For TT, growth volatility reduces GDP growth by 0.1 percentage point in the long run (Khadan, 2016). As shown in Fig. 6.1, TT has the highest level of volatility even when compared with the volatility of other

[1] Some studies found that ethnically diverse economies are prudent regarding fiscal policy (Siddique 2021), and that oil price shocks on the economy are mainly through fiscal policy (Tazhibay et al., 2008).

J. Khadan and I. Jit Ruprah, *Unraveling Race, Politics, and Gender in Trinidad and Tobago's Economic Development*,
https://doi.org/10.1007/978-3-031-54656-3_6

resource-dependent economies. The country's economic growth is lower than all comparator groups (Fig. 6.2). Thus, TT's lower economic growth can be partially attributed to higher volatility.

However, volatility alone does not explain TT's prolonged economic contraction and stagnation periods. Other microeconomic and macroeconomic forces are at play, particularly those contributing to the country's falling productivity and competitiveness and an undiversified economic structure. As shown in Fig. 6.3, the main turning points of the country's boom-and-bust episodes are associated with changes in commodity prices, which are often accentuated by the fiscal policy stance (pro-cyclical) during commodity booms and lethargic policy responses after a negative price shock.[2] In its post-independence history, TT has experienced two primary commodity cycles, with the most recent one leaving the economy stagnating for over a decade.

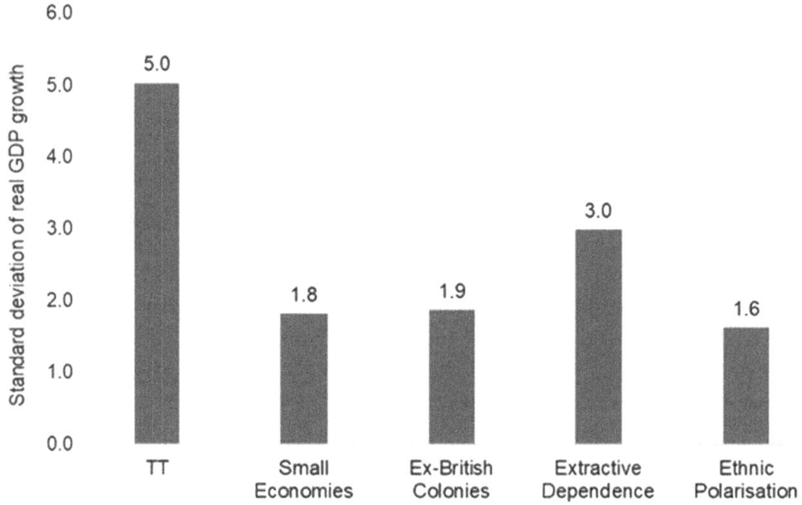

Fig. 6.1 Volatility, TT, and Comparators (*Note* Volatility is measured by the standard deviation of economic growth for 1962–2020, *Source* Authors' estimates from World Development Indicators [2021])

[2] See Ramlogan and Sookram (2018) for procyclical fiscal policy and inadequate coordination with monetary policy in TT.

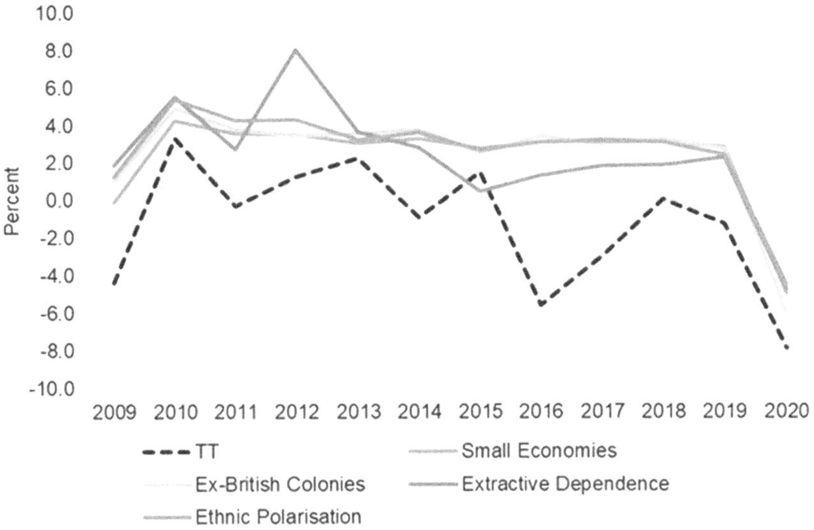

Fig. 6.2 Economic Growth, TT, and Comparators (*Source* Authors' estimates from World Development Indicators [2021])

We now turn to examine these boom-and-bust cycles in some detail. After discussing the boom–bust episodes, we discuss structural impediments to growth, namely the Dutch Disease and lack of diversity in exports and supply-side issues, including low productivity.

6.2 Booms and Busts

Since the 1970s, we can distinguish the following boom–bust episodes: boom from 1973 to 1982, bust from 1983 to 1989, recovery from 1990 to 1999 despite falling oil prices, boom from 2000 to 2018, and bust from 2019 to 2020. For each episode, we chart the evolution of the main variables: oil or gas price and production, economic growth, GDP per capita, inflation, unemployment, and the fiscal and current account of the balance of payments.[3]

[3] See Premdas and Ragoonath (2020) for details on the booms and busts cycles during the period 1962 to 2008.

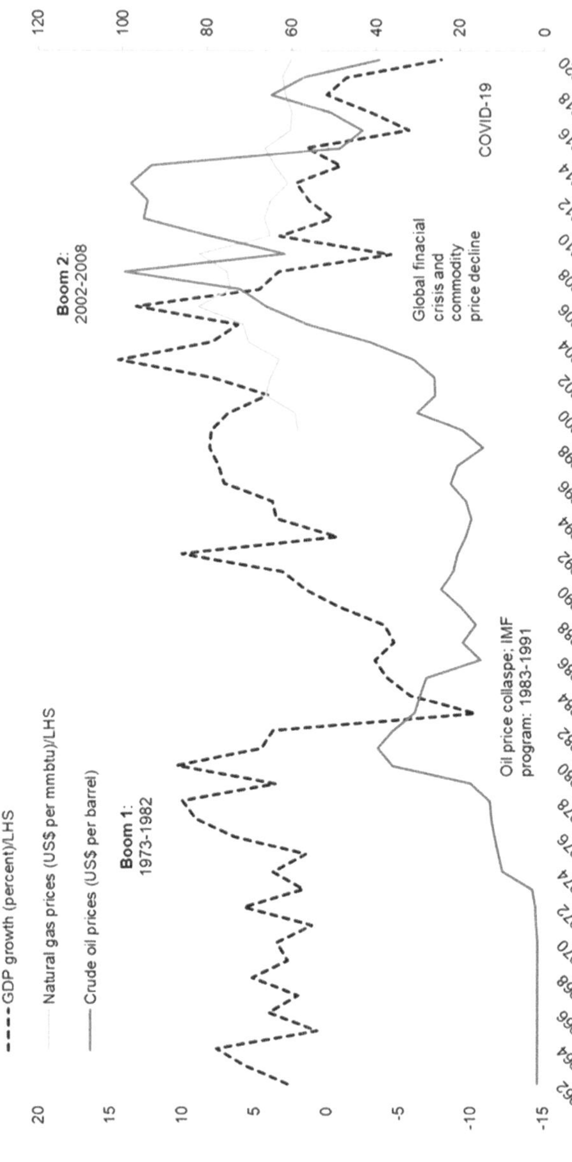

Fig. 6.3 Economic Growth and Commodity Prices (*Source* Authors' estimates from World Development Indicators [2021] and World Economic Outlook [2021])

Boom 1 was based on the crude oil boom from 1973 to 1982 (Fig. 6.4). As an independent country, TT's first oil boom was due to increased crude oil production and international oil prices. Crude oil output increased from 140,000 barrels per day in 1972 to 177,000 in 1982, peaking at 230,000 barrels per day in 1978. External forces, particularly the Yom Kippur War of 1973, led to a rapid and persistent increase in international oil prices from US$1.90 per barrel in 1972 to US$35.5 per barrel in 1982. As a result, economic growth accelerated to double digits, reaching 10 per cent in 1978 and 1980. TT's overall financial performance during the boom period was among the region's best. Over the period 1973–1982, economic growth averaged 5.5 per cent, GDP per capita increased by almost five-fold, and unemployment fell from 15 per cent to 10 per cent. The fiscal and current account balances as a per cent of GDP averaged 3.7 per cent and 4.6 per cent, respectively, and import cover increased to more than 12 months in 1982. TT was referred to as the Arabs of the Caribbean.

What did TT do with the boom? The oil sector operated as an economic enclave, with fiscal policy being the main link to the rest of the economy. As expected, the oil boom led to a surge in government revenues, and while the government showed restraint initially, public spending accelerated in subsequent years. Government revenues doubled over the boom period, reaching 40 per cent of GDP in 1981, and spending rose to a historic high of 49.4 per cent in 1982. The increase in public spending was concentrated on sticky current account items such as subsidies and transfers to households and public enterprises, public wages, and capital expenditure through an ambitious public works programme. The most significant increase was in transfers and subsidies, which grew by almost 34 per cent from 1972 to 1982. These were followed by loans and grants to public utilities (30.6 per cent) and capital expenditure (28 per cent). The latter partially reflects policies to reduce the economy's reliance on petroleum in the long term as the government invested part of the windfall revenues in large steel and petrochemical projects.

The glory days of the 1970s and early 1980s came to a painful end by the mid-1980s (see Fig. 6.5). Crude oil prices retreated swiftly to pre-boom levels. The oil price fell from its peak of US$39.6 per barrel in 1981 to US$15 per barrel in 1986. This fall was due to an oil glut in the global market and a slowdown of economic activity in industrial countries. This fall led to a reversal of the country's commodity fortunes. The TT economy, heavily reliant on crude oil for its revenue and export earnings,

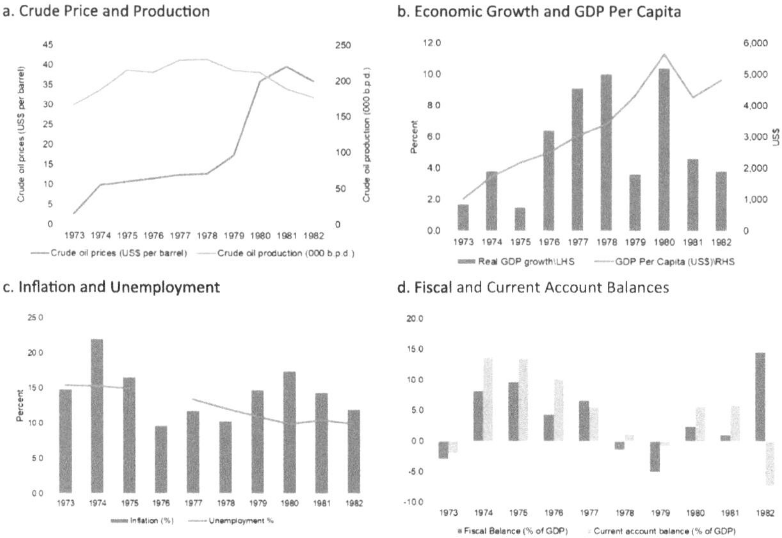

Fig. 6.4 Oil Boom 1973–1982 (**a**) Crude price and production (**b**) Economic growth and GDP Per Capita (**c**) Inflation and unemployment (**d**) Fiscal and current account balances (*Source* The authors' calculations are based on data from the Central Bank of Trinidad and Tobago)

was thrown into a deep recession that lasted for seven years: real GDP growth contracted by an annual average of 4.7 per cent over the period 1983–1989, with dire consequences for the rest of the economy. Consequently, the fiscal and current account balances turned to and remained in deficit for the entire period. The unemployment rate reached a high of 22 per cent, GDP per capita fell almost two-fold, and the country ran through a large stock of international reserves in a relatively short period.

TT policymakers were slow to adjust to the shock and initially continued to accumulate large deficits on the fiscal and external accounts. The country became accustomed to a lifestyle financed and subsidised by oil rents, making it politically difficult for the government to cut the current expenditure bill. The initial response was to scale back capital spending, which was insufficient to offset the adverse revenue shock. The financial sector also took a significant hit. The non-performing loans to

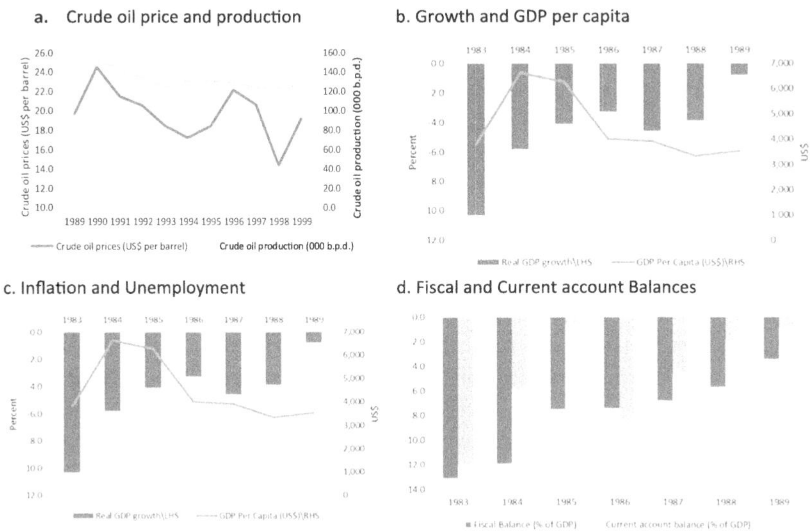

Fig. 6.5 Bust 1983–1989 (**a**) Crude oil price and production (**b**) Growth and GDP per Capita (**c**) Inflation and unemployment (**d**) Fiscal and current account balances (*Source* Central Bank of Trinidad and Tobago)

gross loans reached a historic high of 25 per cent in 1989, as real estate prices collapsed, taking down several financial institutions.

The economic crisis of the 1980s coincided with a change in the country's leadership. The PNM retained power in the November 1981 elections after the death of Eric Williams in March 1981 but under the leadership of George Chambers. The new Prime Minister inherited an economy facing a deep recession and mounting allegations of corruption and wastage associated with government projects. The Chamber's government attempted some adjustments. These included reducing subsidies, increasing utility rates, cutting capital expenditure, establishing a dual exchange rate, imposing import controls, and eventually devaluing the exchange rate by 50 per cent in December 1985. However, a recovery never materialised under his administration. The political cost associated with those economic adjustments and overall dissatisfaction with the PNM administration at that time was severe. After controlling the government for over three uninterrupted decades, the PNM retained only three seats (out of 36) in the country's Parliament in the 1986 general elections. The new party, NAR, overwhelmingly won the elections.[4]

Then, there occurred a period of further adjustments and reforms. The NAR, made up of former PNM members and opposition parties, won the December 1986 elections with broad national support, obtaining 66 per cent of the votes cast. The new coalition government, led by Arthur N. R. Robinson, quickly corrected the economic imbalances and stabilised the declining economy. By 1987, the government started accelerating the implementation of fiscal austerity measures: some of the critical policies included the suspension of cost-of-living allowances and merit pay for public officers,[5] deep cuts to transfers and subsidies, a 10 per cent cut to public-sector wages, reduction in public-sector employment via voluntary separation programme, increases in utility rates, and divestment of state-owned enterprises. The government revised the oil tax regime to incentivise companies to increase exploration and production.

Moreover, the government undertook a comprehensive overhaul of the tax system by simplifying taxes (moving from 11 to 4) and introducing a VAT in 1990. At the same time, international reserves were almost depleted (less than one month of import cover in 1989), and TT was experiencing great difficulty meeting external obligations. By January 1989, the government turned to the IMF for a Stand-By Arrangement. The structural reforms and adjustments continued under the IMF programme, including fiscal, monetary, and exchange rate reforms.

However, doing the "right thing" had devastating political costs. The NAR lost coalition members and retained only the two Tobago seats in Parliament in the 1991 elections.[6] After the IMF programme, the new PNM government continued to enact structural reforms by focusing on industrial and trade liberalisation policies to support economic growth. PNM reaped the benefits of the structural adjustments enacted under the NAR government.

[4] For developments in the 1980s and the political transition, see Ryan (1989).

[5] This action was subsequently reversed by the industrial court.

[6] There were also internal disputes over government posts and economic policies, and an attempted coup in 1990. Together, these developments weakened and fractured the NAR, which never recovered. After the ULF left the NAR in 1988 it went on to form the Caucus for Love, Unity, and Brotherhood (CLUB 88), which then evolved into the United National Congress (UNC) in 1989.

These adjustments and reforms led to a recovery (Fig. 6.6) despite falling oil production and prices. The economy started to respond favourably to the reforms and adjustment measures in the early 1990s, and by 1994, economic growth of 3.6 per cent was obtained. The recovery marked the beginning of a period of relatively balanced growth (1994 to 1999), where developments in the energy sector along with macroeconomic and structural reforms resulted in sustained economic recovery: the annual average growth rate for the non-energy and energy sectors was 6 per cent and 8 per cent, respectively. Real GDP growth remained robust from 1994 onwards, reaching 8.1 per cent by 1998. GDP per capita partially recovered, unemployment fell from 22 per cent to 13 per cent, and inflation fell to low single digits. The restrictive policy was successful as the large and persistent fiscal and current account deficits were reduced to manageable levels.

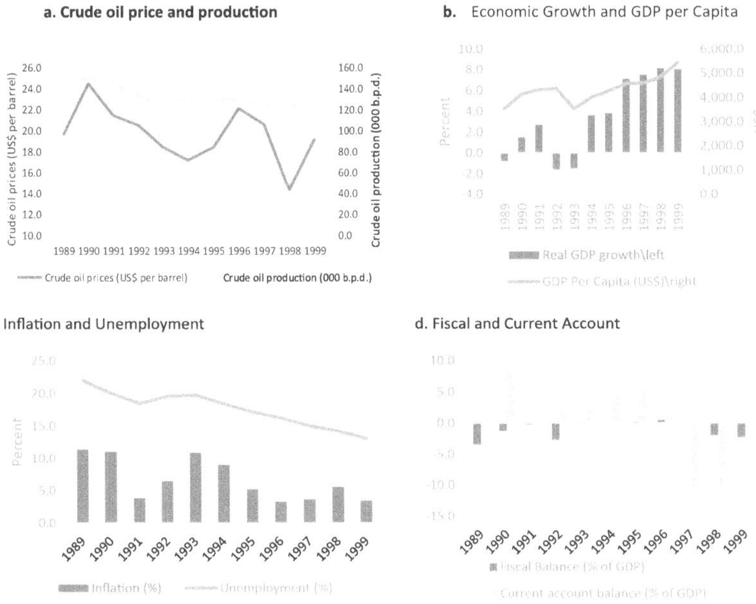

Fig. 6.6 Recovery 1989–1999 (**a**) Crude oil price and production (**b**) Economic growth and GDP per Capita (**c**) Inflation and unemployment (**d**) Fiscal and current account (*Source* Central Bank of Trinidad and Tobago)

The second major boom was due to a surge in natural gas production and prices, Fig. 6.7, from 2000 to 2008. The investments in developing the natural gas and petrochemical sectors helped TT transition to a natural gas-based economy in the 2000s. Natural gas production increased from 15,346 M.cu. Metres in 2000 to 41,483 M.cu. Metres in 2008.

On the other hand, crude oil production experienced a persistent decline, from 230,000 barrels per day (bpd) in 1978 to 144,000 bpd in 2008. As a result, the share of oil exports in government revenues declined from 63 per cent in 1978 to 54 per cent in 2008. In 2000, oil exports as a share of total energy exports were close to 46 per cent. Still, this share declined to about 16 per cent in 2008, and natural gas and petrochemical exports accounted for roughly 70 per cent of total energy exports.

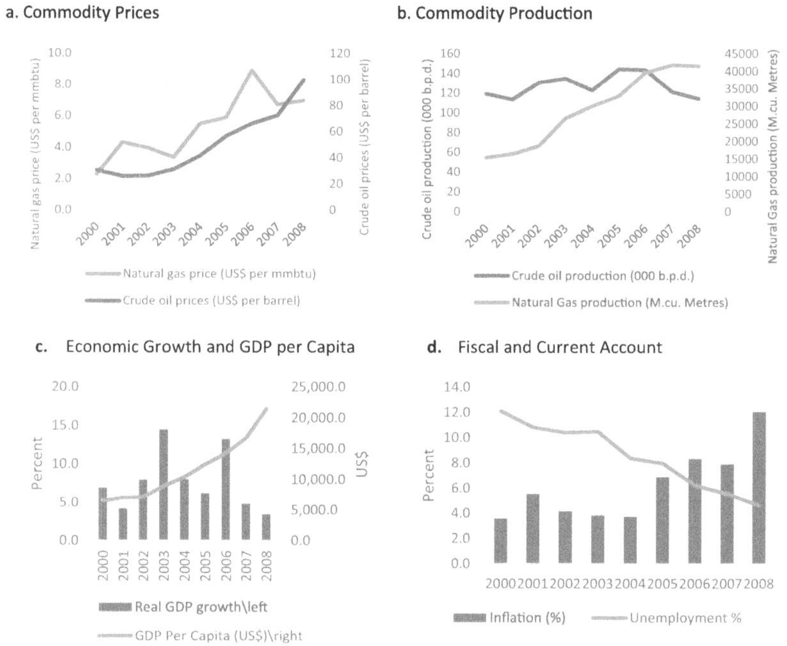

Fig. 6.7 Boom 2000–2018 (**a**) Commodity prices (**b**) Commodity production (**c**) Economic growth and GDP per Capita (**d**) Fiscal and current account (*Source* Central Bank of Trinidad and Tobago)

As the commodity super cycle of the 2000s unfolded, TT became one of the wealthiest nations in Latin America and the Caribbean on a GDP per capita basis.[7] International oil and gas prices reached historic highs during the boom period. With TT's exports and revenues still heavily dependent on oil and gas, this positive shock meant a bonanza for the government coffers. Economic growth accelerated to double digits (again), reaching 14 per cent in 2003. Over the period 2002–2008, economic growth averaged 8.3 per cent. GDP per capita increased three-fold, unemployment fell from 10 per cent to 4.6 per cent, and the fiscal and current account balances as a per cent of GDP averaged 3.4 per cent and 19.8 per cent, respectively. Import cover of foreign reserves increased to almost 12 months in 2008.

But a tale similar to the previous oil boom ensued. The government's response to the energy windfall was cautious initially, but as energy revenues surged, government spending increased. Government revenue increased fourfold (from TT$14 billion to TT$57 billion) from 2002 to 2008, while government expenditure rose three-fold (from TT$14 billion to TT$46 billion) over the same period. The most significant increase in expenditure was in current transfers and subsidies to households and public entities. The government offered numerous public programmes, often duplicating programmes across government agencies, to achieve poverty alleviation, employment creation, human capital development, social welfare assistance, and micro-enterprise development. These were in addition to generous fuel and electricity subsidies, mostly favouring the wealthy.[8] During the boom period, capital expenditure increased by an annual average of 60 per cent as the government pursued an aggressive infrastructural development programme with several mega-construction projects. The number of state-owned enterprises exploded during that period, becoming the government's preferred vehicle for capital projects, presumably avoiding the public-sector bureaucracy. However, some projects were often marred by cost overruns and recurring allegations of corruption and wastage. Nonetheless, the state played a significant role in driving economic activity as it extended itself across essential sectors of the economy.

[7] TT had the 5th highest GDP per capita in Latin America and the Caribbean over the period 2002–2008.

[8] See IMF (2016) for an analysis of the fuel subsidies' fiscal, distributional, and environmental impacts.

Though well-intentioned, most social programmes fell short in achieving their desired results and often compromised various elements of long-term macroeconomic stability. As discussed in the following sections, some programmes helped reinforce structural constraints to growth and created new ones. Nevertheless, learning from the mistakes of the previous boom, TT formalised the Interim Revenue Stabilization Fund by creating a Heritage and Stabilization Fund in 2007. At the end of the boom, the HSF had almost US$3 billion in savings.[9]

In the late 2000s, "the lost period" began, see Fig. 6.8. The TT economy experienced several shocks following the 2002–2008 commodity boom. These included the global financial crisis (2008–09),[10] three commodity price shocks (2009, 2016, and 2020), and the COVID-19 pandemic (2020). These shocks largely impacted the TT economy through the international trade channel, except for the pandemic, which was more broad-based and included both external and internal elements. Furthermore, unlike the last boom period, oil and gas production has been steadily declining: crude oil production continued to 56,000 barrels per day (bpd), and natural gas production dropped to 31,177 M.cu. Metres in 2020 are 42 per cent and 30 per cent less than their 2010 levels. These recurring shocks led to a volatile and low economic growth period: TT's GDP growth averaged 1.2 per cent from 2009 to 2020.

The central government's general policy stance remained unchanged after the global financial crisis and the 2009 commodity shock. There were changes to taxation policy to incentivise exploration and production in the energy sector and improve non-energy revenue collection through tax amnesties. However, government spending continued to outpace government revenues, leading to persistent fiscal deficits from 2010 to 2020. Because of persistent primary deficits and negative economic growth, TT's debt-to-GDP ratio ballooned to 81.9 per cent of GDP in 2020 from 35 per cent in 2010. The external sector weakened significantly from a current account surplus of almost 20 per cent to 0.05 per cent of GDP, and import cover of foreign reserves fell from more than

[9] See IMF (2018) for the shortcomings of the Heritage and Stabilisation Fund and the need for counter cyclical fiscal policy.

[10] Related to the global financial crisis, the country was faced with the collapse of its largest insurance company which required a government bailout to prevent a systemic crisis.

Fig. 6.8 Bust 2019–2020 (**a**) Commodity prices (**b**) Energy production (**c**) Economic growth and GDP per Capita (**d**) Inflation and unemployment (**e**) Fiscal and current account (*Source* Central Bank of Trinidad and Tobago)

13 months to 8.5 months over the same period. Nonetheless, unemployment remained low, supposedly supported mainly by several public work programmes and public spending.

After the 2016 shock and the pandemic, gradual fiscal retrenchment appears to be taking hold. The government has been eliminating fuel subsidies and cutting back on some areas of social spending to curb public spending. Interestingly, although faced with repeated shocks, the impact on the broader economy has been less severe when compared to previous commodity price shocks. For instance, the TT economy emerged from the pandemic with relatively adequate fiscal savings (HSF has 26.5 per cent of GDP), international reserves, and a banking sector that remains well-capitalised, liquid, and profitable. Nevertheless, the heavy hand of the government in the economy masks several socioeconomic and structural challenges that continue to weigh negatively on economic growth. Thus, the main challenge would be restoring economic growth while preserving fiscal sustainability and improving social conditions.

6.3 Dutch Disease in Trinidad and Tobago

We will now explore the Dutch disease explanation for sluggish economic growth, a topic briefly discussed in Chapter 1. The Dutch disease, encompassed within the broader resource curse hypothesis, investigates the phenomenon wherein countries abundant in natural resources experience slower economic growth compared to those with fewer resources (Auty, 1994; Auty & Gelb, 1986; Wenner et al., 2018). While this may initially seem counterintuitive, empirical research has demonstrated that attempts to foster the growth of non-energy tradable sectors in mineral-dependent nations are hindered by unproductive rent-seeking, an overvalued exchange rate (Dutch disease), and revenue volatility (Oomes & Kalcheva, 2007). Even in cases where countries manage to avoid unproductive rent-seeking and corruption, the manufacturing sector may still suffer due to commodity booms causing increases in wages and exchange rates, diminishing the competitiveness of tradable products in global markets. Symptoms associated with Dutch disease comprise an overvalued real exchange rate, sluggish manufacturing growth, accelerated growth in the service sector, and higher overall wages (Oomes & Kalcheva, 2007).

Dutch disease, as outlined by Corden and Neary in 1982, involves two main effects: resource movement and spending. The resource movement effect takes place when a surge in the natural resource sector draws labour and capital away from manufacturing and services, leading to a decrease in output in both areas. Despite the decline in output, the price of manufacturing goods set by the world market remains unchanged. However, there is an increase in the price of services due to excess demand. This shift results in a higher relative price of services compared to manufacturing, causing an appreciation of the real exchange rate.

Even in the absence of the resource movement impact or its insignificance, the spending effect would still induce a real appreciation of the exchange rate. This effect materializes when increased income generated by the booming natural resource industry boosts overall demand and expenditure. If this increased demand is directed towards domestic services, it leads to a relative increase in the price of services compared to manufacturing. Consequently, the overall domestic price level rises, resulting in an appreciated real exchange rate.

6.3.1 *Why Focus on Dutch Disease?*

The significance of Dutch disease for TT is crucial, considering the country's experience with two periods of commodity booms (1973–1982 and 2002–2008) and its heavy reliance on oil and natural gas. If Dutch disease is prevalent, all firms face the challenge of dealing with a higher real exchange rate, diminishing the international competitiveness of non-energy tradables. Concurrently, domestic market producers encounter competition from more affordable imports. Consequently, even technologically advanced goods struggle to be economically viable in a competitive market when Dutch disease is present. If a new business utilizing modern technology is established in a Dutch disease-affected country, under equal competitive conditions, its economic viability hinges on surpassing the productivity achieved by rival businesses in other countries to a greater or equal extent of the exchange rate appreciation induced by Dutch disease (Khadan & Ruprah, 2016). The extent to which non-energy tradables are crowded out depends on the magnitude of energy revenues and the initial technological gap (Cherif et al., 2016).

6.3.2 *Does TT Show Symptoms of Dutch Disease?*

Four exercises are undertaken to determine whether symptoms of Dutch disease are present in TT. First, we construct a relative overvaluation index. Second, we calculate an adjusted real effective exchange rate (REER). Third, we analyse the data for sectoral shifts in the economy. Lastly, we estimate the effect of an increase in the REER on non-energy GDP and the non-energy trade balance.

There are various methods by which one can say that a country's currency is overvalued or undervalued. One approach involves comparing a country's per capita GDP, expressed in US dollars using market exchange rates, with the per capita GDP adjusted for variations in the cost of living at exchange rates. Countries experiencing a lower purchasing power parity (PPP)-adjusted GDP per capita compared to their nominal GDP per capita are deemed to have an overvalued exchange rate. Similarly, another method known as the relative overvaluation index (Rodrik, 2008) considers the Balassa-Samuelson effect by adjusting the domestic price level. The index is determined through a series of steps. Initially, nominal exchange rates and PPP conversion factors from the Penn World Tables are utilized to calculate a "real" exchange rate. Subsequently, a regression analysis of the real exchange rate on GDP per capita reveals a relationship with a coefficient of −0.27 (Rodrick found a value of −0.24), indicating a strong Balassa-Samuelson effect. That is, a 10 per cent increase in income leads to a roughly −2.7 per cent decrease in the real exchange rate. An undervaluation index is derived by comparing the actual real exchange rate with the Balassa-Samuelson-adjusted rate. If the index surpasses (falls below) unity, it signifies undervaluation (overvaluation). The overvaluation index, illustrated in Fig. 6.9, demonstrates that the TT dollar has consistently and significantly been overvalued for most of the covered period.

Policy discussions often centre around Real Effective Exchange Rates (REER), as depicted in Fig. 6.9. These indices aim to gauge a country's overall international competitiveness relative to its trading partners. Typically, REER indices are created by considering a weighted average of a country's nominal and real bilateral exchange rates against a designated set of countries. However, the absence of a universally accepted method for calculating these indexes results in significant variations across countries in terms of weighting methodologies, the inclusion of different types of trade, and the frequency of weight updates. Consequently, these indexes may not be well-suited for addressing current competitiveness issues. The selection of weights essentially comes down to two options: trade-weighting, which relies on direct export shares, import shares, or both, and competition-weighting, where weights account for the fact that a country's exports face competition from both domestic producers in the destination country and exports from other nations (third-market competition). The frequency of updating trade weights varies across countries, typically occurring annually, every three years, or approximately every ten

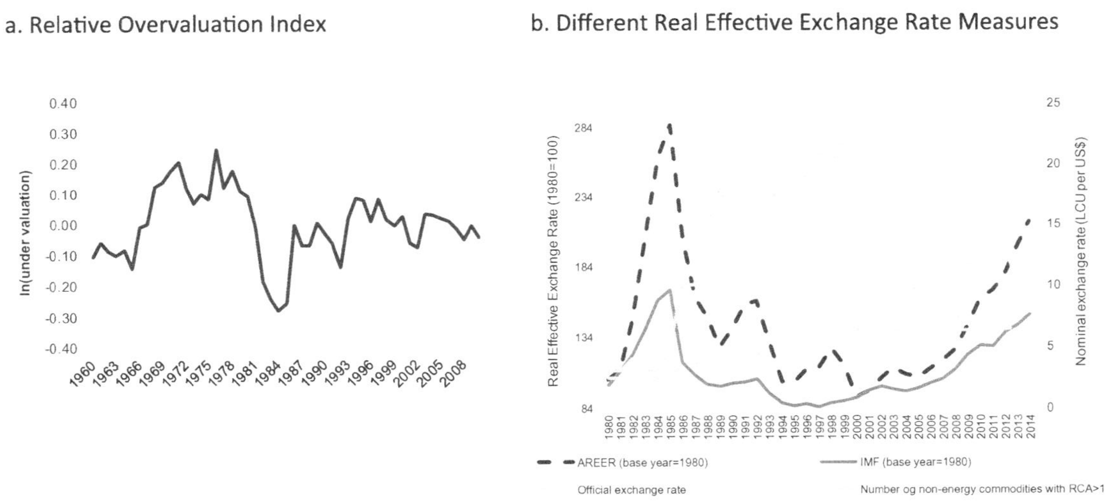

Fig. 6.9 Overvalued real exchange rates (**a**) Relative overvaluation index (*Note* ln (undervaluation) < 1 implies overvaluation, *Source* Author's estimates based on the Penn World Tables 7.1) (**b**) Different real effective exchange rate measures (*Note* AREER = adjusted real effective exchange rate; IMF = International Monetary Fund; LCU = local currency units; RCA = revealed comparative advantage, *Source* Author's estimates based on the World Integrated Trade Solution database, the Central Statistical Office of Trinidad and Tobago, and the World Bank's World Development Indicators)

years. The most used REER is the one published by the International Monetary Fund (IMF). The IMF's REER employs competition weights, encompasses manufacturing goods, primary products (excluding energy), and services (specifically travel), and adjusts the weights roughly every ten years.

Our alternative index, known as the adjusted real effective exchange rate (AREER), incorporates a more extensive range of countries and utilizes annually updated competition-driven weights. These weights, derived from bilateral trade data sourced from the United Nations COMTRADE database, consider TT's bilateral trade with another country and the competitive challenges TT encounters from that country on a product-specific basis in third markets. While trade in energy products is crucial for TT, these items have been omitted from the weight calculations. The exclusion of energy is justified by the fact that global energy markets determine prices, and fluctuations in exchange rates are not anticipated to impact a country's relative competitiveness in primary commodities. This exclusion also serves to minimize fluctuations in trade weights, which could result from significant swings in crude oil prices. Our index focuses on third-market competition, allowing for an evaluation of how changes in exchange rates may influence TT's market shares in key export markets. In comparison to the IMF's REER, the AREER exhibits greater fluctuations and indicates higher appreciation, as illustrated in Fig. 6.9. It provides a more accurate representation of competitiveness: despite nominal devaluations from 1988 to 1999, the AREER appreciated until 1993 and subsequently depreciated, mirroring the currency trends of TT's competitors in export markets.

Figure 6.10 illustrates changes in GDP and employment across various sectors. When Dutch disease is present, one anticipates a reduction in the manufacturing sector (de-industrialization), as discussed earlier. The data reveals a decrease in the proportions of the non-booming tradable sectors (manufacturing and export agriculture) and non-tradable sectors (services), offset by an increase in the share of the booming tradable industry. In 1966, the booming tradable sector contributed 26% to GDP, a figure that rose to 44% by 2013. Conversely, the non-booming tradable sector's GDP share dropped more than two-fold to 6% in 2013, while the non-tradable sector's share decreased from 60 to 50% in the same year. A shift in employment distribution is also evident, with an increase in the non-tradable sector (services) but a decline in the non-booming tradable sector. Notably, there were no substantial changes in the tradable booming industry.

Two tasks are conducted to enhance precision in assessing the impact of an overvalued real exchange rate on the non-energy sector. The first describes the correlation between the AREER and the quantity of non-energy products exported by TT. The second involves estimating the influence of an AREER appreciation on non-energy GDP and the non-energy trade balance, employing a cointegrated vector autoregressive (VAR) model as outlined by Khadan and Ruprah in 2016.

A negative correlation is observed between the AREER and the quantity of non-energy export products. As the AREER increases, there is a delayed decrease in the export of non-energy tradable products. It is important to note that the total non-energy exports considered here meet the criterion of having a Revealed Comparative Advantage (RCA) greater than one. The relative weight of a percentage of total exports of a commodity in a country over the share of world exports of that commodity measures the RCA of a product. A product is considered to have a revealed comparative advantage if RCA is greater than 1. Conversely, a RCA value of less than 1 suggests a revealed comparative disadvantage. A more formal analysis of the relationship between AREER and the non-energy sector involves estimating their elasticity using a cointegrated Vector Autoregressive (VAR) model. The results indicate that a one standard deviation increase in AREER leads to a reduction of 0.04 percentage points in non-energy GDP. Additionally, the non-energy trade balance weakens by 0.12 percentage points with a similar increase in AREER.

Another consequence of the Dutch disease that contributes to the country's volatility is the lack of diversification of exports. TT has gone through several phases to diversify the economy, which reflects the current dominant common wisdom of industrial policy at that time. Three steps can be distinguished (see Hilaire, 1995). The first two phases were dominated by "industrialisation by invitation", which included import-substitution industrialisation (1950–1973) and resource-based industrialisation (1974–1982). However, following the collapse of international oil prices in 1986, which lasted for almost two decades and required a

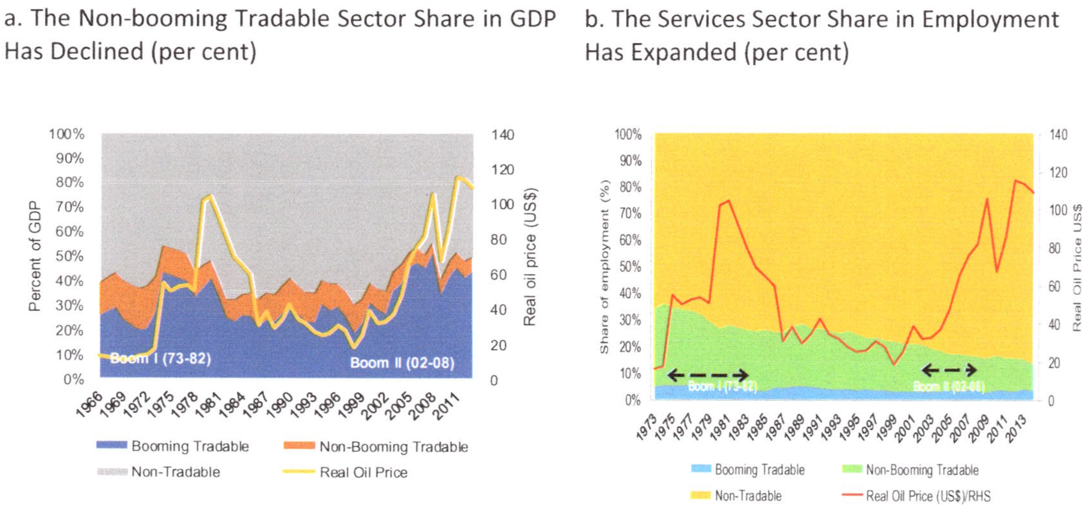

Fig. 6.10 Sectoral Shifts in GDP (**a**) The non-booming tradable sector share in GDP has declined (per cent) (**b**) The services sector share in employment has expanded (per cent) (*Note* Non-booming Tradable Sector = Manufacturing and Agriculture Sectors; Non-Tradable = Services Sector; Booming Tradable = Energy Sector, *Source* Central Bank of Trinidad and Tobago)

balance of payments support, the government of TT entered two successive Stand-by Arrangements with the International Monetary Fund. These led to the third phase: (3) export-led industrialisation (1983-present).[11]

During that period, an interesting parallel, highly relevant to TT, can be drawn from the case of Indonesia. As highlighted by Cherif et al., (2016), Indonesia stands among the trio of oil-exporting nations—alongside Malaysia and Mexico—that effectively diversified their economies. Faced with the collapse of oil prices in the 1980s, Indonesia adopted a strategic shift towards export promotion. This involved attracting Direct Foreign Investment in export-oriented industries, establishing free trade zones, offering tax incentives, and concurrently reducing both tariff and non-tariff barriers. TT underwent a similar policy transformation. However, Indonesia experienced the most significant exchange rate devaluation among developing nations and implemented measures to prevent its currency from appreciating. These policy adjustments occurred against the backdrop of diminishing oil production, ultimately leading Indonesia to transition into a net importer by 2003. Much like Indonesia, the successful diversification of oil-exporting countries unfolded as their oil revenues dwindled—a situation currently confronting TT, where reserves are anticipated to be depleted in the near future.

However, TT has struggled to replicate Indonesia's success in diversifying away from the energy sector into non-oil and gas tradable goods. The Herfindahl–Hirschman index (HHI), a comprehensive gauge of diversification based on goods or markets, illustrates this challenge. A country with a well-diversified export portfolio would exhibit an HHI close to zero, while a country exclusively exporting one product or to a single country would have an index value of 1, indicating the least diversified scenario. The data reveals that diversification has primarily occurred within the energy sector, with continuous expansion in both products and export markets since the late 1970s (Fig. 6.11). Vertical diversification within the energy sector emerged as oil production declined, giving

[11] Hosein, Boodram, and Saridakis's (2022) paper examines measures that can be adopted for a small petroleum-exporting economy to dampen the effect of Dutch disease by promoting non-energy trade. They found that a devaluation of the TT dollar does have a positive impact on non-energy trade and the Marshall–Lerner condition holds. They also recommended other measures to stimulate non-energy exports in the long run. The Marshall–Lerner condition is when the absolute sum of a country's export and import demand elasticities is greater than unity therefore trade balance will improve with a devaluation of the exchange rate.

way to an increase in natural gas production. Natural gas and petrochemical exports have surpassed oil exports by approximately 1.6 times. The country has attained the status of the world's leading exporter of ammonia and methanol, constituting the primary petrochemical products. However, diversification in non-oil and non-petrochemicals, referred to as "non-Energy" tradable goods, has remained consistently low. Despite a modest decrease since the early 2000s, diversification in terms of commodities and markets within this category has remained stagnant.[12]

But why is the economy less diversified than desired, i.e., why have past and current policies failed?

It is because the country is suffering from the Dutch Disease. The country is experiencing the Dutch Disease, which results from a persistent overvaluation of the exchange rate. This overvaluation is driven by the exploitation of oil and gas resources, leading to a currency value that exceeds the level needed for competitiveness in non-oil and gas international trade. Consequently, domestic producers face challenges from inexpensive imports, making it difficult for even technologically advanced goods to thrive in a competitive market. In such a scenario, the establishment of a new business utilizing modern technology in the affected country would only be economically feasible if its productivity surpasses that of competitors in other countries to a greater or equivalent extent, considering the exchange rate appreciation caused by the Dutch Disease.[13] The extent of the displacement of non-oil tradables depends on the magnitude of oil revenues and the initial technological disparity (Cherif et al., 2016). In this specific case, the odds were stacked against the success of the country's diversification efforts due to the substantial oil revenue and a significant technological gap, exacerbating the impact of the Dutch Disease.

[12] See Khadan and Ruprah (2016) for details of non-oil and gas exports and their markets.

[13] Of course, there is another effect of the Dutch Diseases as discussed in previous chapters namely large oil rents lead to an economic and political system dominated by unproductive rent-seeking.

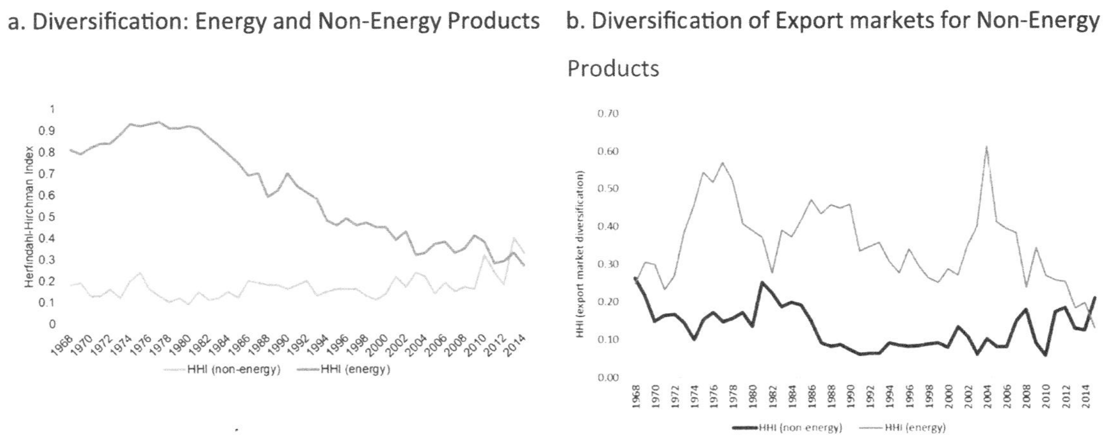

Fig. 6.11 Economic diversification: Products and markets (**a**) Diversification: Energy and non-energy products (**b**) Diversification of export markets for non-energy products (*Note* The HHI was calculated using Standard International Trade Classification (SITC) 2-digit data, *Source* Authors' estimates from World Integrated Trade Solution database and Central Statistical Office, Trinidad, and Tobago)

6.4 Growth Drivers from the Supply Side: Falling Total Factor Productivity

There is consensus and evidence that the growth performance of TT has been mainly influenced by external conditions, particularly commodity prices, and by the growth performance of its major trading partners (which would have influenced demand conditions). However, it is less clear about the growth drivers from the supply side. Economic growth has two sources from the supply side: the accumulation of factors (human capital and fixed capital) and the efficiency of utilising these factor inputs (total factor productivity). While economic theory suggests that all sources are essential, total factor productivity (TFP) is considered the primary sustainable source of long-term growth. This section examines the growth drivers from the supply side using a growth decomposition approach, the impact of growth volatility on growth, investment and growth, expenditure and growth, and labour productivity. A growth accounting exercise is undertaken to examine the supply-side factors that explain the economic growth process of TT. The decomposition of output growth into physical capital, human capital, and total factor productivity is estimated using the Cobb–Douglas production function approach.

Figure 6.12 shows the decomposition of GDP growth for TT using the Cobb–Douglas Production Function. The results indicate that total factor productivity (TFP) was the primary source of growth up to 2008, after which physical capital took over as the main source of growth. The contribution of human capital to GDP growth has remained negligible for the period covered. The share of TFP's contribution increased sharply during 2002–06, except in 2005, where physical capital contributed to almost 72 per cent of growth. The highest contribution of TFP was reported in 2003 and 2006, periods when the energy sector's growth was highest. However, TT's TFP share in growth has remained lower than those experienced by ROSE and ROSE-C (the rest of the small commodity exporters, see Fig. 6.12 and Khadan & Ruprah, 2016). The figure below shows that TT's TFP has declined sharply from the mid-1980s to the mid-1990s relative to ROSE and ROSE-C. Only after 2004 did TT's TFP begin to improve relative to ROSE, but it showed a decline for the period after 2008.

Labour productivity is also important for economic performance falling in TT. The fall can be explained by combining the spending effect of the Dutch disease and Baumol Cost Disease (Baumol, 1967; Hosein,

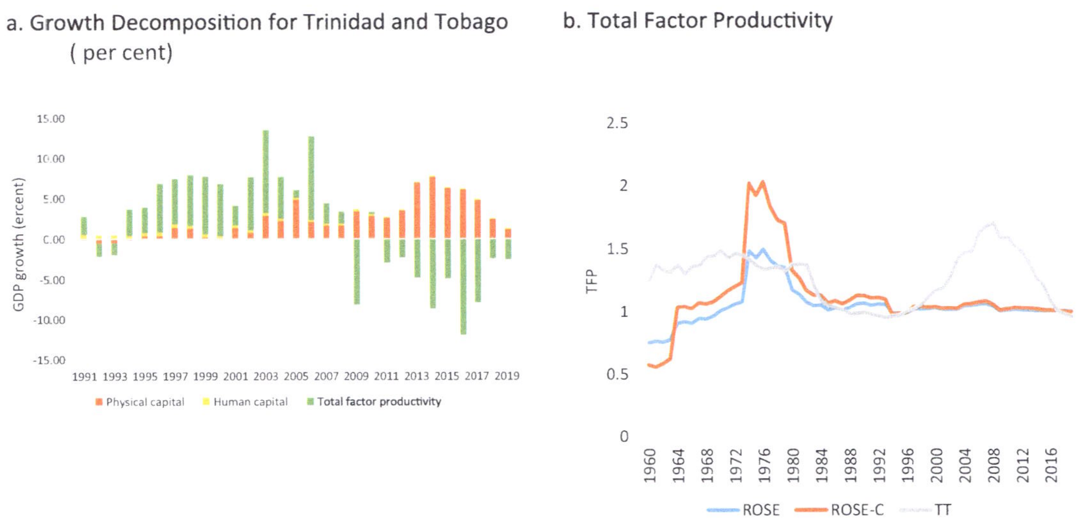

Fig. 6.12 Growth decomposition and total factor productivity (**a**) Growth decomposition for Trinidad and Tobago (per cent) (**b**) Total factor productivity (*Note* ROSE = Rest of Small Economies; ROSE-C = Rest of Small Commodity Dependent Economies, *Source* Authors' estimates from Penn World Table 8.1)

(2021);;, who applies it to the TT case).[14] The spending effect implies that the non-booming tradeable sector loses labour to the non-tradeable sector. Baumol argues that some sectors, like the non-tradeable sector, mainly services, have limited productivity due to technical progress and capital deepening. The Baumol Cost disease is when salaries increase in a non-tradeable sector that experiences little or no productivity increases but realises wage increases on account of increases in productivity in more productive sectors. We saw a trend decrease in the non-booming tradeable sector GDP (Fig. 6.10a) with a simultaneous increase in the service sector increasing share of employment in the service sector (non-tradeable sector). This output pattern implies that per-worker output rises slower than in the non-booming tradeable sector, which has a much higher level of labour productivity than in the non-tradeable sector, trends that give credence to the existence of the Baumol Costs Disease.

This trend is also observable in a shift-share analysis, which breaks down the growth of labour productivity into three elements: the within-sector effect, the reallocation-level effect, and the reallocation-growth effect (Fig. 6.13; Meehan, 2014). The within-sector effect estimates the change in labour productivity within a specific sector. The reallocation-level effect measures the contribution of labour reallocation across sectors. The reallocation-growth effect measures the reallocation of labour into sectors with growing productivity. The findings of this analysis reveal the following outcomes: firstly, a decline in labour productivity; secondly, noteworthy variations in labour productivity across sectors; thirdly, an adverse correlation between structural changes and overall productivity resources; and fourthly, nearly all productivity differences can be explained by the within-sector effect, with a negative impact from the reallocation-growth aspect. A categorization of sectors into four groups based on relative productivity and labour attraction indicates that wholesale and retail trade (comprising 40 per cent of firms in our sample and 33 per cent of non-petroleum GDP), public administration, and transport have a detrimental impact on labour productivity growth. These findings suggest that the productivity of these sectors surpasses national productivity, yet their employment share is diminishing, or their productivity is below national levels, but their employment share is increasing—while other sectors are positively contributing.

[14] Baumol (1967), and Hosein (2021) who develops and applies the Baumol Cost Disease to Trinidad and Tobago.

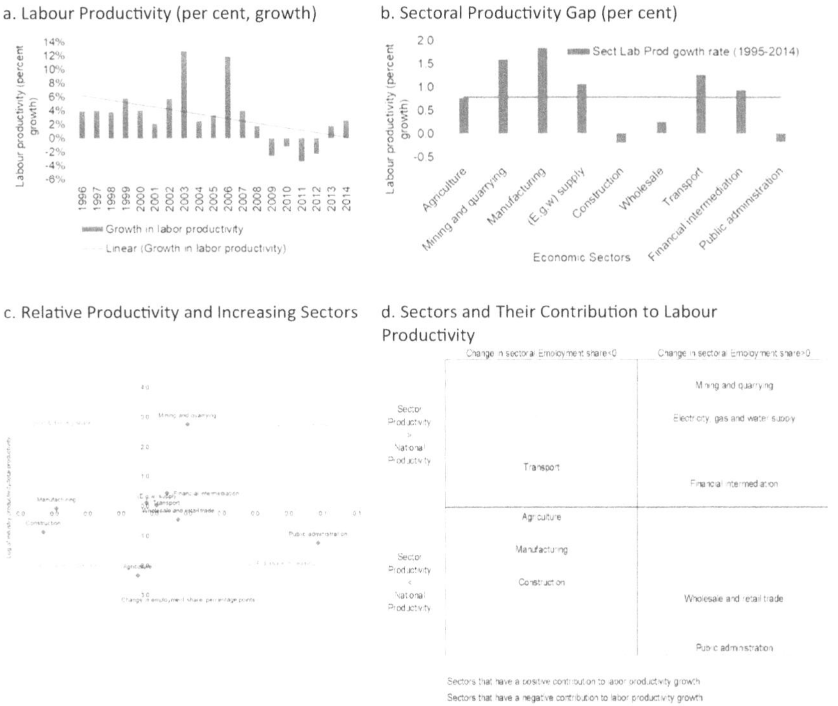

Fig. 6.13 Sectoral labour productivity (**a**) Labour productivity (per cent, growth) (**b**) Sectoral productivity gap (per cent) (**c**) Relative productivity and increasing sectors (**d**) Sectors and their contribution to labour productivity (*Note* pi = industry productivity and total productivity; E, g, and w = electricity, gas, and water, *Source* Authors' estimates are based on data from the Central Statistical Office, Trinidad and Tobago)

6.5 Conclusions

This chapter examines the impact of resource dependency, characterised by volatility and Dutch disease, on TT's economic performance. The analysis reveals various symptoms and effects of Dutch disease in TT, such as an overvalued real exchange rate, slower growth in the manufacturing sector, faster growth in the service sector, and a decline in the contributions of the agriculture and manufacturing sectors to the overall output.

TT's economic growth is highly vulnerable to fluctuations in international commodity prices. TT's economic growth volatility is higher than that of other comparator groups, negatively impacting TT's economic growth and potentially destabilising investment and aggregate demand. However, it is essential to note that volatility alone cannot fully account for the prolonged periods of economic contraction and stagnation experienced by TT. Other contributing factors include declining productivity, decreasing competitiveness, and an undiversified economic structure.

The decline in productivity has also contributed to TT's underperformance. The fall in labour productivity is attributed to changes within sectors, with specific sectors such as wholesale and retail trade, public administration, and transport exerting negative influences on national labour productivity. TFP, a key source of long-term growth, has increased its contribution to growth from 2002 to 2006 but started to decline after 2008, while the contributions of employment and human capital to growth have significantly decreased over time, indicating underinvestment in these crucial areas. Additionally, the business environment in TT poses obstacles to firms' operations, including challenges related to accessing finance, regulatory frameworks, and workforce quality. Together, these factors continue to weigh on the level and quality of TT's growth.

The country has benefitted from two significant commodity cycles, leading to prolonged periods of economic stagnation. Pro-cyclical policies often exacerbate recession episodes, and slow implementation of reforms following adverse shocks. These boom-and-bust cycles and structural constraints can substantially impact poverty, inequality, and labour market outcomes. However, government spending through subsidies and transfer programmes has generally mitigated the adverse effects of these price shocks on households.

Addressing challenges posed by resource dependency, Dutch disease, and productivity issues while promoting economic diversification and improving the business environment are critical for TT to achieve sustained and inclusive economic growth.

In the following two chapters, we first look at the labour market developments, followed by an analysis of the private non-energy sector.

References

Auty R. (1994). Industrial policy reform in six large newly industrialising countries: The resource curse thesis. *World Development, 22*(1).

Auty, R., & Gelb, A. (1986). Oil Windfalls in a Small Parliamentary Democracy: Their Impact on Trinidad and Tobago. *World Development, 14*(9), 1116–1175.

Baumol, W. (1967). Macroeconomics of Unbalance Growth: The Anatomy of Urban Crisis. *The American Economic Review, 57*(3), 415–426.

Cherif, R., Hasanov, F., & Zhu, M. (2016). *Breaking the Oil Spell: The Gulf Falcons' Path to Diversification*. IMF.

Corden, W. M., & Neary, J. P. (1982). Booming Sector and De-Industrialisation in a Small Open Economy. *The Economic Journal*, *92*(368), 825–48. *JSTOR*, https://doi.org/10.2307/2232670

Hilaire, A. (1995). Commercial Policy in Trinidad and Tobago. Insights into an Emerging Financial Structure: The Experience of Trinidad and Tobago, ed. R. Ramsaran, and Mottley W. (2008) Trinidad and Tobago Industrial Policy 1959–2008, Ian Randle Publishers.

Hosein, R., Boodram, L.,& Saridakis, G. (2022). Stimulating Non-Energy Exports in Trinidad and Tobago: Evidence from a Small Petroleum Economy Experiencing The Dutch Disease. *Journal of Risk and Financial Management, 15*(1).

Hosein, R. (2021). *Oil and Gas In Trinidad and Tobago: Managing The Resource Curse in a Small Petroleum Exporting Economy*. Palgrave.

IMF. (2016). *Fuel Subsidies in Trinidad and Tobago: Fiscal, Distributional and Environmental Impacts*. Trinidad and Tobago Selected Issues, 16/205, IMF.

IMF. (2018). *Trinidad and Tobago Selected Issues*. IMF.

Khadan, J. (2016). *An Econometric Analysis of Energy Revenue and Government Expenditure Shocks on Economic Growth in Trinidad and Tobago*, IDB Publications (Working Papers), 8025, Inter-American Development Bank.

Khadan, J., & Ruprah, I. (2016). *Diversification in Trinidad and Tobago*. Waiting for Godot, Policy Brief No IDB-PB-256.

Meehan, L. (2014). *Structural Change and New Zealand's Productivity Performance*, New Zealand Productivity Commission Working Paper 2014/4.

Omes, Ni.,& Kalcheva, K., (2007). *Diagnosing Dutch disease: Does Russia have the symptoms?* No 7/2007, BOFIT Discussion Papers, Bank of Finland, Institute for Economies in Transition.

Philippe, M., & Rogers, C. (1995). Long-Term Growth and Short-Term Economic Instability, No 1281, CEPR Discussion Papers, CEPR Discussion Papers.

Premdas, R., & Ragoonath, B. (2020). *From Boom to Bust and Back: The Trinidad Experience with the Resource Curse*, Special Edition WP2020, No. 1. UWI, Cave Hill Campus.

Ramey, G., & Ramey, V. A. (1995). Cross-country Evidence on the Link Between Volatility and Growth. *American Economic Review, 85*(5), 1138–1151.

Ramlogan, A., & Sookram, S. (2018). *Coordination of Monetary and Fiscal Policy in Trinidad and Tobag*. WP/02/2018, Central Bank of Trinidad and Tobago.

Ryan, S. (1989). *The Disillusioned Electorate: The Politics of Succession in Trinidad and Tobago*. Port of Spain: Inprint Caribbean Ltd.

Rodrik, D. (2008). The Real Exchange Rate and Economic Growth. *Brookings Papers on Economic Activity*, 2008(2), 365–412. *Project MUSE*. https://doi.org/10.1353/eca.0.0020

Siddique, A. (2021). Does ethnic diversity hurt fiscal sustainability? *Economics Bulletin, 41*(2), 532–543.

Tazhibayeva, K., Husain, A., & Ter-Martiroysan, A. (2008). *Fiscal Policy and Economic Cycles in Oil-Exporting Countries*. WP No 2008/253, IMF.

Wenner, M., Bollers, E., & Hosein, R. (2018). *The Dutch Disease Phenomenon and Lessons For Guyana: The Trinidad and Tobago Experience*. Technical Note, No. IDB TN-1470, IDB.

CHAPTER 7

Economic Development: The Labour Market

7.1 Introduction

Labour market outcomes are crucial for a country's socioeconomic performance. A well-functioning labour market promotes job creation, lowers unemployment, boosts productivity, and reduces income inequality. Fair and inclusive labour market practices, such as equal pay for equal work and non-discrimination, create opportunities for all individuals, fostering social cohesion and reducing disparities based on background, gender, or other socioeconomic characteristics. Moreover, policies prioritising labour market reforms that promote access to employment and skill development and minimise distortions help to support sustainable and inclusive socioeconomic development.

This chapter reviews the stylised facts of TT's labour market by gender and race. Issues affecting the unemployment rate, labour force participation rate, wages, and the distribution of occupations are explored.[1] We review possible discrimination from both gender and race perspectives.

[1] We do not explicitly analyse the informal sector. Maurin, Sookram and Watson (2006) find that the size of the hidden economy rose from a low of about 14% of measured GDP in the early 1970s to a high of 36% in 1981 and was about 20% of measured GDP at the end of the nineties.

J. Khadan and I. Jit Ruprah, *Unraveling Race, Politics, and Gender in Trinidad and Tobago's Economic Development*,
https://doi.org/10.1007/978-3-031-54656-3_7

We end the chapter with a discussion of poverty, income inequality, and the distribution of economic growth across various groups.

7.2 Labour Demand and Supply

Labour supply is determined by the growth of the economically active population. The economically active population includes both employed (employees and self-employed) and unemployed people, but not the economically inactive, such as school children, pensioners, and those not actively looking for a job. Labour force participation rates are *calculated by dividing the labour force, individuals who are either employed or actively seeking employment, by the total working-age population.* The participation rate is an important labour market indicator, representing the labour resources available to produce goods and services. Figures 7.1 and 7.2 show the labour force participation rates by gender and race. The two key features are that males have a higher participation rate than females, as do ATTs compared to ITTs. However, female participation in the labour market increased from 47.4% in 1991 to 58.9% in 2015, and male participation decreased from 82.8% to 79.1% over the same period. Labour force participation rates of ATTs and ITTs grew from 1991 to 2015. The increase was almost twofold higher for ATTs.

More striking is the continuous fall in the unemployment rate: a fall in unemployment that holds for females, males, ATTs, ITTs, and MTTs (Figs. 7.3 and 7.4). The national unemployment rate fell from almost 20% in 1991 to 3.4% in 2015, initially due to a sustained period of economic growth. However, the relationship between unemployment and the business cycle has significantly weakened. The Okun ratio, which measures the elasticity of unemployment to economic growth, is approximately zero, see Mercer-Blackman and Salazni (2014). Figure 7.5 shows no relation between the unemployment rate and economic growth. The latter can be attributed to numerous public programmes that offer employment and training. These programmes absorb unemployed individuals and are reported as not seeking jobs; hence, they are not in the official unemployment statistics. While they aim to provide short-term employment, these programmes have been associated with labour market distortions.

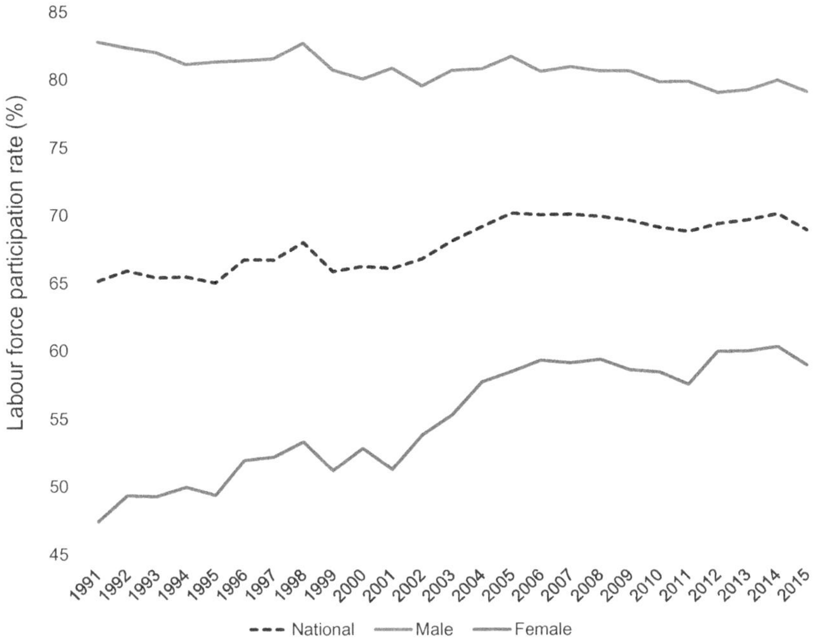

Fig. 7.1 Participation rates (gender) (*Source* Authors' based on the Continuous Sample Survey of Population [CSSP, 1999–2015])

7.3 Are There Wage Differentials in TT's Labour Market?

Wage differentials refer to variations or disparities in wages or salaries earned by individuals in the labour market. Wage differentials among labour market participants can occur for several reasons. These may include differences in education and skills, work experience, occupation or industry, supply and demand dynamics, bargaining power, government policies or discrimination and bias based on gender, race, or other socioeconomic factors. When there are no discernible productivity differences, wage differentials can reduce output, labour market participation, and weaken workers' ability to cooperate in their self-interest (Breza et al., 2018).

Wage differences (mean ITT to ATT wage ratios) are shown separately in Fig. 7.6 for the economy and public and private sectors. We observe

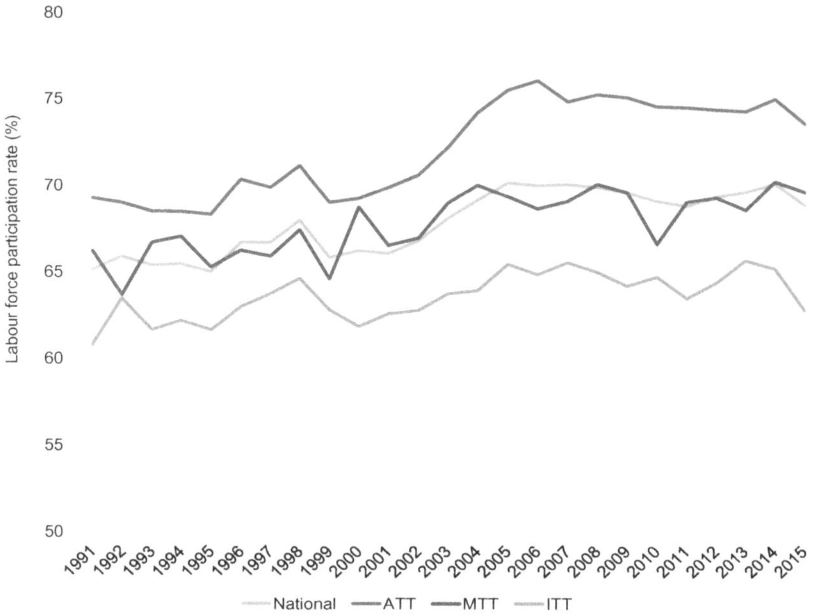

Fig. 7.2 Participation rates (race) (*Source* Authors' based on the Continuous Sample Survey of Population [CSSP, 1999–2015])

no persistent wage differential between the two ethnic groups. There was virtually no wage difference between 1999 and 2005 when considering only public-sector employment. However, from 2006 to 2011, the situation changed significantly, as the public-sector wage difference between ATTs and ITTs reached 15% in 2011 in favour of ITTs. Afterwards, the disparity gradually diminished. These results align with the catch-up of ITTs in terms of educational attainment shown in Fig. 7.12. We also observe a relatively large wage differential favouring males in private employment, especially for ATT males.[2] However, the mean wage differential of ATT and ITT males (in relation to females in the same

[2] Sookram and Watson (2008) in an analysis of the informal market find that formal sector workers earn more than informal sector workers and that men tend to work for higher wages than women in the informal sector. Most of the observed difference may be attributed to wage discrimination rather than to human capital differences between females and males.

Fig. 7.3 Unemployment rates (gender) (*Source* Authors' based on the Continuous Sample Survey of Population [CSSP, 1999–2015])

ethnic group) converged at the end of the sample period (see Fig. 7.7). There was no significant difference in wage differential by gender in the public sector for ATTs. However, for ITTs, the wage differential favoured females until 2011, then they converged.

Wage differentials between ATTs and ITTs can also vary across income levels. We examine plots of the logarithm of wage income for both ethnic groups over the income distribution for 1999 and 2015 in Figs. 7.8 and 7.9. These figures show that differences between mean income vary across ethnic groups—indicated by different coloured bars that do not overlap consistently over the wage income distribution. There has been a shift towards ITT-favoured wage differentials across most income levels, except for the lowest segment of the distribution. Moreover, the distribution of

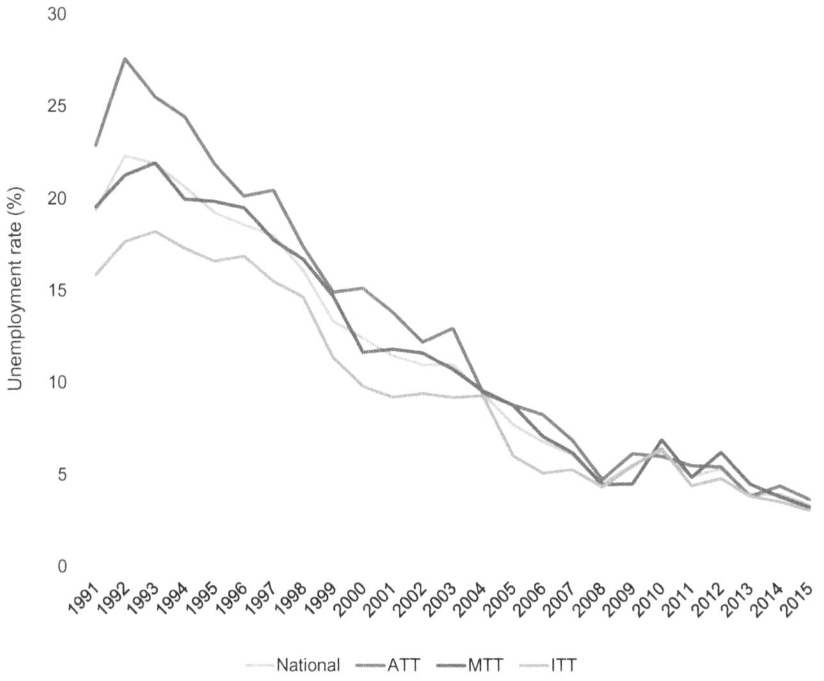

Fig. 7.4 Unemployment rates (race) (*Source* Authors' based on the Continuous Sample Survey of Population [CSSP, 1999–2015])

wage income has become even more dissimilar over time. The latter holds regardless of whether one analyses the reported income distribution or the corrected wage income selection (see Figs. 7.10 and 7.11).[3]

7.4 Labour Protection

Several factors temper the supply and demand pressures in the labour market. The TT labour market is governed by many regulations prioritising job security and ensuring significant benefits to formal sector workers. While the legal framework intends to reach high standards for

[3] The selection corrected income figures are corrected for selection into the labour market and wage employment (for details see Schimanski et al. (2018).

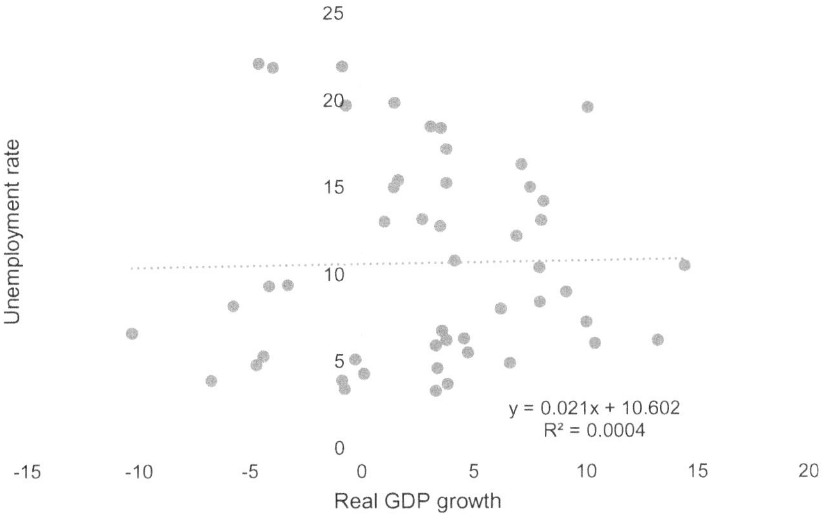

Fig. 7.5 Real growth and change in unemployment (*Source* Central Statistical Office of Trinidad and Tobago and World Bank)

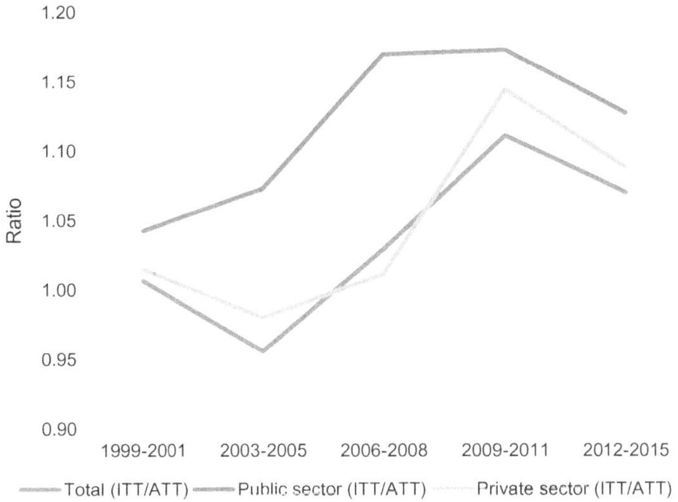

Fig. 7.6 Differences in mean real income by race (*Source* Authors' estimations based on CSSP 1999–2014)

Fig. 7.7 Differences in mean real income by gender (*Source* Authors' estimations based on CSSP 1999–2014)

the workers' well-being, they contributed to creating a segmented market with a significant presence of public-sector jobs and poor mobility. In addition, government employment programmes and other conditions in the low-skill segment of the market appear to validate the existence of considerable levels of underemployment.

The three most crucial labour laws are the Industrial Relations Act, the Retrenchment and Severance Benefits Act, and the Minimum Wage Act. The Industrial Relations Act sets forth legislation concerning strikes and the registration and certification procedures for trade unions; the Retrenchment and Severance Benefits Act guarantees severance payments as a function of the length of uninterrupted service in the case of dismissal due to redundancy; and the Minimum Wage Act created a national minimum remuneration in 1998 at an initial level of TT$7.00 per hour (US$1.10). In 2023, the minimum wage was raised to TT$19.50 (US$2.9) per hour, up from TT$15.00 in 2015, placing TT's minimum wage among the highest in the Caribbean region. Also, TT counts on the National Insurance Board (established in 1971) to provide social security services for employees (self-employed are not covered). Among other major labour laws is the Equal Opportunity Act (in 2000, amended

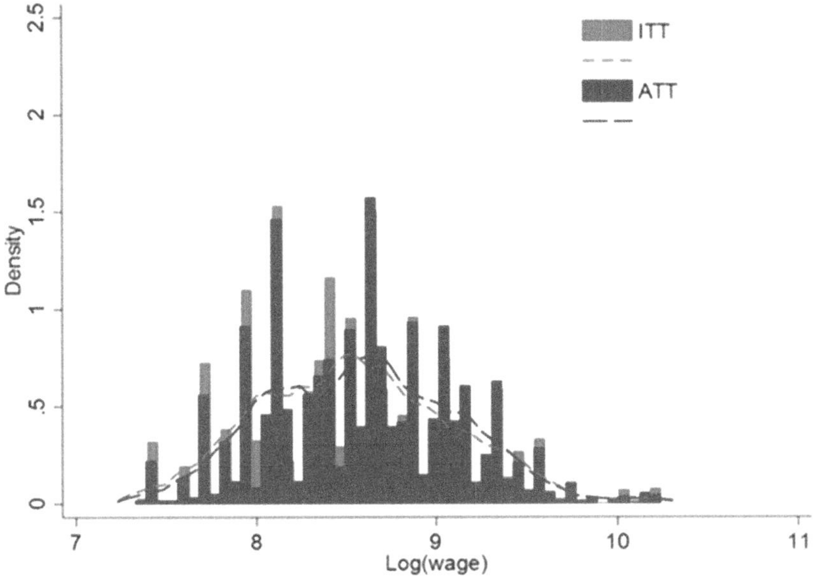

Fig. 7.8 Wage distribution 1999 (*Source* Authors' estimations based on CSSP 1999–2014)

in 2001), which established an Equal Opportunity Commission and an Equal Opportunity Tribunal. The law prohibits discrimination based on sex, race, ethnicity, origin, religion, marital status, or disability in employment, training, education, and other fields. In addition, the Maternity Protection Act (1998), the Occupational Safety and Health Act (enacted in 2004, amended in 2006), and the Trade Union Act (1933) also protect workers' rights. As a member of the International Labour Organization (ILO) since 1963, TT has ratified 22 ILO Conventions.

Collective bargaining takes place fundamentally at the firm level. There are more than 80 registered trade unions in TT, with the size of memberships reaching into the tens of thousands for the largest union. Per the Industrial Relations Act, all collective agreements in TT must cover at least three years and no more than five years. The recent experience shows that unions tend to negotiate wage increases to cover three years but with considerable lags (e.g., in late 2012, the wage negotiation for 2008–10

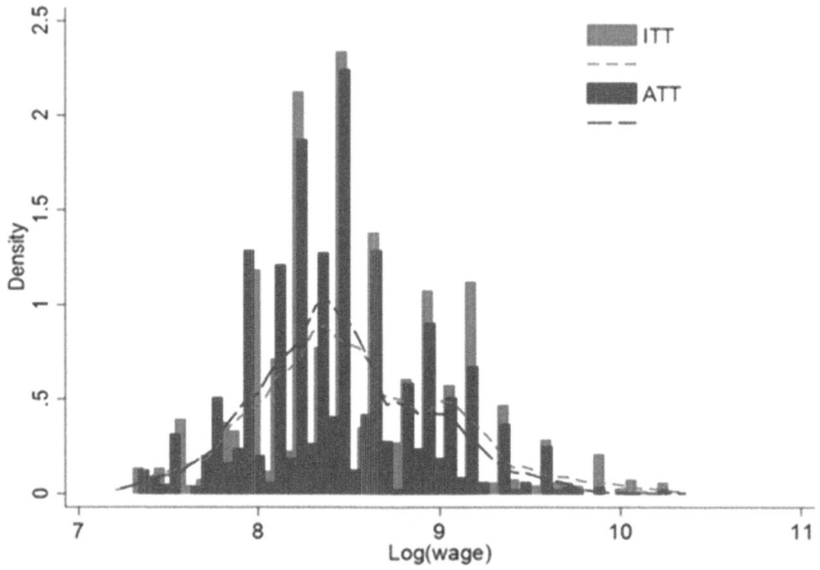

Fig. 7.9 Wage distribution 2015 (*Source* Authors' estimations based on CSSP 1999–2014)

was concluded) and with retroactive benefits.[4] While some researchers have found that minimum wages exert sizeable effects on the rest of TT's labour market, mainly by shifting the entire wage structure upwards and negatively affecting formal sector employment (Rambarran, 1998), two other studies concluded that labour market regulations do not impact employment significantly. Downes (2006) and Downes et al. (2004) analysed the impact of minimum wage, contribution to the national insurance system, and severance payment on employment. They found that they do not impact employment significantly, although the lack of changes in labour regulations during their study period may explain such findings.

Recent evidence suggests that the employment rate has been relatively stable through the economic cycle and that government-sponsored employment programmes have served to buffer the impact of economic

[4] In 2023, several trade unions accepted a 4% wage increase offer following wage negotiations for the period 2014–2019.

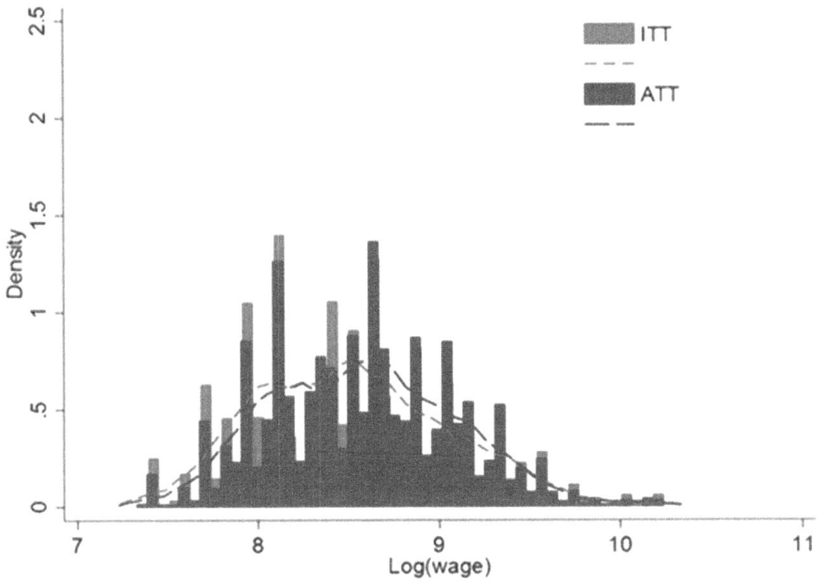

Fig. 7.10 Selection corrected income separated by Race 1999 (*Source* Authors' estimations based on CSSP 1999–2014)

volatility on the unemployment rate. In the past decades, the government introduced various employment support and training programmes under the Social Sector Investment Program (SSIP) to reduce unemployment in certain disadvantaged population segments. The two most notable programmes are the Unemployment Relief Program (URP) introduced in 1992 and the Community Environment Protection and Enhancement Program (CEPEP) introduced in 2002. Both programmes provide unskilled or semi-skilled people with temporary jobs for less than 8 hours per day, resulting in average hourly wages surpassing the minimum wage. The URP usually provides three consecutive two-week jobs and allows re-registration after a three-month break. The CEPEP jobs can last from 1–3 years. While these programmes have an essential role in the country's social safety net and reduce measured unemployment, their de facto non-transitory nature and the associated remuneration levels distort the labour market and appear to contribute to the relatively high underemployment in TT compared with other developing countries. The Continuous

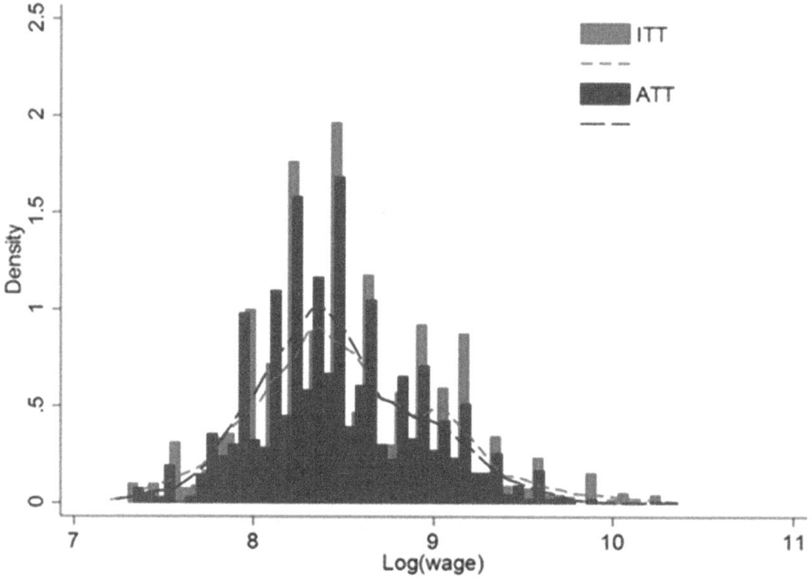

Fig. 7.11 Selection corrected income separated by Race 2015 (*Source* Authors' estimations based on CSSP 1999–2014)

Sample Survey of the Population (CSSP) provides some direct evidence that underemployment was severe in the Community Social and Personal Service sector, the sector that includes the URP and CEPEP, as in 2011, it accounted for 45% of the total employees who worked less than 33 hours/week for the specific reason of having "no more work to do". Finally, the prevalence of underemployment in TT's labour market is likely aggravated by informal activities and temporary migration from other countries, especially outside the main cities.

7.5 Occupational Composition of Employment

Labour market composition refers to the distribution of workers across occupations, industries, and sectors based on characteristics like age, education, ethnicity, gender, race, and skill level. Labour market segregation could result from many factors, including social norms and stereotypes, educational and occupational choices, or discrimination and bias, among other issues. Segregation of labour markets can perpetuate social inequalities and discrimination, hamper economic growth and productivity, and undermine workplace diversity and inclusion.

Table 7.1 shows that there have been no or only very marginal changes in the composition of the labour market over the sample period.[5] The patterns slightly shift from elementary and craft-related occupations to professionals, legislators, senior officials, and managers.

Instead, occupations are distributed over the ethnic groups, as Table 7.2 shows. Although the concentration of ethnic groups in some occupational categories persisted over time, we observed an increasing share of ATTs in agricultural, forestry and fishery workers and craft and related workers, while ITTs share in legislators, senior officials and managers category increased by about 10% from 1999–2001 to 2011–2013.

Figure 7.12 illustrates that the labour market is more segregated along gender than racial lines, as one can observe more differences between the figures in the middle and right column than when comparing the

Table 7.1 Share of Occupations in the economy

	1999–2001	*2011–2013*
No occupation	1.3	2.3
Legislators, Senior Officials, and Managers	1.7	2.0
Professionals	4.7	8.7
Technicians and Associate Professionals	17.0	17.7
Clerks	16.3	18.3
Service Workers and Shop and Market Sale	12.0	12.0
Agricultural, Forestry, and Fishery Workers	0.7	0.0
Craft and Related Workers	8.3	6.7
Plant and Machine Operators and Assemblers	5.3	5.0
Elementary Occupations	33.0	27.3

Note These shares present (Table 7.1) the total shares of ATTs and ITTs working in a respective occupation of all ATTs and ITTs (Table 7.2) the share of ATTs among all ATTs and ITTs working in the separate occupation
Source Authors' estimations based on CSSP 1999 2014

[5] These marginal changes could be attributed to survey bias.

Table 7.2 ATTs as a proportion of ATTs and ITTs (per cent)

No occupation	86.0	88.7
Legislators, Senior Officials and Managers	63.0	53.7
Professionals	47.3	46.7
Technicians and Associate Professionals	51.7	54.0
Clerks	57.0	59.0
Service Workers and Shop and Market Sale	74.7	70.7
Agricultural, Forestry, and Fishery Workers	22.3	30.0
Craft and Related Workers	65.3	73.3
Plant and Machine Operators and Assemblers	51.7	53.3
Elementary occupations	59.3	63.0

Note These shares present (Table 7.1) the total shares of ATTs and ITTs working in a respective occupation of all ATTs and ITTs (Table 7.2) the share of ATTs among all ATTs and ITTs working in the separate occupation

Source Authors' estimations based on CSSP 1999–2014

upper to the lower figures in the left column, which depict the differences across races.[6] Nevertheless, there are some noteworthy differences across ethnicities. In particular, female youth (between 15 and 24 years) of ITT origin accounted for a much higher share of occupations, such as legislators, senior officials, managers, professionals, technicians, and associates, than their ATT peers, who hold just over 10% of those types of positions. Apart from being among the oldest age group, where racial differences are similarly extreme, this difference is not as substantial for the middle-aged groups. ATT women are more likely to be employed as service workers and shop and market sellers. Likewise, the share of service, shop and market sales personnel among the males of ATT origin is significantly higher than among those of ITT origin. Males seem to have some heterogeneity across age groups; a higher share of ATTs are working as technicians and associate professionals, while among older ITTs, this does not seem to be such a prevalent occupation.

[6] See Schimanski et al. (2016) who analyse occupational segregation in four Caribbean countries.

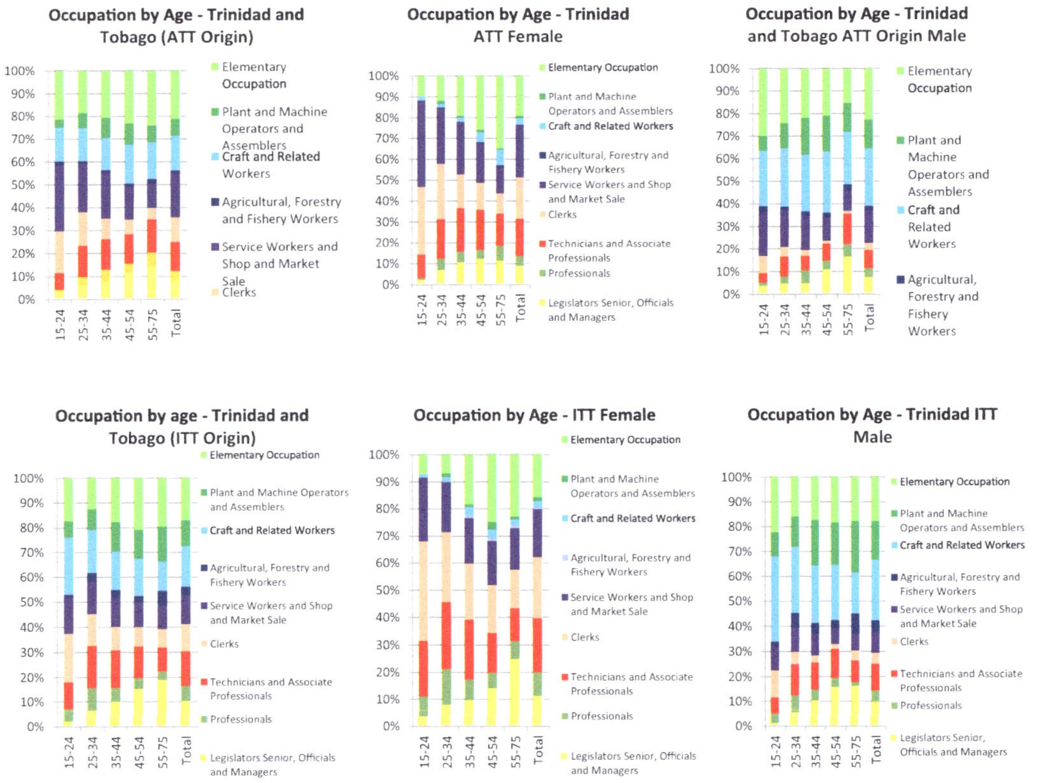

Fig. 7.12 Occupation by Age and Race aggregated and separated by Gender (*Source* Authors' calculations based on CSSP 1999–2014)

7.6 Is There Any Discrimination in the Labour Market?

A key question is whether there is discrimination in the labour market. There are several ways to answer this question. One approach is to ask if a person has felt discriminated against. In the LAPOP surveys, the respondents were asked if they felt discriminated against in public places, schools, work, or government offices. More ATTs followed by MTTs than ITTs thought they had been discriminated against in all three options in 2012.

Another approach is to determine whether labour market outcomes reveal discrimination by gender or race. Typically, a premise of the oft-used human capital approach is that the earnings of various groups are mainly explained by their average education, training, and experience. If the human capital model correctly captures the representation of the labour market, gender, and race play no significant role once the human capital of individuals is controlled for; that is, the coefficients of education/training and labour market experience in an earnings function should be equal for all ethnic/gender groups. The payoffs of investing in education should be the same for all groups (Fig. 7.13).

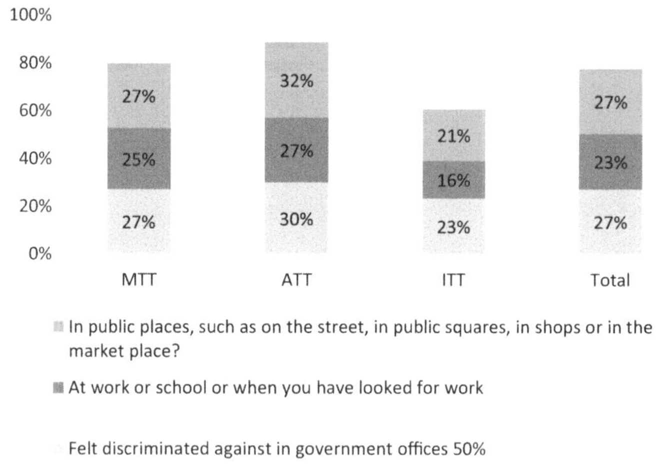

Fig. 7.13 Felt Discriminated Against (*Source* LAPOP [2012])

The Brown, Moon and Zoloth (1980) decomposition,[7] Fig. 7.14, reveals that the decrease over time in gender wage gaps is explained primarily by reduced vertical segregation, i.e., the differences in wage structures within occupations (or unexplained intra-occupational component). The differences in observed characteristics exist primarily across occupations, with female workers employed disproportionately in more skilled professions, which would justify higher female wages on average. Finally, horizontal segregation represents a minor issue which modestly favours women over time.

The analysis of the mean wage gap reveals that its reduction has been driven by changes in characteristics, primarily increasing female education, while the unexplained component, indicative of discrimination, has been declining but remains positive and statistically significant. The unexplained component relates to occupational segregation, as males receive higher wages compared to women, and even more disproportionate returns when employed in heavily female-dominated occupations.

7.7 Poverty, Labour Income Inequality, and Distribution of Economic Growth

Poverty and income inequality are critical measures of labour market outcomes.[8] High poverty levels may indicate that a substantial portion of the labour force cannot secure employment or earn sufficient wages, leading to lower living standards and reduced economic mobility.

We construct poverty and inequality measures based on data from the CSSP surveys for 1999–2014. There are some caveats to our estimations. The CSSP surveys only provide labour income data but do not

[7] The Brown, Moon and Zoloth (1980) technique decomposes wage gaps additionally into within and between occupation components based on the assumption that the characteristics that determine wages do not perfectly coincide with those that determine occupations. Occupational choice is likely influenced by personal characteristics and circumstances as well as discrimination regarding entry into particular occupations for a given gender. By combining the traditional wage gap literature and segregation literature techniques, the Brown, Moon and Zoloth (1980) decomposition can disentangle the share of the wage gap that can be attributed to explained and unexplained variation in wages within occupations by gender called, "vertical segregation" and the part of the wage gap which is a result of justifiable and unjustifiable differences in wages across occupations, the "horizontal segregation".

[8] See Caribbean Development Bank (2016) for an analysis of the Caribbean countries.

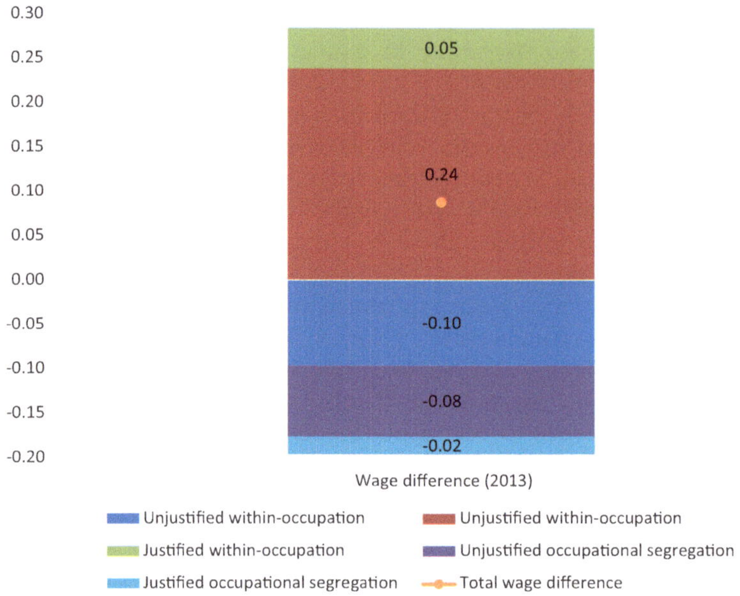

Fig. 7.14 Decomposition of mean wage gaps (*Note* The Brown, Moon and Zoloth [1980] decomposition used here is based only on those who reported income in the 2013 CSSP using gender-separated OLS earnings equations. *Source* Authors' estimations)

contain information on non-labour income and transfers, neither for those working, unemployed, or out of the labour force. Public transfers and remittances will likely vary between households of different ethnic groups. Therefore, using these datasets, only the returns from employment with a positive income can be estimated among those who report their income in the survey.

During the segregation and wage gap analysis we conducted before, we used only the first observation in each year of the sample. We dropped the remaining as duplicates, and this restriction is relaxed in this part of the analysis to avoid seasonality bias. Doing so increases the likelihood that one of the household members would be dropped as an observation, further biasing the results by underestimating total household income. Unlike household surveys, the labour force survey does not include a question on total household income. Still, it is computed as the labour income of all household members who report an income figure. As individual household members may decide not to report income independently, it remains unknown whether the total household labour income figures are complete concerning all household members and may therefore include some bias. Even in random non-response of household members across races, this aspect may induce bias, as the mean income of certain ethnicities is higher than others, so leaving out a person's income has a multiplicative effect in the inequality measure.

Nevertheless, using these estimates as a basis for analysing the return to working and inequality of labour income across ethnicities gives a broad indication of the country's current situation. It underscores the need for annual household income data, including non-labour income and transfer information.

We find poverty and extreme poverty generally low, with less than one per cent, in all years (1999–2014) for individuals living in households earning and reporting positive labour income.[9] The average poverty gap has been decreasing over time, as has the squared poverty gap—which indicates that despite having at least one working household member, poor households are not as poor in the later years as in the initial ones, with fewer extremes among them. The most significant annual decrease is observed from 1999 to 2000.

Regarding the poverty headcount ratio, OTTs appear to be the poorest ethnic group, followed by ATTs and ITTs (Fig. 7.15). Surprisingly, though, among those who are poor, more ITTs are extremely poor, showing the slightly highest headcount ratio (FGT 0, Foster-Greer-Thorbecke (1984) poverty indices) of 0.9% compared to 0.8% for ATTs and OTTs. When looking more specifically at FGT poverty measures for each ethnic group, it becomes clear that this observation is even more extreme for the squared poverty gap, which expresses the severity of poverty—ATT households' poverty does not seem to be as severe as that of the other races in any year. Poverty severity for OTTs became more volatile, with an initial increase and a short decrease during the early 2000s before stabilising later at around 0.3% to 0.4%. The ITTs' extreme poverty has been slightly more volatile, increasing till the mid-2000s after an initial decrease and then decreasing and seemingly stabilising at a lower

[9] However, Kedir A. and S. Sookram (2013) using the 1995 Survey of Living Conditions find that the poverty rate is higher than the existing estimates and socioeconomic and demographic characteristics play significant roles in poverty and household welfare.

level. The same relationship as extreme poverty also holds for poverty (Fig. 7.16).

The relationship looks remarkably different regarding the poverty headcount ratio based on a relative poverty line of 60% of median income and 30% of median income. The display barely any change in poverty and

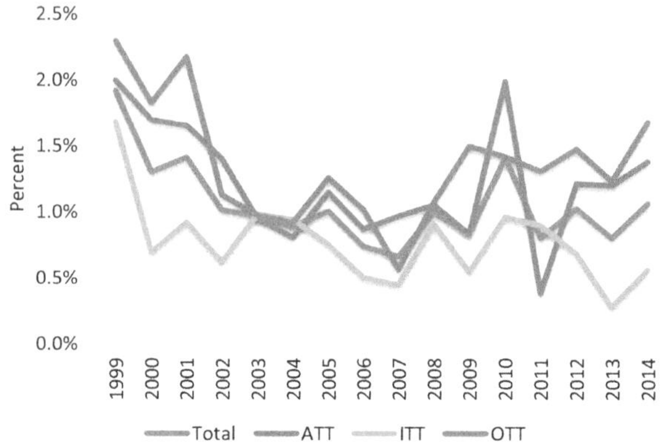

Fig. 7.15 Poverty (*Source* Continuous Sample Survey of Population [CSSP] 1999–2014)

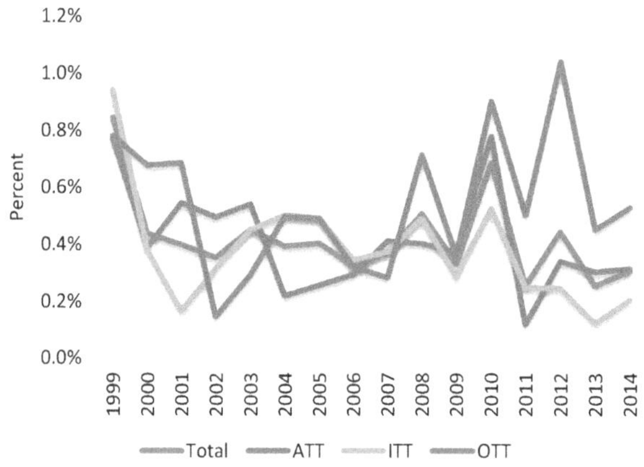

Fig. 7.16 Extreme poverty (*Source* Continuous Sample Survey of Population [CSSP] 1999–2014)

extreme poverty. Instead, regarding the relative poverty line, OTTs seem to become slightly poorer over time. Only the share of ITTs in extreme poverty and the severity of their poverty measured by the squared poverty gap seem to have decreased somewhat according to this relative measure.

Labour income inequality refers to the unequal distribution of earnings among individuals or groups in the labour market. It is measured by the Gini index that ranges from zero, indicating perfect equality, to a hundred, which shows ideal inequality.

We construct Gini indices by ethnic groups and for the total labour force. The national Gini index indicates that inequality has fallen over 1991–2014 in the total labour force and for each ethnic group separately (Fig. 7.17). OTTs experienced the sharpest fall in inequality among their working households, followed by ITTs, which had the lowest level of inequality for most of the period. In contrast, inequality among the ATT working households decreased till the mid-2000s but rose from 2011 onwards.[10]

Lastly, we examine the growth incidence curves (GIC) to assess how income at each percentile changed over the sample period. GICs are used to explore the distributional aspects of economic growth. They provide insights into how different segments of the population benefit from economic growth and whether the benefits are shared equitably or disproportionately. A negative sloping curve suggests that the income of the poorer deciles increases more than that of richer deciles. The GIC from 1999 to 2014 is given in Fig. 7.18 by household ethnicity. For all ethnic groups, economic growth has benefited those at the lower end of the income distribution and has even negatively impacted the top-end incomes. Economic growth has, therefore, been partly redistributive. The higher and steeper GIC at the lower end of the distribution for ITTs and OTTs categories suggest that growth has benefited their incomes most.

[10] Kelly (2023) using census data from 1970 to 2011 looks at the white advantage and if socioeconomic parity has been achieved between the two major ethno-racial groups of Trinidad: ATTs and ITTs. The results reveal that whites, along with other (numerical) smaller ethno-racial groups, continue to outperform ATTs.

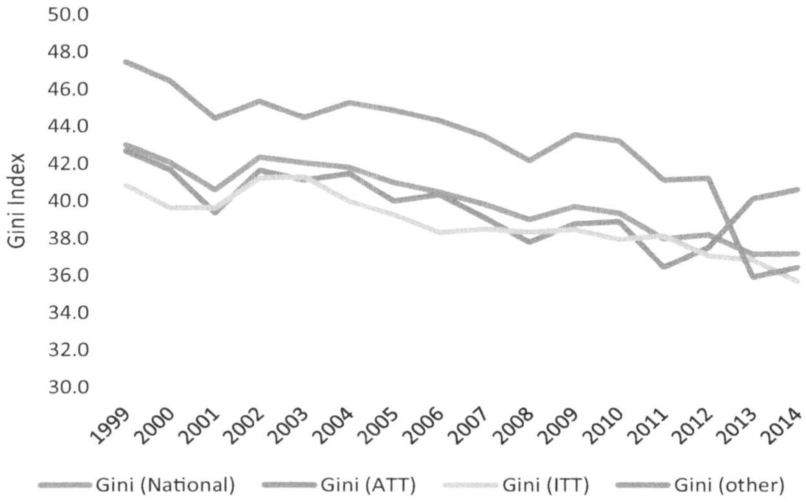

Fig. 7.17 Labour income inequality (*Source* Continuous Sample Survey of Population [1999–2014])

7.8 Conclusion

This chapter examined gender and race disparities in labour participation, wages, occupational segregation and composition, and poverty and income inequality outcomes in the TT labour market. Over the period 1991–2015, males have had a higher labour force participation rate than females—although female labour force participation increased by almost 25% over the same period. ATTs had a higher participation rate than ITTs. There has been a continuous decrease in unemployment rates over time for all groups, even during periods of subdued economic activity, supported by generous public employment and training programmes. Only marginal changes in the ethnic composition of occupational categories have been observed. However, there are significant differences in the distribution of occupations across genders.

Wage differentials among labour market participants were not systematically different between the two ethnic groups. However, there were significant wage differentials in favour of ITTs in the public sector. Wage differentials in the private sector were more prominent than in the public sector and favoured males of ATT and ITT origin. The mean wage gap

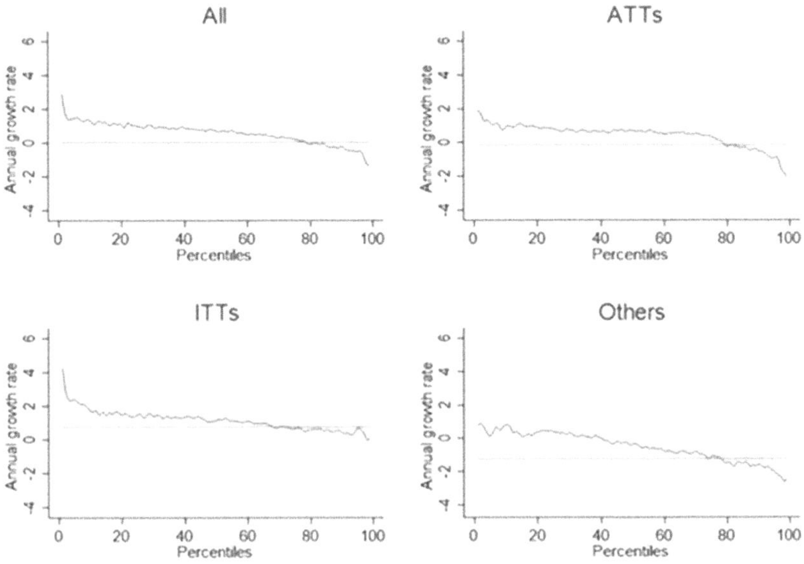

Fig. 7.18 Growth incidence curves (*Source* Continuous Sample Survey of Population [1999–2014])

has declined over time, driven by changes in characteristics, primarily increasing female education. However, a significant unexplained portion of the wage gap is still linked to occupational segregation, with men earning higher wages, especially in female-dominated professions.

Economic growth has been partly redistributive, with all ethnic groups benefitting, especially those at the lower end of the income distribution. Lastly, there are indications that although TT's generous government employment programmes, such as URP and the CEPEP, have helped stabilise the employment rate and mitigate the impact of economic volatility on unemployment, they may be contributing to distortions in the labour market.

References

Breza, E., Kaur, S., & Shamdasani, Y. (2018). The Morale Effects of Pay Inequality. *The Quarterly Journal of Economics, 133*(2), 611–663.

Brown, R. S., Moon, M., & Zoloth, B. S. (1980). Incorporating Occupational Attainment in Studies of Male-Female Earnings Differentials. *Journal of Human Resources*, 3–28.

Caribbean Development Bank. (2016). *The Changing Nature of Poverty and Inequality in the Caribbean*: New Issues, New Solutions, Caribbean Development Bank.

Dabri-Alai, P., & Odekon, M. (1998). *Economic Liberalisation and Labour Markets*. Greenwood Press.

Downes, A., (2006). *Caribbean Labour Market: Challenges and Policies*. CEPAL Series, United Nations.

Downes, A., Mamingi, N., & Belle Anotione, R. (2004). Labour Market Regulation in the Caribbean in Heckman J. and C. Pages (Eds.), *Law and Employment in Latin America and the Caribbean*. University of Chicago Press.

Kedir, A., & Sookram, S. (2013). Poverty and Welfare of the Poor in a High Income Country: The Case of Trinidad and Tobago. *Journal of International Development, 25*(4), 520–535.

Kelly, M. (2023). The Changing Terrain Of Racial Inequality in Trinidad and Tobago. *Research on Social Stratification and Mobility, 86*, 1970–2011.

Mercer-Blackman, V., & Salazni, M., (2014). *Does Okun's Law Apply to Trinidad and Tobago?* IDB Policy Brief IDB-PB-229.

Rambarran, A. (1998). Labor Market Adjustment in an Oil-Based Economy: The Experience of Trinidad and Tobago. *Economic Liberalisation and Labour Markets*, 197–223.

Schimanski, C., Chagalj, C., & Ruprah, I. S. (2018). *Race-Based Educational, Occupational and Industry Segregation and Wages Gaps in Trinidad and Tobago* (No. IDB-WP-955). IDB Working Paper Series.

Schimanski, C., Chagalj, C., & Ruprah, I. S. (2016). *Gender–based Educational Occupation Segregation in the Caribbean*. IDB Working Series, No.931.

Sookram, S., & Watson, P. (2008). The Informal Sector and Gender in The Caribbean: The Case of Trinidad and Tobago. *Journal of Eastern Caribbean Studies, 33*(4), 43–68.

CHAPTER 8

Economic Development: The Private Sector

8.1 Introduction

TT's non-energy sector has been increasing in importance over the past decades. Before the 2002–2008 commodity boom, the non-energy sector accounted for 72% of GDP in 2001 and rose to 77% by 2019 (Fig. 8.1). In the non-energy sector, services account for an outsized share of non-energy GDP—about 87% in 2019. Manufacturing is the second most important non-energy sub-sector, followed by agriculture, forestry, and fishing (Fig. 8.2). The relative importance of these three sectors to non-energy sector output has remained stable for the decade ending in 2019. A more detailed examination of TT's non-energy sector in Fig. 8.2 indicates that trade and repairs contributed to one-third of non-petroleum

This chapter draws on "Private sector challenges in Trinidad and Tobago", unpublished, by Jeetendra Khadan and Ricardo Sierra.

J. Khadan and I. Jit Ruprah, *Unraveling Race, Politics, and Gender in Trinidad and Tobago's Economic Development*,
https://doi.org/10.1007/978-3-031-54656-3_8

GDP,[1] followed by finance, insurance, and real estate (14%), food, beverages, and tobacco products (8.8%), transportation, communication, and storage (8%), and construction (7.6%).[2] The share of the non-energy sector in total output fell from about three-quarters in 2019 to nearly two-thirds in 2022, following the impact of the pandemic on economic activity.

One of the key challenges for TT's growth is weak linkages between the energy sector and the non-energy private sector. Hydrocarbon industries, such as oil and gas, tend to operate as economic enclaves with narrow direct links to the real economy. The industry's capital-intensive nature undermines its ability to create jobs and generate high value-added backward and forward linkages with other industries in the economy. Nonetheless, the non-energy sector can potentially benefit indirectly through higher domestic spending during commodity booms. In the

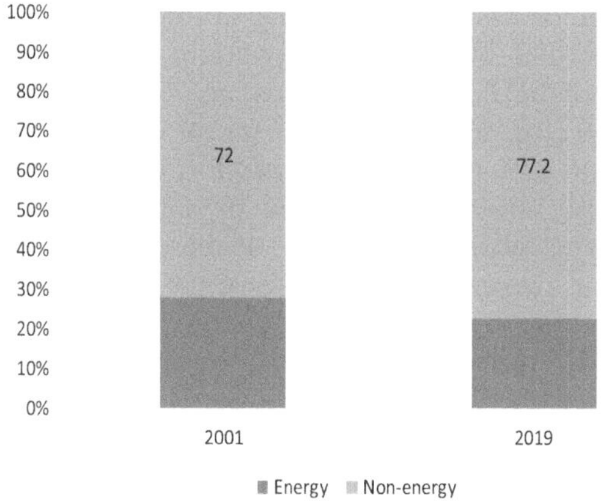

Fig. 8.1 Structure of the economy in Trinidad and Tobago (*Source* Central Bank of Trinidad and Tobago)

[1] Petroleum GDP refers to activity in the energy sector related to exploration and production, refining, petrochemicals, service contractors, distribution, and asphalt production. Non-petroleum GDP includes activity related to agriculture, manufacturing, and services.

[2] These calculations omit public administration which accounted for 8% of total GDP in 2019.

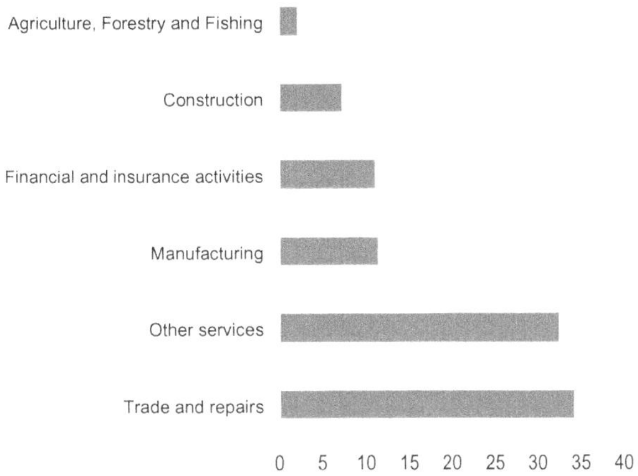

Fig. 8.2 Share of non-petroleum GDP (2019)[3] (*Source* Central Bank of Trinidad and Tobago)

case of TT, however, it has been observed that the non-energy sector remains largely unaffected when the energy sector experiences a boom. This suggests a further weakening in the relationship between the energy and non-energy sectors. The latter seems to imply the presence of obstacles that prevent the non-energy sector from capitalising on growth in the energy sector, even via indirect channels. To illustrate, between 1996 and 2001, the energy sector grew by 9.5%, while the non-energy industry grew at a rate of 6.2%. However, from 2002 to 2007, amidst a significant surge in energy prices and domestic production, the energy sector expanded by an average of 14.2%, yet the non-energy sector remained stagnant (Fig. 8.3). Conversely, when oil prices dipped in 2008 and gas prices continued to decline, the growth rate in the energy sector averaged -0.3%, and non-energy sector growth came in at 1.2%. Broad-based weakness in both sectors continued after the 2015 decline in energy prices and subsequent recovery, and then again during the pandemic.

[3] Other services include electricity and gas, water supply and sewerage, transportation and storage, accommodation and food service, information and communication, real estate activities, professional, scientific, and technical services, administrative and support services, education, health and social work, arts, entertainment and recreation, and domestic services.

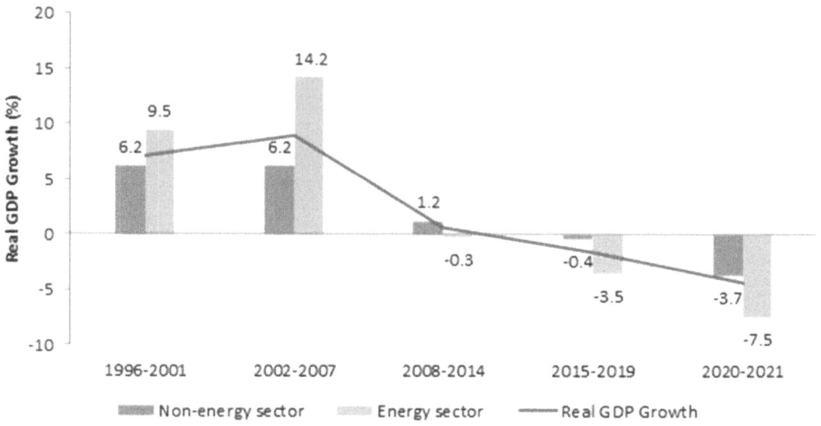

Fig. 8.3 Weak relationship between energy and non-energy growth (*Source* Central Bank of Trinidad and Tobago)

Non-energy sector activity shrank further in 2020 following the COVID-19 pandemic. The data in Table 8.1 provides a detailed breakdown of economic growth by sector from 2019 to 2022. Out of the 21 non-petroleum sectors, nine contracted in 2019 and almost all contracted in 2020. Only a few sectors, such as construction and manufacturing, had substantially recovered by 2021–2022. The recent weakness in non-energy sector activity represents an extension of contractions in the five years (2015–2019) preceding the pandemic, where non-energy sector GDP declined by an average of 0.44%. In the next section, we explore the underperformance of the non-energy private sector using firm-level data.

Table 8.1 Real GDP Growth by Sector (per cent)

Activity	*Average (2015–2019)*	*2020*	*2021–2022*
Agriculture, Forestry and Fishing	−1.0	−12.2	−11.5
Mining and Quarrying	−4.9	−12.1	0.8
Manufacturing	−1.4	−12.1	6.1
Food, Beverages and Tobacco Products	2.7	−8.2	31.7
Textiles, Clothing, Leather, Wood, Paper and Printing	−5.7	−11.1	15.8
Petroleum and Chemical Products	−2.3	−13.5	−2.1
Other Manufactured Products	0.8	−9.3	−2.9
Electricity and Gas	−1.3	−10.8	−0.9
Water Supply and Sewerage	0.2	2.7	−0.5
Construction	−3.7	−12.8	4.3
Trade and Repairs	−5.0	−12.2	6.1
Transportation and Storage	−3.9	−28.0	27.5
Accommodation and Food Service	−1.2	−19.2	19.0
Information and Communication	1.9	−1.6	0.3
Financial and Insurance Activities	2.3	−2.0	−3.1
Real Estate Activities	0.7	−0.7	−0.4
Professional, Scientific and Technical Services	0.9	−10.4	47.6
Administrative and Support Services	1.7	−2.2	1.5
Public Administration	0.4	0.7	−0.5
Education	0.3	−0.6	−0.1
Human Health and Social Work	0.1	−0.3	0.4
Arts, Entertainment and Recreation	0.1	−0.4	0.5
Other Service Activities	1.7	−4.1	−1.3
Domestic Services	1.2	1.1	0.8
GDP	−2.7	−9.1	1.5

8.2 Firm's Profile and Performance[4]

The dynamism of TT's private sector can be assessed by analysing sales growth and total factor productivity of firms. Total factor productivity is not only a key source of economic growth but also an important performance metric. It measures the ability of firms or countries to generate greater value or output with fewer or similar amounts of inputs (Francis et al., 2020). The total factor productivity indicator is estimated using a Cobb–Douglas production function with three factors of production: capital, labour, and intermediate goods. Output is measured by firm sales in 2019; capital is measured by the replacement value of machinery, vehicles, and equipment declared by the firms in the survey; labour is measured by the total income of workers, including wages, salaries, and bonuses; and the value of intermediate goods is determined by the cost of raw and intermediate materials (or the cost of finished goods and materials purchased for sale by retail sector firms). The residual term of the production function is used as the measure of total factor productivity. Sales growth is calculated using firm's total sales from 2017 to 2019.

The average sales growth for Caribbean firms is 9.84% (Fig. 8.4).[5] This figure is well above the average for TT, which has a sales growth of 3.1%.[6] This represents the second lowest sales growth rate among Caribbean countries, only above Dominica which had an average negative sales growth rate of 11.1%.

Firms can be classified according to their sales performance into declining (negative sales growth), stagnant (favourable growth rates but under 10%), and expanding (over 10% growth rates). The distribution of firms in TT according to their sales performance is presented in Fig. 8.5. Most firms (52.2%) had negative growth rates and 19.3% experienced moderate growth rates. Only 28.5% of the firms could be classified as expanding firms. This distribution contrasts with the 2014 results

[4] The following analysis uses the Innovation, Firm Performance and Gender survey (IFPG) that was conducted in 2020 from a random sample of formal firms in 13 Caribbean countries. Given that this data captures the effect of COVID-19, where relevant we compare the findings with those in Khadan (2017) who used the 2014 Productivity Technology and Innovation Survey.

[5] We used Caribbean countries as a comparator to TT due to data limitations.

[6] For a comparison with firm behaviour in other Caribbean countries see Nicolson and Lashley (2016), and Garvey and Shirley (2015). The latter analyses family-owned businesses.

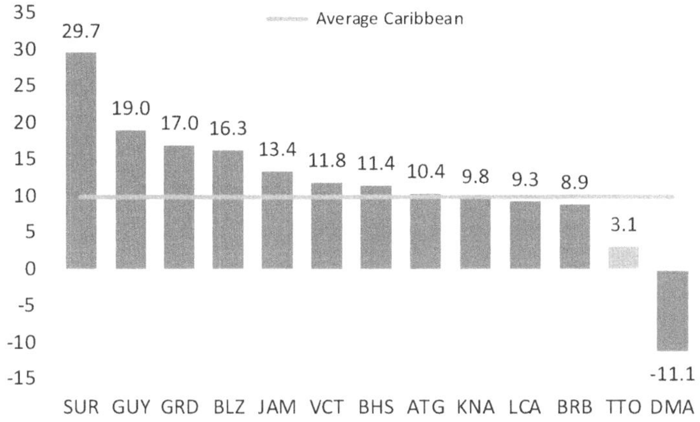

Fig. 8.4 Sales growth by country (2017–2019) (*Source* Innovation, Firm Performance and Gender Survey [IFPG, 2020])

presented in Khadan (2017) based on the 2014 PROTEqIn data, where declining, stagnant, and expanding firms represented 23, 59, and 18%, respectively.[7]

The classification of sales growth performance could be combined with basic profile variables of firms to better understand performance differences among different types of firms. The data shows that small firms had the worst sales growth metrics. Two-thirds of all small firms had "declining" sales growth, 14% had "stagnant" sales growth rates, and only 20% of the small firms in the TT sample had "expanding" sales growth rates (Fig. 8.6). The disaggregation by firm's age does not follow a clear pattern, and the few foreign-owned firms in the sample had all positive performances in sales growth.

As pointed out by Ruprah and Sierra (2016), TFP is one of the main determinants of long-run economic growth, and firm-level TFP growth is perhaps the most telling indicator of a firm's health. It captures the

[7] One caveat on the comparisons and estimates between Khadan (2017) which is based on the 2014 PROTEqIn data and IFPG online survey that should be kept in mind throughout this chapter is the differences in sample size. The 2020 IFPG online survey is based on a sample of 180 firms, while the 2014 PROTEqln survey is based on a sample of 340 firms.

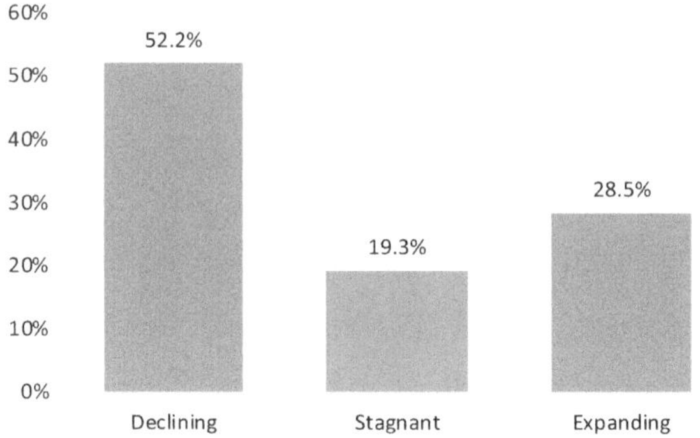

Fig. 8.5 Expanding, declining, and stagnant firms in TT (*Source* Innovation, Firm Performance, and Gender Survey [IFPG, 2020])

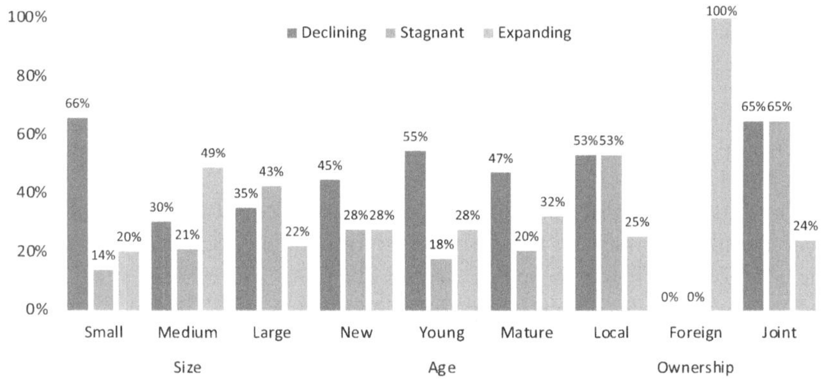

Fig. 8.6 Expanding, declining, and stagnant firms by characteristics (*Note* Small firms are those with 20 employees or less, medium-sized firms have more than 20 and up to 100 employees, and large firms have more than 100 employees. New firms are those that have been established for less than three years, a young firm is one that has been operation for 3 to 10 years, and a mature firm is one that has been operation for more than 10 years. *Source* The Innovation, Firm Performance and Gender Survey [IFPG, 2020])

efficiency with which capital and labour inputs are used and is a reasonable proxy for the return on capital for firms in an economy. Hence, it is important to complement the previous performance analysis with this metric.

While TT is ranked second to last in sales growth among Caribbean countries, it performs relatively better in terms of TFP. The average TFP value for all Caribbean firms is 2.85 (Fig. 8.7), and firms in TT had an average TFP of 2.74. This figure is higher than the TFP values observed for Grenada (2.71), The Bahamas (2.64), Dominica (2.57), and Barbados (2.45).

Firm's performance based on sales growth and TFP, by age and size, is shown below. Small firms exhibit the lowest average sales growth rate at 0.2%, whereas medium and large firms demonstrate average sales growth rates of 8.6% and 4.7%, respectively. The TFP metric follows a similar pattern[8]: small firms underperform (2.5), medium-sized firms have the best results (3.3), and large firms have a moderate performance (2.8). The latter suggests that firms with over 20, but less than 100, employees

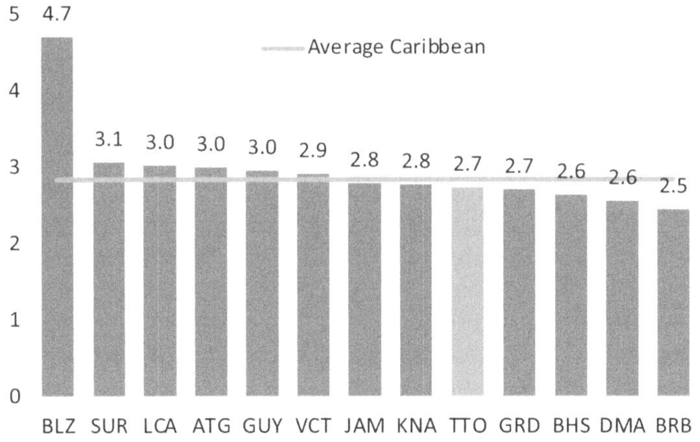

Fig. 8.7 Total factor productivity by country (*Source* Innovation, Firm Performance and Gender Survey [IFPG, 2020])

[8] This pattern is different for the rest of Caribbean firms in terms of sales growth: medium-sized firms are the best performers, but these firms are followed by small instead of large firms.

(medium-sized firms) are among the best-performing firms in TT, based on sales growth and TFP.

Note: Small firms are those with 20 employees or LESS, medium-sized firms have more than 20 and up to 100 employees, and large firms have more than 100 employees.

Sales growth is significantly different between new and mature firms: While new firms had an average decline of 7.8% during 2017–2019, the latter had an average growth rate of 6.1%. The average at the country level was 3.1 (Fig. 8.8), which is closer to the average observed for young firms (3.34). On the other hand, TFP was also the lowest among new firms (2.5), and the difference between young and mature firms is marginal, at 0.1 percentage points (Fig. 8.9).

8.3 Obstacles Affecting the Firm's Operations

A growing body of literature has identified many factors that negatively affect the environment for business operations (Ruprah & Sierra, 2016). These factors include access to telecommunications, electricity, transportation, access to land, tax rates, tax administration, customs and trade regulations, labour regulations, the workforce, business regulations, access to finance, the cost of finance, and the political environment, among others. Many of these factors not only affect day-to-day business operations but they can have long-term impacts on firms' performance.

To allow for adequate comparisons with the 2010 World Bank Enterprise Survey (WBES) and the 2014 PROTEqIn survey, the IFPG module on investment climate included a question that details all factors that were included in the previous surveys and added additional obstacles that are more relevant to the pandemic, like access to digital payments.

Figure 8.10 shows the proportion of firms that consider each item to be an obstacle to their operations, and these are ranked from the one that represents the most burden (access to finance) to the one that has the lowest proportion of firms considering it to be an obstacle (business licensing and permits). Remarkably, 65% of firms in TT consider access to finance to be a significant obstacle to their operations, followed by an inadequately educated workforce (63%) and customs and trade regulations (54.2%).

Furthermore, the IFPG survey provides data to evaluate how businesspersons subjectively rank obstacles to their innovation activities, and

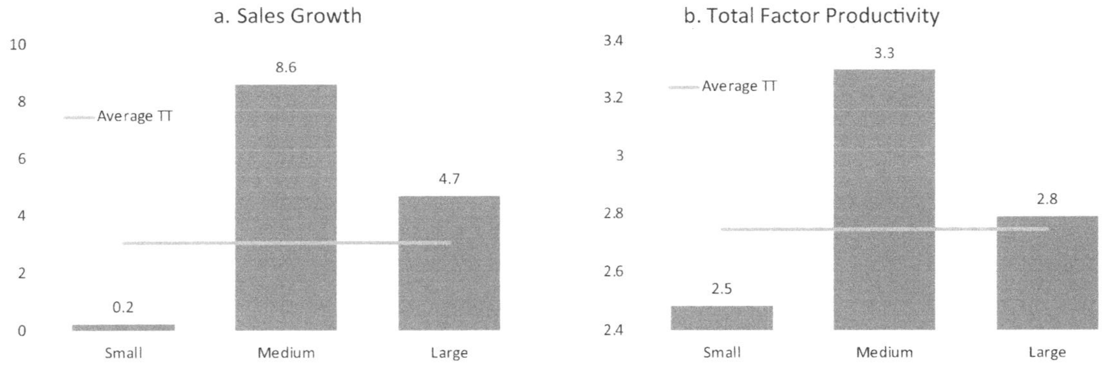

Fig. 8.8 Firm size and performance (**a**) Sales growth (**b**) Total factor productivity (*Source* Innovation, Firm Performance and Gender Survey [IFPG, 2020])

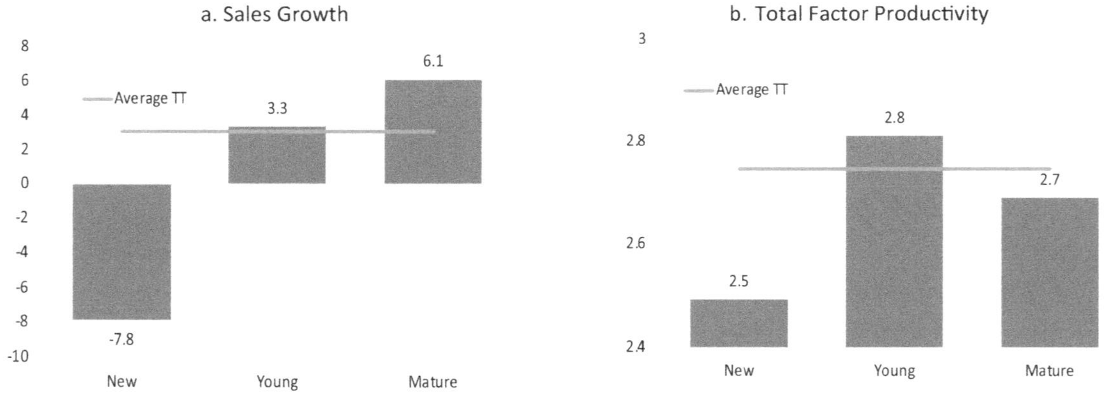

Fig. 8.9 Firm age and performance (**a**) Sales growth (**b**) Total factor productivity (*Note* New firms are those that have been established for less than three years, a young firm is between 3 and 10 years of operation, and a mature firm is one that has been operation for more than 10 years. *Source* Innovation, Firm Performance and Gender Survey [IFPG, 2020])

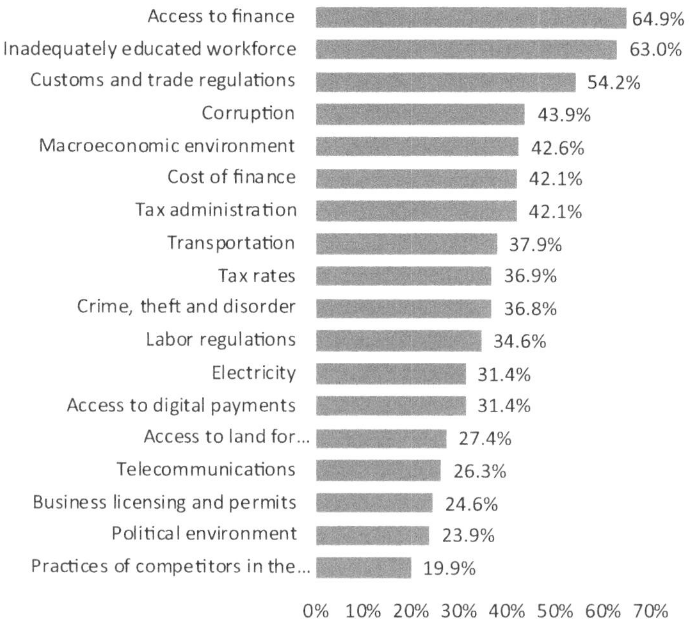

Fig. 8.10 Most serious obstacles affecting business operations in TT, 2019 (*Source* Innovation, Firm Performance and Gender Survey [IFPG, 2020])

how the pandemic affected those innovation decisions. Of the 14 potential barriers to innovation that were provided in the survey, employee qualification stood out as the primary obstacle hindering firms' innovation activities. This result correlates with Fig. 8.10, which ranks an undereducated workforce as the second most significant barrier to business operations in general. Figure 8.11 shows that, in the absence of the COVID-19 pandemic, 75.7% of firms in TT considered employees' qualifications as an obstacle to innovating, followed by the market size (i.e., the market size is too small given the cost of innovating). These two factors remained as the major obstacles after considering the impact of COVID-19 (blue bars in Fig. 8.11). The percentage of firms that viewed employees' qualifications as an obstacle post-COVID-19 increased to 93.4%, while the share of firms that state market size as an obstacle for innovation increased to 89%. The share of firms reporting the cost of innovating as an obstacle increased the largest in the context of COVID-19: While only 15.2% of firms saw this as an obstacle to innovating before COVID-19, 73.5% of firms saw it as an obstacle after the pandemic started.

A well-educated and appropriately skilled labour force is fundamental for productivity and business development. The literature suggests that a firm's productivity increases with the quality of its human capital stock, and most of the analysis related to mincer equations follow this literature. The share of firms that see an inadequately educated workforce as a significant obstacle affecting their operations rose from 41% in 2014 (Khadan, 2017) to 58.9% in 2020 (see Fig. 8.12 for the distribution of responses across different types of firms).

Fig. 8.11 Obstacles to innovation activities and the COVID-19 crisis (*Source* Innovation, Firm Performance and Gender Survey [IFPG, 2020])

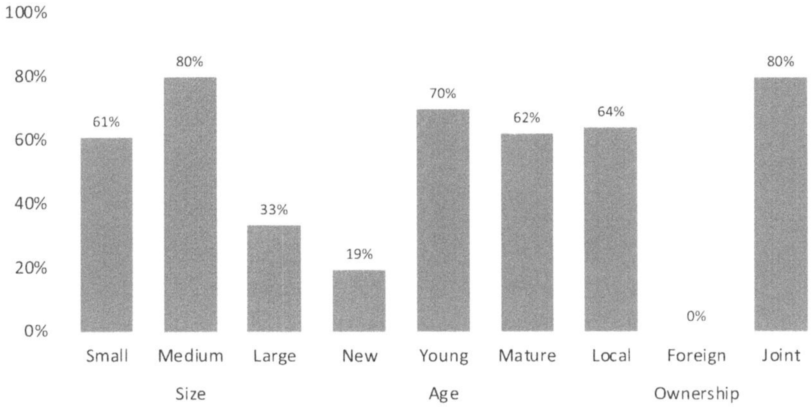

Fig. 8.12 Firms affected by an inadequately educated workforce (per cent of firms) (*Note* Small firms are those with 20 employees or less, medium-sized firms have more than 20 and up to 100 employees, and large firms have more than 100 employees. New firms are those that have been established for less than three years, a young firm is one that has been operation for 3 to 10 years, and a mature firm is one that has been operation for more than 10 years. *Source* Innovation, Firm Performance and Gender Survey [IFPG, 2020])

Skills shortages also affects TT's private-sector capacity to innovate (Khadan, 2018). However, there are no significant differences between the perception of skills shortage for innovation in TT and the rest of the Caribbean. 61.6% of firms in TT identified that skills shortages represented an obstacle to innovation activities before the COVID-19 crisis, compared to 62.7% in the rest of the Caribbean (Fig. 8.13). Undoubtedly, the pandemic greatly affected businesses worldwide, and the Caribbean is no exception. The percentage of firms asserting a lack of skills as an obstacle to innovation, since the start of COVID-19, has increased to 84.2% in TT and 83.2% in the rest of the Caribbean countries.

However, the labour force composition within firms in TT's private sector suggests that TT has more skilled workers that the average for the rest of the Caribbean. A comparison among three categories of full-time employees—management workers, production staff, and non-production workers (the latter comprising skilled and unskilled labour)—shows the following breakdown: In TT, the percentage of employees in management roles stands at 20.8%, closely aligned with the Caribbean's 21.8%.

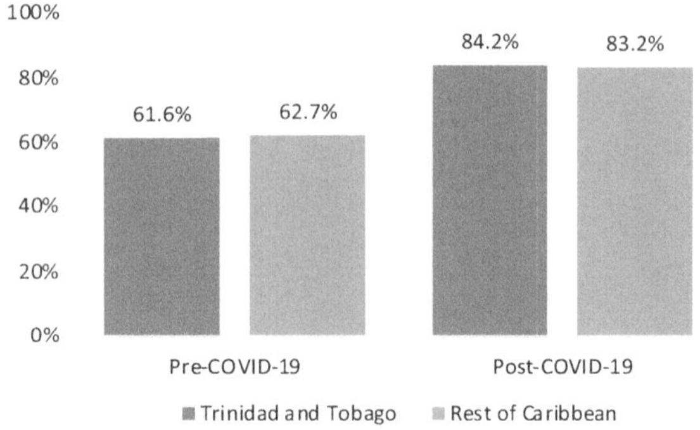

Fig. 8.13 Lack of skills for innovation (per cent of firms) (*Source* Innovation, Firm Performance and Gender Survey [IFPG, 2020])

However, the share of skilled and unskilled workers is different. 51.3% of workers in TT are classified as skilled, compared to 46.2% in the Caribbean. Conversely, according to the IFPG survey, the proportion of unskilled workers is lower in TT: only 27.9%, compared to 32.1% in the comparator group (Fig. 8.14).

The IFPG survey's Human Resource Management section delves into potential reasons for the perceived skills shortage in the Caribbean as highlighted by firms. Seven reasons are presented to survey respondents

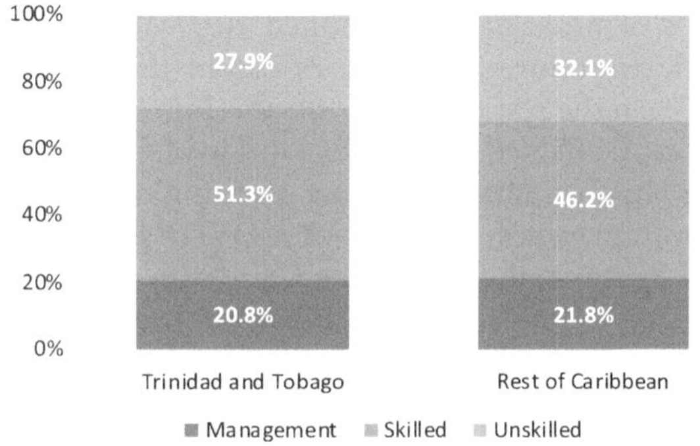

Fig. 8.14 Labour force composition within firms (*Source* Innovation, Firm Performance and Gender Survey [IFPG, 2020])

to assess their importance regarding the skills shortage issue.[9] These potential causes were ranked according to their importance level and shown in Fig. 8.15. According to the private sector, the quality of education and training offered by local educational institutions is perceived to be the most important cause of the country's skill shortage. This is followed by the lack of necessary personal soft skills offered by local institutions (average of 3.6), and a shortage of local professionals (average of 3.5).

TT businesspersons have identified a lack of access to finance as the most important constraint they face in their daily operations. Inadequate finance has been consistently cited as one of the main obstacles to a firm's

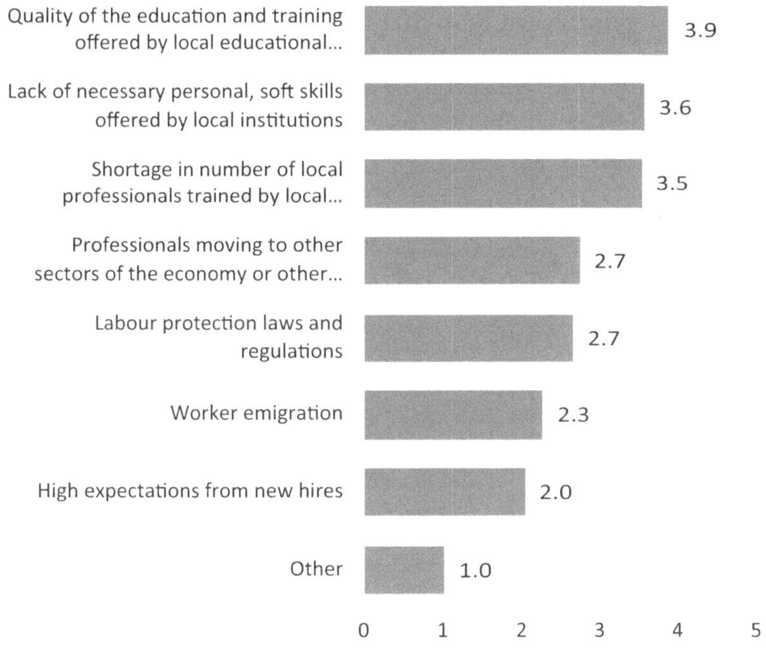

Fig. 8.15 Factors causing skills shortage (*Source* Innovation, Firm Performance and Gender Survey [IFPG, 2020])

[9] These were coded as: Not important (1), Slightly important (2), Important (3), Very important (4), and Critical (5).

performance (Khadan, 2017; Ruprah, 2016), and empirical evidence has shown that insufficient access to finance impairs firm productivity. While 65% of firms cited access to finance as a major obstacle for their operations (Fig. 8.16), the disaggregation by firm size, age, and ownership reveals some variations from the average.

Small and large firms have a worse perception regarding access to finance than their medium-sized counterparts. Firms that have been operating the longest view access to finance, due to collateral, as the most "major obstacle" (68% of firms). The perception of this obstacle is similar for young firms (66%) but lower for new firms (45%). Eighty-five per cent of joint-ownership (local and foreign) firms sees access to finance as a significant problem. The former represents the highest proportion among the characteristic of firms in Fig. 8.16, and it contrasts with 65% observed for locally owned firms in TT.

As pointed out in Khadan (2017), firms in TT rely heavily on retained earnings as a source of financing. Since access to finance is the biggest constraint firms face, it is important to examine how firms source funding

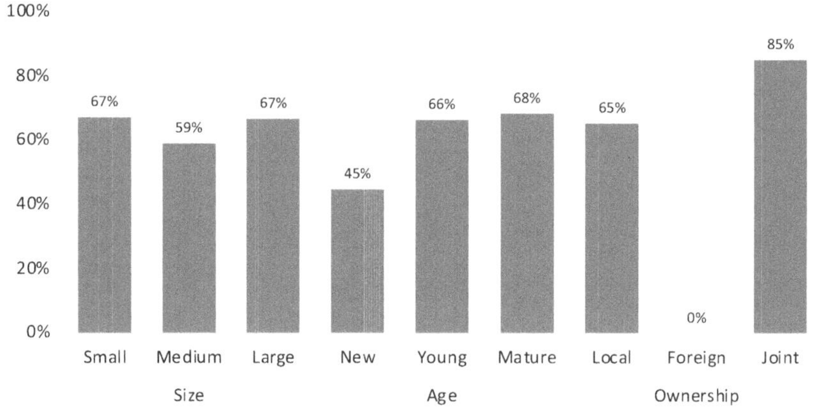

Fig. 8.16 Firms perceiving access to finance as an obstacle (per cent of firms) (*Note* Small firms are those with 20 employees or less, medium-sized firms have more than 20 and up to 100 employees, and large firms have more than 100 employees. New firms are those that have been established for less than three years, a young firm is one that has been operation for 3 to 10 years, and a mature firm is one that has been operation for more than 10 years, *Source* Innovation, Firm Performance and Gender Survey [IFPG, 2020])

for their working capital. The financing structure is determined by firm-specific characteristics that may vary across countries and by the constraints posed by countries' level of financial development and their institutional environment. 47.1% of firms in TT rely on internal funds and retained earnings as their primary sources of financing, followed by credit from their suppliers and advances from customers (34.6%), which is informal and highly unreliable—notably, only 10% of firms borrowed from private commercial banks to finance working capital (Fig. 8.17).

The results from the 2014 PROTEqIn survey (Fig. 6.9 in Khadan, 2017) differ from the ones presented in Fig. 8.17.[10] The percentage of firms that used internal funds and retained earnings in 2014 was 53.5, compared to 47.1 in 2020. While there was a slight decrease in the use of internal funds during the pandemic, relying on credit and customer advances has gained much traction since 2014. This form of funding represented 7.6% of firms in 2014, and the proportion of firms using it as a source of funding for their working capital increased by more than four times and now stands at 34.6%. The share of firms that borrow from private commercial banks remained similar: 10.9% in 2014, compared to 10% in 2020. Table 8.2 highlights the profile of firms that experience financing constraints using four indicators: loan demand, loan denial, "constrained" firms, and "discouraged" firms, following Presbitero and

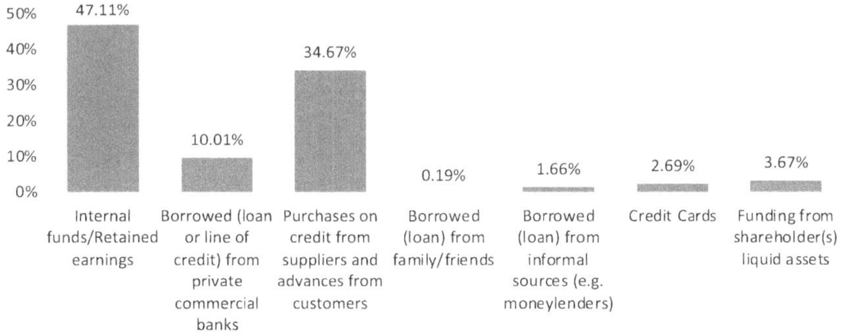

Fig. 8.17 Financing structure of working capital (*Source* Innovation, Firm Performance and Gender Survey [IFPG, 2020])

[10] The 2014 PROTEqIn survey is available here: https://publications.iadb.org/en/productivity-technology-innovation-caribbean.

Rabellotti (2014). Most firms were either discouraged from applying for loans or were constrained (i.e., their loan application was rejected).

We now turn to assess the role of crime on private-sector operations in TT. Crime constrains productivity, private-sector investment, firm sales, profitability, and economic growth (Fiestas & Sinha, 2011). The effects of crime on economic growth are well documented in the literature. Firm-level evidence shows that increases in crime and violence are associated with significant declines in revenue, employment, and hours worked (Montoya, 2016). These effects are heterogeneous across firm sizes and sectors, with the most significant impact on small firms (Montoya, 2016). Crime acts as a deterrent to firm entry, which can lead to less dynamic industries (Mahofa et al., 2016) and underperformance. Crime can also negatively impact the investment climate, deter or delay domestic and foreign investment, and dampen economic growth (Ruprah & Sierra, 2016). It can increase the cost of doing business because of the need to employ different forms of security, hence diverting investment away from business expansion and productivity-enhancing investments.

While crime was not ranked in the top 5 obstacles to a firm's operations, more than one-third of firms identified it as the most serious

Table 8.2 Firm characteristics associated with financing constraints (per cent of firms)

		Credit demand (%)	*Loan denial (%)*	*Discouraged (%)*	*Constrained (%)*
Size	Small	0.7	0.7	82.4	83.1
	Medium	7.0	0.8	72.1	72.9
	Large	25.9	0.0	29.7	29.7
Age	New	0.0	0.0	68.1	68.1
	Young	6.1	0.3	70.1	70.4
	Mature	6.5	1.9	83.3	85.2
Ownership	Local	4.5	0.8	78.5	79.3
	Foreign	20.0	0.0	0.0	0.0
	Joint	7.4	0.0	63.0	63.0
Overall		**5.5**	**0.7**	**73.3**	**73.9**

Note Small firms are those with 20 employees or less, medium-sized firms have more than 20 and up to 100 employees, and large firms have more than 100 employees. New firms are those that have been established for less than three years, a young firm is one that has been operation for 3 to 10 years, and a mature firm is one that has been operation for more than 10 years

Source Innovation, Firm Performance and Gender Survey (IFPG, 2020)

obstacle to their performance. Crime is also an issue at the national level that affects decisions for potential investors and businesspersons in TT (see Chapter 11). Figure 8.18 shows how larger firms perceive crime as a harsher obstacle (50%, compared to 33% among small firms), but no clear pattern is associated with firm age and crime perception. Finally, locally owned firms (36%) tend to perceive crime as a lesser burden than firms jointly owned by local and foreign individuals (56%).

Theft is one of the most frequent crimes committed on the firms' premises, according to IFPG data (Fig. 8.19): 31% among all firms in TT, followed closely by deliberate damage/vandalism and robbery. 24% of firms reported burglary as the crime committed in the fiscal year before the IFPG survey, and 21% of firms reported assault and threats as the crime committed on their premises.[11]

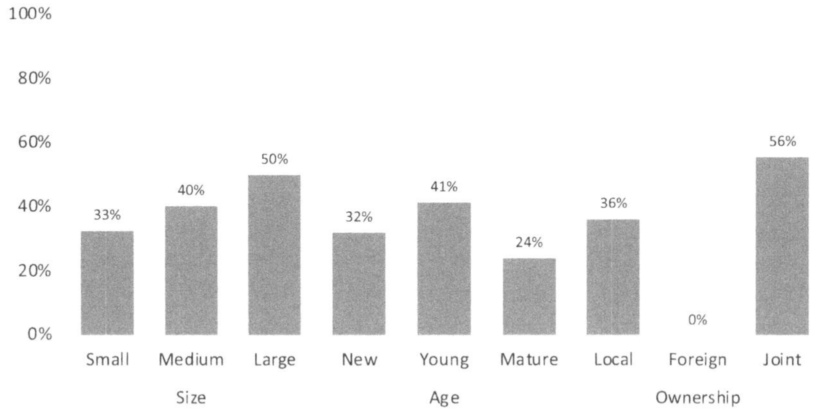

Fig. 8.18 Firms perceiving crime as an obstacle (per cent of firms) (*Note* Small firms are those with 20 employees or less, medium-sized firms have more than 20 and up to 100 employees, and large firms have more than 100 employees. New firms are those that have been established for less than three years, a young firm is one that has been operation for 3 to 10 years, and a mature firm is one that has been operation for more than 10 years, *Source* The Innovation, Firm Performance and Gender Survey [IFPG, 2020])

[11] Perception of crime is highly correlated with crime incidence. Constructing a variable for any type of crime committed in the firm's premises, the country's average stands at

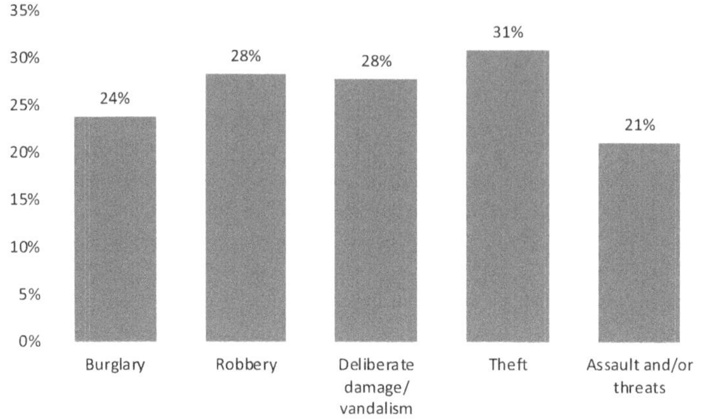

Fig. 8.19 Incidence of crime by type (*Source* Innovation, Firm Performance and Gender Survey [IFPG, 2020])

Since a significant proportion of firms is affected by any type of crime, it would be natural that firms would allocate resources to increasing security. The latter would entail spending on equipment, insurance, personnel, or professional security services that could lead to a decrease the crimes suffered by such firms; unsurprisingly, over three-quarters of firms spent on security during the fiscal year before the IFPG survey. A relatively higher proportion of medium (87%) and large-sized (85%) firms report positive expenditures on crime compared to small firms (74%), and all foreign-owned firms report expenditures on security, compared to 80% of firms that are locally owned (Fig. 8.20). While all foreign-owned firms in the sample incur security outlays, their perception of crime as an obstacle to their operations is better than that of the firms (locally owned or jointly owned) in TT.

Finally, the value of these expenditures is far from insignificant in TT. An average firm spends 3.8% of its total annual sales on security, and these expenditures are heterogeneous across firm size (Fig. 8.21). Small firms spend an average of 4% of their total sales on security, compared to 2.5% for large firms. The latter could result from either more considerable costs

34%. However, this proportion is different between firms that perceive crime as an obstacle (45%) than for those that don't see crime as a burden for their operations (28%).

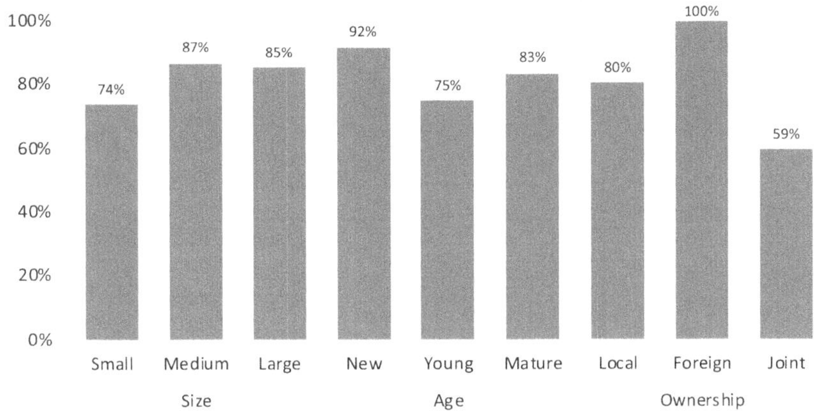

Fig. 8.20 Expenditure in security (per cent of firms) (*Note* Small firms are those with 20 employees or less, medium-sized firms have more than 20 and up to 100 employees, and large firms have more than 100 employees. New firms are those that have been established for less than three years, a young firm is one that has been in operation for 3 to 10 years, and a mature firm is one that has been in operation for more than 10 years. *Source* Innovation, Firm Performance and Gender Survey [IFPG,2020])

faced by small firms or a smaller denominator (lower sales compared to large firms). Nevertheless, it is significant for small firms trying to compete in any market. While all foreign-owned firms in the sample stated that they incurred security expenditures, these expenditures amount to only 2% of their total annual sales. This proportion is half what small firms (regardless of ownership status) report as security expenditures percentage of total yearly sales.

We classify firms into four groups following Seker (2009) and Khadan (2017): (i) firms that import material inputs or supplies and with at least 10% of direct exports (two-way traders), (ii) firms that only export (only-exporters); (iii) firms that only import (only-importers); (iv) firms that do not engage in international trade (non-traders). The IFPG survey data shows that 32% of firms engage in two-way trade, 0.2% are only-exporters, 66% are only-importers, and only 1.8% do not engage in foreign trade

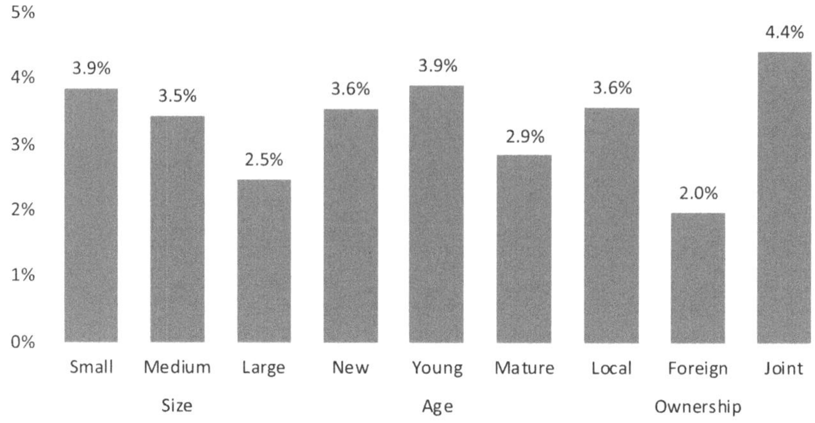

Fig. 8.21 Expenditure in security (per cent of annual sales) (*Note* Small firms are those with 20 employees or less, medium-sized firms have more than 20 and up to 100 employees, and large firms have more than 100 employees. New firms are those that have been established for less than three years, a young firm is between 3 and 10 years of operation, and a mature firm is one that has been in operation for more than 10 years. *Source* Innovation, Firm Performance and Gender Survey [IFPG, 2020])

(Fig. 8.22).[12] The latter contrasts remarkably with the 2014 PROTEqIn data and results presented in Khadan (2017). There is a clear improvement among TT firms and their engagement in international trade. Non-traders amounted to 27% in 2014 and currently represent less than two per cent. Furthermore, there was a shift from only exporting firms to two-way trading firms during this time since the share of only-importers remained very similar (69% in 2014 compared to 66% in 2020).

The shift from 9 to 32% in two-way traders requires further analysis. A country ranking based on the share of two-way traders sheds light on the degree of trade openness across Caribbean countries. Figure 8.23 shows that TT (32%) is very close to the regional average (31.1%) regarding the share of two-way traders. However, it is still far from Belize, the country

[12] One caveat on in interpretation of these comparison and estimates is that they are from different sample sizes. The 2020 IFPG online survey is based on a sample of 180 firms, while the 2014 PROTEqIn survey is based on a sample of 340 firms.

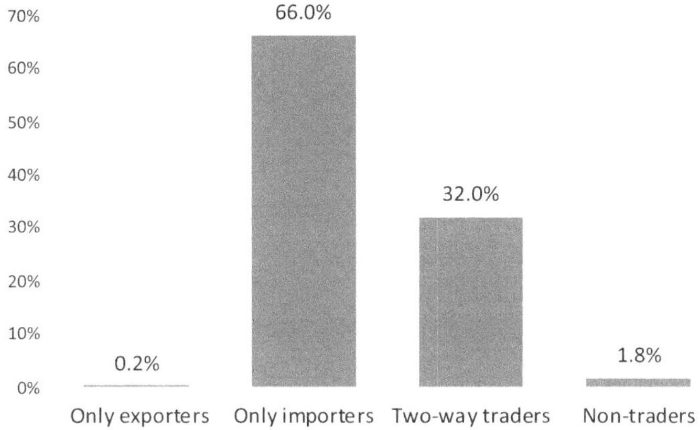

Fig. 8.22 Firms engaged in trade (*Source* Innovation, Firm Performance and Gender Survey [IFPG, 2020])

in the sample with the largest proportion of two-way traders in the region, at 47.5%.

Figure 8.23 puts TT's trade openness in perspective. There are only slight differences in the proportion of two-way traders across the age and size of firms (Fig. 8.24), but significant differences between local and jointly owned firms. The share of small and large firms that are two-way traders are similar, but medium-sized firms demonstrate a slightly higher proportion of such activity, at 36%. Moreover, new and young firms comprise 34% and 29% of two-way traders, whereas mature firms account for 42% of such traders. The difference between local firms and joint ventures is considerable, at 26 percentage points.

The IFPG data reveals that TT firms have relatively lower fuel and electricity costs. The average fuel cost (as a per cent of sales) for firms in TT is three times lower than in the rest of the Caribbean—0.3% of total sales for TT compared with 1% for the rest of the Caribbean (Fig. 8.25). A similar difference is observed for electricity costs. While firms in TT spend 0.9% of annual sales on electric bills, the comparator firms spend 2.6%, on average. These lower costs should support firm competitiveness and help reduce the performance gap described in Sect. 8.1, at least among firms that intensively use energy for production.

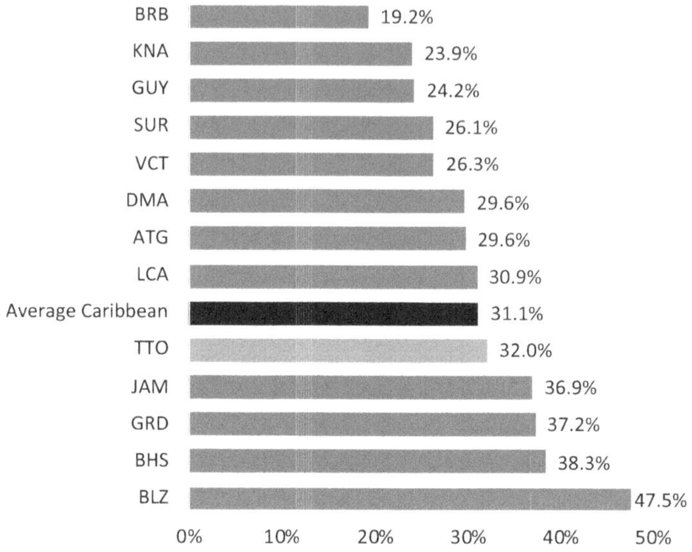

Fig. 8.23 Share of two-way traders by country (*Source* Innovation, Firm Performance and Gender Survey [IFPG, 2020])

One way to gauge the level of digitalisation among TT's firms is by examining the extent to which they employ technological tools to enhance sales, broaden market reach, and establish efficient connections with both customers and suppliers. The marketing and sales module of the IFPG survey asks questions on the use of mobile phones, e-mail, social media, and whether firms have a website. Table 8.3 shows how almost all (98%) firms use mobile phones for their operations in TT. A slightly lower share of firms (96.9%) use e-mail to communicate with their clients or suppliers. However, the proportion of firms that use social media and a website for their operations relatively lower (62%).

Men-led firms tend to have higher usage of technological tools. There is evidence that women typically run smaller firms and face more considerable obstacles regarding access to finance. These issues could affect the performance of digitalisation efforts. Concerning size, there is evidence that the use of social media and a website for firms' operations increases with firm size. The difference between small and large firms using social

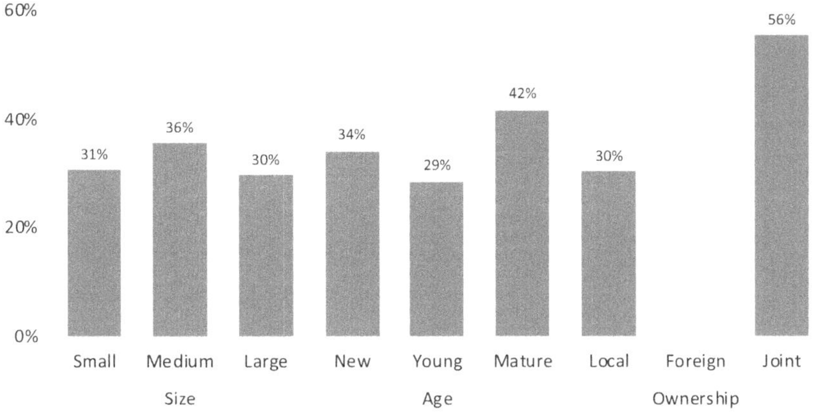

Fig. 8.24 Share of two-way traders within TT (*Note* Small firms are those with 20 employees or less, medium-sized firms have more than 20 and up to 100 employees, and large firms have more than 100 employees. New firms are those that have been established for less than three years, a young firm is one that has been in operation for 3 to 10 years, and a mature firm is one that has been in operation for more than 10 years. *Source* Innovation, Firm Performance and Gender Survey [IFPG, 2020])

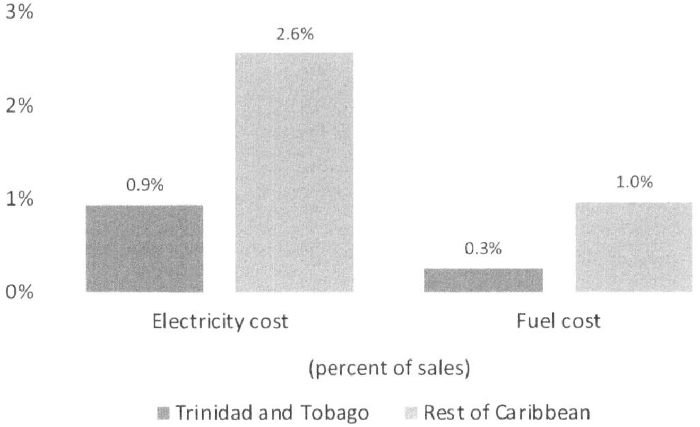

Fig. 8.25 Cost of fuel and electricity for firms (*Source* Innovation, Firm Performance and Gender Survey [IFPG, 2020])

Table 8.3 Technology use by firms in TT

		Overall (%)	*Women-led firms (%)*	*Men-led firms (%)*	*Small (%)*	*Firm size Medium (%)*	*Large (%)*
Does this establishment…	…use mobile phones for its operations?	**98.0**	95.9	98.6	96.7	100.0	100.0
	… use email to communicate with clients or suppliers?	**96.9**	95.9	97.2	96.7	96.1	100.0
	… use social media?	**62.0**	62.8	61.8	54.5	69.8	81.5
	… use a website?	**62.0**	47.4	66.0	56.0	63.5	88.8
	% of sales paid online	**3.4**	1.0	4.1	3.3	2.4	6.5
	% of firms dedicating efforts in advertising on digital media (Google ads, Facebook, Instagram, etc.)	**53.3**	43.3	56.0	52.0	51.1	64.8
	% of annual advertising budget dedicated to digital media*	**19.4**	20.0	19.3	20.1	20.5	14.7
Have you heard of the following payment methods (**% YES**)	Mobile money (e.g. ApplePay, Bitt)	**55.7**	70.1	51.8	39.6	79.0	81.5
	Electronic payments through a mobile phone	**40.8**	49.4	38.4	23.8	60.5	79.6
	Electronic payments through a money transfer service (e.g. payment Western Union)	**77.8**	79.4	77.4	72.2	84.4	90.7
	International processors such as Paypal, Stripe	**26.5**	27.8	26.2	8.07	49.6	64.8
	Cryptocurrency (e.g. Bitcoin, Ethereum)	**16.0**	18.5	15.3	4.8	23.3	55.5

		Overall (%)	*Women-led firms (%)*	*Men-led firms (%)*	*Small (%)*	*Firm size Medium (%)*	*Large (%)*
Currently accept the following payment methods (% **YES****)	Mobile money (e.g. ApplePay, Bitt)	**14.6**	11.7	15.6	12.0	23.5	0.0
	Electronic payments through a mobile phone	**35.0**	27.1	37.7	50.7	29.5	20.9
	Electronic payments through a money transfer service (e.g. payment Western Union)	**14.4**	6.5	16.5	17.8	14.7	0.0
	International processors such as Paypal, Stripe	**45.4**	48.1	44.7	59.1	45.3	37.1
	Cryptocurrency (e.g. Bitcoin, Ethereum)	**0.0**	0.0	0.0	0.0	0.0	0.0

* Among firms who dedicate efforts to advertising on digital media

** This applies only to firms who answered that they had heard of the corresponding payment method

Note Small firms are those with 20 employees or less, medium-sized firms have more than 20 and up to 100 employees, and large firms have more than 100 employees

Source Innovation, Firm Performance and Gender Survey (IFPG, 2020)

media amounts to 27 percentage points and up to 32.8 percentage points for website use.

While firms use these technological tools for their daily operations, the percentage of sales paid online is meagre, at only 3.4%.[13] Again, there is room for improvement in gender since only 1% of women-led firms accept online payments for their sales, compared to 4.1% among male-led firms. Additionally, improvements could be made to advance firms' digital media marketing efforts since only 53.3% of TT firms in the survey has dedicated efforts to this end.

Firms are aware of different payment methods that require basic digital use/skills, but awareness does not necessarily translate into use. The lower panels of Table 8.3 show how electronic payments through money transfer services (such as Western Union) are widely (77.8%) known among businesspeople in TT. However, only 14.4% of the firms in the sample implements this payment method. An awareness campaign on the use of digital payments could benefit MSMEs in TT. Still, the final objective of such campaigns should relate to deploying digital technologies available at reasonable prices and broader acceptance of innovative payment methods.

Another approach to measure digital competency at the firm level is by analysing subjective responses to statements related to digital tools, training, and equipment within the firms in the sample. These statements could shed light on the causes behind the underuse of digital tools. Figure 8.26 shows how training on digital competency should not be considered the most critical factor affecting digital use in TT. 40% of the firms agree with the statement that they provide training on digital competencies to their employees. In contrast, only 27.8% of firms believe that they provide equipment and devices to deploy digital competency fully, and 33% stated that their firms choose the most appropriate digital tools to solve their technological needs. The latter suggests that providing the right equipment and digital tools seems to be a more significant obstacle to digital competency than training in digital skills. Statements regarding proper equipment and choosing the appropriate digital tools reveal substantial differences across gender groups, where women-led firms lag in providing adequate equipment to deploy digital competency fully.

[13] To provide context, this figure is 24% for Belizean firms within the same IFPG survey.

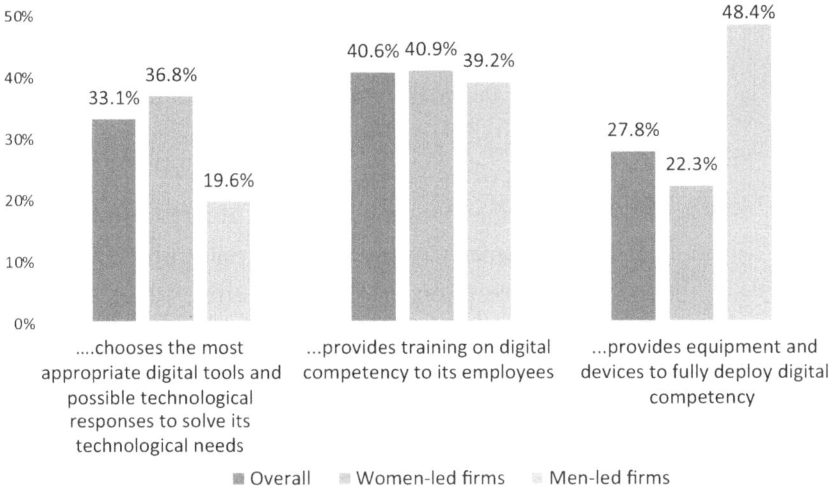

Fig. 8.26 Digital competency in TT (*Source* Innovation, Firm Performance and Gender Survey [IFPG, 2020])

8.4 Putting It All Together: Identifying Key Problems and Policy Options

Previous sections of this chapter shed light on the macroeconomic and microeconomic hurdles encountered by TT's private sector, based on comparisons with other Caribbean countries. Policymakers confront the arduous task of rejuvenating a stagnant private sector, empowering it to assume a more substantial role in bolstering domestic investment, fostering employment growth, and strengthening its impact on the country's export earnings and revenues. This section delves deeper by undertaking an empirical analysis to identify key areas for policy intervention.

The approach employed to prioritise policy interventions assesses how each constraint impacts a firm's performance, specifically its sales growth. We use simple regression analyses to investigate the impact of firm characteristics, microeconomic constraints, and sector-specific dummy variables on sales growth. The contribution of each factor to predicted sales growth is then used to rank constraints. The data is derived from the 2021 IFPG firm-level survey. The model used for this analysis is as follows:

$$\begin{aligned} \textit{Sales growth} = {} & \beta_0 + \beta_1\text{Age} + \beta_2\text{Age}^2 + \beta_3\text{Size} + \beta_4\text{Size}^2 \\ & + \beta_5\text{Local owned} + \beta_6\text{Privately held} \\ & + \beta_7\text{Sole Proprietorship} + \beta_8\text{Partnership} \\ & + \beta_9\text{Limited Partnership} + \beta_{10}\text{Exporter} \\ & + \beta_{11}\text{Importer} + \beta_{12}\text{Female Manager} \\ & + \beta_{13}\text{Crime Constraint} + \beta_{14}\text{ Labor Constraint} \\ & + \beta_{15}\text{Finance Constraint} + \beta_{16}\text{Innovation} \\ & + \beta_{17}\text{Corruption} + \beta_{18}\text{Infrastructure} + \theta_s + \varepsilon \end{aligned}$$

This model is estimated using data from a sample of 175 TT firms across the manufacturing and services sectors. It incorporates several explanatory variables, including measurements of microeconomic constraints, features of individual firms, and sector-specific fixed effects. These findings quantify how much each constraint or firm characteristic contributes to predicted sales growth.

The regression analysis shows that firm-related attributes contribute more negatively to performance than microeconomic challenges and sector-specific factors. Specifically, characteristics such as the company's size, legal structure, gender composition, and involvement in international trade (whether as an exporter or importer) emerge as the main factors negatively affecting sales growth. In contrast, ownership (locally owned) and age positively contributed to predicted sales growth. Microeconomic constraints, such as access to financing, crime rates, corruption levels, infrastructure quality, innovation capacity, and labour-related issues, were the second most significant negative contributors to predicted sales growth. The sector-specific factors had a less favourable influence on predicted sales growth, as illustrated in Fig. 8.27.

In order of importance, as depicted in Fig. 8.28, the main hindrances to sales growth include a lack of innovation (even for firms with an innovation department), inadequate infrastructure, crime, corruption, and access to finance. Notably, these constraints deviate from the perceptions of businesspersons, albeit only in terms of their priority. Regarding their impact on sales growth, the following factors contribute negatively to predicted sales growth: innovation constraint (47%), inadequate infrastructure (17%), and the crime constraint (17%). The negative impact of financial and labour constraints on predicted sales growth showed a similar magnitude. It's important to note that these results should not be interpreted as causal effects.

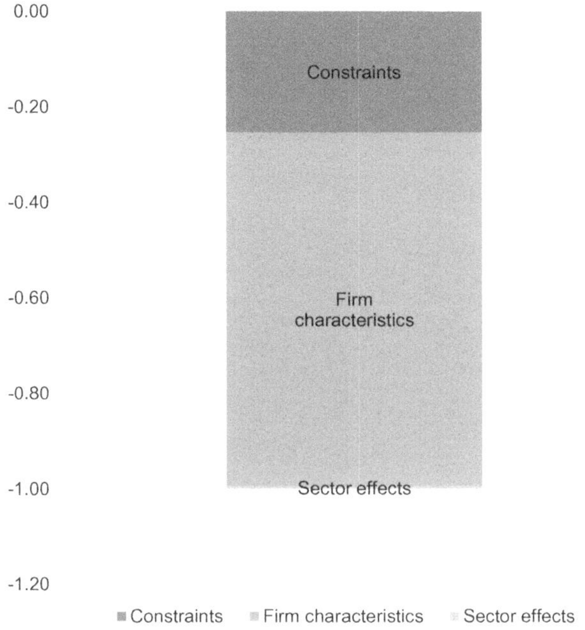

Fig. 8.27 Contribution to predicted sales growth (per cent) (*Note* Predicted sales growth does not include the reference category of the dummy variables. *Source* Author's estimates using The Innovation, Firm Performance and Gender Survey [IFPG, 2020])

The legal structure, size of a company, gender of managers, and its trade orientation are all associated with adverse effects on predicted sales growth, as illustrated in Fig. 8.29. Legal form is categorised into sole proprietorships, privately held companies, and partnerships. When it comes to size, the coefficient is negative, but when size is squared, it turns positive, suggesting a possible performance premium for larger firms in the market. It is worth noting that the trade estimate combines importer and exporter variables. Importers positively contribute to sales growth, but surprisingly, exporter status is associated with a negative contribution. In contrast, the coefficient for age is positive, but when age is squared, it turns negative, suggesting that firms' performance wanes as they mature.

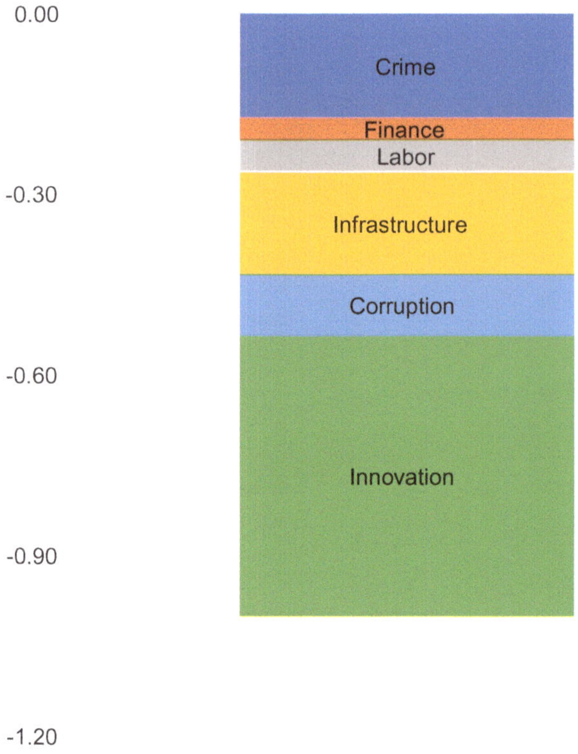

Fig. 8.28 Relative importance of firm constraints on sales growth (per cent) (*Source* Author's estimates using The Innovation, Firm Performance and Gender Survey [IFPG, 2020])

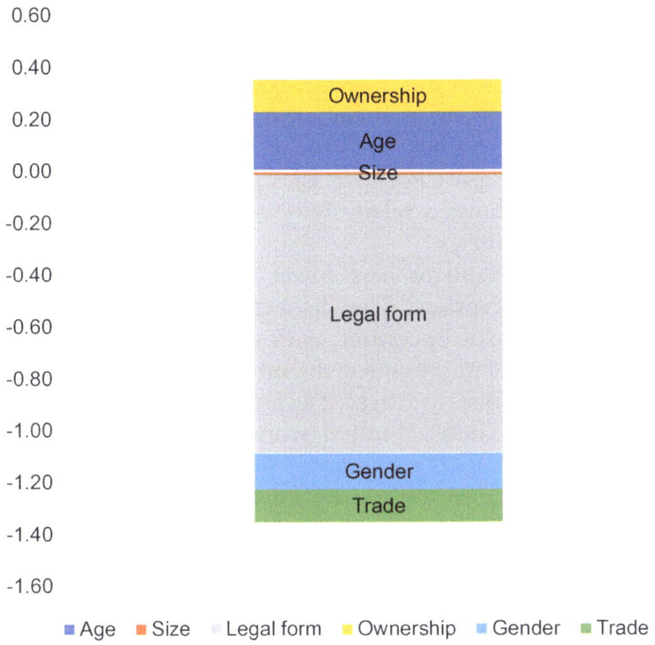

Fig. 8.29 Relative importance of firm characteristics on sales growth (per cent) (*Source* Author's estimates using The Innovation, Firm Performance and Gender Survey [IFPG, 2020])

8.5 Conclusion

This chapter examines TT's non-energy private sector by assessing several dimensions of its performance and prioritising policies to support its growth. The non-energy sector has become more important to the TT economy, with services being the dominant sub-sector. However, the non-energy sector performance has deteriorated recently, particularly during the COVID-19 pandemic, followed by a sluggish recovery. This downturn follows a continuation of the sector's underperformance that had already become evident over the decade preceding 2019. Furthermore, the weakening relationship between the energy sector and the rest of the economy further undermines non-energy sector growth. Growth of the energy sector often fails to provide the desired stimulus for the non-energy sector. Conversely, downturns within the energy sector are associated with negative growth in the non-energy sector.

While a few industries in the non-energy sector have shown resilience and growth—particularly in manufacturing and services, performance disparities are evident across firm sizes and ages. For example, a substantial portion of small firms report negative sales growth. On the other hand, TFP at the firm level shows a relatively better picture for TT compared to some Caribbean countries.

Overall, small firms tend to have lower sales growth and TFP than medium and large enterprises. The distinction in performance is also apparent in firms' years of operation, with mature firms outperforming their newer counterparts in sales growth and TFP.

Several factors continue to affect TT firms' performance. Access to finance and an inadequately educated workforce remain as substantial hurdles for firms in TT, with a significant proportion of firms reporting them as a major obstacle to their operations. Crime is a major concern, affecting firms' investment decisions. Theft, vandalism, and robbery are common crimes that cause businesses to divert resources from other productive activities to enhance security.

The impact of COVID-19 is evident on firms, with businesses perceiving market size and the cost of innovating as increasingly significant obstacles since the pandemic's onset. Relatedly, digitalisation emerged as an essential aspect of infrastructure to support business continuity during the pandemic. The data shows that there is ample room for growth in online payment systems and enhancing digital marketing efforts in TT.

Our regression results show that the profile of the private sector—an important determinant of firms' performance—is unfavourable in terms of age, size, legal form, and trade orientation. Microeconomic constraints, including access to finance, crime, corruption, inadequate infrastructure, and insufficient innovation, also affect firms' performance. Among these, the lack of innovation emerges as the most significant hindrance, followed by inadequate infrastructure and crime. Addressing these challenges can create a more favourable environment for business growth.

Annex 1: Description of Variables

- ***Sales growth***: Firm-level outcome (sales growth, purchasing power parity adjusted).
- ***Age***: Firm age in years.
- ***Age***^{2}: Firm age in years squared.
- ***Size:*** Number of employees.
- ***Size***^{2}: Number of employees squared.
- ***Foreign-owned***: Dummy equal to one if the firm is predominately foreign-owned.
- ***Joint owned***: Dummy equal to one if the firm is owned jointly by local and foreign entities.
- ***Privately held:*** Dummy equal to one if the firm is a private limited liability company.
- ***Sole proprietorship***: Dummy equals one if the firm is a sole proprietorship.
- ***Partnerships***: A dummy equals one if the firm is a partnership.
- ***Limited partnerships***: Dummy equal to one if the firm is a limited partnership.
- ***Female manager***: Dummy equals one if a female manages a firm.
- ***Exporter***: Dummy equal to one if the firm is an exporter.
- ***Importer***: Dummy equal to one if the firm is an importer.
- ***Corruption***: A dummy equals one if the firm identified corruption as a significant and severe obstacle to its performance.
- ***Innovation***: A dummy equals one if the firm has an innovation department.
- ***Crime constraint***: Dummy equals one if firms report losses (per cent of sales) due to crime.
- ***Labour constraint***: Dummy equals one if the firm identified an inadequately educated workforce as a major and severe obstacle to their performance.
- ***Credit constraint***: Dummy equals one if identified access to finance as a major and severe obstacle to their performance.
- ***Infrastructure:*** Dummy equals one if the firm identified electricity, telecommunications, and transportation as major and severe obstacles to their performance.
- $\boldsymbol{\theta_s}$: sector-specific fixed effects.
- $\boldsymbol{\mu_c}$: country-specific fixed effects.

References

Binos, M. A. J., Vigonte, F. G., & Abante, M. V. (2023, May 28). *International Trade: Impact in Economic Growth*. Available at SSRN: https://ssrn.com/abstract=4461422 or https://doi.org/10.2139/ssrn.4461422.

Czabanski, J. (2008). *Estimates of Cost of Crime: History, Methodologies, and Implications*. Springer Science & Business Media.

Fiestas, I., & Sinha, S. (2011). Constraints to Private Investment in the Poorest Developing Countries Review of the Literature. *London, UK: Nathan Associates London*.

Francis, D. C., Karalashvili, N., Maemir, H., & Rodriguez Meza, J. (2020). *Measuring Total Factor Productivity Using Enterprise Surveys. A Methodological Note*. Policy Research Working Paper; No. 9491. World Bank, Washington, DC.

Garvey, M., & Shirly, G. (2015). *Beyond Sun and Sea: International Strategy and Entrepreneurship in Caribbean Firms*. The University of West Indies.

IFPG (Innovation, Firm Performance and Gender). 2020. Innovation, Firm Performance and Gender, *Inter-American Development Bank*, 2020–2021.

Khadan, J. (2017). *Are Oil and Gas Smothering the Private Sector in Trinidad and Tobago?* Inter-American Development Bank.

Khadan, J. (2018, May). Estimating the Effects of Human Capital Constraints on Innovation in the Caribbean. *Economies, MDPI, 6*(2), 1–18.

Mahofa, G., Sundaram, A., & Edwards, L. (2016). Impact of Crime on Firm Entry: Evidence from South Africa. *Economic Research South Africa (ERSA) Working Paper*, *652*.

Montoya, E. (2016). *Violence and Economic Disruption: Firm-level Evidence from Mexico*. Working Paper. https://are.berkeley.edu/sites/default/files/job-candidates/paper/JMPMontoya.pdf.

Nicholson, L., & Lashley, J. (2016). *Understanding The Caribbean Enterprises: Insights from MSMEs and Family Owned Businesses*, Palgrave.

Presbitero, A., & Rabellotti, R. (2014). *Is Access to Credit a Constraint for Latin American Enterprises? An Empirical Analysis with Firm-Level Data*. Money & Finance Research Group Working Paper No. 101.

Ruprah, I., & Sierra, R. (2016). *Engine of Growth?: The Caribbean Private Sector Needs More Than an Oil Change*. Inter-American Development Bank.

Seker, M. (2009). *Importing, Exporting and Innovation in Developing Countries*. Policy Research Working Paper 5156. The World Bank.

CHAPTER 9

Social Development: Education

9.1 Introduction

Education is an essential determinant of a country's political and socioeconomic performance (Kimenyi, 2011). Education supports the accumulation of human capital, which is strongly associated with higher economic growth and boosting levels of social capital such as civic engagement, political engagement, voting, trust, and tolerance. A justification for large expenditures on education is social, not just economic, given the purported benefits an educated electorate brings to civil society.

This chapter first examines the resources dedicated to and the outcomes of the country's education system relative to those worldwide and in comparator country groups. Second, we discuss how TT's education system is organised and the differences in value-added of different school types. Finally, we examine differences in educational outcomes by gender and race.

9.2 International Comparison

It is well-established that higher spending on education is associated with better student outcomes (Jackson et al., 2016). The three often used measures of educational resources available in a country are government education spending as a proportion of GDP, per capita, and per pupil.

J. Khadan and I. Jit Ruprah, *Unraveling Race, Politics, and Gender in Trinidad and Tobago's Economic Development*,
https://doi.org/10.1007/978-3-031-54656-3_9

Given that the size of the school-aged population changes over time and differs between countries, looking at overall education spending (expenditure as a proportion of GDP or per capita GDP) can give misleading information about the resources available to students. One should analyse expenditures per pupil to assess whether spending changes have led to more resources per student over time. We find that total government expenditure on education as a share of GDP and per pupil is higher in TT than other comparator groups (Figs. 9.1 and 9.2).

We use two indicators to gauge the country's education system's relative performance. The first is the United Nations Development Program (UNDP) education index, which is calculated using the mean years of education and the expected years of schooling. We also use test scores to compare the performance of TT students with those in other countries. TT participated in two international assessments that facilitated such a comparison. TT participated, the only Caribbean country to do so, in the Progress in International Reading Literacy Study (PIRLS) in 2006, when

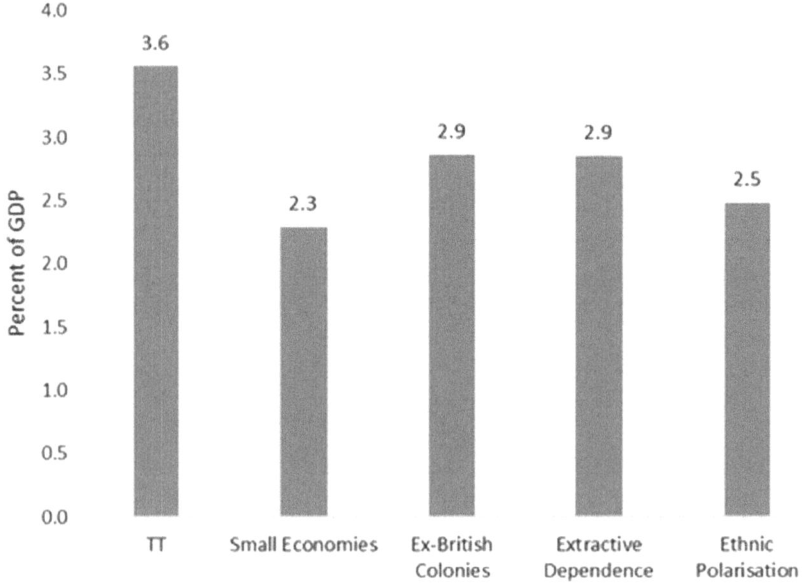

Fig. 9.1 Government expenditure on education (% of GDP) (*Source* World Development Indicators)

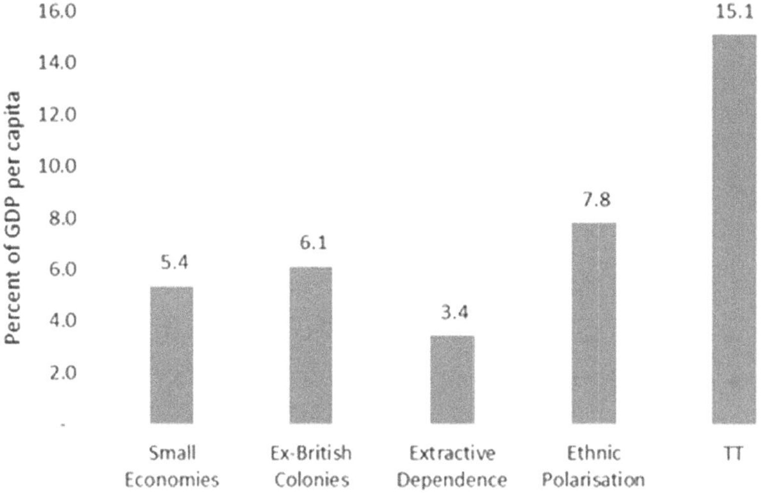

Fig. 9.2 Government expenditure per student, primary (% of GDP per capita, 2009) (*Source* World Development Indicators)

there were 36 participants; the latest was in 2011, with 53 participants. The PILRS is an international comparative study of the reading literacy of young students in grade 4. The second test began in 2009 when TT participated in the Program for International Student Assessment (PISA). The PISA is a triennial international survey that tests the skills and knowledge of 15-year-old students. These tests are designed to assess students' ability, at the end of compulsory education, to apply their knowledge to real-life situations and be prepared for full participation in society.

TT's Education Index has improved over time. In 2013, TT was ranked 64 out of 187 countries on the UNDP education index. TT was above the median and the world average. The country did better than all the comparator country groups (Fig. 9.3). However, patterns of both PISA and PIRLS tests show a different story (Figs. 9.4 and 9.5).

Regarding PIRLS, in 2006, TT was ranked 34 out of 39 nations; in 2011, TT's ranking fell to 36 of 53 countries. TT PIRSL scores were lower than those implied by its GDP per capita in both cases. TT has a sizable negative outlier status (countries with lower test score performance than their economic outcomes would suggest). A feature TT shares with other oil producers. In 2009, the year TT participated, the emphasis of

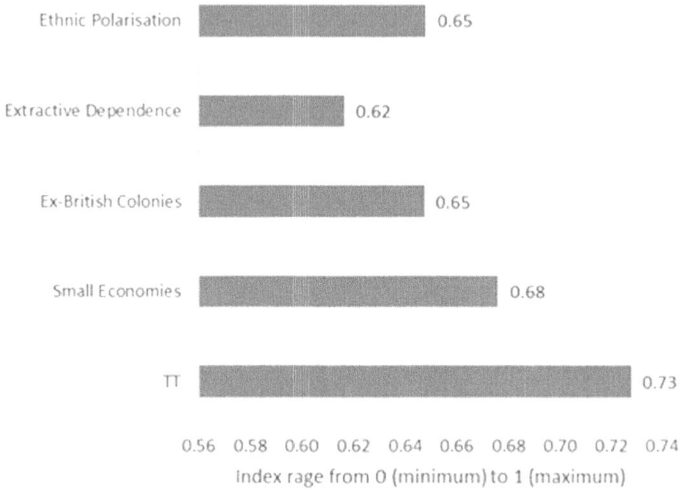

Fig. 9.3 Education Index (2019) (*Source* United Nations Development Programme)

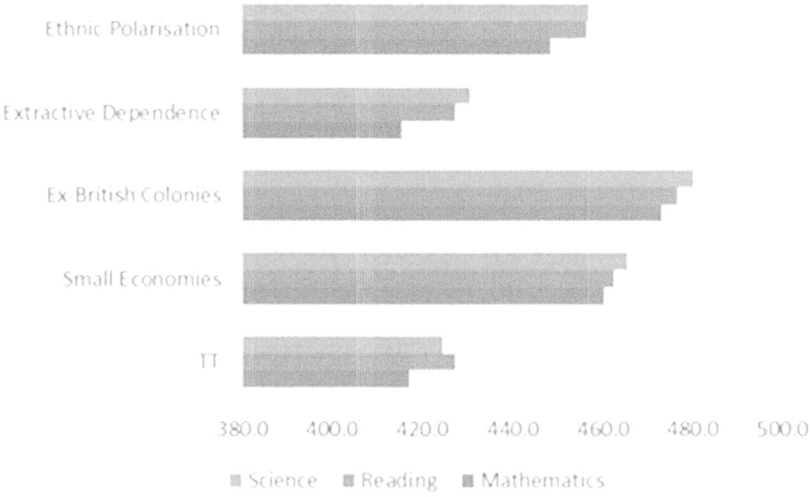

Fig. 9.4 Program for International Student Assessment (2015) (*Source* Organisation for Economic Co-operation and Development)

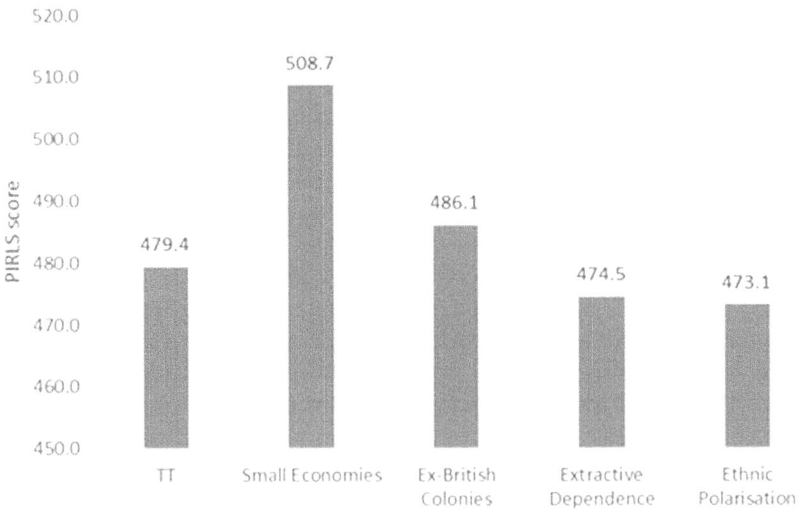

Fig. 9.5 Progress in International Reading Literacy Study (2016) (*Source* International Association for the Evaluation of Educational Achievement)

the PISA was on Mathematics. In the 2009 PISA results, TT scored below the average of other participating nations on the PISA tests and below that of other countries with similar per capita income levels.

Thus, while the mean years of education have improved over time, the quality of education outcomes leaves much to be desired. One possible explanation for the lower-than-expected performance on these international assessments is that spending levels in TT are below that of nations at similar levels of economic development. TT spends less on public education as a fraction of GDP than most high-income nations and less per student than most high-income nations.

9.3 Within Country: The Basics and Performance

The school system has three levels: pre-primary or early childhood care and education (ECCE), primary, and secondary (see Fig. 9.6). Children from 0 to 3 years attend nurseries at the pre-primary level, while those from 3 to 5 years attend kindergartens, pre-schools, or ECCE centres. Children between the ages of 5 and 11 participate in primary school. At the end of primary school, students can sit the Secondary Entrance Assessment (SEA) examination to obtain placement into a secondary school.[1] Students aged 11+ attend secondary school for five years before sitting for the Caribbean Secondary Education Certificate (CSEC). Depending on one's grades on the CSEC examination, students also have the option to remain in a secondary school for an additional two years to pursue the Caribbean Advanced Proficiency Examinations (CAPE), which is usually a prerequisite for acceptance into a university.

Primary and secondary schools fall into government, government-assisted, and private schools. The difference between government and government-assisted schools is that the former is fully funded and operated by the government, while private bodies, usually religious boards, manage the latter. Most primary schools are classified as government-assisted schools (62%), followed by government schools (26%) and private schools (12%). In contrast, at the secondary level, the majority are government schools (56%), followed by government-assisted schools (33%), with the remainder being private schools (Ministry of Education, Trinidad and Tobago).

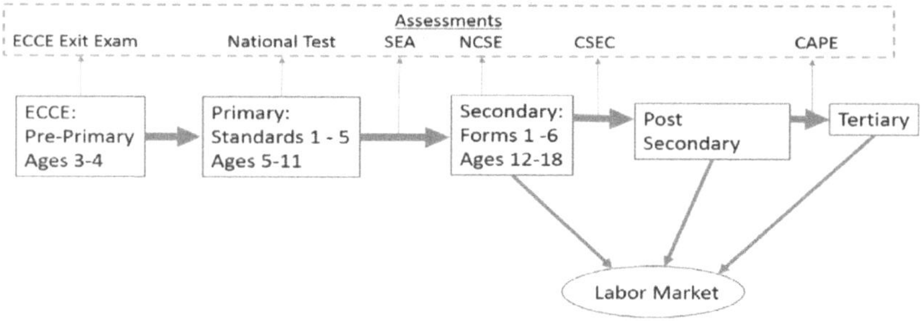

Fig. 9.6 Schematic outline of education levels and exams. *Note* ECCE stands for Early Childhood Care and Education, SEA is Secondary Entrance Assessment, NCSE is National Certificate of Secondary Education, CSEC is Caribbean Secondary Education Certificate and CAPE is Caribbean Advanced Proficiency Examination (*Source* Authors based on the Ministry of Education, TT)

[1] Students are allocated to secondary schools by the Ministry of Education based on the SEA scores and the school preferences submitted at SEA registration using a deferred acceptance mechanism.

There is free access to public education. Education is compulsory at the primary and secondary levels and free of cost for all citizens between 3 and 18 years of age. At primary and secondary schools, students can access other benefits such as subsidised meals, school bus service, and textbooks. Tertiary education is heavily subsidised through the Government Assistance for Tuition Expenses (GATE) programme. Students enrolled in undergraduate studies at accredited local and regional institutions receive free tuition, and post-graduate students can benefit from tuition coverage up to a maximum of 50% of their tuition fees. Also, university students can access soft loans through the Higher Education Loan Program (HELP) to fund other aspects of their tertiary education. In return, tertiary graduates are expected to commit to working in the country for an agreed period at the end of the programme. The government also provides a full government scholarship for citizens to undertake studies up to the PhD level at local and international tertiary-level institutions based on a student's academic achievements.

Facilitated by the policies mentioned above, access to education has markedly improved, as reflected in increasing enrolment rates at primary, secondary, and tertiary levels. TT achieved universal access to primary education in the 1960s and universal secondary education in 2000. Gross enrolment, which measures the ratio of total enrolment, regardless of age, to the age group population that officially corresponds to the primary school level, increased from 95% in 1990 to 106% in 2010. At the secondary school level, the gross enrolment rate was estimated to be 89% in 2011 (Beuermann et al., 2015). Moreover, gross enrolment rates at the tertiary level increased from 7% in 2001 to 65% in 2013, above the average for Latin America, the Caribbean, and other small countries (43% and 23%, respectively).[2]

A key issue is whether there is a difference in performance between these three types of schools. It is, and for both primary and secondary schools. We consider three high-stakes tests to assess student performance differences between government-assisted schools, government schools, and private schools. The value-added for primary school reflects gains in test scores between the National Test in standard one and the SEA at the end of primary school. Individuals from the 2009 SEA cohort are linked to those who took the NCSE assessment (Form 3) from 2010 through

[2] Ministry of Education and Skills Training the Future of Tertiary Education and Skills Training 2015–2025 Port of Spain: 2015.

2014 to construct value-added measures for secondary schools. Based on averages, private school students outperform government-assisted schools, and both outperform students from government schools'. A caveat, however, is needed. Regarding primary schools, the average value-added value at government schools was −3.47, that for assisted schools was 0.11, and that for private schools was 9.17. Regarding secondary schools, the average value-added of government schools was −0.05, while that for government-assisted schools was 0.167. The lowest value-added schools are more likely to be government schools, and the highest value-added schools are more likely to be government-assisted schools. However, many government schools have higher value-added than the average government-assisted school, and several government-assisted schools are worse than the average government schools (see Beuermann et al., 2015).

A further cautionary note is needed. Exam results on high-stakes tests are an underestimation of valuable outcomes for schools. Also important are non-academic outcomes, such as reducing criminality, teen motherhood, and increased labour market participation. These long-term non-academic outcomes are not necessarily correlated with exam results. Beuermann et al. (2023) study this issue and find that the choices of high-achieving students are more strongly related to schools' estimated impacts on high-stakes exams than non-academic outcomes.

In contrast, the options of low-achieving students are more strongly associated with the school's effects on non-academic outcomes than those on the high-stakes exam. School impacts on test scores are not necessarily the best measure of a school's impacts on longer-run outcomes. Noting this drawback, we next analyse test results by ethnic groups.

9.4 Educational Outcomes by Gender and Ethnicity

Within TT, marked differences exist between students of different religious groups (a proxy for ethnicity) in educational performance at the secondary level (Figs. 9.7, 9.8, 9.9 and 9.10). Information regarding the ethnic composition of students sitting the Caribbean Secondary Education Examination was unavailable. However, data on religion exists. TT's 2011 population census data shows that most ITTs were Hindu or Muslim, while ATTs predominately belonged to Christian-oriented religions. So, religion can be used as a reasonable proxy for ethnicity.

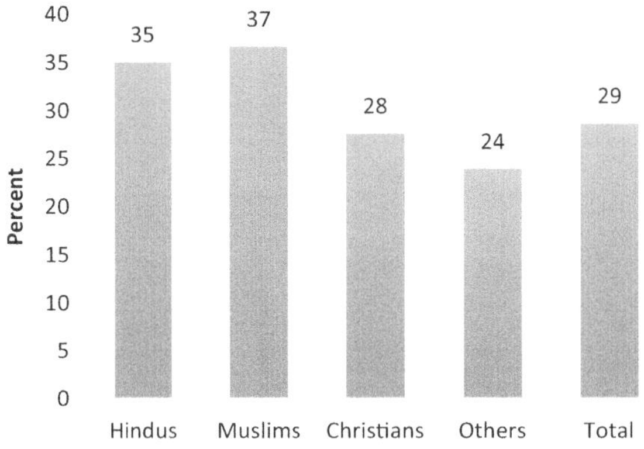

Fig. 9.7 CSEC certificate by religions, all cohorts (2000–2015). *Note* Christians refer to Pentecostals, Presbyterians, and Roman Catholics (*Source* Ministry of Education, Trinidad and Tobago)

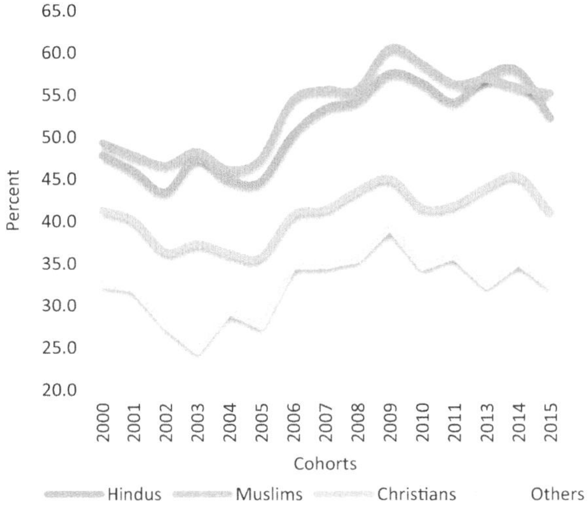

Fig. 9.8 Percentage obtaining CSEC certificates within each religious group. *Note* Christians refer to Pentecostals, Presbyterians, and Roman Catholics (*Source* Ministry of Education, Trinidad and Tobago)

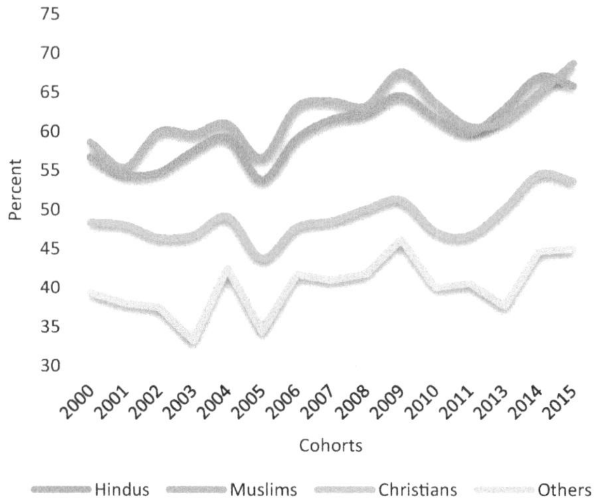

Fig. 9.9 Percentage obtaining a pass (Grades I–III) in Mathematics within each religious group. *Note* Christians refer to Pentecostals, Presbyterians, and Roman Catholics (*Source* Ministry of Education, Trinidad and Tobago)

From 2000 to 2015, only 29% of all students sitting for the CSEC examination obtained a CSEC certificate at the national level. Most students obtaining a certificate were Muslims and Hindus (i.e., mainly ITTs), followed by Christians (i.e., mainly ATTs) and other groups. Similarly, while all religious groups have shown improvements over time, the disparity in achievement by ethnic groups is becoming more prominent. The ratio of ITTs (Hindus and Muslims) to non-ITTs obtaining a passing grade was 1.1 in 2000 and 1.2 in 2015 for English, and 1.2 and 1.3 for mathematics for both years respectively.

A snapshot of the labour market differentiated by education levels (primary or less with or without training, incomplete secondary without or with training, complete secondary with or without training, and university degree) and by race, gender, and age reveals several clear patterns (see Figs. 9.11, 9.12, 9.13 and 9.14). Considering different age groups, the rise in the mean level of education reflects a decline in the primary with or without training, incomplete secondary with or without training, and an increase in all other higher categories.

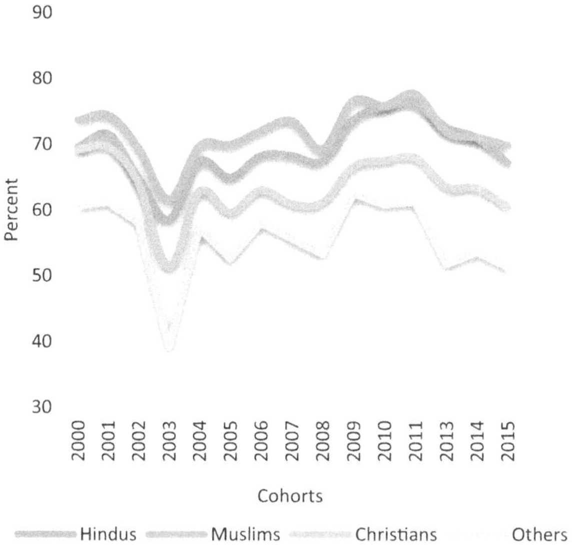

Fig. 9.10 Percentage receiving a pass (Grades I–III) in English within each religious group. *Note* Christians refer to Pentecostals, Presbyterians, and Roman Catholics (*Source* Ministry of Education, Trinidad and Tobago)

However, the national data masks differences by gender and race. More females across both ethnic groups have a university degree: 15% of ATT females have a university degree compared to 8% of ATT males, and 19% of ITT females have a university degree compared to 9% of ITT males. The disparity in educational outcomes is even more significant for the age group 25–34[3]: 20% of ATT females have a university degree compared to 7% of ATT males, 26% of ITT females, and 13% of ITT males. The only group where attaining a university degree has fallen is for ATT males. Significant gains were made between 55–75- and 25–34-year groups for secondary education with "Ordinary levels" and with or without training. The most significant increase was for ITT females (33%), followed by ATT females (27%), such that for the younger age group, they are over 50% for each category. Men have also improved, though at slower rates, and remain less than 50% for each category. The disparities across gender

[3] This age group would have benefited the most from the GATE programme.

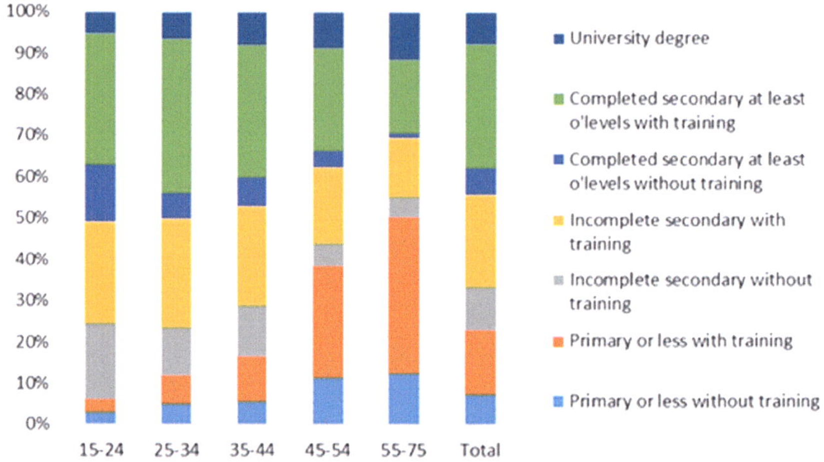

Fig. 9.11 Educational category by age (ATT males) (*Source* Authors based on the Continuous Sample Survey of Population (1999–2014), Trinidad and Tobago)

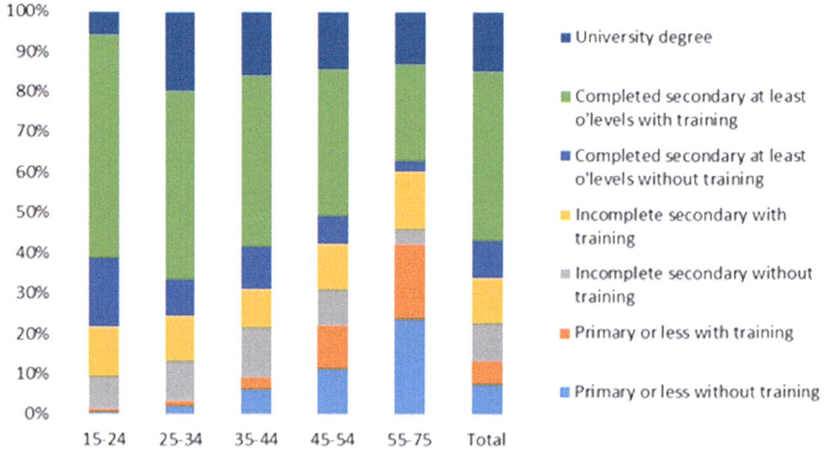

Fig. 9.12 Educational category by age (ATT females) (*Source* Authors based on the Continuous Sample Survey of Population (1999–2014), Trinidad and Tobago)

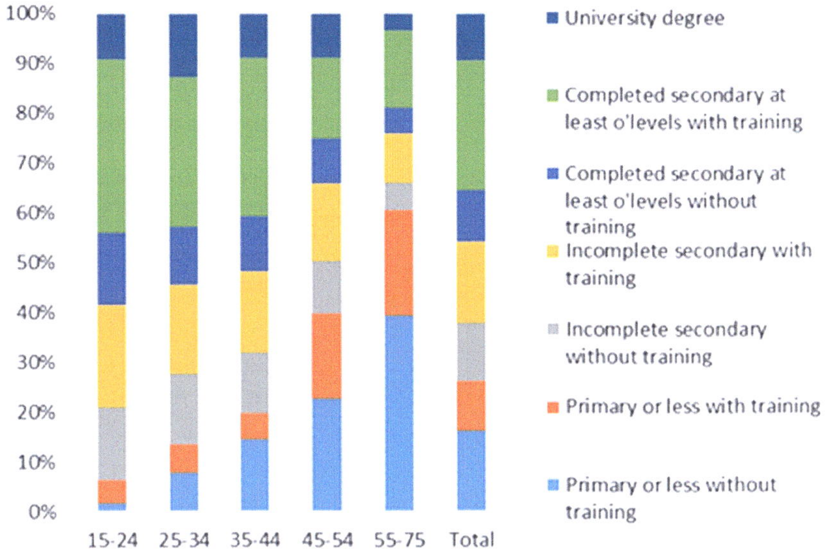

Fig. 9.13 Educational category by age (ITT males) (*Source* Authors based on the Continuous Sample Survey of Population (1999–2014), Trinidad and Tobago)

and race are becoming more prominent, with ITT males and females outperforming ATTs.

The gender imbalance will only increase in the future. Figure 9.15 shows that the number of female entrants in UWI has risen steadily. In 1981, women replaced men as the majority and, since then, have increasingly replaced men. The latter is also true in academic disciplines. Other than engineering, women increasingly dominate in all other fields (Fig. 9.16).

9.5 Conclusions

Education is an essential determinant of a country's political and socioeconomic development. Education supports economic growth and is strongly associated with boosting social capital. Therefore, educational expenditures are justified for both social and political reasons, not only economic.

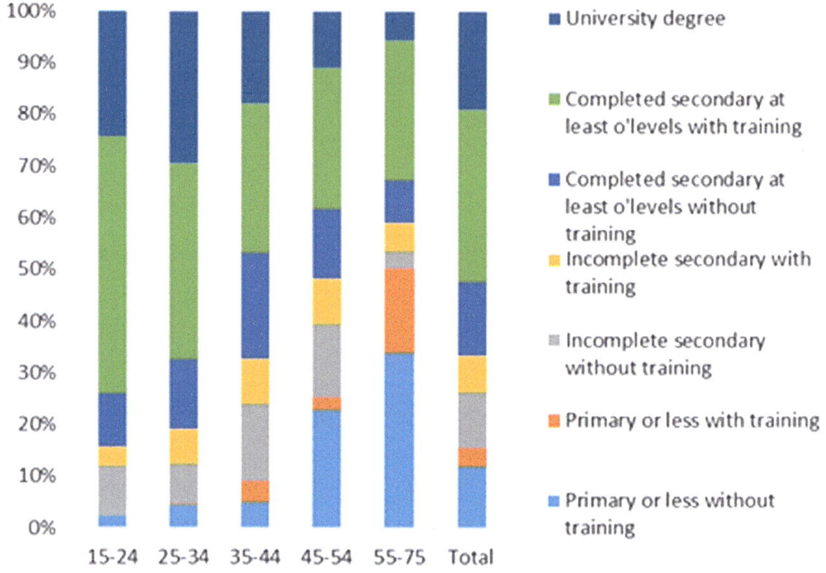

Fig. 9.14 Educational category by age (ITT females) (*Source* Authors based on the Continuous Sample Survey of Population (1999–2014), Trinidad and Tobago)

TT has more significant public education expenditure than comparator countries. There is free access to public education. Education is compulsory and free of cost for all citizens between the ages of 3 and 18. Students can access other benefits such as subsidised meals, school bus service, and textbooks. Tertiary education is also heavily subsidised through the Government Assistance for Tuition Expenses programme. The government also provides a full scholarship for citizens to undertake studies up to the PhD level at local and international tertiary-level institutions.

Over time, TT's Education Index (the mean years of education and the expected years of schooling) has improved. The country did better than all the comparator country groups. However, there is room to improve the education quality. Regarding Progress in International Reading Literacy, TT's ranking has fallen to 36 of 53 countries. TT has a sizable negative outlier status (countries with lower test score performance than their economic outcomes would suggest). TT scored below the average of other participating nations on the Programme for International Student

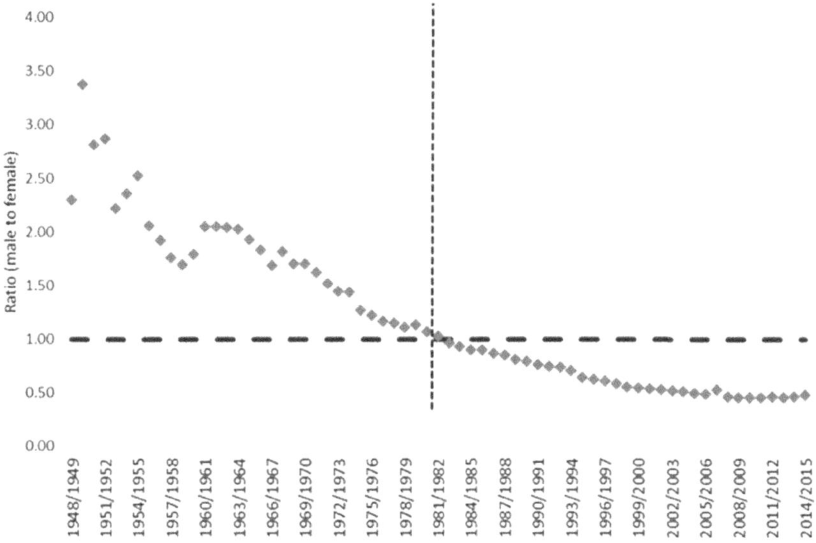

Fig. 9.15 Enrolment in the University of West Indies by gender. (*Source* University of the West Indies enrolment reports [various years])

Assessment tests (for mathematics) and below that of other countries with similar per capita income levels.

Educational outcomes differ according to the type of school attended, gender, and student's race. Based on averages of national tests, private school students outperform government-assisted schools, which outperform government schools' students. There are marked differences in educational performance between religions (a proxy for ethnicity). Of all the students sitting for the CSEC examination, most students obtaining a certificate were Muslims and Hindus (i.e., mainly ITTs), followed by Christians (i.e., mainly ATTs) and other groups. Although students' performance in all religious groups has improved over time, this disparity in achievement by religious groups is becoming more evident.

There is also an increasing gender imbalance. TT female entrants in the UWI have steadily increased over time. In 1981, women replaced men as the majority and, since then, have increasingly replaced men. Other than in engineering, women increasingly dominate in all fields. More females across both ethnic groups have a degree at the university level.

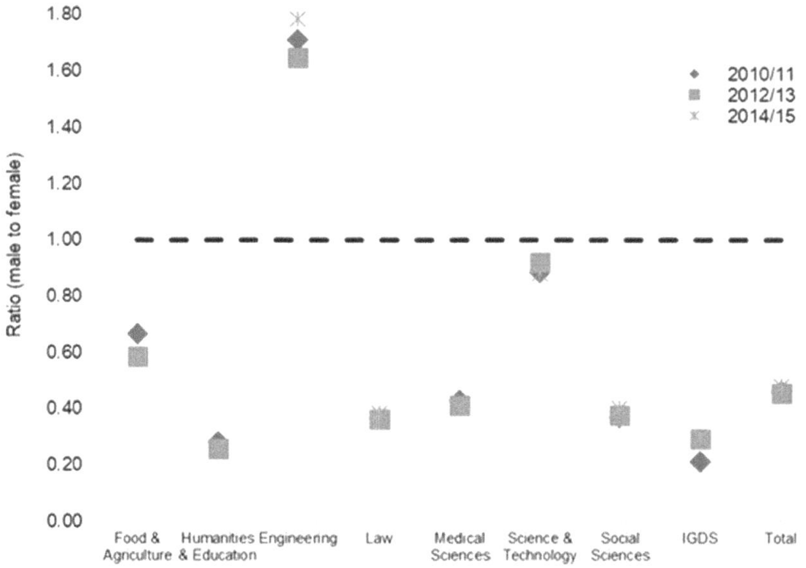

Fig. 9.16 Entrants by discipline and gender. *Note* IGDS = Institute for Gender and Development Studies (*Source* University of the West Indies enrolment reports [various years])

The disparities in educational outcomes across gender and ethnic groups are becoming more apparent, with ITT males and females outperforming ATTs.

References

Beuermann, D. W., Jackson, C. K., Navarro-Sola, L., & Pardo, F. (2023). What is a good school, and can parents tell? Evidence on the multidimensionality of school output. *The Review of Economic Studies, 90*(1), 65–101.

Beuermann, D. W., Jackson, C. K., Sierra, R. (2015). *Privately managed public secondary schools and academic achievement in Trinidad and Tobago: Evidence from rule-based student assignments*. IDB Working Paper Series, No. IDBWP-637, Inter-American Development Bank (IDB), Washington, DC. http://hdl.handle.net/11319/7308

Jackson, K. C. K., Johnson, R. C., & Persico, C. (2016). The effects of school spending on educational and economic outcomes: Evidence from school finance reforms. *The Quarterly Journal of Economics, 131*(1), 157–218.

Kimenyi, M. S. (2011). Contribution of higher education to economic development: A survey of international evidence. *Journal of African Economies, 20*(3), 14–49.

Ministry of Education, Trinidad and Tobago. *List of schools in Trinidad and Tobago.* https://moe.gov.tt/school-listing-2/

CHAPTER 10

Social Development: Health

10.1 Why Is Health Important for Development?

Empirical studies have shown a positive correlation between income levels and life expectancy, an indicator often used to judge a country's overall health. The hypothesis is that countries with high income levels will have greater access to inputs that improve health outcomes, for example, food, sanitation, medical care, and education. Macroeconomic research has shown that improved health extends the economically active years of workers, boosting labour force participation and productivity. Health also affects life satisfaction and happiness. For example, Angner et al. (2009, 2013) directly measured the degree to which disease disrupts daily functioning, and they found a one-point increase in the freedom-from-debility score was associated with a three per cent reduction in the odds of reported unhappiness.

In this chapter, we first review the basics of TT's health care system, i.e., financing and provision. We then review health outcomes.

This chapter draws on "TT: Health Sector" IDB, unprocessed, by Ian Ho-A-Shu.

J. Khadan and I. Jit Ruprah, *Unraveling Race, Politics, and Gender in Trinidad and Tobago's Economic Development*,
https://doi.org/10.1007/978-3-031-54656-3_10

Both sections highlight differences in international comparison (with comparator country groups) and within TT by gender and race.

10.2 Health Care System: The Basics

TT operates under a two-tier healthcare system. Namely, both private healthcare and public healthcare facilities exist. However, private insurance covers only 2.8% of total health expenditures and is a luxury. Insurance coverage by race is 36% for ATT, 30% for ITTs, and 7% for MTTs. Private health insurance is available from insurers such as Guardian Life of the Caribbean, a subsidiary of the Guardian Holdings Group, and Sagicor Life, a part of Sagicor Financial Corporation. These providers generally cover about 90% of medical expenses. The private healthcare system is relatively small, and patients are expected to prove their ability to pay before treatment can be received—even in emergencies. It comprises a handful of private facilities to treat common health problems. At the same time, they appear to offer better care than their public counterparts; private facilities in the country can handle serious illnesses, injuries, and long-term care.

The public-sector health services were financed through general tax revenue. However, as of 2015, the system is funded by a "pay as you earn" income tax surcharge from the state coffers. Through the Chronic Disease Assistance Programme (CDAP), drugs are distributed for free to patients with certain conditions, including diabetes, asthma, cardiac diseases, arthritis, glaucoma, depression, high blood pressure, an enlarged prostate, epilepsy, hypercholesterolemia, Parkinson's disease, and thyroid diseases.

As a per cent of GDP, total health expenditures have risen but remain below comparator country groups (Fig. 10.1). Of total health expenditure, about half is private expenditure, a figure much higher than that of all comparator country groups (Fig. 10.2). Of the latter, only a small percentage is from pre-paid plans (Fig. 10.3). Thus, most health expenditure is out-of-pocket (Fig. 10.4). Further, current public spending to address NCDs is concentrated on treatment rather than prevention (Theodore, 2011). Given the significant growth in health spending due to NCDs, TT has yet to adopt more cost-effective interventions, such as an integrated NCD prevention and control model (Jamison et al., 2006).

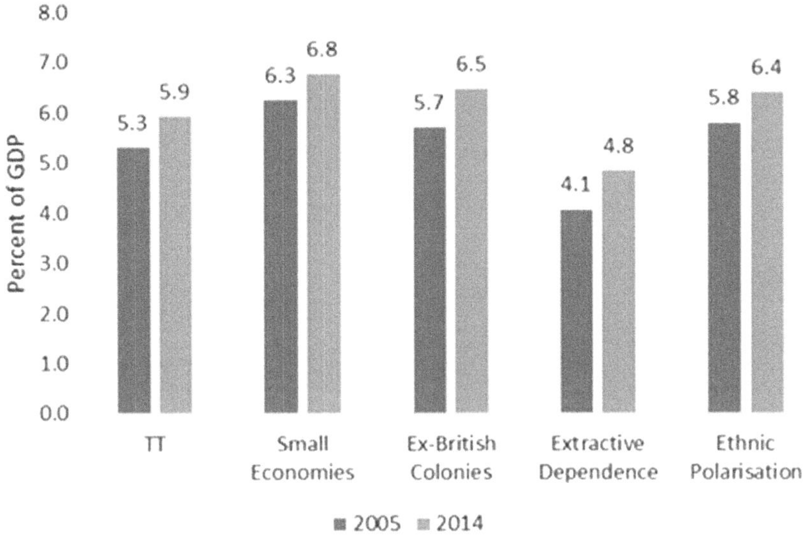

Fig. 10.1 Total health expenditure (as a per cent of GDP) (*Source* World Health Organization, http://apps.who.int/nha/database/DataExplorerRegime.aspx)

The public healthcare system in TT is based on universal access, and citizens can access free healthcare at public facilities where health insurance is not required. In addition, medicines are free at all public health facilities. Since 2005, CDAP has provided citizens with free prescription drugs and other pharmaceutical items for the treatment of the following chronic conditions: diabetes, asthma, cardiac diseases, arthritis, glaucoma, mental depression, high blood pressure, benign prostatic hyperplasia, epilepsy, Parkinson's disease, and thyroid diseases. These drugs are dispensed through over 250 pharmacies (public and private) across the country.

Public healthcare services are delivered through five Regional Health Authorities (RHAs), which manage a network of 11 hospitals, six District Health Facilities (DHFs), and 97 health centres. While the Ministry of Health does not directly manage health facilities, it plays a key role in ensuring they are adequately administered by setting policies, goals, and targets for the RHAs. The Ministry focuses on policy development,

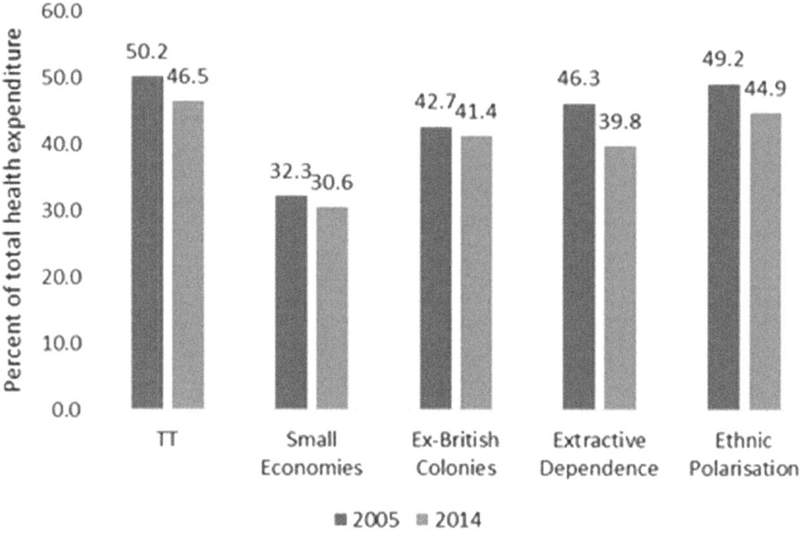

Fig. 10.2 Private health expenditure (as a per cent of total health expenditure) (*Source* World Health Organization, http://apps.who.int/nha/database/DataExplorerRegime.aspx)

planning, monitoring and evaluation, and regulation. The Ministry also allocates resources to the RHAs to finance their operations.

Despite investments in expanding primary care centres in TT, improving their quality remains unsatisfactory. Challenges with the primary care system include long waiting times for some services due mainly to shortages of primary care physicians and nurses. A 2013 Human Resources for Health assessment study showed a 55% vacancy in the positions opened for physicians and a 34% vacancy for nurses (PAHO/MoH, 2013). The study indicated that the main reasons for these shortages are (i) weak recruitment due to non-competitive remuneration, (ii) poor retention due to the absence of a structured career path and financial and non-financial incentives, and a lack of continued educational opportunities. In addition to nurses leaving the public sector for the private sector, the situation is compounded by overseas recruiters who target nurses, resulting in "a nursing brain drain" (OAS, 2009). Several short-term remedial efforts have been made recently: recruiting doctors from India and Nigeria, recruiting nurses from the Philippines, and utilising

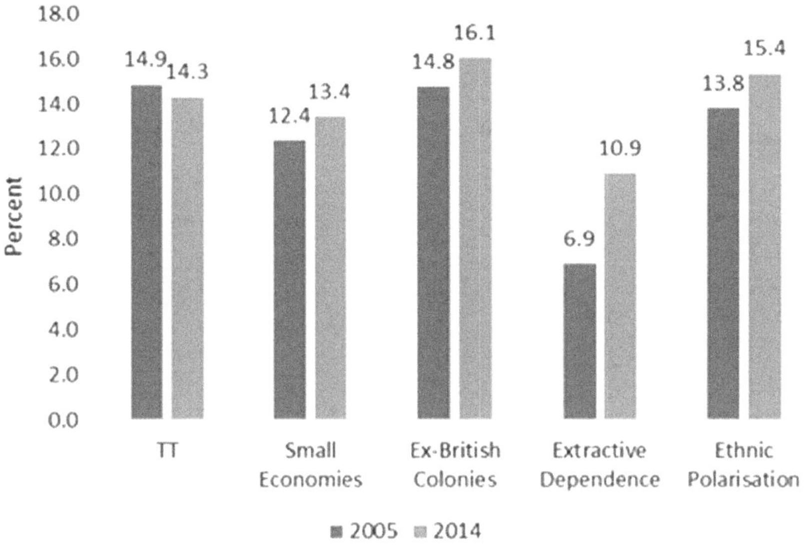

Fig. 10.3 Private pre-paid plans as a cent of private expenditure on health (*Source* World Health Organization, http://apps.who.int/nha/database/DataExplorerRegime.aspx)

United Nations Volunteer doctors. However, the shortage persists. International evidence shows that competitive remuneration and professional development opportunities are critical elements to hiring, retaining, and boosting the productivity of nurses and physicians (IDB, 2013). The dearth of healthcare professionals in public facilities results from migration to foreign healthcare markets and drifting away from the public-sector healthcare system to more profitable private practices.

Discussions on the shortage of healthcare professionals, particularly in public facilities, have sometimes taken on worrying racial overtones.[1] Hence, the health staff's racial profile is interesting (Fig. 10.5). Doctors are mainly ITTs (45%), followed by MTTs (28%), with only 23% being ATTs. Nurses are mainly ATTs (60%), followed evenly by ITTs and MTTs with 20% each. If this represents a trend of decreasing diversity, this bodes ill for health. Diversity in healthcare benefits both healthcare professionals

[1] 'See: PoS General, an African hospital' | TT News Blog.

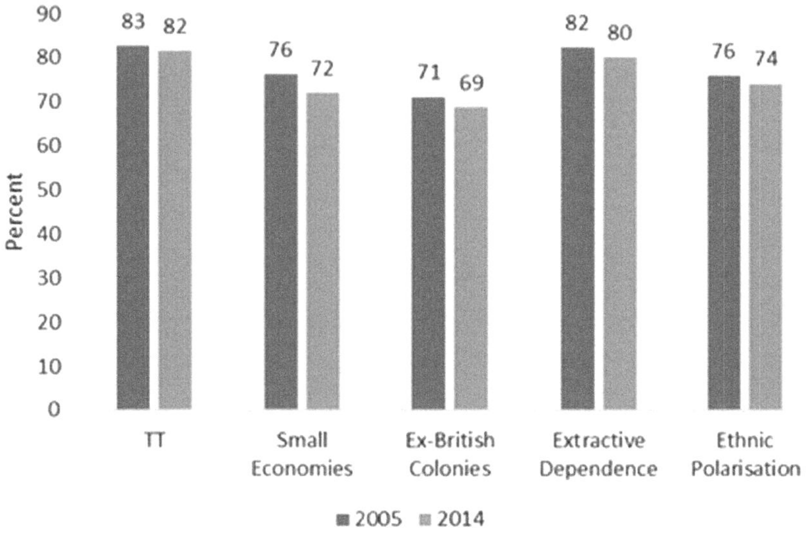

Fig. 10.4 Out-of-pocket expenditure as per cent of private expenditure on health (*Source* World Health Organization, http://apps.who.int/nha/database/DataExplorerRegime.aspx)

and patients. There are several advantages to having a diversity of health-care professionals. There is evidence that students who have trained at diverse schools are more comfortable treating patients from ethnic backgrounds other than their own. A more diverse healthcare professional will better understand colleagues' and patients' belief systems. Patients of colour may be more likely to seek care. A Stanford University study found that Black male patients treated by Black doctors were more likely to seek preventative services, compared to being treated by non-black doctors (Alsan et al., 2019).

This disparity may reflect the racial profile of higher education (Fig. 10.6). The UWI St. Augustine Campus graduates roughly 250 medical students annually, and graduates are automatically qualified to work anywhere in CARICOM countries. The medical school has 20 graduate programmes, including obstetrics, gynaecology, family medicine, emergency medicine, psychiatry, and anaesthetics. Other institutions in the country also train medical staff: the College of Science Technology

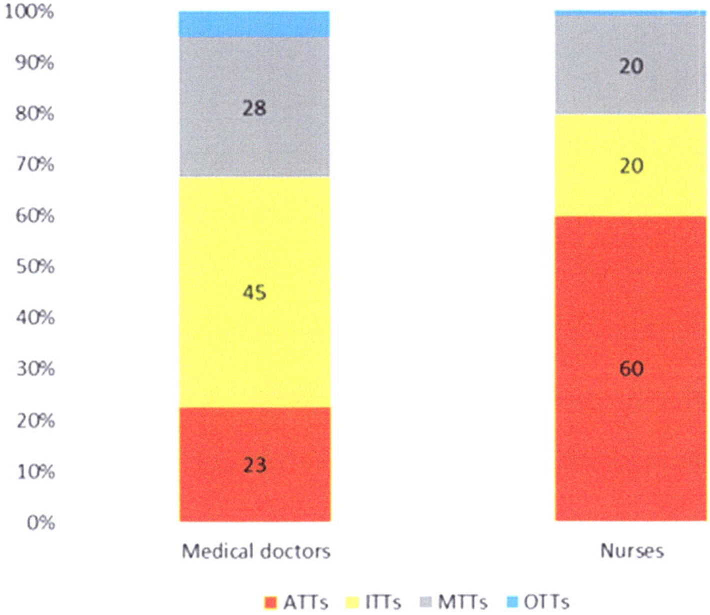

Fig. 10.5 The racial profile of health care professionals (*Source* Authors based on Survey of Living Conditions for Trinidad and Tobago [2005 and 2014])

and Applied Arts of TT, for example, runs an Academy of Nursing and Allied Health.

At the UWI's Faculty of Medical Sciences, the student body is dominated by TT nationals. One of the main reasons cited for this pattern is that TT students in their final year of school tend to outperform their peers in the Caribbean Advanced Proficiency Examination (CAPE). Administered by the Caribbean Examinations Council, the CAPE is the rough equivalent of A-Level exams in the UK. Each year, there are around 500 applicants for the faculty's medical programme with relevant results from CAPE (or, in some cases, first degrees from a university). Students are selected based on their grades and their involvement in co-curricular activities.

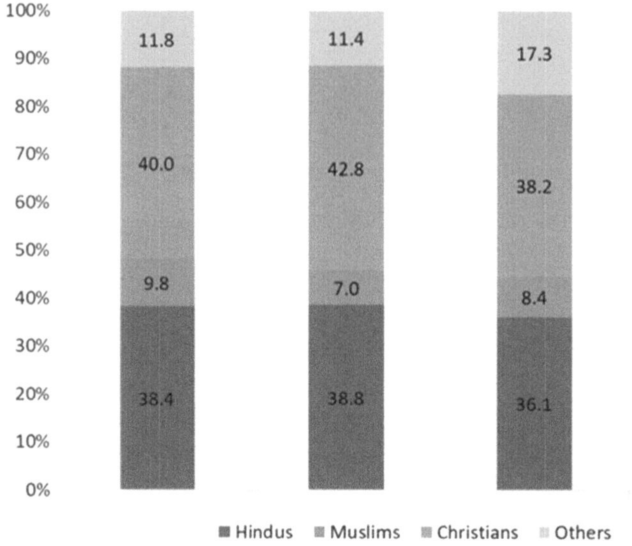

Fig. 10.6 Religious profile of students achieving qualifications to enter medical faculty (*Source* Authors based on the Ministry of Education, Trinidad and Tobago data)

10.3 How Well Does TT Do in Terms of Health Outcomes?

Figure 10.5 shows the positive relationship between per capita income and life expectancy for 248 countries in 2013. TT is below the average, meaning the country is underperforming relative to its income level (Fig. 10.7). On the other hand, the evidence on the relationship between government expenditure on health and growth is mixed. The health-led growth hypothesis treats health as capital and argues that investments in health can increase economic growth (Mushkin, 1962). However, there is no consensus on the direction of causality between health spending and economic development (Devlin & Hansen, 2001; Hartwig, 2010).

TT's performance relative to comparator country groups reveals the following. The country is on par with other small economies regarding life expectancy and has a lower mortality rate than other small economies. The life expectancy rate gradually improved from 68 years in 2001 to 70 years in 2013, marginally below the global average of 71 years. The infant

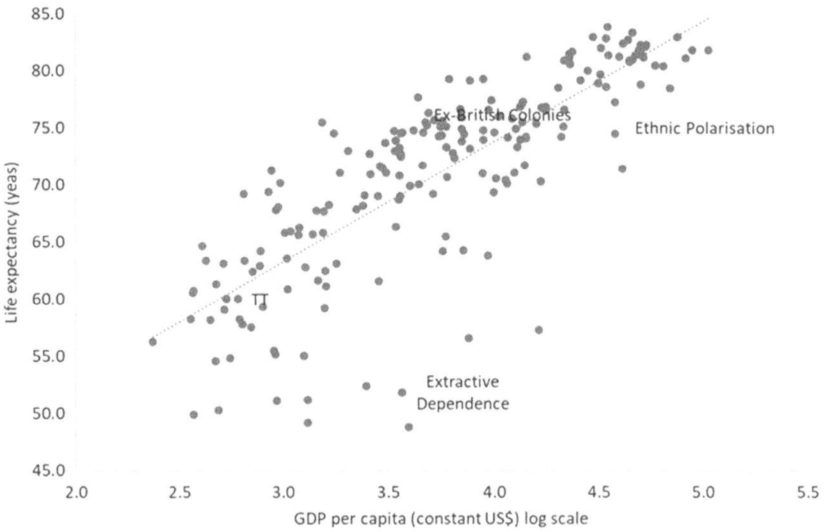

Fig. 10.7 Income and life expectancy: average 2011–2015 (*Source* World Bank Development Indicators)

mortality rate (per 1000 live births) has also dropped from 24 in 2001 to 19 in 2012 and is well below the global average (32 per 1000 live births) and the rest of small economies (21 per 1000 live births). However, TT lags in the number of physicians per 1000 people, nurses and midwives per 1000 people, and hospital beds per 1000 people (see Table 10.1).

The burden of diseases is high. TT had an annual loss of 542,600 disability-adjusted life years (DALYs) in 2015. The DALY is a metric that quantifies the burden of morbidity and mortality, i.e., it measures how many years of healthy life are lost. DALY can measure the gap between current health status and an ideal health situation where the entire population lives to an advanced age, free of disease and disability. The DALYs for a disease or health condition are calculated as the sum of the Years of Life Lost (YLL) due to premature mortality in the population and the Years Lost due to Disability (YLD) for people living with the health condition or its consequences. With 1.3 million people, TT loses 510 thousand DALYs (Table 10.2), higher than small economies but lower than other comparator country groups. The primary health problem is non-communicable diseases. Losses from communicable diseases are less

Table 10.1 Selected health indicators for TT and comparators (2015)

	TT	*Small economies*	*Ex-British colonies*	*Extractive dependence*	*Ethnic polarisation*
Hospital beds (per 1000 people)	2.1	3.7	2.4	3.0	2.4
Mortality rate, infant (per 1000 live births)	21.0	23.8	210.9	36.6	33.4
Nurses and midwives (per 1000 people)	3.6	4.1	3.6	3.5	2.9
Physicians (per 1000 people)	1.2	1.5	1.1	1.5	1.2

Source World Bank Development Indicators

than those of comparator country groups. Non-communicable conditions in TT DALYs are higher than in all other country groups. Unintentional injuries are lower than in comparator countries, but intentional injuries are more elevated.

Table 10.2 Estimated disability-adjusted life year (DALY) ('000) by cause (2015)

		TT	*Small economies*	*Ex-British colonies*	*Extractive dependence*	*Ethnic polarisation*
All Causes		510	405	21,189	14,752	11,973
Communicable, maternal, perinatal and nutritional conditions		12.9	35.1	40.3	30.4	25.8
A	Infectious and parasitic diseases	36.1	51.7	44.1	42.8	42.1
B	Respiratory Infectious	18.4	15.5	16.5	17.9	19.0
C	Maternal conditions	1.1	1.9	2.4	2.3	2.1
D	Neonatal conditions	30.3	23.2	28.3	27.4	27.3
E	Nutritional deficiencies	14.2	7.7	8.8	9.6	9.5

(continued)

(continued)

		TT	*Small economies*	*Ex-British colonies*	*Extractive dependence*	*Ethnic polarisation*
Noncommunicable diseases		75.8	54.7	48.9	58.9	63.1
A	Malignant neoplasms	13.7	15.2	12.0	16.1	17.1
B	Other neoplasms	0.7	1.5	1.2	1.2	1.3
C	Diabetes mellitus	16.6	6.8	4.7	4.1	4.4
D	Endocrine, blood, immune disorders	1.9	1.8	2.4	1.8	1.7
E	Mental and substance use disorders	9.0	11.1	11.1	10.8	11.3
F	Neurological conditions	4.5	5.0	5.8	5.5	5.2
G	Sense organ diseases	3.0	3.4	4.5	4.0	3.7
H	Cardiovascular diseases	26.2	26.9	23.4	26.5	27.5
I	Respiratory diseases	4.7	5.1	8.7	7.3	6.5
J	Digestive diseases	4.3	5.2	7.0	5.3	4.6
K	Genitourinary diseases	3.7	3.7	4.3	3.8	3.6
L	Skin diseases	1.3	1.5	1.5	1.4	1.5
M	Musculoskeletal diseases	6.0	6.4	7.0	7.0	6.8
N	Congenital anomalies	3.0	4.8	5.2	3.9	3.6
O	Oral conditions	1.1	1.2	1.0	1.1	1.1
P	Sudden infant death syndrome	0.1	0.2	0.2	0.1	0.1
Injuries		11.3	10.2	10.8	10.6	11.1
A	Unintentional injuries	40.7	69.2	75.2	75.4	72.5
B	Intentional injuries	59.3	30.8	24.8	24.6	27.5

Source World Health Organization (2014)

Within TT, there are marked differences between ethnic groups by type of illness (Fig. 10.8). ITTs suffer more than ATTs from obesity (43%), heart disease (60%), and diabetes (54%). However, they have the same proportions of cancer and mental disorders.

Over the past decade, the country's demographic profile has undergone a transition marked by a declining fertility rate (1.63 in 2020 from 5.3 in 1960), a decrease in the under-15 population, an increase in the over-60 age group, and an increase in the dependency ratio. TT is also experiencing an epidemiological transition, with a decline in communicable diseases and a rise in chronic non-communicable diseases.

NCDs claim more lives than infectious diseases. Data indicates that six common NCDs—heart disease, hypertension, cerebrovascular disease (collectively referred to as cardiovascular disease, CVD), diabetes, cancer, and chronic respiratory illness—account for 60% of all deaths in TT (Fig. 10.9; Healthy Caribbean Coalition, 2014), with NCDs overall accounting for 78% of all deaths (World Health Organization, 2011). TT's CVD mortality rate is one of the highest in the Americas (289/100,000), and it should be noted that TT has high rates of premature deaths due to NCDs compared to other countries in the region

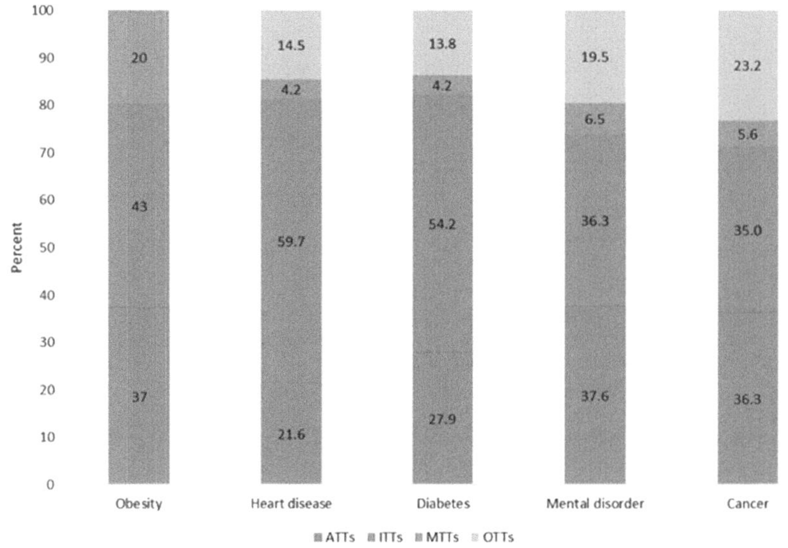

Fig. 10.8 Incidence of illness by race (*Source* Authors based on TT Census 2010 and Survey of Living Conditions 2005)

(Gawryszewski & Souza, 2014). A significant portion of the NCD burden occurs among the working-age population, causing estimated annual losses of 383,254 DALYs. Also, recognising that gender and life-course determinants affect NCD prevalence, exposure to risk, access to health services, and health outcomes, it is essential to note that men in TT have the highest overall NCD death rates (World Health Organization, 2014). Men in TT are less prone to seek preventative health services. Therefore, they are less likely to be screened or treated for NCDs, suggesting the need to explore gender-based barriers to NCD prevention and management uptake (Babwah et al., 2006). Childhood obesity is also a growing concern in TT. A study conducted by the Caribbean Food and Nutrition Institute (CFNI) from 2009 to 2010 found that 23% of primary school children and 25% of secondary school children in TT were overweight or obese (CFNI, 2010). This number significantly increased in 2011, when 8.5% of children were overweight or obese (Teelucksingh, 2013).[2]

Modifiable behavioural risk factors are an unhealthy diet, harmful alcohol use, tobacco use, and physical inactivity, which cause most NCDs. In contrast, intermediate-risk factors include elevated blood pressure, raised blood glucose levels, and obesity (WHO, 2010). In TT, 59% of females and 52% of males are overweight or obese.[3] Harmful alcohol use, another key risk factor, is reported by 40% of the population, while 21% of adults and 10% of children report tobacco use (TT MoH/PAHO, 2012). Forty-six (46%) adults are physically inactive, and over 75% of children and adolescents have a sedentary lifestyle.

In comparison, 70% of children drink one or more high-sugar beverages daily. Statistics also indicate that females have a higher prevalence of risk factors (physical inactivity and obesity), except for smoking, with a

[2] Another study conducted by the University of the West Indies (UWI) and the Diabetes Education Research and Prevention Institute (DERPI) in 2009 demonstrated a significant increase in the number of children aged 5 to 17, who were diagnosed with Type II diabetes or identified to be at high risk of developing diabetes. The elevated childhood obesity rates are worrisome, not only because they are a precursor to adult obesity, but also because they have both immediate and long-term effects on health and well-being, including a heightened risk for cardiovascular diseases, cancers, and diabetes. There is also significant concern that NCDs will not only cause even deeper poverty among the poor and vulnerable resulting with worse health outcomes, but people would likely develop NCDs at younger ages, and possibly suffer longer with preventable complications.

[3] This is particularly high given that the average obesity rates among adults in the Caribbean is between 35% to 40%.

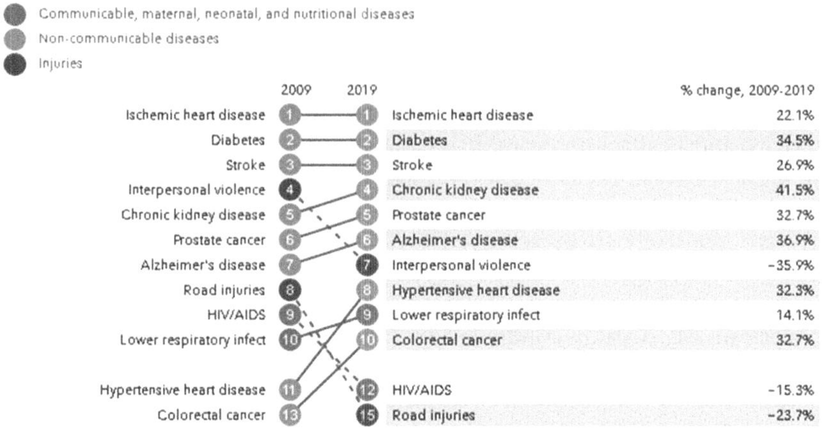

Fig. 10.9 Leading causes of years of life lost to Premature Death (*Source* The Institute for Health Metrics and Evaluation)

tobacco prevalence of 34% for males compared to 9% for females. This gap is considerably reduced among the youth: 20% of boys and 16% of girls 13 to 15 years old engage in smoking (Ministry of Health, 2011). Figure 10.10 illustrates the leading risk factors in TT.[4]

Risk factors differ between races (Fig. 10.11). ITTs have a greater risk than other ethnic groups as they smoke and drink alcohol more than others. Alcohol is a contributing factor in over 200 diseases (CDC, 2022). Among these are non-communicable diseases, including cirrhosis, cancer, high blood pressure, heart disease and stroke, osteoporosis, and pancreas inflammation. Further, it is often the underlying cause of broken bones from trips and falls, injuries from fights, suicide, and driving accidents. Estimates show smoking increases the risks for coronary heart disease by 2 to 4 times, stroke by 2 to 4 times[1], men developing lung cancer by 25 times, and women developing lung cancer by 25.7 times[1]. Smoking causes diminished overall health, increased absenteeism from work, and increased healthcare utilisation and cost.[5] Many of which are more prevalent among ITTs.

[4] Institute for Health Metrics and Evaluation.

[5] See Smoking and Tobacco USE, CDC, Health Effects of Cigarette Smoking | CDC.

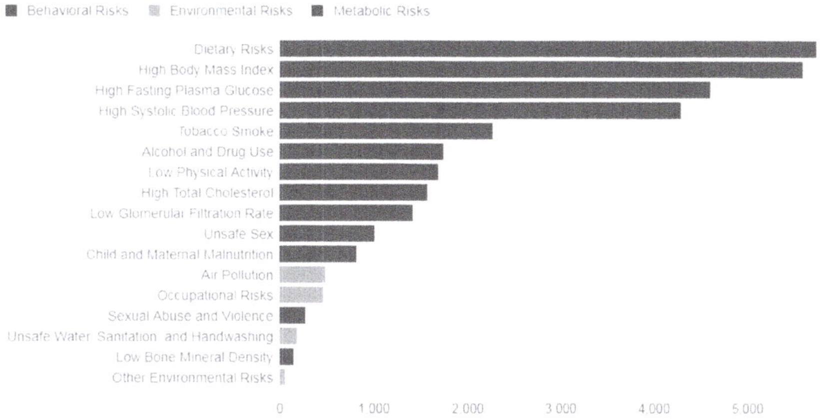

Fig. 10.10 Leading risk factors of NCDs (*Source* World Health Organization, 2016)

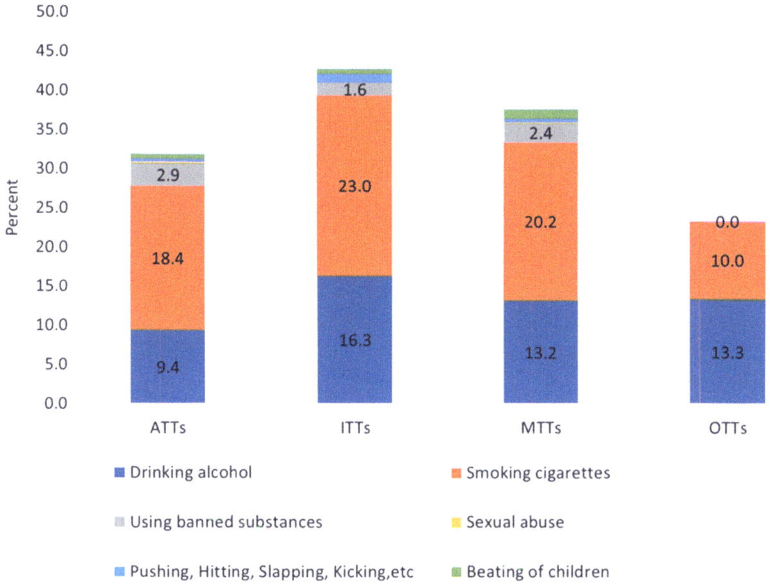

Fig. 10.11 Risk factors by race (*Source* Authors based on Survey of Living Conditions for Trinidad and Tobago [2005 and 2014))

Physical activity has been shown to have significant health benefits. As Warburton et al. (2006) conclude: "We confirm that there is irrefutable evidence of the effectiveness of regular physical activity in the primary and secondary prevention of several chronic diseases (e.g., cardiovascular disease, diabetes, cancer, hypertension, obesity, depression, and osteoporosis) and premature death". Physical activity has gained more relevance with the increase in chronic non-communicable diseases in TT. However, in TT, non-pro-health behaviour is similar across ethnic groups, where about 70% do not engage in physical activity (Fig. 10.12). Lack of physical activity is more damaging to ITTs as they engage in more risk factors.

Productivity loss for health-related reasons presents a severe economic burden for employers. Productivity loss involves three types of failures. The first type of loss is absence from work, i.e., absenteeism. The second type of loss is work limitation while at work, known as presenteeism. The third type of loss is the complete inability to be employed. Unfortunately, available data does not allow such a detailed analysis. However, TT's Continuous Population Sample Survey asks respondents if they did not look for work due to a disability or illness. There is a marked difference by race in the percentage of those who did not work due to disability or illness (Fig. 10.13). Of the total, 51% were ITTs, followed by 30% ATTs. ITTs contribute more to the loss of productivity.

10.4 Conclusions

Over the past decade, TT's demographic profile has undergone a transition marked by a declining fertility rate, a decrease in the under-15 population, an increase in the over-60 age group, and an increase in the dependency ratio. At the same time, the country is experiencing an epidemiological transition, with a decline in communicable diseases and a rise in chronic non-communicable diseases. The latter now claims more lives than infectious diseases. The DALY, a metric that measures how many years of healthy life are lost, reveals that TT loses 510 thousand DALYs annually (higher than small economies but lower than other comparator country groups). Communicable diseases are less than other comparator country groups. Non-communicable conditions in TT's DALYs are higher than in all other country groups.

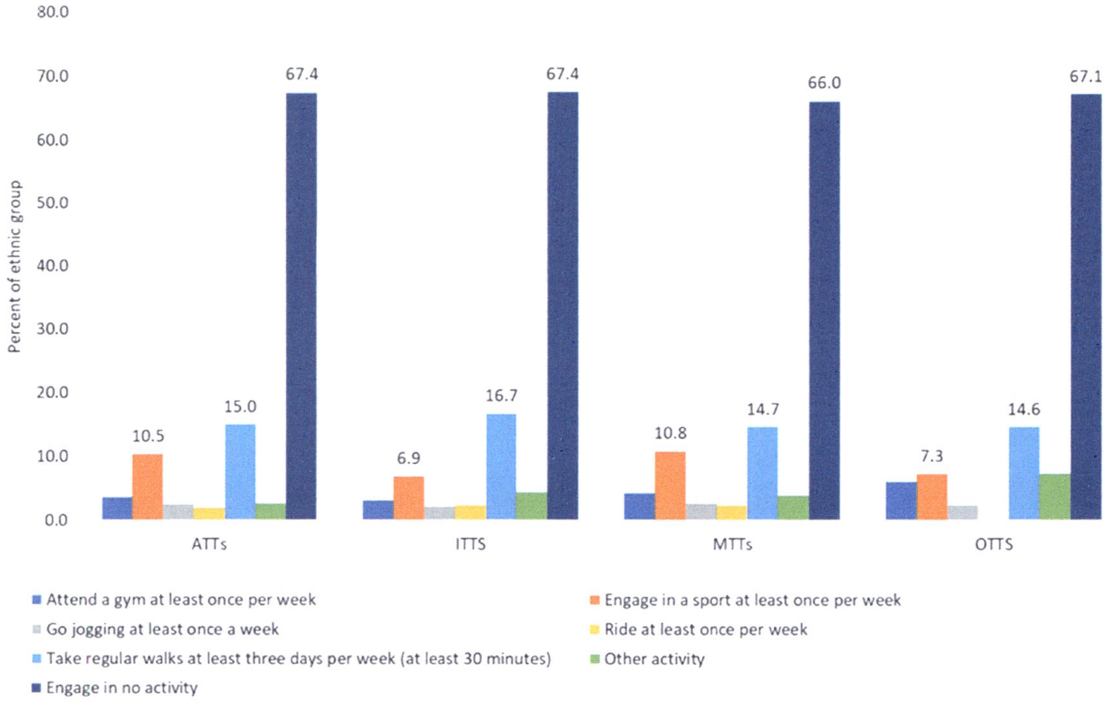

Fig. 10.12 Pro-health behaviour (*Source* Authors based on Survey of Living Conditions for Trinidad and Tobago [2005 and 2014])

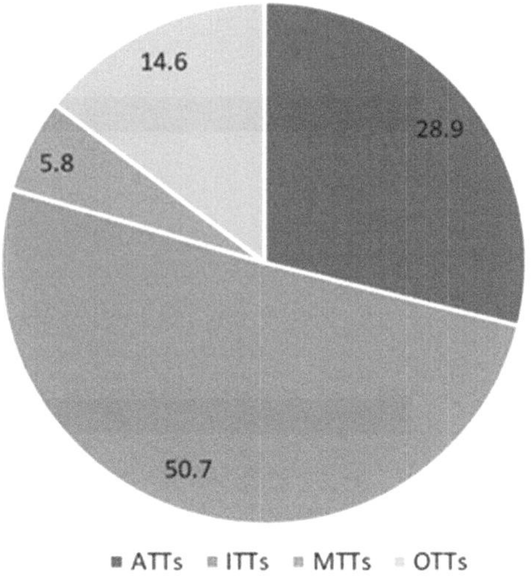

Fig. 10.13 Did not look for work due to disability or illness by race (*Source* Authors based on Continuous Sample Survey of Population for Trinidad and Tobago)

Most NCDs are caused by modifiable behavioural risk factors, including an unhealthy diet, harmful alcohol use, tobacco use, and physical inactivity. Within TT, there are marked differences between the races with respect to illness types. Incidence of obesity, heart disease, and diabetes are higher among ITTs than ATTs. But they have the same proportions of mental disorders and cancer. Risk factors differ between races. ITTs have a greater risk than other ethnic groups as they smoke and drink alcohol more than others. Physical activity has gained more relevance with the increase in chronic non-communicable diseases in TT. However, in TT, the lack of pro-health behaviour is similar across ethnic groups, where about 70% do not engage in physical activity. Lack of physical activity is more damaging to ITTs as they engage in more risk factors. There is a marked difference by race in the percentage of those who did not work due to disability or illness, with ITTs being affected the most.

References

Alsan, M., Garrick, O., & Graziani, G. (2019). Does diversity matter for health? Experimental evidence from Oakland. *American Economic Review, 109*(12), 4071–4111.

Angner, E., Ghandhi, J., Williams Purvis, K., Amante, D., & Allison, J. (2013). Daily functioning, health status, and happiness in older adults. *Journal of Happiness Studies, 14*, 1563–1574.

Angner, E., Ray, M. N., Saag, K. G., & Allison, J. J. (2009). Health and happiness among older adults: A community-based study. *Journal of Health Psychology, 14*(4), 503–512.

Babwah, F., Baksh, S., Blake, L., Cupid-Thuesday, J., Hosein, I., Sookhai, A., Poon-King, C., & Hutchinson, G. (2006). The role of gender in compliance and attendance at an outpatient clinic for type 2 diabetes mellitus in Trinidad. *Revista Panamericana De Salud Pública, 19*(2), 79–84.

Centers for Disease Control and Prevention (CDC). (2022). *Alcohol and public health: Alcohol-related disease impact (ARDI)*. Annual average for United States 2015–2019 alcohol-attributable deaths due to excessive alcohol use, all ages [Internet]. CDC. [cited 2022 April 26]. https://nccd.cdc.gov/DPH_ARDI/Default/Default.aspx

CFNI (Caribbean Food and Nutrition, 2010). *Interim report on the findings of the evaluation of school meal options in TT*. Pan American Health Organization. World Health Organization. Regional Office for the Americas.

Devlin, N., & Hansen, P. (2001). Health care spending and economic output: Granger causality. *Applied Economics Letters, 8*(8), 561–564. https://doi.org/10.1080/13504850010017357

Gawryszewski, V. P., & Souza, M. D. F. M. D. (2014). Mortality due to cardiovascular diseases in the Americas by region, 2000–2009. *Sao Paulo Medical Journal, 132*, 105–110.

Hartwig, J. (2010, March). Is health capital formation good for long-term economic growth?—Panel Granger-causality evidence for OECD countries. *Journal of Macroeconomics, 32*(1), 314–325.

Healthy Caribbean Coalition. (2014). *Responses to NCDs in the Caribbean Community*.

IDB. (2013). *Health and nutrition sector framework document (GN-2735-3)*.

Jamison, D. T., Breman, J. G., Measham, A. R., Alleyne, G., Claeson, M., Evans, D. B., Jha, P., Mills, A., & Musgrove, P. (Eds.). (2006). *Disease control priorities in developing countries*. The International Bank for Reconstruction and Development/The World Bank; Oxford University Press.

Ministry of Health. (2011). *Global youth tobacco survey*. Trinidad and Tobago.

Mushkin, S. J. (1962). Health as an investment. *Journal of Political Economy, 70*(5), 129–157. http://www.jstor.org/stable/1829109

OAS. (2009). *Brain drain and the impact on development*. Special Committee on Migration.

PAHO/MoH. (2013). *2nd assessment of TT's progress towards the achievement of the goals for HRH*.

Teelucksingh, S. (2013). *A case for universal screening for diabetes in pregnancy in TT*. UWI.

Theodore, K. (2011). Chronic non-communicable diseases and the economy. IDB non processed.

TT MoH/PAHO. (2012). *TT chronic non-communicable diseases risk factor survey [STEPS]*.

Warburton, D. E., Nicol, C. W., & Bredin, S. S. (2006, March 14). Health benefits of physical activity: The evidence. *CMAJ, 174*(6), 801–810. https://doi.org/10.1503/cmaj.051351.PMID:16534088;PMCID:PMC1402378

World Health Organization (WHO). (2010). *Package of essential NCD interventions for primary health care in low-resource settings*.

World Health Organization (WHO). (2011). *Non communicable diseases country profiles 2011*.

World Health Organization (WHO). (2014). *WHO Global Infobase*. www.who.int/infobase

World Health Organization (WHO). (2016). *World health statistics 2016: Monitoring health for the Sustainable Development Goals (SDGs)*. World Health Organization.

CHAPTER 11

Social Development: Crime

11.1 Introduction

Crime and violence can impact a country's economic and social development. Many studies have found that crime hurts economic activity (Bannon and Collier, 2003; Gaibulloev & Sandler, 2008; Peri, 2004). There is considerable evidence of the adverse impact of crime on the growth of the informal economy, women, and the private sector (Camacho & Rodriguez, 2013; Dell, 2015). Crime also endangers economic diversification, as some industries, especially non-extractive industries (Ashby & Ramos, 2013; Driffield et al., 2013; Maher, 2015a, 2015b; Mihalache-O'Keef & Vashchilko, 2010), are less resilient to the effects of crime (Rios, 2015). For the private sector, research shows that crime and violence are associated with declines in revenue, unemployment, and hours worked, reduced profitability, and lower private investment (Montoya, 2016).

This chapter first reviews the facts of crime and violence in TT, followed by the cost of crime. Finally, we present citizens' evaluation of the justice system through their revealed level of vertical trust.[1]

[1] This chapter draws on work by Heather Sutton on crime in the Caribbean. See Sutton and Ruprah (2017).

J. Khadan and I. Jit Ruprah, *Unraveling Race, Politics, and Gender in Trinidad and Tobago's Economic Development*,
https://doi.org/10.1007/978-3-031-54656-3_11

11.2 Crime and Violence: The Facts

Intentional homicides represent a good indication of a country's overall level of security or lack thereof. Information on homicides also lends itself to global comparability since it is produced by national authorities worldwide. The country has the sixth-highest intentional homicide rate globally (in 2015), Fig. 11.1. TT's homicide rate, of 31 per 1000,000, is significantly higher than in other small countries, ethnically diverse societies, other ex-British colonies, and other extractive-dependent economies.

Drugs, gangs, and guns are critical factors influencing safety and security. TT's location between the cocaine suppliers of South America and cocaine consumers in North America and Europe makes it a desirable target for trafficking illicit drugs and firearms. The symbiotic relationship between the illegal drug trade and guns has contributed to the emergence of gun-related violence in many communities in TT. Firearm-related homicides increased significantly during the last two decades, from less than one-third before 2000 to 78.6% of all murders in 2013. In other

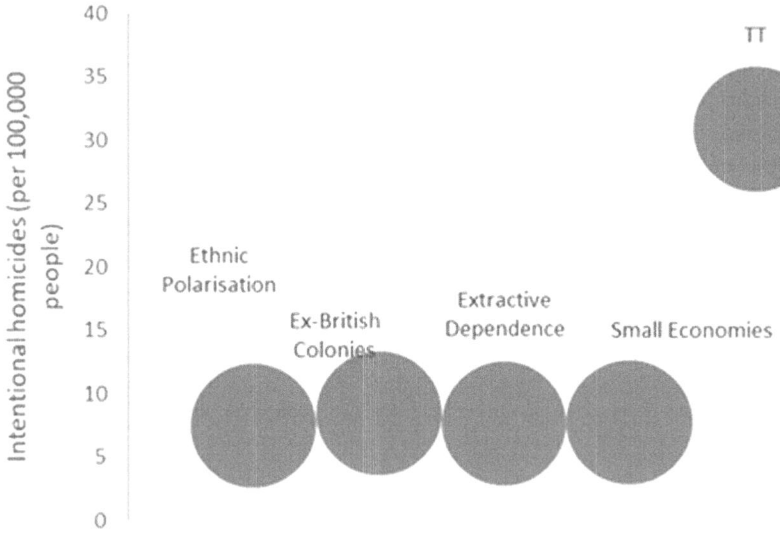

Fig. 11.1 Intentional homicides (per 100,000 people; 2015) (*Source* World bank indicators [2017])

crimes, such as woundings and shootings, 50.9% were committed with firearms from 2001 to 2013 (Seepersad, 2016).

The emergence of criminal gangs, also partly fuelled by the drug trade, and illegal firearm trade has contributed to the country's high homicide rate: during 2000–2013, TT recorded 4743 murders, of which 30.5% were reported to be gang-related. The last two decades saw a proliferation of criminal gangs in some parts of the country. In a 2006 survey of gangs in TT, Katz and Choate (2006) found roughly 95 gangs with approximately 1269 gang members involved in some form of criminal activity. The number of criminal gangs increased to 102 by 2012. Katz and Choate (2006) noted that these gangs were mainly concentrated in Port of Spain, Western, and Northern Police Divisions, predominantly persons of African descent (83%), male-dominated, and most gangs (74%) started after 2000. Most gangs are reported to frequent alcohol, drugs, drug sales, robbery and firearm activity, and two-thirds are involved in fights with rival groups.

In 2014, 68% of individuals in TT identified security as the country's most critical problem. The historical trends clearly show that detection rates of most violent crimes have been declining while the incidence of violent crimes has been increasing. There were 84 reported murders in 1990, with a detection rate of 69, compared to 407 in 2013, with a detection rate of 13. Woundings and shootings also significantly increased from 391 to 542, while the detection rate fell from 61 to 24%. A similar trend was observed for larcenies and larcenies of motor vehicles and robberies. However, detection rates for burglaries and break-ins remained relatively high and were associated with a rapid decline in incidences.

Violence in the home, particularly against women, is multifaceted and endemic worldwide. Violence against women takes many forms, including intimate partner violence (physical, sexual, and emotional abuse), sexual violence, trafficking of girls and women, forced and early marriages, honour killings, and female genital mutilation (World Health Organization, 1997). The victims often have to contend with long-lasting physical discomfort and psychological distress, which may lead to undesirable behavioural changes such as alcohol consumption, addiction to tobacco or other illegal drugs, and may even attempt to commit suicide (Andrews & Brown, 1988; Koss, 1990; Plichta, 1992; Rawlins, 2000).

In TT, inter-partner violence is the main form of domestic violence. Seepersad and Williams (2012) noted that the most frequently reported forms of domestic violence in TT are murder, assault by beating, wounding, threats, and breach of a protection order. Frequently reported sexual violence includes rape, indecent assault against girls, sexual intercourse primarily against girls under 14 and between 14 and 16, and incest. Assaults and beatings during the period 2000 to 2013 accounted for more than half of the 19,078 incidences of domestic violence that were reported, followed by threats (28%), breach of a protection order (5.6%), and wounding and sexual abuse accounted for 3.5 and 3.3%, respectively. Moreover, 8.4% of all homicides committed from 1995 to 2013 were due to domestic violence. The majority of victims of domestic violence from 2009 to 2012 were almost evenly distributed between ATTs (41.2%) and ITTs (40.3%), with the MTTs accounting for 13.3% of the victims' Fig. 11.2). Most (56%) of the victims were concentrated mainly within 20–40 years of age.

Child abuse and violence in schools are prevalent in TT. The World Health Organization identifies five subtypes of child abuse: physical abuse, sexual abuse, neglect and negligent treatment, emotional abuse, and

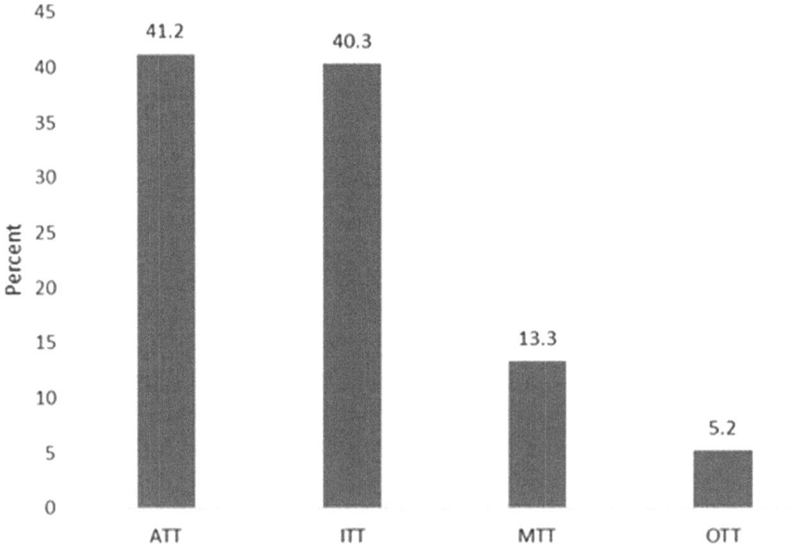

Fig. 11.2 Ethnicity of victims of domestic violence (*Source* Crime and problem analysis branch of the Trinidad and Tobago police service. *Note* Data represents the average for the period [2009–2012])

exploitation. In TT, most of the literature has focused on child sexual abuse and, to a lesser extent, corporal punishment and other types of abuse.[2] Of the 6950 reported offences against children during 2000–2013, the majority were sexual offences of various types: 24.2% were sex with a female between the ages of 14 and 16, 21.9% were sex with a female under 14, 17.2% were rape, and 16.7% grievous sexual assault.

The use of violence to discipline children is widespread. The data shows that physical punishment and psychological aggression are the two most prevalent forms of child abuse, with roughly 77% of children aged 2–14 affected. Similar incidences were reported for males and females. As revealed by survey data, there are also high levels of peer violence in schools. The 2011 Global School-based Health Survey found that 33% of youths reported being physically attacked at school, 36% were involved in physical fights, and 40% were seriously injured (World Health Organization, 2011). At the primary school level, Seepersad's (2014) evidence revealed that other students hit 78% of children, 65% were kicked, 40% were relieved of their money, and an object hurt 55%.

Within TT, there are marked differences between religious groups (a proxy for ethnicity) regarding the perpetrators of crime (Fig. 11.3).[3] Most persons committing most crimes were Christians (i.e., mainly ATTs). A similar pattern, Fig. 11.4, is also observed for persons arrested for crimes at age 16.

There is evidence of relatively high social tolerance of partner and family violence in TT. Most respondents (61%) in the 2012 LAPOP survey accepted that physical punishment is necessary when children are disobedient.[4] This high level of acceptance of beating one's child is consistent across the three major ethnic groups, with the highest being ATTs (79%), followed by MTTs (77%) and ITTs (69%; Fig. 11.5). Similarly, 49% of respondents in the LAPOP survey accept physical

[2] The International Labour Organization (ILO) has examined child labour and other issues that can be considered to amount to child abuse.

[3] Information regarding the ethnic composition of the perpetrators of crime in T&T was not available for this study, however, data on religion is available. From census data, we observe that the majority of ITT's were either Hindus or Muslims, while ATT's belonged to predominantly Christians oriented religions and faiths. So, on average, religion can be used as a reasonable proxy for ethnicity.

[4] Acceptance is calculated using LAPOP data for 2012 by adding those that approved and those that don't approve but understand.

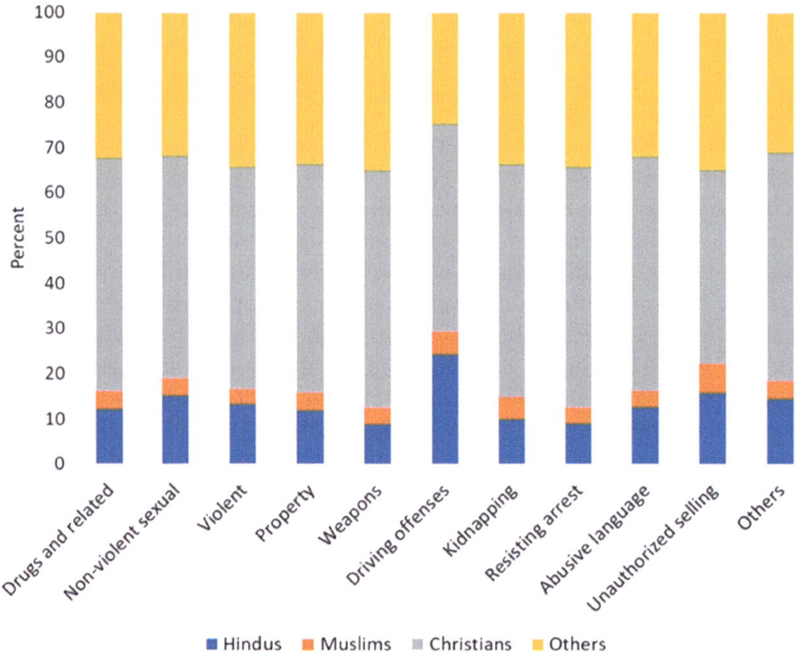

Fig. 11.3 Crimes committed by religion of the perpetrator (*Source* Authors based on Beuermann et al. (2016) compilation of Trinidad and Tobago criminal offence administrative data)

punishment for wives when they are unfaithful. While the level of acceptance is high among ATTs and ITTs, the MTTs have a high disapproval rate: 68% of MTTs do not approve or understand (Fig. 11.6). The tolerance of violence outside of the home is also high. Seventy-three per cent of the survey respondents think it is justified to kill someone who kills another person or rape someone's child: the approval of such a response is high among ATTs and ITTs, but lower for MTTs (Fig. 11.7). Police torture is primarily accepted, especially among ITTs: 74% of the survey respondents believe it is justified to torture criminals to get information about very dangerous organised crime, with 83% of ITTs surveyed reporting acceptance of this behaviour from the police (Fig. 11.8). The acceptance of violence is also evident in schools. One reaction to this

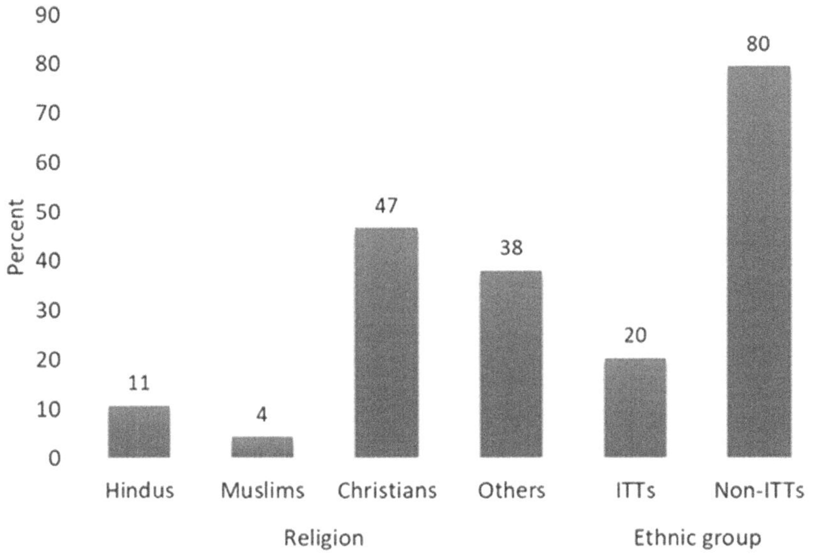

Fig. 11.4 Arrested at age 16 by religion and race

hostile school environment has been a call by some for corporal punishment to be reintroduced formally in schools, which further illustrates the societal tendency to respond to violence with more violence. Similar calls have been made to continue hanging murderers to address the country's crime problem.

11.3 Impact of Crime on the Economy

The high levels of crime and violence described above affect the well-being of citizens and take a heavy toll on the economy. Crime and violence have high costs to the government as it requires significant investments of public resources in law enforcement, prisons, and courts. Businesses also incur losses from theft and vandalism, losses in sales, and spending additional resources on hiring security. There are also personal costs to the victims of crime and violence. While no studies have attempted to apply the accounting approach to estimate the cost of crime in TT, it is possible to estimate specific costs (by type of crime and sector).

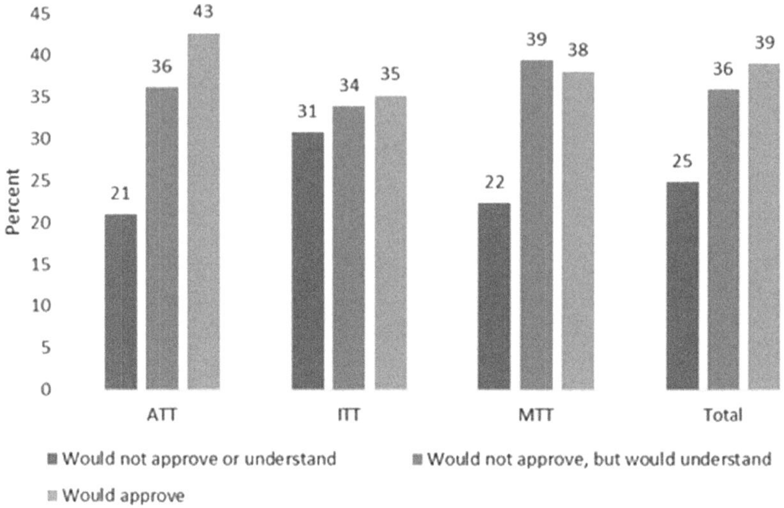

Fig. 11.5 Beating children when they are disobedient (*Source* LAPOP [2012])

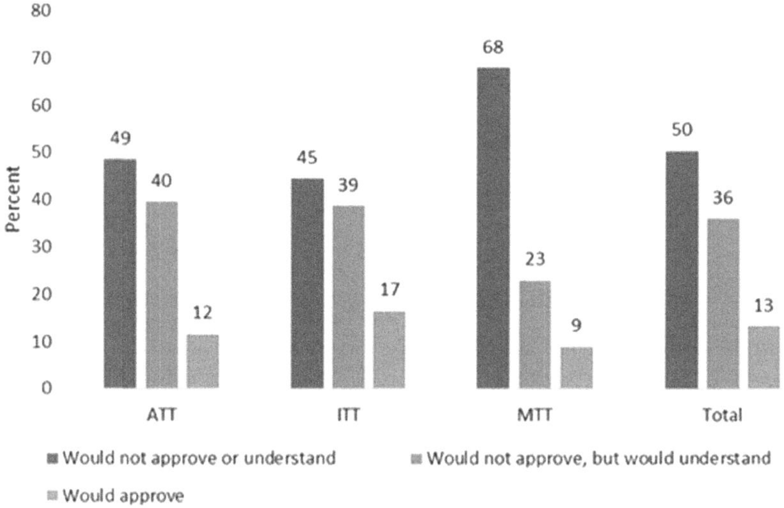

Fig. 11.6 Beating wife when unfaithful (*Source* LAPOP [2012])

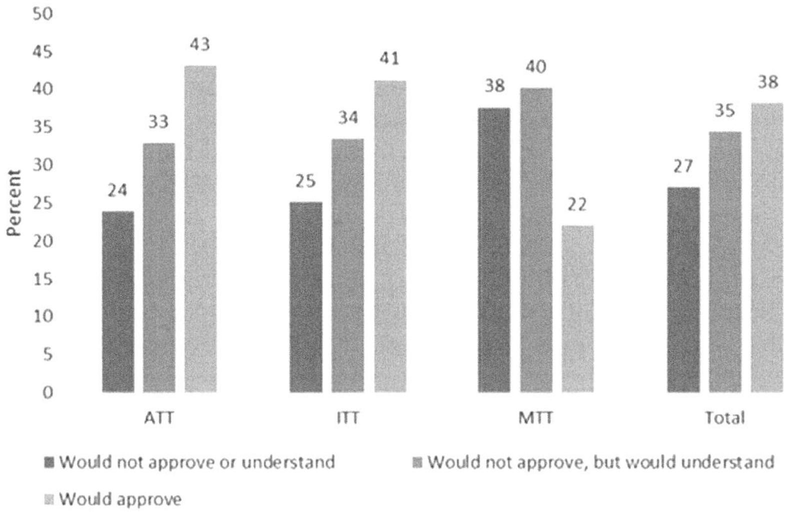

Fig. 11.7 Approval of killing of criminals (*Source* LAPOP [2012])

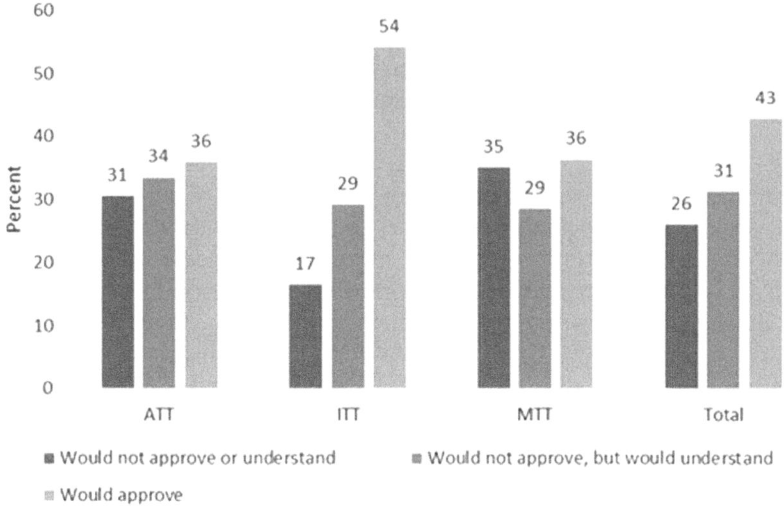

Fig. 11.8 Approval of police torture (*Source* LAPOP [2012])

We examine the cost of youth violence, sexual and intimate partner violence, government expenditure on national security, and business costs. The annual cost of youth violence, including direct costs, forgone earnings, tourism revenue and opportunity cost, is estimated at 2.8% of GDP. Sexual and intimate partner violence, both direct and indirect costs of sexual abuse and domestic violence, is estimated at 0.51% of GDP (2005). Government expenditure on national security in TT is the highest in the Caribbean: 13.9% of the budget and 12% of GDP. In the private sector, twenty-six per cent of businesses reported being victims of crime, with financial losses of 2.1% of annual sales. Moreover, 80% of firms reported spending, on average, almost 2% of annual sales on private security measures.

The cost of crime has been found to harm economic growth. The growth effects approach to measuring the cost of crime has the advantage that, in principle, it summarizes the long-run effects of crime through various channels. Simulation results show that an increase of 1 in a country's homicide rate per 100,000 is associated with a 0.8 percentage point reduction in economic growth worldwide. Suppose TT had the same homicide growth rate as the global average between 1995–2011 (–0.009). In that case, the regression results suggest potential gains from a reduction in violence: GDP growth in TT could have been 2.1% higher (3.88 pp instead of 3.8 pp) for the period (Khadan, 2016).

TT firms ranked crime as their third most serious obstacle to performance after an inadequately educated workforce and access to finance: almost 18% of firms report that crime is the most critical factor that affects their performance. Crime appears to be a bigger problem for small and medium-sized enterprises (SMEs), mature firms, locally owned firms, and firms in the services sector. The crimes frequently committed against firms during or after working hours include vandalism, theft, attempted robbery, and burglary. The data shows that 17% of firms were victims of deliberate damage and destruction, 13.5% were victims of theft, 11% were victims of attempted burglary, 10% were burglary victims, and 9.1% were robbery victims. Theft and vandalism occurred roughly three times per year, while burglary, attempted burglary, and robbery occurred, on average, twice yearly. Attempted robberies and theft mainly occurred during working hours, while vandalism occurred outside of working hours. Firearms were the most used weapon in robberies, burglaries, assaults and threats, and knives were the primary weapon used for theft and vandalism. The perpetrators of these crimes were mainly gangs or groups of criminals. Money and goods or stocks were the main targets of criminals.

Firms mostly report to the police incidents of burglary, robbery, attempted robbery and theft. The data shows that while all firms reported burglary incidents, only 24% reported attempted burglary. The reporting rate for robberies was 84% of firms, although 80.5% report attempted robberies. Most deliberate damage/vandalism incidents go unreported, as only 21% of firms report this type of crime to the police. Similarly, only 29% of firms report assaults and threats to the police. Some firms choose not to report some types of crime for different reasons. Poor police response was one of the main reasons firms opted not to report attempted burglary incidents. Concerning the robberies, the main reasons for the lack of reporting included small losses, insufficient time to file a report, frequent crimes, fear of reprisals, and negative publicity. The main reasons for not reporting attempted robberies were a potential increase in insurance costs, poor police response, and frequent attempted robberies. Minor losses and a lack of police resources were why most firms did not report deliberate damage or vandalism. Concerning theft, minor losses, the inability to contact police, and the effect on insurance costs were among the reasons firms did not file a report. Poor police response and fear of negative publicity were again the main factors influencing firms not to report assaults and threats.

In addition to relying on the police service, most firms engage in self-protection. The 2014 PROTEIN survey found that 85% of firms have spent money on security. Firms spent, on average, about 2% of their annual sales on hiring security and lost 2% of annual sales due to crime (Khadan, 2017). The impact varies according to firm size, with medium-sized and large firms spending roughly 2% of their annual sales on security, compared to 1.1% for small firms. Moreover, foreign firms spent approximately 6% of their annual sales on security compared to 2% for local firms and 1% for jointly owned firms.

11.4 Trust in the Criminal Justice System

Given the situation described above, it is no surprise that public trust in the justice system, police and Supreme Court is low (Figs. 11.9 to 11.14). In the 2012 LAPOP survey, most residents revealed low trust in the police: on one extreme, 29% do not trust the police. Conversely, only 4% have a lot of trust in the police. There is a marginally higher level of trust in the Supreme Court. On one extreme, 11.6% do not trust the Supreme Court at all, while on the other extreme, 14.1% have a lot of trust in the Supreme Court. Trust in the justice system is also marginally higher: on one extreme, 13.5% do not trust the justice system at all, while on the other extreme, 9.4% have a lot of trust.

The level of trust, however, varies by ethnic group. Generally, ITTs have higher trust than ATTs, with MTTs at an intermediate level. ATTs trust the police less than other ethnic groups: 19% of ATTs have no trust compared to 15% of MTT and 7% of ITT. Concerning ethnic groups, 24% of ITTs have a lot of trust in the Supreme Court compared to only 5.8% of ATTs and 14.3% of MTTs. Similarly, only 4.5% of ITTs do not trust the Supreme Court compared to 17.5% of ATTs and 12.9% of MTTs. Fourteen% of ITTs reported a lot of trust in the justice system compared to only 5.4% of ATTs and 10.7% of MTTs. On the other hand, only 7.3% of ITTs do not trust the Supreme Court compared to 19.2% of ATTs and 14.7% of MTTs.

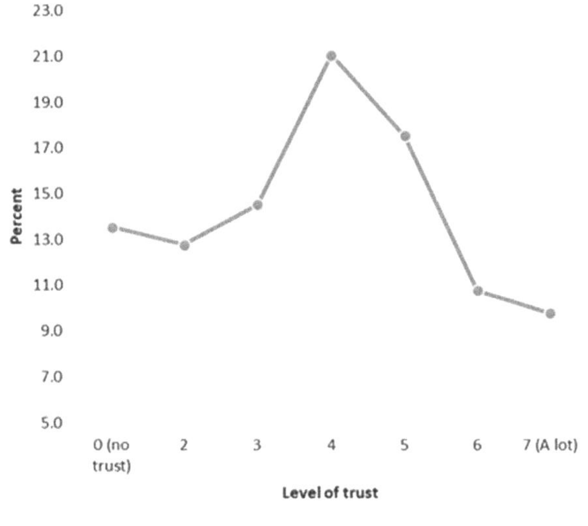

Fig. 11.9 Trust in the justice system (*Source* LAPOP [2012])

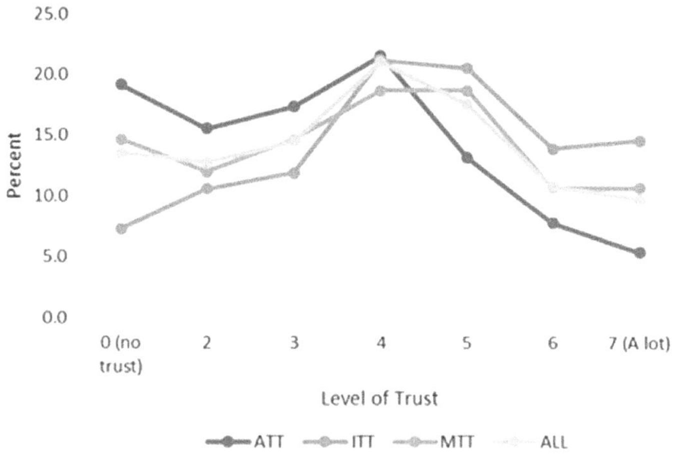

Fig. 11.10 Trust in the justice system by race (*Source* LAPOP [2012])

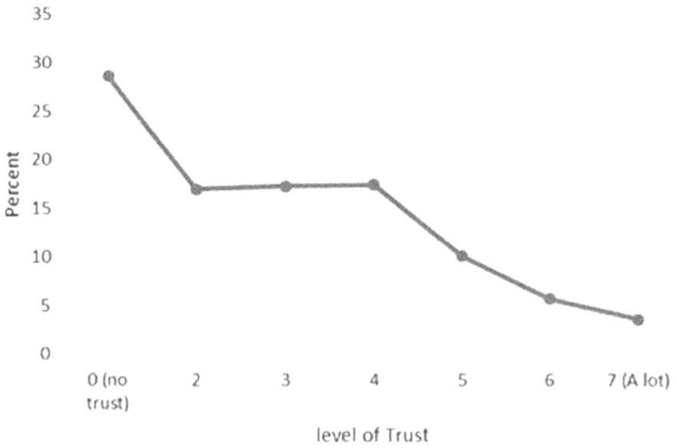

Fig. 11.11 Trust in the police (*Source* LAPOP [2012])

11.5 Conclusions

Most TT citizens identified security as the most critical problem facing the country. The country's homicide rate, 31 per 1000,000, is significantly higher than in other small countries, ethnically diverse societies, other ex-British colonies, and extractive-dependent economies.

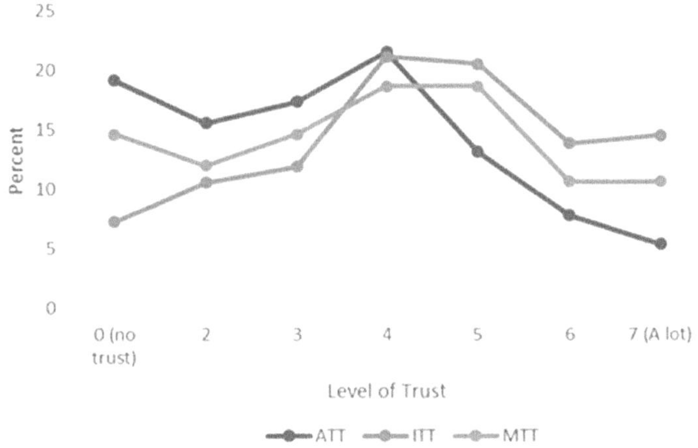

Fig. 11.12 Trust in the police by race (*Source* LAPOP [2012])

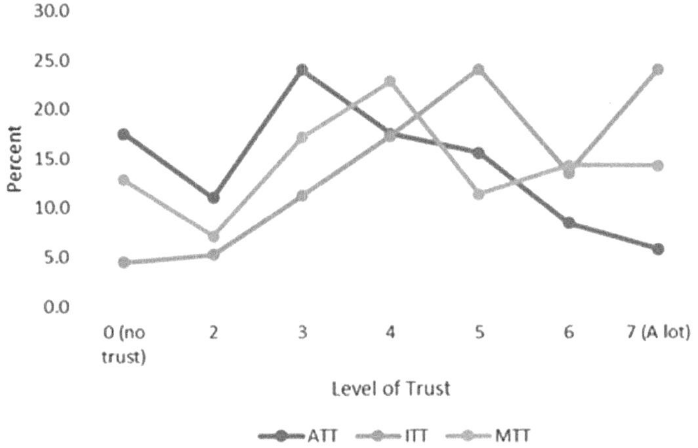

Fig. 11.13 Trust in the supreme court (*Source* LAPOP [2012])

The emergence of criminal gangs, partly fuelled by the drug gun and trade, has contributed to the country's high homicide rate. The crisis in Venezuela has accentuated the drug and arms problems. Further, inter-partner violence is the main form of domestic violence. Assaults and beatings accounted for more than half of the incidences of domestic

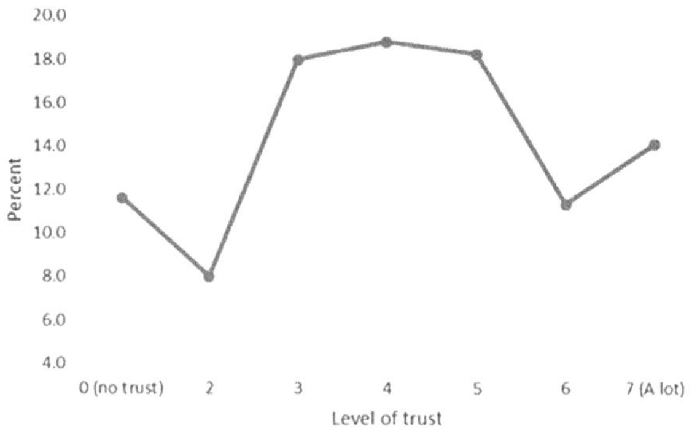

Fig. 11.14 Trust in the supreme court by race (*Source* LAPOP [2012])

violence, followed by threats, breach of a protection order, wounding, and sexual abuse. Child abuse and violence in schools are also prevalent. Within TT, there are marked differences between religions (a proxy for ethnicity) regarding the perpetrators of crime.

Evidence of relatively high social tolerance of partner and family violence and violence in general exists. Most respondents accepted that physical punishment is necessary when children are disobedient. The latter is consistent across the three major ethnic groups, with the highest being ATTs, followed by MTTs and ITTs. Similarly, most accept physical punishment for wives when they are unfaithful at similar rates among ATTs and ITTs. The tolerance of violence outside of the home is also high. The majority think it is justified to kill someone who kills another person or rape someone's child: the approval of such a response is high among ATTs and ITTs, but lower for MTTs. Police torture is primarily accepted, especially among ITTs.

The cost of crime and violence is high. The annual cost of youth violence, including direct costs, forgone earnings, tourism revenue and opportunity cost, is estimated at 2.8% of GDP. Direct and indirect costs of sexual abuse and domestic violence are estimated at 0.51% of GDP. Government expenditure on national security in TT is the highest in the Caribbean: 13.9% of the budget and 12% of GDP. In the private sector, twenty-six per cent of businesses reported being victims of crime, with financial losses of 2.1% of annual sales. Moreover, 80% of firms reported spending, on average, almost 2% of annual sales on private security measures.

Given the situation described above, it is no surprise that public trust in the justice system, police and Supreme Court is low. Most residents revealed low trust in the police. There is a marginally higher level of trust in the Supreme Court. Trust in the justice system is also marginally higher. The level of trust varies by ethnic group. Generally, ITTs have higher trust than ATTs, with MTTs at an intermediate level.

References

Andrews, B., & Brown, G. W. (1988). Marital violence in the community: A biographical approach. *The British Journal of Psychiatry, 153*(3), 305–312.

Ashby, N. J., & Ramos, M. A. (2013). Foreign direct investment and industry response to organized crime: The Mexican case. *European Journal of Political Economy, 30*, 80–91.

Bannon, I., & Collier, P. (Eds.). (2003). *Natural resources and violent conflict: Options and actions*. World Bank Publications.

Beuermann, D., Rieble-Aubourg, S., & Zarate-Barrera, T. (2016). *Matching educational and criminal records at the individual level in Trinidad and Tobago: Methodology and implementation*. Inter-American Development Bank.

Camacho, A., & Rodriguez, C. (2013). Firm exit and armed conflict in Colombia. *Journal of Conflict Resolution, 57*(1), 89–116.

Dell, M. (2015). Trafficking networks and the Mexican drug war. *American Economic Review, 105*(6), 1738–1779.

Driffield, N., Jones, C., & Crotty, J. (2013). International business research and risky investments, an analysis of FDI in conflict zones. *International Business Review, 22*(1), 140–155.

Gaibulloev, K., & Sandler, T. (2008). Growth consequences of terrorism in Western Europe. *Kyklos, 61*(3), 411–424.

Katz, C. M., & Choate, D. (2006, January). *Diagnosing Trinidad and Tobago's gang problem*. In Annual meeting of the American society of criminology, Los Angeles, CA.

Khadan, J. (2017). *Are oil and gas smothering the private sector in Trinidad and Tobago?* Inter-American Development Bank.

Khadan, J. (2016). *Trinidad and Tobago: Country development challenges (CDC)*. Inter-American Development Bank.

Koss, M. P. (1990). The women's mental health research agenda: Violence against women. *American Psychologist, 45*(3), 374.

Maher, D. (2015a). The fatal attraction of civil war economies: Foreign direct investment and political violence, a case study of Colombia. *International Studies Review, 17*(2), 217–248.

Maher, D. (2015b). Rooted in violence: Civil war, international trade and the expansion of palm oil in Colombia. *New Political Economy, 20*(2), 299–330.

Mihalache-O'Keef, A., & Vashchilko, T. (2010). Chapter seven: Foreign direct investors in conflict zones. *Adelphi Series, 50*(412–413), 137–156.

Montoya, E. (2016). Violence and economic disruption: Firm-level evidence from Mexico. Berkeley.

Peri, G. (2004). Socio-Cultural variables and economic success: Evidence from Italian provinces 1951–1991. *The B.E. Journal of Macroeconomics, 4*(1), 1–36.

Plichta, S. (1992). The effects of woman abuse on health care utilization and health status: A literature review. *Women's Health Issues, 2*(3), 154–163.

Rawlins, J. M. (2000). Domestic violence in Trinidad: A family and public health problem. *Caribbean Journal of Criminology and Social Psychology, 5*(1/2), 165–180.

Rios, V. (2015, June 27). *The impact of crime and violence on economic sector diversity*. (Working Paper).

Seepersad, R., & Williams, D. (2012). *A report citizen security, Trinidad and Tobago 2012*. Human Development and the shift to better citizen security, UNDP.

Seepersad, R. (2014). *Bullying and victimization in selected primary schools in North Trinidad*. Citizen Security Programme, Ministry of National Security and Ministry of Education.

Seepersad, R. (2016). *Crime and violence in Trinidad and Tobago: IDB series on crime and violence in the Caribbean*. Inter-American Development Bank.

Sutton, H., & Ruprah, I. (Eds.). (2017). *Restoring paradise in the Caribbean: Combating violence with numbers*. Inter-American Development Bank.

World Health Organization. (1997). *Violence against women—Health consequences*. WHO.

World Health Organization. (2011). *Global school-based health survey data. Trinidad and Tobago*. WHO.

CHAPTER 12

Social Development: Who We Are? The Value and Happiness

In the introduction, we identified the five features—small size, energy-dependent, ethnically diverse, an ex-British colony, and a democratic political system—that we previously asserted needed to be kept in mind to understand the country's political, economic, and social development. One could argue this assertion misses the defining feature of TT: the country's values and culture. Citizens' intra-country shared cultural values define a country and its people. In addition, we have not discussed whether race and cultural identities perfectly overlap. They may not; hence, cultural identity, not only race, is what matters. Further, it could be argued that our measures of success—political, economic, and social indicators—are merely intermediate objectives; what individuals and societies pursue is happiness. Hence, we need to consider the values and happiness of Trinbagonians relative to other countries and verify if they are different by ethnicity within TT.

12.1 Culture and Values

The phrase country's culture has many meanings. Popular understanding means festivals, food, and music and the degree to which they are shared among different groups in the country. Among the sixteen national holidays, with many religious ones, Carnival, Christmas, and Diwali are

J. Khadan and I. Jit Ruprah, *Unraveling Race, Politics, and Gender in Trinidad and Tobago's Economic Development*,
https://doi.org/10.1007/978-3-031-54656-3_12

the biggest celebrations in the country. All ethnic groups, to a large extent, celebrate them as Naipaul (1969) expressed the sharing of festivals: "*...everybody, Hindus, Muslims looking on it, if anything, with greater awe. Hindus and Muslims celebrate Christmas and Easter...everybody celebrated the Muslim festival of Hosay*". In addition, TT has rich culinary diversity, as the cuisine is a blend of African, Arabian, Cajun, Chinese, Creole, Indian, European, and Spanish. Doubles (flatbread filled with curried chickpeas) are unique to TT.

Regarding music, calypso and soca originated in the country. Another music style that evolved in TT is Chutney Soca, a blend of Indian music and calypso rhythms. The steelpan, the only new musical instrument invented in the twentieth century, originated in TT and is used by various ethnic groups in their cultural celebrations.

This rosy picture of a shared culture contrasts the voting by race identified previously and the many differential outcomes in the labour market, education, and health. David Rudder's calypsonian song "How we vote is not how we party" picks up this apparent contradiction. Perhaps the answer lies in that commonality hides a latent problem. The roti vs chicken nuggets controversy is an example[1]; an article comparing the calories of both dishes exploded into an interpretation of insulting assertions against an entire culture, presumably the ITT one. The debate missed the article's main point, the number of calories of the two dishes, which is pertinent when obesity is a problem in the country, particularly among ITTs, with 43% vs. 37% among ATTs who are obese.

This chapter considers the beliefs and behaviours shared by the members of a given society and its groups. It is through a culture that societies and groups define themselves. Thus, culture includes many societal aspects, values, mores, rules, organisations, and institutions. Common institutions are the family, education, and religion. Cultural identity belongs to a group, i.e., a person's self-conception of ethnicity.[2]

Culture matters because economic development is partially associated with culture. There is a growing consensus that economic growth will take more than an increase in investment in capital, more than importing the latest technology, and more than having reliable political and economic

[1] WATCH: Trinis outraged as roti declared too big for one meal | Loop Trinidad & Tobago (loopnews.com).

[2] See Woolcock (2014) for a criticism of this approach.

institutions. Cultural values, including horizontal and vertical trust, are another critical ingredient. Acemoglu and Robinson (2001, 2006) tackle the issue of causality, i.e., determine whether economic development leads to democracy or democratic institutions lead to economic growth. They conclude that economic development and democracy are attributable to "fixed national effects", reflecting a country's institutional and cultural heritage. Their findings suggest that culture plays a vital role in development. In that vein, Farrell (2012, 2017) argues that culture lies at the root of the economic under-achievement of TT. Thus, in this chapter, we also analyse Trinbagonian culture vis-a-vis the culture of other countries and within TT by race.[3]

A convenient framework for comparing values and development across countries is provided by Inglehart and Welzel's (2005) modernisation theory. Woolcock's (2014) theory is that economic, political, and social life transitions occur sequentially. As countries become more "modern", these transitions would yield incremental institutional and behavioural convergence. Their analysis of the World Values Survey asserts two significant dimensions of cross-cultural variation: traditional versus secular-rational values and survival versus self-expression values.[4] Higher economic development is associated with higher values of self-expression and secular values. Lower economic growth is related to higher values of survival and traditional values. Thus, this data allows us to empirically test the validity of Farrell's (2017) argument that culture lies at the root of the economic under-achievement of TT. If true, TT should have high survival-traditional values shared among ethnic groups rather than high secular self-expression values.

Their framework contains two main dimensions. One dimension involves traditional vs. secular values. Traditional values emphasise the importance of religion, parent–child relationships, and authority. People who embrace these values reject abortion, divorce, euthanasia, and suicide. These societies exhibit high levels of national pride. Secular-rational values represent the other extreme. They tend to relate to liberal ways of thinking. Societies that hold these values place less importance on

[3] Happiness and cultural values are obtained from surveys. We use two data sources: World Values survey found at WVS Database (worldvaluessurvey.org), and Latin American public Opinion Project, LAPOP found at LAPOP | Vanderbilt University.

[4] For details about the construction method, see: http://www.worldvaluessurvey.org/WVSContents.jsp.

religion, traditional family values and authority. Instead, divorce, abortion, euthanasia, and suicide are seen as acceptable. Engelbrekt and Nygren have described the shift from conventional to secular-rational values as "essentially replacing religion and superstition with science and bureaucracy". The change from traditional to secular values represents the transition from an industrial society to a post-industrial society and the embracing of democratic values.

The other dimension involves survival vs. self-expression. Survival values emphasise economic and physical security. They are linked with an ethnocentric superiority of one's own group's outlook and low levels of trust and tolerance. Self-expression values prioritise subjective well-being, self-expression, and quality of life. Some values are more common in societies that embrace these values. These include environmental protection, growing tolerance of foreigners, gays and lesbians and gender equality, rising demands for participation in decision-making in economic and political life (autonomy and freedom from central authority), interpersonal trust, political moderation, and a shift in child-rearing values from an emphasis on hard work towards imagination and tolerance. The change from survival to self-expression also represents the transition from an industrial society to a post-industrial society embracing democratic values.

The global cultural map, Fig. 12.1, shows how scores of countries are located on these two dimensions; Fig. 12.2 does so for TT and the comparator country groups. Moving upward in Fig. 12.1 reflects the shift from traditional to secular-rational values, and moving rightward captures the change from survival values to self-expression. In the southwest quadrant of the figure lie high traditional-high survival countries. In the northeast quadrant are countries with high secular-high self-expression.

Regarding the traditional vs. temporal dimension, Sweden has the highest self-expression, with Iraq on the opposite side with high survival values. Ghana lies at the traditional end, with Sweden at the extreme secular end. TT lies in the high survival-traditional space (southwest quadrant of Fig. 12.1). In terms of survival, TT lies between Ghana and Vietnam. Regarding conventional vs. secular values, TT lies between Colombia and Rwanda. As shown in Fig. 12.2, TT lies further towards traditional survival values than the average values of countries classified into ex-British colonies, small economies, ethnically polarised, and extractive dependent. Small economies lie in the northwest quadrant. TT has higher values along the traditional secular dimension and a lower survival dimension than extractive-dependent countries. Figure 12.2 also contains

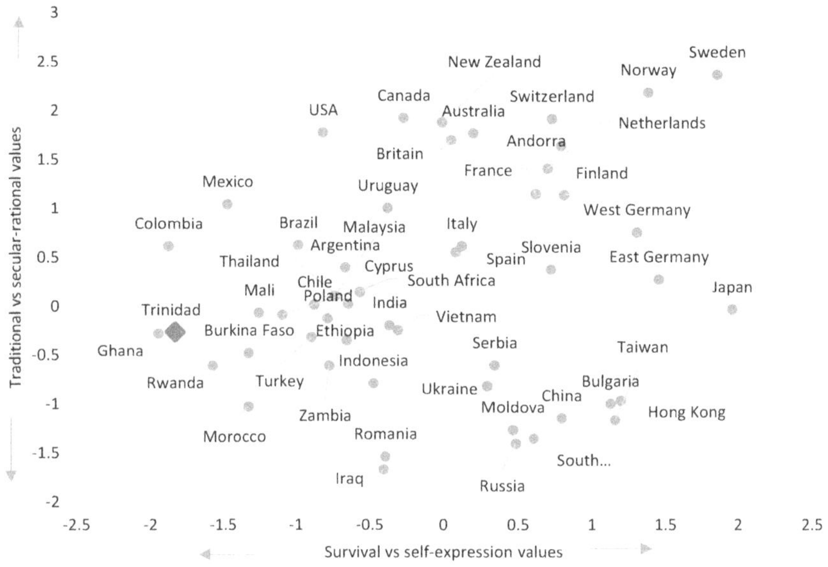

Fig. 12.1 Global culture map by country (*Source* Authors using data from the world values survey (Wave 5). WVS Database (worldvaluessurvey.org))

the numbers for ATTs, ITTs, and MTTs separately. There appear to be no significant differences between the three ethnic groups in both value dimensions. They seem to have similar values.

Inglehart and Welzel (2005) argue that socioeconomic development strongly correlates with a country's cultural values. High-income countries rank relatively high on both dimensions (self-expression-rational values) and are in the upper right-hand corner of Fig. 12.1). Conversely, low-income countries fall into a zone on the lower left (high survival-traditional values), where TT lies. Socioeconomic development tends to move countries in a common direction, regardless of their cultural heritage. Hence, TT remains in the traditional survival space associated with lower economic development. Thus, the shared cultural values of different ethnic groups may be hindering the country's development, providing empirical support to the arguments by Farrell (2017).

These two cultural value dimensions are aggregated from several sub-values. Figures 12.3 to 12.9 show the values for TT, comparator countries

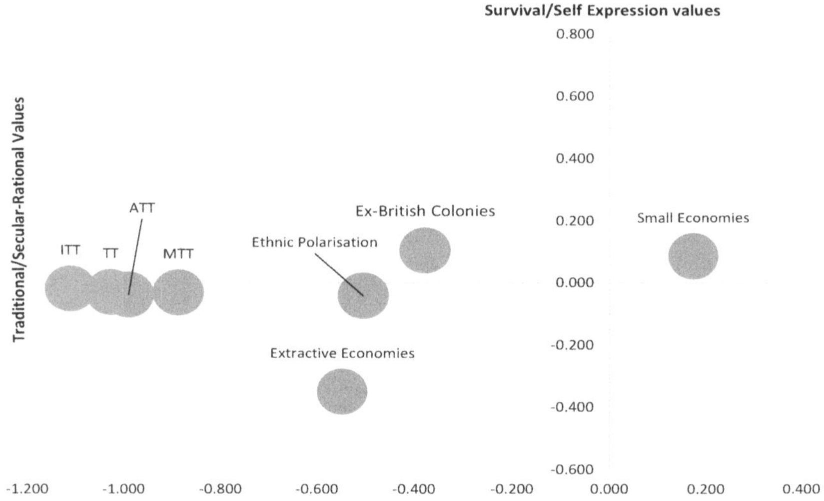

Fig. 12.2 Global culture map by country groups and TT (*Source* Authors using data from the world values survey (Wave 5). WVS Database (worldvaluessurvey.org))

and by race within TT. TT stands out in its high Scepticism and Equality indices and low Autonomy and Choice indices.

The scepticism index measures a national culture's distance to "sacred" sources of authority in order institutions (army, police, courts). Values range from 0, no respect for such institutions, to 1, i.e., very high respect for the police, army, and courts. Country values are equal to the population average. TT's average and the values of all three racial groups reveal a higher level of scepticism than the comparator country categories (Fig. 12.3). There is no significant difference between the racial groups within TT. The equality index measures a national culture's emphasis on universal freedoms in gender equality (support of women's equal access to education, jobs, and power) ranging from 0 to 1, i.e., from the least to most emancipative position. TT lies at the higher end of universal freedom in gender equality than comparator country groups (Fig. 12.4). ITTs have a lower value, i.e., less belief in gender equality.

The voice index, Fig. 12.5, measures a national culture's emphasis on universal freedoms in the domain of people's voice, i.e., priorities for freedom of speech and people's say in national and local affairs. The index

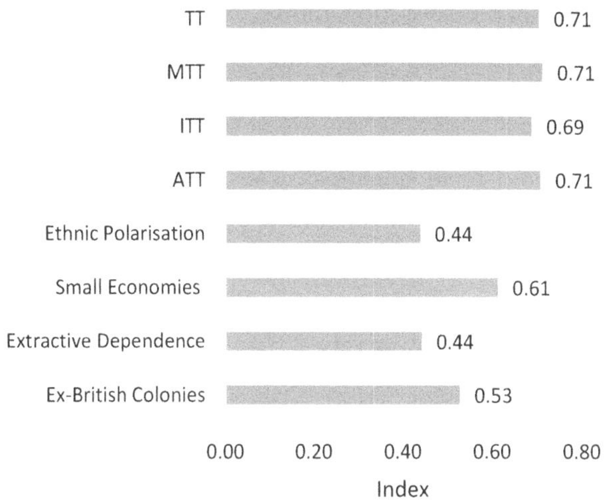

Fig. 12.3 Scepticism index (*Source* Authors using data from the World Values Survey (Wave 5). WVS Database (worldvaluessurvey.org))

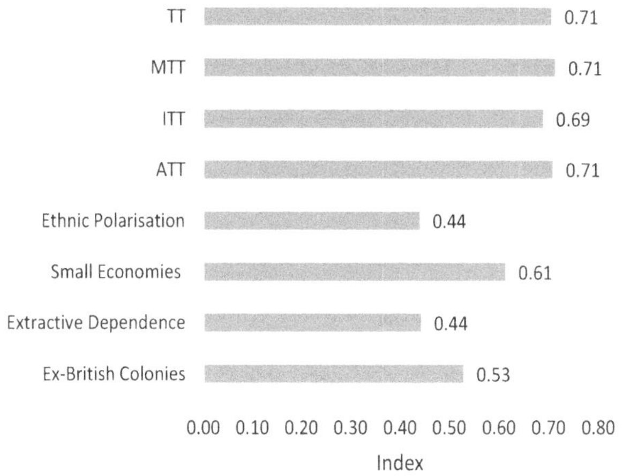

Fig. 12.4 Equality index (*Source* Authors using data from the World Values Survey (Wave 5). WVS Database (worldvaluessurvey.org))

varies from 0 to 1, i.e., from most minor to most emancipative positions. TT lies between small economies closest to one and extractive dependence and polarised countries. ITTs have a lower value than do ATTs. The autonomy index, Fig. 12.6, measures a national culture's emphasis on universal freedoms in personal autonomy (independence and non-obedience as desired child qualities). The autonomy index ranges from 0, no belief in universal freedoms, to unity, i.e., firm belief in universal ideas. Hence, TT is at the lower end of secular beliefs in the least to most secular positions. It has lower autonomy than all five comparator country groups. Lower autonomy also holds for all racial groups within TT. However, ITTs have lower values than do ATTs.

The defiance index, Fig. 12.7, measures a national culture's distance to "sacred" sources of authority in patrimonial authority (the nation, the state, the parents). The values of 0 to 1 are the least to the most secular position. The disbelief index measures a national culture's distance to "sacred" sources of authority in the domain of religious authority (faith, commitment, practice). Except for ex-British colonies, TT lies closer to

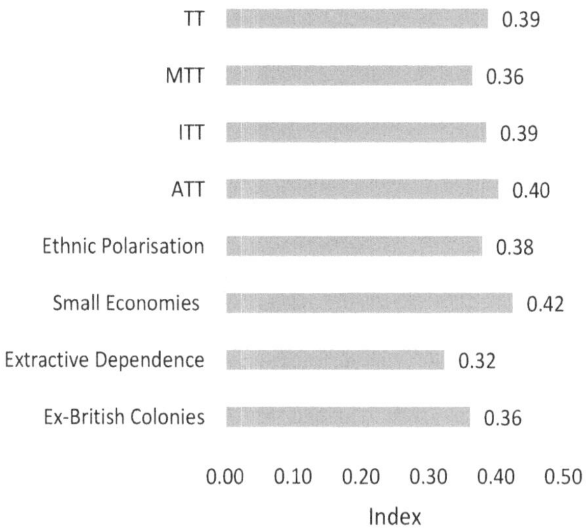

Fig. 12.5 Voice index (*Source* Authors using data from the World Values Survey (Wave 5). WVS Database (worldvaluessurvey.org))

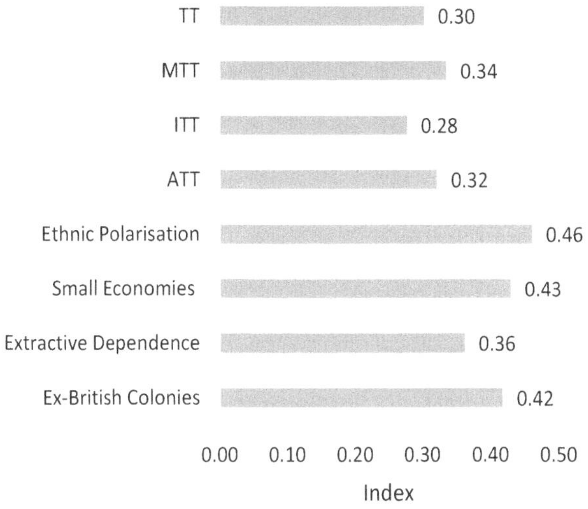

Fig. 12.6 Autonomy index (*Source* Authors using data from the World Values Survey (Wave 5). WVS Database (worldvaluessurvey.org))

zero, i.e., less secular than small economies and extractive-dependent countries. ITTs have a lower value compared to ATTs. The disbelief index, Fig. 12.8, measures a national culture's distance to "sacred" sources of authority in the domain of religious authority (faith, commitment, practice). The index ranges from a minimum of zero when the least secular position is taken to a maximum of 1 when the most secular position is taken. TT lies closer to zero, the least secular value compared to comparator countries. However, ITTs have a value closer to zero compared to ATTs.

The choice index, Fig. 12.9, measures a national culture's emphasis on universal freedoms in reproductive choices (acceptance of divorce, abortion, homosexuality). This index varies from 0, no choice, to 1, full choice. TT and all its ethnic groups fall near the no-choice value, systematically below the average values of comparators.

These sub-indices are generally consistent with the overall traditional survival classification of TT. However, this holds marginally more for ITTs than for ATTs. These findings of no significant differences between ethnic groups suggest that it is not race that matters but values.

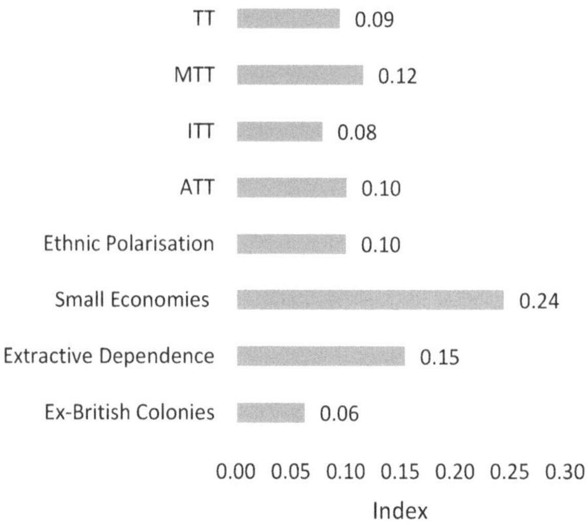

Fig. 12.7 Defiance index (*Source* Authors using data from the World Values Survey (Wave 5). WVS Database (worldvaluessurvey.org))

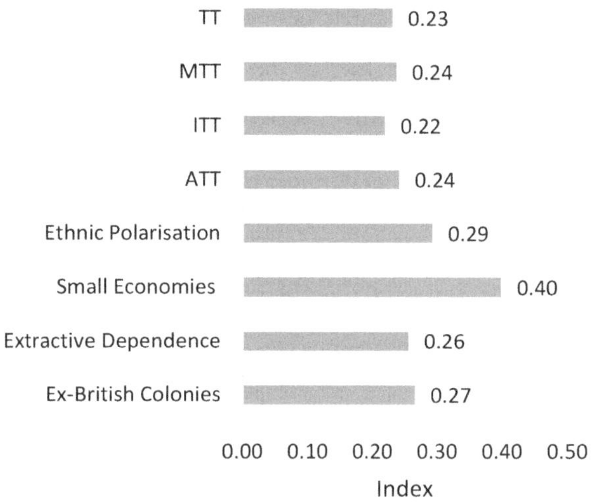

Fig. 12.8 Disbelief index (*Source* Authors using data from the World Values Survey (Wave 5). WVS Database (worldvaluessurvey.org))

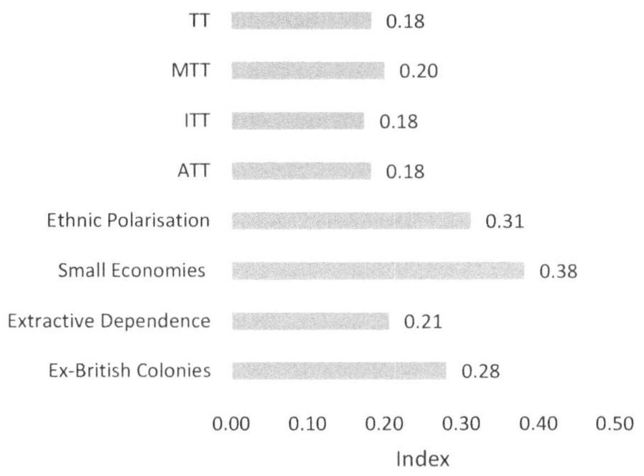

Fig. 12.9 Choice index (*Source* Authors using data from the World Values Survey (Wave 5). WVS Database (worldvaluessurvey.org))

12.2 It Is Not Race but Culture that Matters

So far, we have taken a primordial viewpoint, i.e., assumed that ethnicity is associated with differences in cultural values. The concern over ethnic divisions assumes that people agree about values and norms within ethnic groups and disagree across ethnic groups. Hence, ethnic differences may exacerbate social and political antagonism. However, an alternative–constructivist—viewpoint argues that ethnic identities are the endogenous result of shifting patterns of power. The association between ethnic identity and cultural differences, if any, would be context-dependent. Indeed, Desmet et al. (2017) argue that there are three different possibilities between culture and race: First, cultural antagonism, i.e., where antagonism arises from cultural differences and where ethnicity plays no role. Second is ethnic antagonism, i.e., where antagonism only stems from ethnic differences. The value of others' does not matter. What matters is if they are from the same ethnic group. The third is the overlap between culture and ethnicity. The latter is where individuals feel antipathy towards other ethnic groups, but only to the degree that those other groups are culturally different from their own.

Why does it matter? In countries where ethnicity strongly predicts culture, violent conflict is more likely, and public goods provision will be less. Thus, social antagonism is more significant in societies where individuals differ in ethnicity and culture, and political economy outcomes will worsen. Ethnic conflict and the possible solutions are perceived along ethnic lines. The conflict is usually not about ethnic differences per se but political, economic, social, cultural, or territorial matters. Among the best-known conflicts are those in the Balkans, Rwanda, Chechnya, Iraq, Indonesia, Sri Lanka, India, Darfur, and Israel.

To measure the extent of overlap between culture and ethnicity, Desmet et al. (2017) use a chi-squared (χ^2) index that captures the average distance between the answers of each ethnic group and the answers in the overall population. It is based on comparing average answers for a given group to the distribution of answers in the general population. A low index value indicates that groups reflect the country-wide distribution of responses. If the distribution of answers in a given ethnic group is the same as in the entire population, then knowing a person's ethnic identity conveys no information about his cultural attributes. A high value indicates a lot of group specificity. In this case, the distributions are distinct; then, there is an overlap between ethnic identity and cultural attributes. The second index, developed in population genetics, is known as a fixation index, F_{ST}. It captures the between-group variance in answers to survey questions as a share of the overall variance—the ratio of between-group cultural heterogeneity to total heterogeneity: A zero value indicates no informational content to know an individual's ethnic identity. In this case, cultural cleavages and ethnic cleavages are cross-cutting. In contrast, a value unity suggests that an individual's ethnic identity can perfectly predict answers to cultural questions. Knowing someone's ethnic identity allows a perfect prediction of their cultural attributes.

If F_{ST}, i.e., overlap, is high, then knowing someone's ethnicity provides much information about the person's culture. On the other hand, if the overlap is low, knowing someone's race tells little about the person's culture. What is the value of the overlap in TT? TT's χ^2 and F_{ST} take on low values, 0.03 and 0.01, respectively. The values indicate that most cultural heterogeneity is within ethnic groups, i.e., between-ethnic group cultural variation is a small part of overall cultural variation and that most of this variation occurs within ethnic groups. This result indicates why TT has avoided communal violence and inadequate public good provision. Desmet et al. (2017) find that "… *to the extent that ethnic divisions matter for conflict, they only do so when they overlap with cultural cleavages*". They do not overlap in TT; hence, the country has largely avoided ethnic-based violent conflict.

12.3 Happiness

A possible criticism of the measures used to gauge success in the previous chapters is that they are intermediate objectives. Instead, life satisfaction-happiness is the appropriate standard of success for a country and an individual. Happiness and GDP per capita can show societal well-being and ranking. But why prefer happiness to GDP? Easterlin and O'Connor (2020) lists four reasons why they differ.

First, happiness is a more comprehensive measure of well-being. It considers a range of concerns, while GDP is limited to one aspect of the economic side of life, that is, the output of goods and services. Second, happiness is evaluated by people whose well-being is being assessed. For GDP, the judgement on well-being is made by outsiders, the "experts", and may not be an objective measure of the economy's output. The judgements involved in measuring GDP have long been recognised.[5] Third, happiness is a measure people can personally identify, while GDP is an abstraction with little personal meaning for individuals. Fourth, happiness is a measure in which everyone has a single vote. Everyone in the adult population counts equally in measuring society's well-being. Thus, the happiness measure reveals how a society satisfies the concerns of people's everyday lives. GDP only measures one aspect of life: producing material goods and services. If happiness were to replace GDP as a leading measure of societal well-being, public policy might be moved in a direction more meaningful to people's lives (Frey & Gallus, 2016).

Happiness measures are obtained from surveys. Under the broad concept of well-being, the literature uses happiness and life satisfaction interchangeably (Medvedev & Landhuis, 2018). While the three concepts

[5] GDP does not directly account for leisure, environment, health and education, non-market activities, changes in inequality of income, increases in variety, increases in technology, or the—positive or negative—value that society place on certain types of output and services.

are somewhat different, responses in various surveys are highly correlated. Several validation studies suggest that the happiness questions reveal something meaningful regarding well-being. Self-reported happiness has high test–retest correlations and correlates well with the psychometric analysis variables.[6] Thus, self-reported happiness scores measure actual utility with a high signal-to-noise ratio.

This section compares TT's happiness values with other countries and then looks within TT. We also look at the key determinants of happiness and TT ranking.

So, how happy are Trinbagonians? In 2020, out of 153 countries, TT was the 42nd happiest country between Lithuania and Poland (Helliwell et al., 2020). The national-level data primarily uses people's reports of the quality of their lives, as measured on a scale with 10 representing the best possible life and 0 for the worst. In comparing TT with the averages of the comparator country groups, TT stands out as being much happier (Fig. 12.10).

Helliwell et al. (2016) estimate the contributions of several variables to happiness. These include:

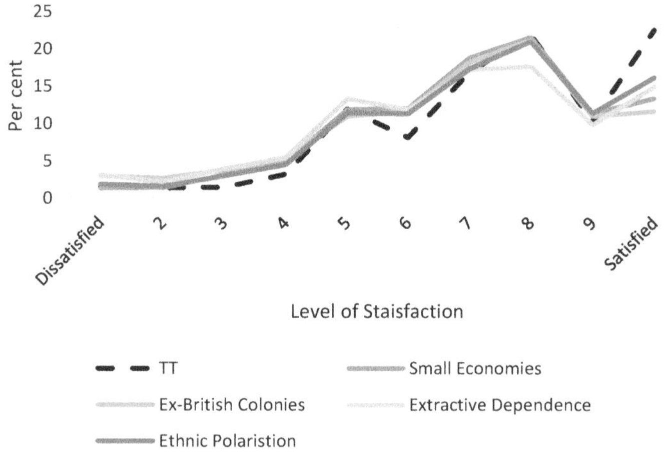

Fig. 12.10 Happiness in TT and comparators (*Source* World Happiness Report (2016))

[6] For the happiness measure's reliability and construct validity van Hoorn (2016).

i. Purchasing power adjusted GDP per capita,
ii. Social support (or having someone to count on in times of trouble) is the national average of the binary responses (either 0 or 1) to the question, "If you were in trouble, do you have relatives or friends you can count on to help you whenever you need them, or not?"),
iii. healthy life expectancy at birth,
iv. freedom to make life choices (is the national average of binary responses to the question "Are you satisfied or dissatisfied with your freedom to choose what you do with your life?"), generosity (is the residual of regressing the national average of responses to the question "Have you donated money to a charity in the past month?"),
v. perceptions of corruption (the average of binary answers to two questions: "Is corruption widespread throughout the government or not?" and "Is corruption widespread within businesses or not?").[7]

Table 12.1 shows the contribution of these concepts to life satisfaction for TT and the comparator group of countries. TT has the highest GDP per capita, social support and freedom to make life choices. The contribution of generosity is only higher in ex-British colonies, and healthy life expectancy is higher only in small economies.

We can delve deeper within TT on happiness by income, gender, race, and skin colour to determine if and what differences exist between different groups.

There is the oft-stated adage that money cannot buy happiness. However, empirical research finds that it can do so, but only up to a certain income level, beyond which higher income does not imply higher happiness (Jebb et al., 2018; Kahneman & Deaton, 2010). What about TT? Fig. 12.11 shows life satisfaction and income; increasing income is associated with increased happiness with no upper plateau. Figure 12.12 reports on happiness and whether the respondents responded positively or negatively to whether household income is enough. Not enough income is associated with higher levels of unhappiness.

[7] The coefficients of the regression used to generate the values can be found in Table 2.1 of Helliwell et al. (2016).

Table 12.1. Factors influencing happiness

	Happiness	*Log GDP per capita*	*Social support*	*Healthy life expectancy*	*Freedom to make life choices*	*Generosity*	*Perceptions of corruption*	*Dystopia + residual*
TT	6.19	1.17	1.41	0.66	0.55	0.20	0.02	2.19
Small economies	5.48	0.87	1.16	0.69	0.47	0.19	0.13	1.98
Ex-British	5.03	0.83	1.10	0.60	0.49	0.23	0.14	1.64
Extractive dependence	5.07	0.87	1.12	0.57	0.41	0.17	0.11	1.82
Ethnic polarisation	5.37	0.83	1.09	0.66	0.47	0.20	0.12	2.01

Source World Happiness Report (2016)

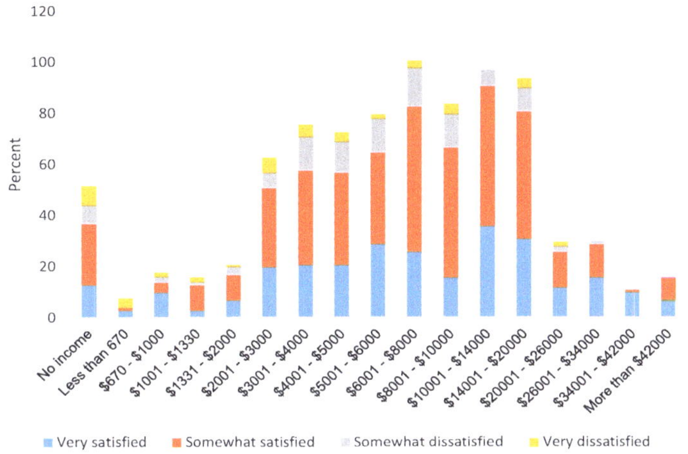

Fig. 12.11 Happiness and income

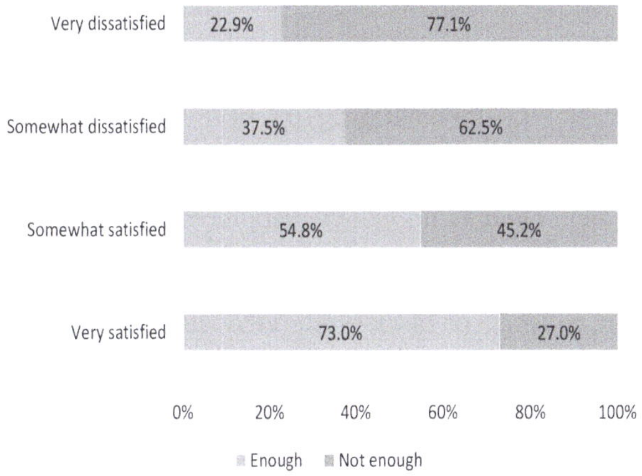

Fig. 12.12 Happiness and if income is enough (*Source* LAPOP [2012])

One common but counterintuitive finding in the life satisfaction literature is that women worldwide report higher levels of life satisfaction than men. While this finding applies across countries on average, it does not exist in countries where gender rights are compromised (Graham, 2020; Stevenson & Wolfers, 2009). Further, there is the paradox of "declining female happiness" after gender rights have improved. Greater happiness is counterintuitive as gender inequality remains. Women have not yet gained gender equity. Women are often discriminated against in health, education, political representation, the labour market, etc.—with negative consequences for developing their capabilities and freedom of choice. Hence, this discrimination may reduce happiness. One measure of how women are hindered from reaching their potential is the gender inequality index.[8] It measures gender inequalities in three aspects of human development. First, reproductive health is measured by maternal mortality ratio and adolescent birth rates. Second, empowerment is measured by the proportion of parliamentary seats occupied by females and the proportion of adult females and males aged 25 years and older with at least some secondary education.

Third, economic status is expressed as labour market participation and measured by the female and male populations aged 15 years and older labour force participation rate. The index ranges from zero, i.e., no inequality, to one, i.e., absolute disparities—the inequality values for TT and comparator country groups are given in Fig. 12.13. Gender inequality has been falling over time for TT and in all comparators. TT has the lowest level of gender inequality relative to comparator country groups except for 2017 to 2019, when it falls below the value of small economies. However, women in TT have the same distribution of life satisfaction as men (Fig. 12.14). There is no gender happiness gap.

Is there a race happiness gap? Many studies, particularly in the USA, find a race gap, although they also note that it is shrinking over time and attribute it to levels of black-white inequality having declined; there has been some narrowing of the gap in educational attainment, poverty, life expectancy, and residential segregation and neighbourhood economic conditions (Iceland & Ludwig-Dehm, 2019). In TT, there is no overwhelming evidence of racial discrimination on the scale found in the USA, so we would not expect a happiness race gap. There are no major differences in life satisfaction across races (Fig. 12.15), although there is a

[8] The Gender Inequality Index is an index for measurement of gender disparity that was introduced in the 2010 Human Development Report, 20th edition by the United Nations Development Programme.

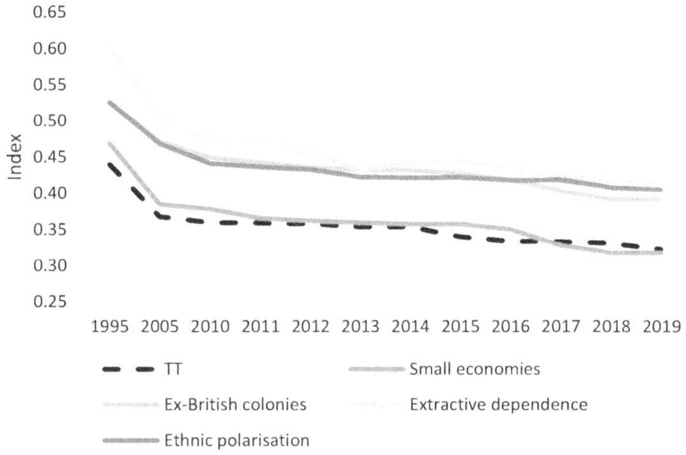

Fig. 12.13 Gender inequality index (*Sources* United Nations Development Programme (UNDP) and LAPOP (2014))

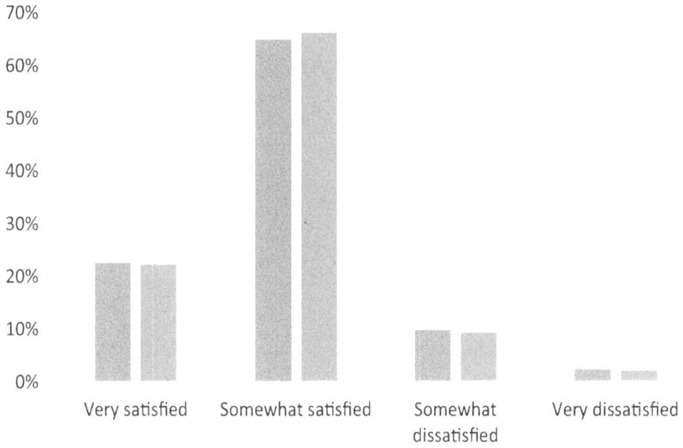

Fig. 12.14 Happiness by gender (*Sources* United Nations Development Programme (UNDP) and LAPOP (2014))

marked difference in median income levels (Fig. 12.16) of the survey's respondents grouped by ethnicity.

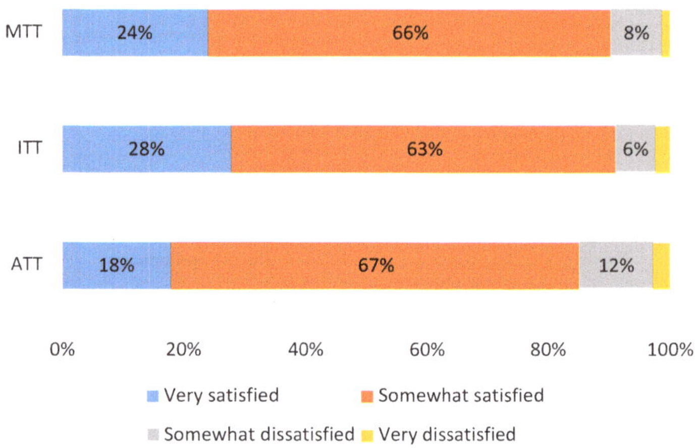

Fig. 12.15 Race and happiness (*Source* LAPOP [2014])

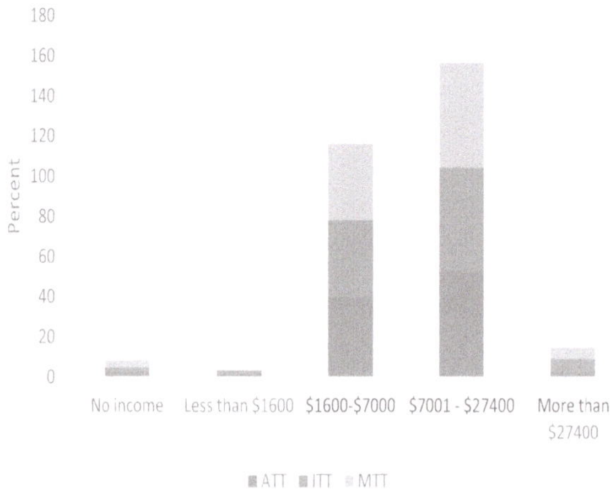

Fig. 12.16 Race and income (*Source* LAPOP [2014])

However, we found that skin colour matters. Lighter-skinned persons are happier than darker-skinned persons (Fig. 12.17). There is possibly a colour happiness gap. First, the lighter the skin, the more a person is considered socially beautiful, hence the search for a whitening cream. The latter can be traced back to colonial times. As Lewis (2004, page 60) puts it: "*A value system grew up emphasising skin colour and ethnic affiliation as the badges of social respectability*". Which resulted in "*...a vast and disproportionate volume of individual thought and energy to be consumed in search for acceptance by the light-skinned and white groups*". Second, skin colour is inverse to income; the darker the skin, the lower the monthly median income (Fig. 12.18).

That colour still permeates society is best illustrated by opposition leader Kamal Persad-Bissessar, who, less elegantly than Fanon (1952), said: "*They tried to own me, but I sent them packing. They have their Oreo now, who is their guy in Keith Rowley, and that's how the one per cent*

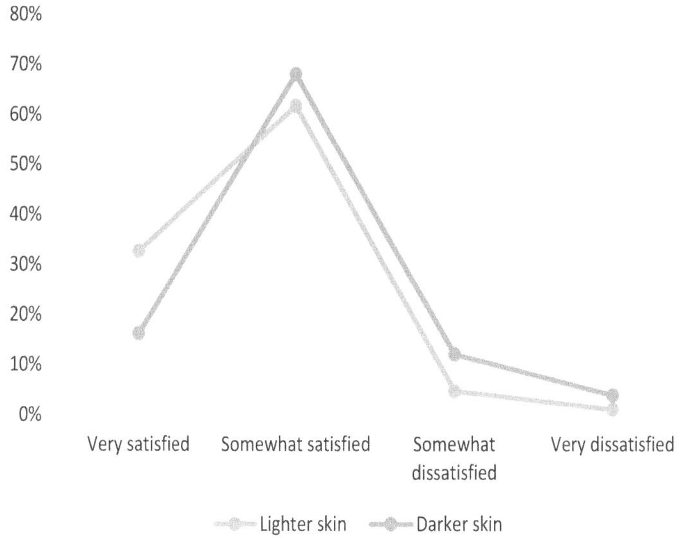

Fig. 12.17 Skin colour and happiness (*Source* LAPOP [2012])

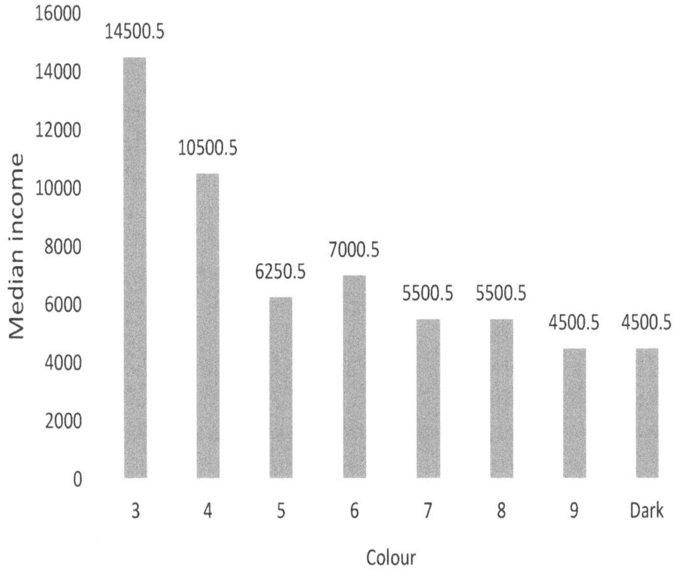

Fig. 12.18 Colour of skin and median income (*Source* LAPOP [2012])

friends and family of Rowley control him".[9] Although she was immediately widely condemned for her remarks.

Collectively, Trinbagonians are happier than the people in comparator countries. Within TT, there appears to be increasing happiness with increasing income, with no plateauing at higher income levels. There are no gender and race gaps. There is, however, a possible colour gap in terms of happiness.

12.4 Conclusions

In this chapter, we reviewed culture and happiness. Culture matters for the country's economic development as socioeconomic outcomes strongly correlate with a country's cultural values. Higher economic development is associated with higher values of self-expression and secular

[9] See: Kamla slammed for calling the PM an 'Oreo'—Trinidad Guardian, the term "one per cent", is used in the country to refer to the Syrian/Lebanese community,

values. Lower economic growth is related to higher values of survival and traditional values. TT has low (high) self-expression (survival) and high (low) traditional (secular) values. There appear to be no large differences between the three ethnic groups in both value dimensions. Thus, the shared cultural values represent a drag on development. The fact that most cultural heterogeneity is within ethnic groups, i.e., between-ethnic group cultural variation, is a small part of overall cultural variation and that most of this variation occurs within ethnic groups. This result indicates why TT has avoided communal violence despite race-based voting and differential outcomes in education, health, and labour market outcomes. Cultural identity, not only race, is what matters.

TT stands out as much happier when comparing TT with the averages of the comparator country groups. Comparing the common factors' contribution to life satisfaction in TT and the comparator group of countries reveals why. TT has the highest GDP per capita and social support. At the same time, the contribution of generosity is only higher in ex-British colonies, and a healthy life expectancy is higher only in small economies. Interestingly, there is neither a gender nor race happiness gap. There is, however, a colour happiness gap; lighter-skinned people are happier than dark-skinned people.

References

Acemoglu, D., & Robinson, J. A. (2001). A theory of political transitions. *American Economic Review, 91*(4), 938–963.

Acemoglu, D., & Robinson, J. A. (2006). *Economic origins of dictatorship and democracy*. Cambridge University Press.

Desmet, K., Ortuño-Ortín, I., & Wacziarg, R. (2017). Culture, ethnicity, and diversity. *American Economic Review, 107*(9), 2479–2513.

Easterlin, R. A., & O'Connor, K. J. (2020). *"The easterlin paradox. Bonn:" IZA Institute of Labour Economics* (No. 13923). IZA Discussion Paper.

Fanon, F. (1952). *Black skin, white masks*. (C. Markmann, Trans). Grove Press.

Farrell T. (2012). *The underachieving society: Development strategy and policy in Trinidad and Tobago 1958–2008*. UWI Press.

Farrell T. (2017). *We like it so? The cultural roots of economic underachievement in Trinidad and Tobago*. CreateSpace.

Frey, B. S., & Gallus, J. (2016). Happiness: Research and policy considerations. In *Advances in happiness research: A comparative perspective* (pp. 9–21). Springer Japan.

Graham, C. (2020). *Are women happier than men? Do gender rights make a difference?* Brookings Institution. Retrieved from https://policycommons.net/artifacts/4142125/are-women-happier-than-men-do-gender-rights-make-a-difference/4950591/ on October 07, 2023. CID: 20.500.12592/2wvhfr.

Helliwell, J. F., Huang, H., Wang, S., & Norton, M. (2020). *Statistical appendix for chapter 2 of World Happiness Report 2020.*

Helliwell, J. F., Layard, R., & Sachs, J. D. (2016). *World happiness report 2016-update* (Vol. 1). Sustainable Development Solutions Network.

Iceland, J., & Ludwig-Dehm, S. (2019). Black-white differences in happiness, 1972–2014. *Social Science Research, 77*, 16–29.

Inglehart, R., & Welzel, C. (2005). *Modernisation, cultural change, and democracy: The human development sequence* (Vol. 333). Cambridge University Press.

Jebb, A. T., Tay, L., Diener, E., & Oishi, S. (2018). Happiness, income satiation and turning points around the world. *Nature Human Behaviour, 2*(1), 33–38.

Kahneman, D., & Deaton, A. (2010). High income improves evaluation of life but not emotional well-being. *Proceedings of the National Academy of Sciences, 107*(38), 16489–16493.

Lewis, G. (2004). *The growth of the modern West Indies*. Ian Randel.

Medvedev, O. N., & Landhuis, C. E. (2018). Exploring constructs of well-being, happiness and quality of life. *PeerJ, 6*, e4903.

Naipaul, V. (1969). *The suffrage of Elvira*. Penguin.

Stevenson, B., & Wolfers, J. (2009). The paradox of declining female happiness. *American Economic Journal: Economic Policy, 1*(2), 190–225.

van Hoorn, A. (2016). *Reliability and validity of the happiness approach to measuring preferences*. 16008-GEM, University of Groningen.

Woolcock, M. (2014). Culture, politics, and development. In *The oxford handbook of the politics of development.*

CHAPTER 13

Conclusions

TT is unique because it is the only country that meets five criteria: it is a small country, oil and gas-dependent, ethnically polarised, an ex-British colony, and a democracy. However, it is not the fact that the country is unique that matters, but according to the literature, each feature implies generally adverse structural forces on diverse aspects of the country's development. These characteristics suggest that forces are stacked up against success. Uniqueness also creates problems in selecting comparator countries. In this book, we compare TT's performance to the average performance of country groups satisfying each characteristic separately.

However, the forces derived from the country's structural features reveal there is not necessarily an unambiguous linear, unidirectional effect on development. The effects are not clear and could involve various factors, making the relationship between the country's structure and development more complex. Often, even the sign of the impact on development is unclear. Nonetheless, in general, the forces derived from the structural features may create additional problems for development compared to their absence. The general thrust of our literature review emphasised the adverse effects of TT's structural characteristics, suggesting that TT would underperform in political, economic, and social

J. Khadan and I. Jit Ruprah, *Unraveling Race, Politics, and Gender in Trinidad and Tobago's Economic Development*,
https://doi.org/10.1007/978-3-031-54656-3_13

development. Does it? We attempt to answer this question by analysing the country's political, economic, and social development.

13.1 Political Development

TT's political system is organised with an elected president as the head of state, a bicameral legislature consisting of a Senate and a House of Representatives, and a cabinet headed by the prime minister. The country's political system is based on a single-member constituency, with a Westminster model, using a first-past-the-post voting system and an ethnic-based political party system. Its democracy is classified as flawed by the Economist Intelligence Unit democracy index largely due to an underdeveloped political culture and low levels of political participation, despite having free and fair elections and fundamental civil liberties.

TT's political development has been influenced by the two political parties, the PNM and the UNC. Both have historically dominated the political landscape, attracting support primarily based on race. The electoral results indicate predictable patterns and potential shifts, especially after the 1990s, reflecting the country's evolving political dynamics. The PNM held power for a significant portion of the country's history. Both political parties do not significantly differ regarding ideology, classified as left or right-leaning, or by class defined by income or education. Instead, the political parties are race-based, as voting patterns in the general elections show a strong correlation between race and party affiliation. The pattern of race and party affiliation is high among the youth, which suggests that race-based politics is likely to persist.

The electoral results in TT since independence have seen both parties winning elections, with the PNM dominating the early years and the UNC forming governments during specific periods. The election system based on single-seat electoral districts has resulted in some seats switching between parties in different elections. The latter indicates that not all electoral districts are preordained by race-based politics. Marginal seats have played a crucial role in determining several general election outcomes. The number of marginal seats has increased over the years, indicating a more competitive electoral landscape. Switching of seats between parties has also occurred in past elections, highlighting the potential for shifts in voter preferences, especially when they are presented with a coalition among political parties.

TT's structural features imply a substantial yet substandard public sector, meaning it is both inefficient and ineffective. The predictions are generally borne out. Whichever measurement is used, public expenditure, investment, or the wage bill, TT has a larger public sector than comparator country groups. TT underperforms the average of comparator country groups regarding public institutional quality. This relative underperformance holds for property rights, intellectual property protection, diversion of public funds, trust in politicians, irregular payments and bribes, favouritism in decisions of government officials, the wastefulness of government spending, burden of public regulation, the efficiency of the legal framework in settling disputes, and transparency of government policymaking. TT performs relatively well in only one area (judicial independence). Survey data show that public trust in politicians is shallow in TT, and there is a perception of favouritism in decisions made by government officials (usually perceived as favouring well-connected firms and individuals).

Countries with more capable bureaucracies, more institutionalised congresses, independent judiciaries, and institutionalised political parties tend to have more stable, adaptable, coherent, efficient, and publicly regarded policies. Generally, TT performs worse regarding the quality of public institutions (congress capabilities, judicial independence party institutionalisation) than the comparators, except for civil service, where it performs better than all the comparator groups.

However, TT generally performs on par with other comparators regarding the quality of policies, which can be assessed through various dimensions. These include stability—the extent to which policies are stable over time, in which TT does better; the quality of implementation and enforcement—the degree to which policies are implemented and enforced correctly after approval in Parliament, in which TT does worse; efficiency—the extent to which policies reflect an allocation of scarce resources that ensures high returns, in which TT does better; and public regardedness—the degree to which policies pursue the public interest, where TT does worse.

We explored the relationship between political development, voter base payoffs, and corruption. The findings suggest the country can be classified as an ethnic-based patronage democracy. Voters in patronage democracies primarily choose parties based on ethnic headcounts rather than political platforms or ideologies. The analysis using survey data shows that changes in employment composition by race between different administrations tend to favour the ethnicity of the voter base of that political party that holds power, and this is irrespective of political parties. This finding highlights the rationality of voting based on race, as it can increase the chances of obtaining a public job when one's party wins an election. In terms of benefits to the elites, there also appears to be a common group that benefits from many public contracts, regardless of which political party holds office.

It is not surprising, therefore, to find that corruption and rent-seeking, which often involve bureaucratic corruption, are perceived to be common in TT. At the same time, even though TT has laws in place, such as the Integrity in Public Life Act and the Public Procurement and Disposal of Public Property Act; allegations of corruption persist, particularly during election campaigns. We find that ethnicity and political affiliation can influence individuals' attitudes towards corruption, with insiders being more tolerant of corruption and identity playing a role in how corruption is perceived. Also, trust in the government, known as vertical trust, is low in TT compared to other comparators. However, trust levels vary depending on the ethnic background of the prime minister in power, with shifts observed between administrations. The sore-loser effect, where trust levels change based on the ruling party, appears more pronounced among ITTs.

Addressing corruption and building trust in the government are crucial for TT's development and stability. Strengthening the enforcement of existing laws, promoting transparency in public procurement processes, and fostering a culture of accountability are necessary to combat corruption. Efforts to bridge ethnic divisions and promote inclusivity can also enhance trust in the government and foster a sense of national unity. By tackling corruption and improving vertical confidence, TT can work towards a more transparent and accountable governance system that serves the best interests of its citizens.

13.2 Economic Development

TT's economy has transitioned from a sugar-based plantation economy in the eighteenth century to a hydrocarbon-dependent economy. The discovery of crude oil in 1857 marked a significant turning point for the country's development. The government's efforts to promote industrialisation, exemplified by establishing the Point Lisas industrial park, supported the development of upstream, midstream, and downstream energy sectors and the sector's transition from an oil-based to a natural gas-based economy in the mid-1990s. However, as a mature hydrocarbon jurisdiction with depleting resources, TT is experiencing slowing investments and declining energy exports. These trends have highlighted the urgent need for economic diversification.

We examined the impact of resource dependency, characterised by volatility and Dutch disease, on TT's economic performance. The analysis reveals various symptoms and effects of Dutch disease in TT, such as an overvalued real exchange rate, slower growth in the manufacturing sector, faster growth in the service sector, and a decline in the contributions of the agriculture and manufacturing sectors to the overall output.

TT's economic growth is highly vulnerable to fluctuations in international commodity prices. TT's economic growth volatility is higher than other comparator groups, negatively impacting TT's economic growth and potentially destabilising investment and aggregate demand. However, it is important to note that volatility alone cannot fully account for the prolonged periods of economic contraction and stagnation experienced by TT. Other contributing factors include declining productivity, decreasing competitiveness, and an undiversified economic structure.

The decline in productivity has also contributed to TT's underperformance. The fall in labour productivity is attributed to changes within sectors, with specific sectors such as wholesale and retail trade, public administration, and transport exerting negative influences on national labour productivity. Total factor productivity, a key source of long-term growth, has increased its contribution to growth from 2002 to 2006 but started to decline after 2008, while the contributions of employment and human capital to growth have significantly decreased over time, indicating underinvestment in these crucial areas. Additionally, the business environment in TT poses obstacles to firms' operations, including challenges related to accessing finance, regulatory frameworks, and workforce quality. Together, these factors continue to weigh on the level and quality of TT's growth.

The country has undergone two significant commodity cycles, leading to prolonged periods of economic stagnation. Pro-cyclical policies often exacerbate recession episodes and slow implementation of reforms. These boom-and-bust cycles and structural constraints can substantially impact poverty, inequality, and labour market outcomes. However, government spending through subsidies and transfer programmes has generally mitigated the adverse effects of these price shocks on households.

Overall, addressing challenges posed by resource dependency, Dutch disease, and productivity issues while promoting economic diversification and improving the business environment are critical for TT to achieve sustained and inclusive economic growth.

We follow the boom-bust cycle with an analysis of the labour market, by looking at gender and race disparities in labour participation, wages, occupational segregation and composition, and poverty and income inequality outcomes in the TT labour market. Over the period 1991–2015, males have had a higher labour force participation rate than females—although female labour force participation increased by almost 25% over the same period. ATTs had a higher participation rate than ITTs. There has been a continuous decrease in unemployment rates over time for all groups, even during periods of subdued economic activity, supported by generous public employment and training programmes. Only marginal changes in the ethnic composition of occupational categories have been observed. However, there are significant differences in the distribution of occupations across genders.

Wage differentials among labour market participants were not systematically different between the two ethnic groups. However, there were significant wage differentials in favour of ITTs in the public sector. Wage differentials in the private sector were more prominent than in the public sector and favoured males of ATT and ITT origin. The mean wage gap has declined over time, driven by changes in characteristics, mainly increasing female education. However, a significant unexplained portion of the wage gap is still linked to occupational segregation, with men earning higher wages, especially in female-dominated professions.

Economic growth has been partly redistributive, with all ethnic groups benefiting, especially those at the lower end of the income distribution. Lastly, there are indications that although TT's generous government employment programmes, such as URP and the CEPEP, may have helped to stabilise the employment rate and mitigate the impact of economic volatility on unemployment, they may be contributing to distortions in the labour market.

We follow the labour market analysis by examining the private non-energy sector in detail by assessing several dimensions of its performance and prioritising policies to support its growth. The private non-energy industry has become important, with services being the dominant sub-sector. However, the non-energy sector performance has deteriorated recently, particularly during the COVID-19 pandemic, followed by a sluggish recovery. This downturn follows a continuation of the sector's underperformance that had already become evident over the decade preceding 2019. Furthermore, the energy sector's growing disconnect from the broader economy further undermines the non-energy sector growth. Growth of the energy sector often fails to yield the desired stimulus for the non-energy sector. Conversely, downturns in the energy sector are associated with negative growth in the non-energy sector.

While a few non-energy sectors have shown resilience and growth—particularly in manufacturing and services activities, performance disparities are evident across firm sizes and ages. For example, sales growth varied significantly among firms, with a substantial portion experiencing negative growth rates, especially for smaller enterprises. On the other hand, total factor productivity at the firm level portrays a relatively better picture for TT than other Caribbean countries. Furthermore, small firms have lower sales growth and total factor productivity than medium and large enterprises. The distinction in performance is also apparent in firms' years of operation, with mature firms outperforming their newer counterparts in sales growth and total factor productivity.

Several factors, from access to infrastructure and finance to human capital and crime issues, have affected firms' performance. Access to finance and an inadequately educated workforce remains a substantial hurdle for firms in TT, with a significant proportion of firms reporting them as a major obstacle to their operations. Crime is a significant concern, affecting firms' investment decisions. Theft, vandalism, and robbery are common crimes that cause businesses to allocate resources to enhance security measures.

The impact of COVID-19 is evident on firms, with businesses perceiving market size and the cost of innovating as increasingly significant obstacles since the pandemic's onset. Relatedly, digitalisation emerged as an essential aspect of infrastructure to support business continuity during the pandemic. We find ample room for growth in online payment systems and enhancing digital marketing efforts in TT.

Our regression results show that the profile of the private sector—an important determinant of performance—is unfavourable in terms of age, size, legal form, and trade orientation. Microeconomic constraints, including access to finance, crime, corruption, inadequate infrastructure, and insufficient innovation, also affect firms' performance. Among these, the lack of innovation emerges as the most significant hindrance, followed by insufficient infrastructure and crime. Addressing these challenges can create a more favourable environment for business growth.

13.3 Social Development

Education is an important determinant of a country's political and socioeconomic development. Education supports economic growth and is strongly associated with boosting levels of social capital (civic engagement, political engagement, voting, trust, and tolerance). Therefore, educational expenditures are justified on social and political grounds, not just economic.

TT has higher public education expenditure than comparator countries. There is free access to public education. Education is compulsory and free of cost for all citizens between the ages of 3 and 18. Students can access other benefits such as subsidised meals, school bus service, and textbooks. Tertiary education is also heavily subsidised through the Government Assistance for Tuition Expenses programme. The government also provides a full scholarship for citizens to undertake studies up to the PhD level at local and international tertiary-level institutions.

Over time, TT's Education Index (the mean years of education and the expected years of schooling) has improved. The country did better than all the comparator country groups. However, the story regarding the quality of education is the opposite. Regarding Progress in International Reading Literacy, TT ranks 36 of 53 countries. TT has a sizable negative outlier status (countries with lower test score performance than their economic outcomes would suggest). TT scored below the average of other participating countries on the Programme for International Student Assessment tests (for mathematics) and below that of other countries with similar per capita income levels.

Educational outcomes differ according to the type of school attended, gender, and student's race. Primary and secondary schools are either government, government-assisted or private schools. Looking at averages of national tests, private school students outperform government-assisted schools, which outperform government schools' students. However, a caveat, school impacts on test scores are not the best measure of a school's impacts on longer-run non-academic outcomes, such as reducing criminality, teen motherhood, and increased labour market participation.

There are marked differences in educational performance between religions (a proxy for ethnicity as most ITTs were either Hindus or Muslims, while ATTs are predominantly Christian). Of all the students sitting for the CSEC examination, most students obtaining a certificate were Muslims and Hindus (i.e., mainly ITTs), followed by Christians (i.e., mainly ATTs) and other groups. Although all religious/ethnic groups have improved over time, this disparity in achievement by ethnic groups is becoming more prominent.

There is an increasing gender imbalance. Female entrants in the UWI have steadily increased over time. In 1981, women replaced men as the majority and, since then, have increasingly replaced men. Other than in engineering, women increasingly dominate in all fields. More females across both ethnic groups have a degree at the university level. The disparities between races and genders are becoming more prominent, with ITT males and females outperforming ATTs.

Over the past decade, the country's demographic profile has undergone a transition marked by a declining fertility rate, a decrease in the under-15 population, an increase in the over-60 age group, and an increase in the dependency ratio. Concurrently, the country is also experiencing an epidemiological transition, with a decline in communicable diseases and a rise in chronic non-communicable diseases. The latter now claims more lives than infectious diseases. The DALY, a metric that measures how many years of healthy life are lost, reveals that TT loses 510 thousand DALYs (higher than small economies but lower than other comparator country groups). Communicable diseases lose less than other comparator country groups. The problem is non-communicable diseases. Non-communicable conditions in TT DALYs are higher than in all other country groups. Unintentional injuries are lower than in comparator countries, but intentional injuries are higher. Since 2005, the Chronic Disease Assistance Programme (CDAP) has provided citizens with free prescription drugs and other pharmaceutical items to treat chronic conditions.

However, modifiable behavioural risk factors, including an unhealthy diet, harmful alcohol use, tobacco use, and physical inactivity, cause most NCDs. Within TT, there are marked differences between the races of illness types. ITTs suffer more than ATTs from obesity (43%), heart disease (60%), and diabetes (54%). However, they have similar proportions of cancer and mental disorders. Risk factors differ between races. ITTs have a greater risk than other ethnic groups as they smoke and drink alcohol more than others. Physical activity has gained more relevance with the increase in chronic non-communicable diseases in TT. However, in

TT, the lack of pro-health behaviour is similar across ethnic groups, where about 70% do not engage in physical activity. Lack of physical activity is more damaging to ITTs as they engage in more risk factors. There is a marked difference by race in the percentage of those who did not work due to disability or illness. Of the total, 51% were ITTs, followed by 30% ATTs.

Most TT citizens identified security as the most critical problem facing the country. The country's homicide rate, 31 per 1000,000, is significantly higher than in other small countries, ethnically diverse societies, other ex-British colonies, and extractive-dependent economies.

The emergence of criminal gangs, partly fuelled by the drug trade, has contributed to the country's high homicide rate. The crisis in Venezuela has accentuated the drug and arms problems. Further, inter-partner violence is the main form of domestic violence. Assaults and beatings accounted for more than half of the incidences of domestic violence, followed by threats, breach of a protection order, wounding, and sexual abuse. Child abuse and violence in schools are also prevalent. Within TT, there are marked differences between religions (a proxy for ethnicity) regarding the perpetrators of crime.

Evidence of relatively high social tolerance of partner and family violence and violence in general exists. Most respondents accepted that physical punishment is necessary when children are disobedient. The latter is consistent across the three major ethnic groups, with the highest being ATTs, followed by MTTs and ITTs. Similarly, a plurality accepts physical punishment for wives when they are unfaithful at similar rates among ATTs and ITTs. The tolerance of violence outside of the home is also high. The majority think it is justified to kill someone who kills another person or rape someone's child: the approval of such a response is high among ATTs and ITTs, but lower for MTTs. Police torture is primarily accepted, especially among ITTs.

The cost of crime and violence is high. The annual cost of youth violence, including direct costs, forgone earnings, tourism revenue and opportunity cost, is estimated at 2.8% of GDP. Direct and indirect costs of sexual abuse and domestic violence are estimated at 0.51% of GDP (2005). Government expenditure on national security in TT is the highest in the Caribbean: 13.9% of the budget and 12% of GDP. In the private sector, 26% of businesses reported being victims of crime, with financial losses of 2.1% of annual sales. Moreover, 80% of firms reported spending, on average, almost 2% of annual sales on private security measures.

Given the situation described above, it is no surprise that public trust in the justice system, police and Supreme Court is low. Most residents revealed low trust in the police. There is a marginally higher level of trust in the Supreme Court. Trust in the justice system is also marginally higher. The level of trust varies by ethnic group. Generally, ITTs have higher trust than ATTs, with MTTs at an intermediate level.

Finally, we reviewed culture and happiness. Culture matters for the country's economic development as socioeconomic development strongly correlates with a country's cultural values. Higher economic development is associated with higher values of self-expression and secular values. Lower economic growth is related to higher values of survival and traditional values. TT has low (high) self-expression (survival) and high (low) traditional (secular) values. There appear to be no significant differences between the three ethnic groups in both value dimensions. Thus, the shared cultural values represent a drag on development. The fact that most cultural heterogeneity is within ethnic groups, i.e., between-ethnic group cultural variation, is a small part of overall cultural variation and that most of this variation occurs within ethnic groups. This result indicates why TT has avoided communal violence despite race-based voting and differential outcomes in education, health, and labour market outcomes. Cultural identity, not only race, is what matters.

TT stands out as much happier when comparing the country with the averages of the comparator country groups. Comparing the common factors' contribution to life satisfaction in TT and the comparator group of countries reveals why. TT has the highest GDP per capita and social support. At the same time, the contribution of generosity is only higher in ex-British colonies, and a healthy life expectancy is higher only in small economies. Interestingly, there is neither a gender nor race happiness gap. There is, however, a colour happiness gap; lighter-skinned people are happier than dark-skinned people.

Index

J. Khadan and I. Jit Ruprah, *Unraveling Race, Politics, and Gender in Trinidad and Tobago's Economic Development*,
https://doi.org/10.1007/978-3-031-54656-3

The manufacturer's authorised representative in the EU is Springer Nature Customer Service Centre GmbH, Europaplatz 3, 69115 Heidelberg, Germany. If you have any concerns regarding our products, please contact ProductSafety@springernature.com

Printed and bound by CPI Group (UK) Ltd, Croydon, CR0 4YY
01/10/2026
02225898-0006